KEY CONCEPTS IN SOCIAL RESEARCH METHODS

D0519526

Palgrave Key Concepts

Palgrave Key Concepts provide an accessible and comprehensive range of subject glossaries at undergraduate level. They are the ideal companion to a standard textbook making them invaluable reading to students throughout their course of study and especially useful as a revision aid.

Key Concepts in Accounting and Finance
Key Concepts in Business Practice
Key Concepts in Cultural Studies
Key Concepts in Drama and Performance
Key Concepts in e-Commerce
Key Concepts in Human Resource Management
Key Concepts in Information and Communication Technology
Key Concepts in International Business
Key Concepts in Language and Linguistics (second edition)
Key Concepts in Law
Key Concepts in Leisure
Key Concepts in Management
Key Concepts in Marketing
Key Concepts in Operations Management
Key Concepts in Politics
Key Concepts in Public Relations
Key Concepts in Psychology
Key Concepts in Social Research Methods
Key Concepts in Sociology
Key Concepts in Strategic Management
Key Concepts in Tourism

Palgrave Key Concepts: Literature

General Editors: John Peck and Martin Coyle

Key Concepts in Contemporary Literature
Key Concepts in Crime Fiction
Key Concepts in Medieval Literature
Key Concepts in Modernist Literature
Key Concepts in Postcolonial Literature
Key Concepts in Renaissance Literature
Key Concepts in Victorian Literature
Literary Terms and Criticism (third edition)

Further titles are in preparation
www.palgravekeyconcepts.com

Palgrave Key Concepts
Series Standing Order
ISBN 1–4039–3210–7

(outside North America only)

You can receive future titles in this series as they are published by placing a standing order. Please contact your bookseller or, in the case of difficulty, write to us at the address below with your name and address, the title of the series and the ISBN quoted above.

Customer Services Department, Macmillan Distribution Ltd
Houndmills, Basingstoke, Hampshire RG21 6XS, England

Key Concepts in Social Research Methods

Roger Gomm

First published 2009 by
PALGRAVE MACMILLAN

Palgrave Macmillan in the UK is an imprint of Macmillan Publishers Limited, registered in England, company number 785998, of Houndmills, Basingstoke, Hampshire RG21 6XS.

Palgrave Macmillan in the US is a division of St Martin's Press LLC, 175 Fifth Avenue, New York, NY 10010.

Palgrave Macmillan is the global academic imprint of the above companies and has companies and representatives throughout the world.

Palgrave® and Macmillan® are registered trademarks in the United States, the United Kingdom, Europe and other countries.

ISBN-13: 978–0–230–21499–6
ISBN-10: 0–230–21499–1

This book is printed on paper suitable for recycling and made from fully managed and sustained forest sources. Logging, pulping and manufacturing processes are expected to conform to the environmental regulations of the country of origin.

A catalogue record for this book is available from the British Library.

A catalog record for this book is available from the Library of Congress.

10 9 8 7 6 5 4 3 2 1
18 17 16 15 14 13 12 11 10 09

Printed and bound in Great Britain by
CPI Antony Rowe, Chippenhan and Eastbourne

Contents

Also by Roger Gomm

SOCIAL RESEARCH METHODOLOGY: A CRITICAL
INTRODUCTION 2nd Edition

CASE STUDY METHODS: KEY ISSUES, KEY TEXTS
(editor and author with Peter Foster and Martyn Hammersley)

CONSTRUCTING EDUCATIONAL INEQUALITY
(with Peter Foster and Martyn Hammersley)

EVALUATING RESEARCH IN HEALTH AND SOCIAL CARE
(editor and author with Gill Needham and Anne Bullman)

Acknowledgements

The material from the Office for National Statistics in Table 9 is Crown Copyright and is reproduced here under PSI licence number C2008002495, from Office for National Statistics (2008) *National Statistics Socio-economic Classification,* http://www.ons.gov.uk/about-statistics/classifications/current/ns-sec

Introduction

The reader I have in mind for this book is someone who while reading social research wants a quick reference source for unfamiliar words, or, in writing research needs to check the meaning of terms, and move on fairly quickly. Hence the entries are relatively short. An advantage of brevity is that the glossary can contain a large number of terms, roughly 2000. The idea of speedy reference is carried through to the references. Apart from some seminal works, nearly all the references are electronic. I have prioritised those which are free to screen (the majority) and the remainder are to journals for which most university libraries will have electronic subscriptions. Where possible and appropriate, I have selected references which are practical rather than theoretical. Some references I have drawn on several times. This includes the estimable *Stanford Encyclopedia of Philosophy*, William Trochim's *Social Research Methods Knowledge Base,* John Musalia's beautifully presented statistics course from the University of West Kentucky, the *Statsoft Electronic Textbook*, and others, for which my thanks. I also found Wikipedia useful, but because its content and structure are subject to continual change I have not cited it among the references.

This book covers, or at least touches on the vocabularies of research for anthropology, complexity theory, criminology, cultural studies, demography, some areas of economics, educational research, epidemiology, history, health studies, market research, performance management, policy-oriented research, political science, cognitive and social psychology, socio-linguistics and sociology. It covers both quantitative and qualitative research. With such a wide spread it is inevitable that some of the more esoteric terms of each subject area will be missing.

Cross-referencing between entries is extensive. Among other reasons this was necessarily so because of the prodigious amount of synonymy in the corpus. In compiling the book I began to feel that everyone who has written about social and behavioural research has deliberately avoided existing terms and invented new ones. This is probably true of some who see inventing a new term as the route to fame via citation indices, or where a term brands a proprietary package. There, are, for example, at least 75 named varieties of evaluation, many of which I suspect are really brands for consultancies.. They are not all in the book, however. But, more frequently, synonymy reflects the fact that even within subject disciplines there are multiple and exclusionary conversations wherein and whereby social groups mark themselves off with their own sets of terms, or people invent new terms because they simply don't read the literature of other groups. Promiscuous synonymy seems to characterise both quantitative and qualitative research: there are five terms for regression lines ,seven for the normal distribution, and seven again for 'modern' test theory, just as there are at least twenty two different ways of saying that consciousness is organised, ranging from actor perspectives, through interpretive repertoires, schemata and mazeways to world-views. At this point someone will complain that these latter are not really synonyms at all, and have quite distinctive meanings. This might have been so when the terms were new minted, but the finesse wears off with use.

More problematic than synonymy are words which have more than one meaning. Some of these stray in from adjoining vocabularies. Many of the words featured have common as well as specialist meanings; for example, realistic, idealistic, pragmatic, phenomenal, hypothetical. There are hazards here for anyone trying to use an ordinary dictionary to decode the lexicon of social research, and researchers use terms in both their common and specialist forms. And then there are adjoining specialist vocabularies. For example, many of the words used by social researchers also appear in theology. And artificial intelligence and computing also use many of the same homonyms with different meanings. This makes web searches particularly difficult.

Even in research circles the same word may have different meanings. This includes some which are self-contradictory, such as agent, naturalistic research and naturalism, transparency and phenomenological. And there are words which instead of a definition seem to generate a debate or debates. This is particularly true of terms drawn from epistemology and ontology. Nor is it surprising that these are difficult to pin down. They are made worn and crusty by philosophical debates which have been going on for the last 2,500 years, and there is often a heavy sediment of theology too. The debates don't seem to have progressed very far: post-modernism isn't really very different from ancient Greek scepticism, and realism turns out to be very much what most natural scientists thought they were doing anyway. This probably indicates that the debates revolve around irresolvable issues, important for that very reason, but they have generated a lot of extra words. Some important component terms such as objectivity, subjectivity , reflexivity and real are now so eroded that they are difficult to use without further explication. I forebear to suggest replacements, but hope that my discussion of such terms will be useful.

The structure of the glossary is simple. The entries are in alphabetical order. The main terms are in bold type (for their first usage) and usually head an entry, although some are embedded in the text relating to associated terms. Cross references are given in italics. These are some-times incorporated into expositionary text, in which case for gram-matical reasons, they may not be quite the same parts of speech as the entries to which they refer, or they may be plurals when the referent is singular or vice versa. Nonetheless they should always take readers to the correct place in the alphabetical order.

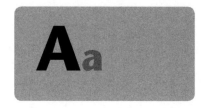

α (alpha)

See *Alpha level, Cronbach's coefficient alpha, Statistical significance, Type 1 and Type 2 errors.*

A&HCI (Arts & Humanities Citation Index)

See *Citation indices.*

A,B,C1,C2,D,E

See *Market research categorisations.*

Abduction/Abductive reasoning

(1) The kind of reasoning which finds the best explanation for a set of given facts, much as with the denouement in detective fiction; may involve sequences of *deductive reasoning, inductive reasoning* and *analytic induction*. Also referred to as 'inference to the best explanation'. Very similar to **Heuristic Thinking** (Arnold 2006) – see also *Reasoning*. (2) Used interchangeably with **retroductive reasoning/ retroduction** and **hypothesis method** to refer to the development of theory through the generation and testing of hypotheses, hence similar in meaning to *hypothetico-deductive method*, but more likely to be used by writers espousing *realism* (Suarez 2005). (3) As above but with abduction reserved for qualitative research – hence similar in meaning to *analytic induction* and *constant comparison*, with **retroductive** reserved for quantitative research (Blaikie 1993). (4) The revision of existing beliefs in the light of additional evidence, as with *Bayesian inference*.

Arnold, T. (2006) 'Heuristic Thinking', *Hyponoetics Philosophical Essays*. www.hyponoesis.org/download/Heuristic_Thinking.pdf

Blaikie, N. (1993) *Approaches to Social Enquiry*, Cambridge: Polity Press

Suarez, M. (2005) 'Experimental Realism Defended: How inference to the most likely cause might be sound'. http://philsci-archive.pitt.edu/archive/00002252/

ABER

See *Arts based inquiry*.

ABI

See *Effect size (ES) measures, Risk, relative and absolute*.

Absissa

See *X-axis*.

Absolute harm increase / decrease

See *Effect size (ES) measures, Risk, relative and absolute*.

Absolute poverty

See *Poverty, absolute*.

Absolute risk, Absolute risk increase / reduction

see *Effect size (ES) measures, Risk, relative and absolute*.

Absolute value

The value of a number ignoring whether it is plus or minus, usually indicated by being enclosed within two vertical bars; |x|.

Abstract empiricism

See *Theory*.

A/B Testing

Market research. Procedure for testing the effectiveness of advertisements and public service information. Responses to one advert (A) compared to responses to another (B).

> Webmaster Tutorials (n.d.) 'A/B testing' www.sitetoolcenter.com/google-adsense-optimization/ab-testing.php

ACASI (Audio Computer Assisted Self-Administered Interview)

See *Questionnaire administration*.

Access

Refers to procedures necessary to contact and work with the subjects of research. See *Criminal records, Ethics committee, Gate-keepers, Key informant.*

Account

(1) Description or explanation of an event or process. (2) In social science specifically, refers to utterances that serve to justify or excuse something which might otherwise be regarded as discrediting. For example, 'It's not usually such a mess, but we've got the builders in' is an account which issues an instruction: 'don't judge us on immediate appearances' (Scott and Lyman 1968). Accounts are of research interest in themselves as an everyday feature of social life, but also as likely to appear as misleading responses to *questionnaires* and *interviews* – see also *Bias, self-serving.*

Buttney, R. (1993) *Social Accountability in Communication,* London: Sage
Scott, M. and Lyman, S. (1968) 'Accounts', *American Sociological Review* (**33**): 46–62

ACORN (A Classification of Residential Neighbourhoods)

Categorisation of neighbourhoods on basis of house size and type, owner-ship and renting, family size, age profile, ethnicity, car and consumer dura-ble ownership and much else, resulting in 17 basic categories and around 56 different neighbourhood types, with titles such as 'Flourishing Families', 'Aspiring Singles', 'Settled Suburbia' and 'Inner City Adversity'. Profiles available for most postcodes in the UK, via the CACI website www.caci. co.uk/acorn/ or the Up-My-Street website www.upmystreet.com. and see:

Businessballs (2007) *Demographics classification,* http://www.businessballs.com/demo-graphicsclassifications.htm

For the alternative system used by the UK Office for National Statistics see *Area classification of output areas.*

A

Acquiescence bias/set

See *Bias, acquiescence.*

Actant

See *Actor network theory.*

Action

Activity explicable in terms of the interpretations of those who perform it, sometimes contrasted with 'behaviour' where that implies reactions beyond someone's control. For some writers a 'social action approach' is roughly synonymous to an *interpretative approach*. However, the term 'social action approach' is also widely used in macro-sociological writing such as American functionalism of the 1930s to 1960s. Different from the 'action' in *action research*. See also *Actor, Behaviourism, Intentionalism, Interpretivism*.

Action research (AR)

Making some real world intervention and studying the results of this. For example, making an organisational change or pursuing a political campaign. At the most rigorous level, action research is modelled on experimental method, with *pre and post measurements*, controls and other devices to avoid *confounding* (see *Control, direct and statistical, Design experiments*). More usually AR researchers are more interested in the practical success of the action than in creating high quality general knowledge. AR is then often indistinguishable from organisational development, political activism, social work, community work or other practical activities. In **educational action research**, the primary objective is usually for the researcher and collaborating subjects to develop skills or have experiences. Then AR is almost indistinguishable from 'practice learning', or 'personal and professional development' and 'organisational development' (McNiff 2002). Action research is commonly associated with *participative* and *emancipatory research*. *Practitioner research* also usually takes an AR form. See also *Consciousness raising, Rapid appraisal, Rapid institutional appraisal*.

McNiff, J. (2002) *Action research for professional development: Concise advice for new action researchers*. www.jeanmcniff.com/booklet1.html#2

The *Reconnect Action Research Kit* from the Australian *Department of Families, Housing, Community Services and Indigenous Affairs* (2003) provides an example of action research procedures. www.facs.gov.au/

Reason, P. and Bradbury, H. (eds) (2001) *Handbook of Action Research*, Sage: Thousand Oaks, CA.

A

Actor

(1) One of the many terms referring to the human subjects of social and psychological research. Implies an interest in what actions mean to those who perform them. See *Action, Agency, Intentionalism, Interpretivism, Subject*. (2) In *Actor network theory* may refer to instruments, documents, committees and so on, as well as to human actors. The term *actant* may be used here instead. See also *Agency*.

Actor network theory (ANT)

A major theory in social studies of science and technology which conceptualises the development of scientific ideas and techniques in terms of networks which involve conjunctions of people, techniques, instruments, buildings and forms of social organisation – so-called **material-semiotic networks.** Thus a laboratory is, at one and the same time, a building furnished with material objects, a social organisation and a site within which meanings are created, and for some purposes can be thought of as 'an actor' (**actant**) with *agency*.

Law, J. (1992) *Notes on the theory of actor networks*, http://www.lancs.ac.uk/fass/sociology/research/resalph.htm

Actor perspectives/ideologies/social theories

Three of a very large number of terms all denoting the ways of understanding characteristic of particular groups of social actors. It is a common aim in social research to discover what these are, to describe them, to explain why they are as they are and to explain what happens in terms of people acting according to the way they make sense of the world. Alternative terms include, *attribution sets*, cognitive maps, connectionist networks, *discourses*, folk-taxonomies, folk-theories, *gaze*, *interpretive repertoires*, knowledge structures, life-worlds, mazeways, mental scripts, prototypes, schemata, schemes of relevance, scripts, sub-cultural ideas, typification schemes, world views, and more. All express the same basic idea that consciousness has a structure, but these terms have different backgrounds and there are some, albeit sometimes subtle, differences between them. See also *Emic and Etic*.

Actuarial

(1) *Demography, epidemiology* and life assurance: pertaining to the calculation of life expectancy. (2) As opposed to **Contractual:** in *ethnomethodology* (Garfinkel 1967) the equivalent to the distinction between factual and *normative*, where actuarial means a description which is factually accurate, and contractual means a description which shows (accurately or otherwise) that a state of affairs was as it should have been, or a process was carried out as it should have been carried out (metaphorically 'as per contract'). 'Contractual' does not necessarily mean untrue, merely that the description is framed prospectively to provide evidence to rebut later claims of malpractice, should they arise.

Garfinkel, H. (1967) *Studies in Ethnomethodology*, Englewood Cliffs: Prentice-Hall

Ad hocing

Making decisions as and when a decision seems required, in the way that seems appropriate at the time. When applied to those being studied, draws attention to the way in which the meaning of words and the likelihood of actions depend greatly on the immediate context. When applied to a researcher this implies haphazard and unprincipled practice. However, in some kinds of research, particularly *ethnographic* or *action research*, or even experimental research in clinical or social work practice, the researcher may have little choice but to ad hoc. The remedy, if there is one, is to recognise ad hoc decisions, record them and theorise their consequences and why they were made as they were. See also *Contingency, Bricolage, Reflexivity.*

Ad hoc sample

See *Sample, convenience.*

Ad hominem argument

Short for **argumentum ad hominem** 'argument against the man': attacking the character of the person making a claim, rather than the claim itself. See also *Genetic fallacy.*

Adjacency pairs

In *pragmatic linguistics* and *conversation analysis*, pairs or suites of kinds of utterances that usually go together. If a first is a greeting, the second will usually be a greeting; a question is usually followed by an answer (or an explanation or apology for failing to answer). If one of an adjacency pair is not followed by another this is usually 'a noticeable absence', something for comment, complaint, apology and such like. See also *Sequential Analysis.*

A

Administrative data (bureaucratic data, official statistics)

Data collected to aid the operation of services and organisations and/or to monitor the implementation of policies or compliance with the law, for example the sickness absence records of a company, or the number of suicide verdicts reached in a coroner's jurisdiction. Much used in research although they are rarely collected in formats and via processes ideal for research usage (Gomm 2008). **Ethnostatistics** is the study of how such data are collected and analysed, though it covers also the collection of data by researchers and is a variety of *social constructionism.*

There has been considerable effort in the last decade to improve the statistics produced by central government. Data quality assurance initiatives may be seen for crime recording in the activities of the Police Standards Unit (PSU) (http://police.homeoffice.gov.uk/about-us/police-crime-standards/), for NHS data(www.connectingforhealth.nhs.uk) and generally on the Office for National Statistics (ONS) website (www.statistics.gov.uk/), for example ONS (2007) *Guidelines for measuring statistical quality*. In 2008 the *UK Statistics Authority* was established as an independent regulator of the quality of central government statistics.

Gomm, R. (2008) 'Using Administrative Data in Research', Chapter 9 in *Social Research Methodology: a critical introduction*, 2nd edn, Basingstoke: Palgrave Macmillan

Affinity diagramming/mapping/sorting

Qualitative techniques of sorting large numbers of items of data or concepts into logical groups, similar in intention to quantitative techniques such as *factor analysis* or *Q methodology*. (1) To facilitate consensus in a *citizen jury* or *nominal group* (Usabilitynet 2006). (2) As an investigative technique to create representations of cognitive or cultural patterns – see *Card sorting, Cognitive anthropology, Concept mapping, Personal constructs*. (3) As mode of qualitative data analysis with or without the assistance of computer software – see *Computer assisted qualitative data analysis (CAQDA)*. (4) Incorporated into some *data mining* software.

Usabilitynet (2006) *Affinity diagramming*, www.hostserver150.com/usabilit/tools/affinity.htm

AFPD

See *Output areas*.

Age, period and cohort effects

For example, if the current older generation is more likely to vote for right wing parties than the current middle-aged generation, is this due to attitudes moving to the right as people age – an **age effect**? Or is it due to differences in the circumstances during which the older people in the past and the younger people more recently formed their political attitudes – a **cohort effect**? Or is it due to something about the circumstances affecting both older and younger people now or in the past – **a period effect**? Sometimes period effects are treated as if they were cohort effects. Analysis to distinguish between the three is termed **Age, period, cohort effect modelling** (APC modelling). See also Flynn effect in *Standardisation*.

Glenn, N. D. (2004) *Cohort Analysis*, Sage: Thousand Oaks, CA

Age standardised morbidity/mortality ratios

See *Standardised morbidity/mortality ratios, Standardisation.*

Agency: agentive action

Implies that someone is the origin of his or her own actions because he or she is able to make genuine choices. The attribution of agency to human beings is sometimes given as reason why social and human behavioural sciences must differ from the natural sciences which deal with entities that lack agency – see *Intentionalism.* The issue of agency is the social and behavioural science version of the philosophical debate about free will versus *determinism.* In psychology the issue arises also in the contrast between *behaviourism* and more interpretative kinds of psychology and in considerations about the relative importance of sentient action as against biologically determined and conditioned behaviour . In sociology and anthropology the equivalent contrast is between agency and structure – see *Action, Structure.* Here the issue is the extent to which people's actions, including the choices they seem to make, are actually determined by social structures, social forces or cultural conditioning, a debate most recently associated with Anthony Giddens (Miller 2007). In *Actor network theory*, complexes of people, objects, buildings and practices are treated as actors (actants) with agency, over and beyond (or despite) the agentive capacity of individuals.

The idea that people have agency is the bedrock of morality (in Western societies at least) because it allows for people to be held responsible for their actions. In psychology in particular, whether or not people see themselves as agentive, and in what respects, may be regarded as an important dimension of personality and, in extreme cases, of psychosis where people believe they are non-agentive and that their actions are determined by someone, or something else. *See also Attribution theory, Action, Agent, Epiphenomenalism, Intentionalism, Motive attribution.*

A

Emirbayer, M. and Mische, A. (1998) 'What is Agency?', *American Journal of Sociology* **104** : 962–1023

Miller, S. (2007) *Social Institutions* (especially section 3:'Agency and Structure') *Stanford Encyclopaedia of Philosophy.* http://plato.stanford.edu

Agent

(1) General usage: someone whose actions are determined by someone or something other than him/herself, as in 'I'm only acting as (another's) agent'. (2) In social and behavioural science: someone whose actions are determined by him or herself: 's/he has agency'. See also *Agency.*

Algorithm **9**

(3) In *computer simulations*: programmable objects able to respond to their electronic environment and learn from experience. For example, in a simulation of belief diffusion, an agent programmed to 'believe' something if two or more of its neighbours in a matrix also 'believe' this. (4) See *Actor network theory*.

Algorithm

Step by step procedures, particularly those implemented in computer programs.

Alpha

See *Cronbach's coefficient alpha*.

Alpha level (confidence level, significance level)

A test for *statistical significance* will be said to show a statistically significant result if what actually happened was unlikely to have happened by chance. But how unlikely? For most purposes a result will be regarded as statistically significant if the odds of a difference as great or greater than that observed, happening by chance, are less than 5 times in 100 ($p < 0.05$). This is a 0.05 level or 5% level, **alpha level** or **significance level**. The **confidence level** is 1 minus the alpha level (or $1 - p$). Hence the 5% or 0.05 level is equivalent to the 95% confidence level and the 99% confidence level is equivalent to the 1% or 0.01 alpha level.

For a researcher to specify an alpha level of (say) 0.05 for a *null hypothesis* is to say that s/he is willing, five times out of a hundred, to reject the hypothesis when it should actually be accepted; that is willing to risk an **alpha error**/ type 1 error – *see Type 1 and Type 2 errors*.

For some purposes researchers choose a more stringent alpha level. For example, a 1% ($p < 0.01$) level is often chosen in research where the results might have life and death consequences, as in medical research. The more tests the same data are subjected to, the more likely it is that one or more of the tests will give what looks like a statistically significant result just by chance. Where such a *family-wise error* is likely, researchers usually select a more stringent alpha level such as the 1% ($p < 0.01$) level or the 1/1000 ($p < 0/001$) level.

See also *Beta error, p values, Statistical power*.

A

ALSPAC

See *Birth cohort studies*.

Alternate/ive (parallel) forms test

Test for the *reliability* of an *instrument* or process composed of pairs of items, developed so that each of them (reliably) produces similar responses from the same subjects. One of each pair then appears in one of a pair of tests. One set can then be used as a *pre-test* or base-line measure, and the other as a *post-test* or outcome measure without fears that memory of earlier responses will confound the results, thus avoiding some forms of *pre-test and post-test sensitivity*. There will inevitably be some differences between the results of the two instruments which can be attributed to the tests themselves, but these can be controlled by

- randomising the subjects – some get one of the alternate forms as a pre-test and some as a post-test, or
- randomising the items – each subject gets a different combination of pairs before and after.

Where an alternate forms test gives similar results on both occasions, the instrument is said to have 'alternate form (or parallel form) reliability'. In test development the degree of similarity is likely to be measured by *correlation*.

Alternative hypothesis

See *Null and alternative hypothesis.*

Analysis

Properly, the breaking down of something into its components, as opposed to synthesis; the drawing together of elements, for example, into an explanation. But often used loosely to refer to everything that happens in research after data collection in order to reach a conclusion, ignoring the fact that the design and execution of research also involves a considerable degree of analysis. See also *Synthesis.*

A

Analysis of covariance (ANCOVA and MANCOVA)

Read the entry for *Analysis of variance* first. The Analysis of Covariance (ANCOVA) is a parametric procedure which controls for the effects of the *covariance* in which the researchers are not interested, and shows the *covariance* in which the researchers are interested – see *Statistics, parametric and non-parametric*. For example, a researcher is interested in what causes differences in aptitude apart from age. The analysis of covariance calculates the covariance of age and aptitude and uses this to reset the values for aptitude as if all athletes were of the same chronological age. This is a form of *standardisation*. Then the relationship between aptitude and other variables can be calculated net of any differences due to age, that is, controlling for age differences. The latter operation is identical to the *analysis of variance* (ANOVA and MANOVA).

MANCOVA, the **Multivariate Analysis of Covariance** is essentially the same as ANCOVA but extended to deal with more than one dependent variable.

ANCOVA/MANCOVA can only be used where groups are being compared with regard to a variable at the interval level, taking values on a continuous scale and where the *variances* are similar – see *Cochran's C test*. Where the comparison is for a *nominal* variable, such as 'yes' or 'no', *logistic regression* may be used instead – see *Data, levels of, Statistics software*.

Analysis of variance (ANOVA and MANOVA)

The *variance* is a measure of the dispersion of scores in a data set. If all the scores were the same, each score would be the same as the *mean* score and the *variance* would be zero.

Suppose three groups of pupils are each taught in different ways, and the aim of the research is to judge which is the most effective way of teaching by comparing their results in the same examination. There will be three kinds of variance in the examination scores. *Total variance* is the variance between all the pupils in their examination scores above and below the *mean* for all pupils. *Between-group variance* (sometimes called 'the main effect') is the variance between the average or *mean* for each group and the *mean* for all pupils. *Within-group variance* (sometimes called 'the error' or 'the *residual*') is the variance of the pupils within each group in relation to the *mean* for that group only. In this example, it would be tempting to assume that the group with the highest average score is the group that has received the most effective tuition. But an alternative interpretation is possible. That is that the pupils are very diverse in their ability, different methods of teaching had a negligible effect and that the group with the highest average score just happens to be the group which by chance was composed of the pupils who were most able at the outset.

ANOVA or the analysis of variance is a parametric procedure – see *Statistics, parametric and non-parametric*. It asks the question: 'Is most of the total variance between the groups?', in which case it is possible that different average examination scores for the groups were due to different methods of teaching. Or 'Is most of the total variance within the groups?', in which case the differences in examination scores between the groups are most likely to be due to the chancy way in which a diverse group of pupils were sorted into different teaching groups at the outset.

A

An ANOVA calculation results in a figure which expresses the difference between the *between-group variance* and the *within-group variance* as a ratio: the *F-ratio*. A high figure for *F* means that there is more variance between the groups than within the groups. Whether the figure for *F* is *statistically significant* is determined by consulting a table for *critical values* for *F*. In this example, a statistically significant figure for *F* would suggest that different methods of teaching (the *main effect*) did have different effects; that the results were not simply due to chance operating when pupils were divided into groups.

ANOVA calculations are used when there are at least three groups to be compared and the variance of the groups are similar – see *Cochran's C test*. If there are only two groups a *t-test* is more usual.

One-way ANOVA compares groups differentiated by one factor only: for example different groups of pupils receiving different styles of teaching. **Two-way, three-way ANOVA** and so on **Multi-factor ANOVA**) compare groups within groups (within groups). For example, for a three-way ANOVA, teaching groups might be compared, and within and between these, girls might be compared with boys, and within the gender groups, minority ethnic pupils compared with ethnic majority pupils. In this case the total variance will be calculated within and between three teaching groups, six gender sub-groups, and twelve ethnic sub-sub-groups. 'Three-way' actually means 21 different comparisons. This would only be sensible with a large data set.

ANOVA only determines if there are *statistically significant* differences between groups, and not the groups which are significantly different from each other. For this *post-hoc* tests are necessary. MANOVA often produces *interaction effects* which can be difficult to interpret.

ANOVA can only be used where groups are being compared with regard to a variable at the interval level that takes values on a continuous scale. Where the comparison is for a *nominal* variable, such as 'yes' or 'no', *logistic regression* may be used instead – see *Data, levels of*. See also *Analysis of covariance (ANCOVA and MANCOVA), Central tendency and dispersion, Statistics software*.

MANOVA (Multi-variate Analysis of Variance) is a similar form of analysis but where several dependent *variables* are analysed: in the example above perhaps, the students' learning and their attitudes to learning might be analysed as outcomes separately and in relation to each other and for boys, girls and teaching methods.

McCreery, C. (2007) 'First year statistics for psychology students through worked examples: 3 Analysis of Variance', *Oxford Forum*: Psychology Paper 2007:3 www.celiagreen.com/charlesmccreery/statistics/anova.pdf

Musalia, J. (2008) *Chapter 14 The Analysis of Variance*, University of West Kentucky www.wku.edu/~john.musalia/soc300

A

Analytic generalisation

See *Generalisation, theoretical*.

Analytic induction

Systematically examining similarities and differences between cases to develop concepts and theories which can be tested by further examination of the same kind. The procedure is as follows:

(1) Produce an initial provisional definition of the phenomenon to be explained.
(2) Find cases of this phenomenon and investigate them, noting down provisional ideas about explanations.
(3) Formulate an hypothetical explanation, which seems to account for common factors found in all cases studied so far.
(4) Investigate further cases.
(5) If the hypothesis does not fit the facts about the new cases, either refine the hypothesis, or redefine the phenomenon, to produce a new hypothetical explanation which is consistent with the common factors in all cases so far.
(6) Repeat the procedure until no known cases of the phenomenon (as now defined) have characteristics which are inconsistent with the *hypothesis*.

Hammersley, M. and Atkinson, P. (2007) *Ethnography: principles and practice*, London: Routledge: 186–88

The procedure is very close to what is often called *constant comparison*.

The term 'analytic induction' is used mainly in the context of *qualitative research* in the social sciences. But as Znaniecki (1934), the originator of the term, points out, this method, while unnamed as such, is widely used in the natural sciences. Indeed it doesn't look too different from a rather informal version of the *hypothetico-deductive method* (or 'scientific method'). Thus it can be doubted whether the term is actually needed, and whether 'induction' alone would not suffice – see *Abductive reasoning, Inductive reasoning, Falsificationism*.

Ratcliff, D (n.d) *Analytic Induction as a Qualitative Research Method of Analysis*, www.vanguard.edu/uploadedFiles/faculty/dratcliff/analytic.html
Znaniecki, F. (1934) *The Method of Sociology*, New York: Farrar & Rinehart

Analytic statements

See *Logical positivism*.

ANCOVA

See *Analysis of covariance (ANCOVA and MANCOVA)*.

Anonymisation

To avoid breaching the *privacy and confidentiality* of subjects (or legal proceedings for defamation) it is typical to protect the identity of individual research subjects on publication, and preferably previously. In quantitative research individual returns, if they are identifiable, must be kept securely (see *Pseudo-anonymisation*) but individual contributions usually disappear into statistical aggregations on publication. However, in government statistics, particularly where small numbers are concerned, anonymisation may be accomplished by aggregating categories or time periods, by **suppression** (not publishing the figures) or by various techniques of *perturbation*. In qualitative research, where the views or actions of individuals may be of interest, code numbers or pseudonyms may be used. It is good practice to do this in field notes and other working documents lest they fall into the wrong hands, and to avoid being legally liable under the *Data Protection Act 1998*. It is doubtful, however, whether *audio or video recordings* can be regarded as anonymous except through using expensive masking and audio distortion techniques (Crow and Wiles 2008). Anonymisation may extend to anonymising the institutions and geographical areas where the research was conducted, including blanking out or pseudo-anonymising any local references in extracts from interview transcripts which are archived or published. In this regard, decisions about whether to represent local dialects in interview transcripts are difficult ones – see *Transcription*. The decision not to anonymise may be taken where the identity of the individuals or the institution studied are themselves of interest, and usually where disclosure is agreed with the research subjects. Anonymising institutions and locations may prevent a researcher from making references to documents and news stories which might serve as evidence, but if referenced would identify the objects of study, and of forestalling other researchers from replicating the research with the same subjects or institutions.

Commitments to anonymise may be made as part of the contract between a researcher and the research subjects, and or be a condition laid down by an *ethics committee* or *Caldicott guardians*. The practice of archiving data complicates the issue – see *Data archives*.

Wiles, R., Crow, G., Heath, S. and Charles, V. (2006) *Anonymity and Confidentiality*, NCRM

Clark, A. (2006) *Anonymising Research Data*, NCRM

Crow, A. and Wiles, R. (2008) *Managing anonymity and confidentiality in social research: the case of visual data*, NRCM

All from http://www.ncrm.ac.uk/research/outputs/publications/
ESDS (2006) *Identifyers and Anonymisation Guidelines*, www.esds.ac.uk/aandp/create/
identifiers.asp 02/06 (Guidelines on anonymising data related to archiving data)

ANOVA

See *Analysis of variance (ANOVA and MANOVA)*.

ANT

See *Actor Network Theory*.

Antecedent variable

See *Variable*.

Anthropologically strange

In *Ethnomethodology*, to attempt not to take for granted that which is culturally familiar. See also *Bracketing*.

Anti-naturalism

See *Naturalistic research*.

Anti-racist research

See *Partisan research*.

Anti-realism

See *Realism*.

APC

See *Age, period and cohort effects*.

Applied social research

See *Social research, pure and applied*.

Archive/Archiving

See *Data archives*. The web site www.a2a.org.uk gives access to the catalogues of the majority of British local authority, museum and university archives containing historical records. See also *Mass observation*.

Area-based inequality measures

See *Deprivation indices, Segregation indices.*

Area classification of output areas

Scheme of classification used by the Office for National Statistics to characterise different areas of the country according to the clustering of 41 *demographic* and socio-economic characteristics – see *Cluster analysis.* There are 7 'super-groups', 21 'groups' –and 52 sub-groups (Rees and Vickers 2006). Supergroups include 1: Blue Collar Communities', '2. City Living' and '4 Prospering Suburbs'. Groups within 1 include '1a Terraced Blue Collar', '1b Younger Blue Collar', '1c Older Blue Collar'. The names are chosen because they are more memorable than numbers, and for each category there are more precise definitions. The units being characterised are the Super Output Areas in terms of which *Census* data are reported: see *Output Areas.*

The main competitor to this system of classification is the CACI *ACORN Classification,* mainly used in market research.

Rees, P. and Vickers, D. (2006) 'Introducing the Area Classification of Output Areas', *Population Trends* **125** (15–24). http://www.statistics.gov.uk/cci/articlesearch.asp

ARI

See *Effect size (ES) measures, Risk, relative and absolute.*

Arithmetic and log scales

On logarithmic scales (Log10), any pair of numbers different by a factor of 10 is separated by the same distance as any other such pair. Thus the distance between 0 and 10 is the same as the distance between 10 and 100. **Semi log scales** (often just called log scales) use a log scale for the vertical and an arithmetic scale for the horizontal. Log scales are used to foreshorten scales to save space on a page and to display greater detail among lower values, but risk giving a misleading impression as to the difference between the lowest and highest values; for example between the richest and the poorest. In Figures 1 and 2 the same data are shown first on an arithmetic scaled graph and second on a semi-log scale. In **log-log scales** both scales are log scales. These are used mainly with *power law distributions.* On a log-log scale the data shown here would form a straight line. Log scaling is not to be confused with *data transformation* by conversion into logarithms or *log normal distributions.*

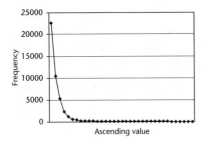

Figure 1 Data shown on arithmetic scale

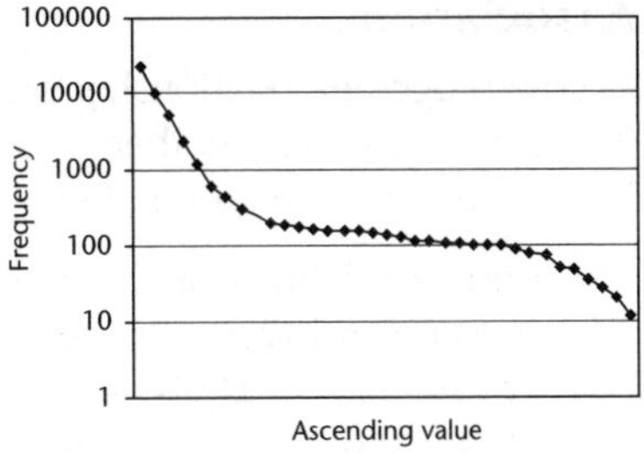

Figure 2 Data shown on semi-log scale

Arm

Of an experiment. One of two or more different treatments or conditions. Synonym for 'condition'. See also *Comparison groups*.

ARR

See *Effect size (ES) measures, Risk, relative and absolute.*

Artefact/Artifact

See *Research artefact.*

Arts-based inquiry (Arts-Based Educational Research (ABER))

One response to the rejection of natural sciences as a model for the social sciences is to base inquiry on artistic pursuits with quality criteria drawn from aesthetics and entertainment. See also *Performance ethnography.*

Von Emmel, T. (2005) '*Methodological approaches; Arts-based research*', http://dreamfish.com/old/vonemmel.ch%204.arts-based%20research.dissertation.pdf

Arts & Humanities Citation Index (A&HCI)

See *Citation indices.*

ASAQ (Audio Self-Administered Questionnaire)

See *Questionnaire administration.*

Ascertainment bias

See *Bias, ascertainment.*

A

Association

A 'going-together' relationship between two variables in a data set, such that one varies with another. Thus being taller is associated with being heavier in any large group of people. Association includes:

- Correlation measures – see *Correlation, Correlation coefficients, Partial correlation, Path analysis.*
- Covariance analysis – see *Analysis of covariance (ANCOVA/MANCOVA)*
- *Proportional reduction of error* measures (Lambda and *Gamma*)
- *Regression analysis* see *Discriminant function analysis, Logistic regression, Multi-level models, Scattergram.*
- *Elasticity* and inelasticity

Asymmetrical and symmetrical

(1) Asymmetrical measures differ according to the order in which data are entered into a formula. *Odds ratios, risk ratios, Lambda* and *Gamma* (see *Proportional reduction of error*) are asymmetrical. Symmetrical measures are the same irrespective of the order in which data are entered. (2) In **symmetrical distributions** of data the shape of the half of the distribution below the *mean, median* or *mode* on a graph, approximately matches the half above.

Asymptotic curve/asymptote

A straight line which approaches a curve but never meets it. In *linearisation* may be used instead of the curve produced by the data.

Atkinson index

See *Indices of inequality.*

Atlas.ti

See *Computer assisted qualitative data analysis.*

Attitude

Psychological predisposition favouring or disfavouring something, which is assumed to underlie behaviour from which the attitude can be inferred. Usually investigated by *questionnaires* in which the responses are scaled, for example, from strongly positive to strongly negative. Attitudes are often conceptualised as components of *values* which are more general pre-dispositions; for example a pro-marriage attitude might be seen as a pro-family value, see also *Guttman scale, Likert scale, Semantic differential, Test theory, Thurstone scale.*

Attractor

In *complexity theory*, a graphical representation of the limits within which some variable of a complex phenomenon fluctuates.

Lucas. C (2004) 'Attractors everywhere – order from chaos', *Complexity: Artificial Life Concept for Self-Organising Systems (CALResCo)* : www.calresco.org/attract.htm

Attributable risk

See *Risk, attributable.*

Attribution sets

One of many terms referring to the structure of consciousness or to habitual interpretative processes. Here the focus is on the way in which people attribute motives and personal characteristics to themselves and others, and in doing this, find explanations for their experience of social life and a basis for their own actions. See also *Actor perspective, Bias, attribution, Motive attribution.*

Attrition (drop out, subject loss)

The number/percentage of subjects initially selected thereafter lost to research, because:

- they cannot be contacted,
- refuse to participate,
- drop out during the research for whatever reason.

(Durnville *et al.*, 2006).

Attrition undermines the effects of the *random allocation* of subjects to *arms* of a *controlled experiment*, the *representativeness* of a probability sample or the comprehensiveness of a purposive sample – *see Sample, probability, Sample, purposive.* In survey research attrition has the same implications as non-response – see *Response rate.* Attrition is a particular problem with long running *longitudinal research* including *cohort studies* (Nathan 1999). See also *Intention to treat.*

Durnville, J.,Torgerson, D. and Hewitt, C. (2006) 'Reporting attrition in randomised controlled trials', *British Medical Journal* **332**: 969–971 www.bmj.com

Nathan, G. (1999) 'A review of sample attrition and representativeness in three longitudinal surveys', *GSS Methodology Series No. 13, Government Statistical Survey.* www. statistics.gov.uk search on 'GSS Methodology'

Audience effect research

Study of the effects of some mass communication on some audience; by *experiment*, by survey or by other techniques.

> Mytton, G. (1999) *Handbook on Radio and Television Audience Research*, Rome:UNESCO/ UNICEF www.cba.org.uk/audience_research/index.php – a how-to-do-it handbook
> Glasgow Media Group: www.gla.ac.uk/centres/mediagroup/

Audience research

Collection, usually by *survey*, and analysis of data on numbers and types of people listening or watching some medium of communication (where printed – **readership research**) The National Readership Survey outlines techniques and definitions for printed media: http://www.nmauk.co.uk/nma/do/live/factsAndFiguresNRSFAQ#m5

The following provide audience/readership figures for the UK. Only some information is available without subscription:

> (TV) Broadcast Audience Research Board www.barb.co.uk/
> Radio Joint Audience Research www.rajar.co.uk
> [local and regional papers] Newspaper Society www.newspapersoc.org.uk and JICREG Joint Industry Committee for Regional Press Research www.jicreg.co.uk
> [Mainly national publications] National Readership Survey www.nrs.co.uk
> Mytton, G. (1999) *Handbook on Radio and Television Audience Research*, Rome:UNESCO/ UNICEF www.cba.org.uk/audience_research/index.php- a how-to-do-it handbook.

Audio and video recording

Important methods of collecting data particularly in qualitative research. See also *Anonymisation, Transcription*.

> Stockdale, A. (2002) 'Tools for digital audio recording in qualitative research', *Social Research Update* Issue 38 http://sru.soc.surrey.ac.uk/
> Shrum, W. (2005) 'Digital video as research practice: methodology for the millenneum', *Journal of Research Practice* 1(1). http://jrp.icaap.org/index.php/jrp
> Ratcliff, D. (2004) *Video and Audio Methods in Qualitative Research*. http://qualitative research.ratcliffs.net/video.htm

Audit trail

A recent adoption into the vocabulary of research from business, referring to making a careful and accurate record of how the research was conducted to give the research procedural objectivity and *replicability* – see *Objectivity, procedural*. See also *Context of discovery and context of justification, Diaries, Memos, Reflexivity*.

Auditability

See *Audit trail, Objectivity, procedural.*

Authenticity

(1) Used by some qualitative researchers as alternative to internal validity, which in that context is very close to the idea of naturalistic or ecological validity, referring to the extent to which a piece of research successfully captures the experience of those who are studied where that experience is not distorted by the process of the research. It is not at all clear how the authenticity of a piece of research can be judged, but reference is often made to *Fallibility testing*, or, where the research is *participatory*, personal testimonies and autobiographies of research subjects may be featured – see *Validity, internal, Validity, naturalistic.* (2) The genuineness of claims of provenance (source) with regard to documents, archaeological and historical artefacts and other kinds of evidence – see *Textual criticism.*

Authorial presence

See *Autoethnography, Reflexivity.*

Autobiography

Facilitating research subjects in writing their autobiographies is sometimes an approach used in *Life history* and *Oral history research.*
　　See also *Autoethnography* and *Reflexivity.*

Autocorrelation

In *time series analysis* the measurement of the extent to which value of a variable at one point in time is correlated with the value of the same variable at (an) earlier point(s) in time. For example, in pursuing the question of whether having a lot of money at one time increased the chances of having a lot at a later date.

Autoethnography

Once meaning an *ethnographic* study of one's own culture, and still sometimes used to refer to the practice of assisting research subjects themselves to write about their own culture. But now more usually an *ethnographic research* report where the author displays his or her own

A

activities, thoughts and (especially) feelings in the field, as well as those of the research subjects (Tenni *et al.* 2003). Such reports are said to show **authorial presence.** Pre-dating the term, such autoethnography has a long history in journalism (for example, Dickens 1995) and travel and memoir writing (for example, Burton 1964), but in social science until recently the researcher's personal engagement in the research, if recorded at all, was presented separately from research findings, as research *diaries* (for example, Malinowski 1989) or 'methodological appendices' (for example, Foote Whyte 1993), or even anonymously and lightly fictionalised as in Laura Bohannan's writing about ethnographic research among the Tiv of Nigeria (Smith Bowen 1988). Thus was the (apparent) objectivity of research reports, rhetorically separated from the subjectivity of the researcher. Autoethography makes no such separation: see also *Introspectionism, Objectivity, Reflexivity, Rhetorical analysis, Subjectivity.*

Burton, R. (2006) *Personal narrative of a Pilgrimage to Al Madinah and Mecca,* (Vol 1), Whitefish MT:Kessinger Publications, and many other editions: originally 1853

Dickens, C. (1995) *Sketches by Boz,* (Edited Walder, D.) *Penguin Modern Classics,* Harmondsworth: Penguin, and many other editions: originally 1836

Whyte, W. F. (1993) *Street Corner Society: the social structure of an Italian slum,* Chicago: U of Chicago Press, and other editions: originally 1943

Malinowski, B. (1989) *A Diary in the Strict Sense of the Term,* Berkeley CA: Stanford University Press (based on unpublished diaries and fieldnotes 1915–1918)

Smith Bowen, E. (Laura Bohannan), (1988) *Return to Laughter: an anthropological novel,* Colchester: Anchor Press, and other editions: originally 1954

Tenni, C. Smyth, A. and Boucher C., (2003) 'The researcher as autobiographer: analyzing data written about oneself', *The Qualitative Report,* **8**(1): 1–12. www.nova,edu/ ssss/QR

Autopoietic system

See *Complex adaptive system.*

A

Availability bias

See *Bias, availability.*

Average

See *Central tendency and dispersion, Mean Median, Mode.*

Average, moving

See *Smoothing.*

Average, weighted

See *Weighted average*.

Axial coding

See *Coding, open axial and selective*.

Axiom

A proposition whose truth is taken for granted to serve as the starting point or *premise* of a deductive argument. Most frequently used in mathematics for propositions such as $2 + 2 = 4$. Sometimes used wrongly to suggest that some proposal is beyond all reasonable doubt, as in claims starting: 'It is axiomatic that...'. Axioms are more properly regarded as propositions accepted 'for the sake of argument'. See *Axiomatic system*, *Deductive reasoning*.

Axiomatic system

System of thought where meanings are determined entirely by its own internal rules, as in mathematics and formal logic. When such systems are used to represent phenomena external to them – such as relationships between social or psychological variables, they are termed **interpreted axiomatic systems.**

A

β (beta)

See *Statistical power, Type 1 and Type 2 errors*.

Backcasting

See *Prediction*.

Bar diagrams

See *Graphs*.

Barnardisation

See *Perturbation*.

Base-line measures

Synonym for *pre-test*.

Basing out

See *Index, to*.

Bayesian inference

So called after the Reverend Thomas Bayes (1701–61).

Bayes' Theorem can be expressed in various ways, for example: see Table 1.

The Bayesian process is one of updating estimates of the likelihood of something being true in the light of additional evidence. The *subjectivity* of this makes it controversial. However, both the evidence and the reasoning on which the subjective judgement is made are transparent, and objective in that sense – see *Objectivity*. Bayesian inference has traditionally

Table 1 Bayes' Theorem

$P(h|e) = \dfrac{(P(h) \times P(e|h)}{P(e)}$	Where: h = hypothesis e = evidence P = probability | = given	P(h) = *prior probability*, the degree of belief in the hypothesis before looking at the current evidence
		P(e|h) = probability that such evidence will exist assuming h is true
	P(h|e) = updated or posterior probability: the probability that can be subjectively allocated to an hypothesis taking all the evidence into consideration	P(e) the probability that the evidence will exist irrespective of whether the hypothesis is true or false

Meaning that the probability of the hypothesis being true after looking at the most recent evidence (the **posterior probability**, or **post**), is equal to the subjective probability assigned to the hypothesis on the basis of previous evidence (the **prior**), times the probability of the current evidence existing if the hypothesis is true, divided by the probability of that evidence existing whether or not the hypothesis is true. Put more simply: if you move to a new house and the dustman arrives on Thursday, you might nonetheless be sensible to assume that there is a one sixth probability- say 17% chance, that they will arrive next Thursday (discounting Sundays). That's your prior. If after six months the dustman has always called on Thursday, you might feel like revising your estimate of them arriving next Thursday to something closer to 100%. That's the posterior probability.

featured in diagnositic medicine and business decision-making – see *Decision analysis*. More recently it has become more popular in other areas, especially in *meta-analysis*. See also *Statistics software*.

Charles River Analytics Inc. (2004) *About Bayesian Belief Networks* www.cra.com/pdf/BnetBuilderBackground.pdf

McCreery, C. (2007) Probability and Bayes' Theorem' *Oxford Forum*, Psychological Paper No. 2007–2. www.celiagreen.com/charlesmccreery/statistics/bayestutorial.pdf

There are three excellent articles on Bayesian topics in the *Stanford Encyclopedia of Philosophy* http://plato.stanford.edu

B

BCS

See *British Crime Survey*.

BCS70

See *Birth cohort studies*.

Behaviourism (logical behaviourism)

A variety of *empiricism*. The view that the study of observable and measurable behaviour is the only valid basis for the scientific study of human activity. This is a version of monism, see *Dualism*. By critics, behaviour as conceived by behaviourists is often contrasted with *action*. Behaviourism usually shows the characteristics of *positivism*, with a belief in the possibility of generating scientific laws (see nomethetic research under *Idiographic research*) about human activity and of *reductionism*, regarding mental events such as intention, understanding, belief and so on, as explicable in terms of underlying biological processes, or as inexplicable and trivial.

Graham, G. (2007) 'Behaviorism' *Stanford Encyclopedia of Philosophy* http://plato. stanford.edu

Philosophy online (n.d.) 'Behaviourism' www.philosophyonline.co.uk/pom/pom_ behaviourism_introduction.htm

BEIRC: British Education Internet Resource Catalogue

Freely accessible database of information about professionally evaluated internet sites which support educational research, policy and practice. http://brs.leeds.ac.uk/~beiwww/beirc.htm

Bell curve

Synonym for *Normal distribution*.

Benchmarking

In *evaluation research, clinical audit* and *performance indication* the comparison of performance of one or more agencies against that of another, or others, chosen as the 'benchmark'.

Beta level

See *Statistical power, Type 1 and Type 2 errors*.

Between group/subjects designs

See *Related and unrelated designs*.

Between-judges variance

See *Inter-rater reliability*.

BHPS

See *British Household Panel Survey.*

Bias

Refers *either* to a deviation from the truth, hence assumes that, relevant to the judgement concerned, there is a single version of the truth which can be deviated from, thus bias is systematic error – (see *Error, random or systematic*). Or a favouring or prejudicing of the interests of some person or group. In *partisan research* and *standpoint epistemology* the two meanings are often not distinguished, and what is thought to be against the interests of the group favoured by the researcher is also regarded as untrue, and vice versa. See also *Bias #, Research artefacts.*

Hammersley, M. and Gomm, R. (2000) 'Bias in social research', in M. Hammersley, *Taking Sides in Social Research: Essays on Partisanship and Bias*, London: Routledge, 151–66

Bias, acquiescence

Attempts by respondents to please an interviewer, rather than to answer honestly. Synonyms: **acquiescence set**, **yea saying set**. Similar in meaning to co-operation bias *(Bias, co-operation).* See *Interviewer effect, Questions, leading.*

Bias, ascertainment

Sometimes called the **lamp-post error**, after the joke about a drunk who searched for his keys under a lamp-post, not because this was where he lost them, but because this was where it was lighter. The bias is in mistaking what is known, as a good guide to that which is unknown, for example thinking that those criminals who get caught are a representative sample of all criminals, known about and unknown. The reciprocal of ascertainment bias is the **dark number problem,** which refers to unenumerated phenomena – for example unreported crimes, unclaimed benefits. See also *Bias, availability, Bias, publication.*

Bias, attribution (fundamental attribution error)

A tendency to explain one's own failings in terms of situational factors and other people's failings with reference to internal factors such as personality, abilities, and feelings. Hence I am late because of a traffic hold up. He is late because he was too feckless to plan his journey with the contingency of a traffic hold up in mind. With regard to successes, the reverse tendency is shown, although some people explain their own

B

successes as due to situational factors and their failures as due to their personal characteristics – see *Bias, self-effacing*. Attribution bias is also called the **correspondence bias** from the assumption that people's behaviour corresponds to their personal attributes. See also *Attribution sets, Bias, self-serving, Motive attribution*.

Bias, attrition

See *Attrition*.

Bias, availability

The error of basing research findings on subjects, documents or data easily to hand (*Sample, convenience, Sample, self-selected, Sample, quota*) rather than representative samples (*Sample, representative*). Note for example the predominance in psychology of data derived from undergraduates, and, to quote Winston Churchill: 'one of the most misleading factors in history is the practice of historians to build a story exclusively out of the records which have come down to them.' Similar in meaning to ascertainment bias (*Bias, ascertainment*). Publication bias is a special case of availability bias (*Bias, publication*).

Bias by selection

See *Regression to the mean*. Not to be confused with selection bias – see *Bias, selection*.

Bias, citation

The number of times a piece of research is cited (referred to) in other publications may be a biased indication of its truth or importance. An exaggerated form of publication bias *(Bias, publication)*.

Bias, compositional

Of *group interviews*, the bias away from representativeness, deriving from the composition of the group. Or referring to the possibility of an error of consensual or majority judgement resulting from the less than ideal composition of a delphi group or nominal group (see *Group interviews*).

Bias, confirmational (or verificationist bias)

Bias shown by researcher towards the collection of, or the analysis of, data that favours what the researcher already believes or wishes to be true. For example, ceasing to collect data at the point at which a preferred result emerges, or discarding data which disconfirms a desired finding: the basis of many *expectancy effects*.

Bias, co-operation

The tendency for respondents to seek to be helpful to interviewers, rather than to provide accurate or honest answers. Synonym: **co-operation set**. Similar in meaning to acquiescence bias (*Bias, acquiescence*). See *Interviewer effect, Questions, leading*.

Bias, correspondence

See *Bias, attribution*.

Bias, exoticism

A tendency to notice and report on the features most unlike one's own society/culture and to ignore similarities. For example this has been suggested as the source of notions that people in contemporary Western cultures are more individualistic than most people elsewhere and in the past (Ouroussoff 1993). The opposite of culture-blindness – see also *Ethnocentrism, Orientalism, Post colonial Anthropology*.

Naroll, R. and Naroll, F. (1963) 'On Bias of Exotic data' *Man*, **LXIII** (Feb): 25
Ouroussoff, A. (1993) 'Illusions of rationality, false premises of liberal tradition', *Man* **28(4)**:281–298

Bias, experimenter

See *Expectancy effect*.

Bias, interviewer

See *Interviewer effect*.

Bias, narrative

The tendency for respondents to provide information in ways that constitute 'a good story', rather than accurately. This is not a problem in those forms of *narrative analysis* where the way stories are told is of central interest. A similar tendency is sometimes shown by researchers telling the story of their research – see *Autoethnography, Reflexivity, Rhetorical analysis*.

Bias, patriarchal

The tendency to see things from a male ('malestream') point of view. **Masculinism** is used in the same way but most often in expressing the

B

view that in claiming superiority for their theories over the ideas of lay people, scientists (male or female), are tyrannical and oppressive.

Bias, positional

Any tendency of respondents to be influenced by the position of a question within a sequence or by the layout of the permitted response options. Includes *error of central tendency* and some *primacy and recency effects* – see also *Question formats*.

Bias, publication

At any one time the research published about a particular topic will not be a *representative sample* of all the research which might be published about that topic, nor even of all the research which has been conducted about it. Deviations from representativeness include the tendencies to favour the publication of definite rather than ambiguous results, and novel results rather than confirmations. There may also be a bias against publishing highly original work, or work by 'outsiders' to a field of study. Thus the corpus of work on a topic is likely to give a misleading picture. This is particularly so with statistical *meta-analysis*, where attempts are made to combine the results of several studies and where the pooled result may be highly biased by publication bias: see *Fail-safe N, Funnel plot, Meta-analysis*.

Department of Health Sciences, University of York (n.d.) 'Meta-analysis: publication bias' http://www-users.york.ac.uk/~mb55/msc/systrev/pub_text.pdf

Scargle, E. (2000) 'Publication bias: the file-drawer problem in scientific inference', *Journal of Society for Scientific Exploration* **14**(1):91–106. http://www.scientificexploration.org/jse/articles/

Bias, recall/retrospective

As well as referring to the frailty of human memory also refers to the tendency for recent events to distort memories of the past. See also *Bias, narrative*.

Bias, sampling

The extent to which a sample deviates from statistical *representativeness*. Includes selection bias, *Bias, selection* and *Sampling error*.

Bias, selection (or selection error)

Not to be confused with bias by selection – see *Regression to the mean*. Usually a deviation from the kind of *representativeness* a sample was supposed to achieve; includes bias arising from *coverage error* and from

B

non-response – see *Response rate*, from *Design effects* and other from other causes, but excludes *sampling error*. See *Bias, sampling, Heckman's procedure, Imputation, Weighting*.

Bias, self-effacing

Said to be more characteristic of people from collectivist cultures, and of women more than men, a tendency for respondents/interviewees to downgrade their own achievements, efforts or status and or to attribute them to fortuitous situations or to the efforts of others. See also, *Bias, attribution*.

Bias, self-serving

Usually of interviewees, or autobiographers; a tendency to show themselves in a preferred way. Not restricted to self-presentation in a conventionally respectable way **(Social desirability bias)**, since some respondents may want to shock, and others to display themselves as victims. See *Bias, attribution, Interviewer effect, Questions, leading*.

Bias, sympathetic (over-rapport, going native)

A researcher coming uncritically to view the world in the same way as those studied/a researcher angling findings to favour those studied to the extent of misrepresentation. Not regarded as a bias by *partisan* researchers and or those engaged in *participatory research*.

Bias, value

Any deviation from the truth, or any prejudice against or in favour of some person or social group due to the moral values held by the researcher, by the researcher's informants, his or her sponsors, or anyone else able to influence the research. Value bias may not be regarded as a problem by *partisan researchers* if it is in favour of a social group they support – see *Value-neutral or value-led research*.

Bibliometrics

See *Citations*.

Bimodal distribution

Frequency distribution showing two peaks.

Bin

Synonym for class interval – see *Frequency distribution*.

B

Binomial distribution

Describes the *probability* of an event occurring where there are two possibilities and where each event is independent of each other: for example the frequency of heads and tails in 100 tosses, or the chances of twins in 1000 births. The **binomial theorem** is used to calculates probabilities in estimating the likelihood of various *combinations and permutations*.

Krysstal (n.d) *Pascal's Triangle* http://www.krysstal.com/binomial.html

Binomial sign test

Non-parametric test of *statistical significance* for nominal level data, from a related design- see *Data, levels of, Statistics parametric and non-parametric, Related and unrelated designs*. All that is taken into account is the direction of difference between pairs of scores. The result tells whether there is a difference in a particular direction greater than could be expected by chance. For calculators and tutorials see *Statistics software*.

Biography

See Life history research, Oral history research.

Birth cohort studies

A series of large scale *longitudinal surveys* of children born in particular years starting in 1946: the major source of information about childhood and subsequent development in the UK. See also *Cohort studies*.

The following can be accessed from www.longitudinal.stir.ac.uk/index.html or www.cls.ioe.ac.uk

- The MRC National Survey of Health and Development (NSHD) (once known as the British 1946 Birth Cohort Study).
- The National Child Development Study (NCDS)- cohort born March 1958.
- The 1970 British Cohort Study (BCS70).
- The Millennium Cohort Study (MCS). The first sweep began in June 2001 and gathered information from the parents of 18,819 babies born in the UK over a 12-month period and living in selected UK wards at age 9 months.

And for The Avon Longitudinal Study of Parents and Children http://www.bristol.ac.uk/alspac/

Bivariate analysis

Analysis concurrently of two variables, as in, for instance, *binominal sign test, contingency tables, t-tests,* χ^2 *tests* and *scattergrams*.

Black box

Part of a process left uninvestigated in a piece of research. For example, a study comparing the morale of people discharged from hospital with their morale on entry, could be said to have 'black boxed' what actually happened in hospital if this was not investigated. All research leaves some boxes black.

Blinding

Subjects and or researchers are deprived of knowledge which, if they had it, might influence their behaviour or judgement causing unwanted *subject reactivity* and *expectancy effects*. In **double blind experiments** experimental subjects <u>and</u> researchers are prevented from knowing which of two treatments subjects are being subjected to; in **single blind experiments,** only the subjects are deprived of this information. In medical research a *placebo* may be used to facilitate blinding. Blinding may also be used at the stage of analysing the results of research and in *inter-rater reliability* tests. **Masking** is an alternative term where blinding is accomplished by anonymising the source or subjects of documents – see also *Random allocation/randomisation*.

BME/BMEG

Black and Minority Ethnic (Groups). A widely used but confusing term which has meaning only if there is an accompanying specification. Sometimes restricted to people of colour in Britain with African, African Caribbean and South Asian origins, sometimes including (some) and sometimes not including (some) people of mixed race; maybe including near eastern, south east Asian and far eastern people, and sometimes and sometimes not including 'white' minorities such as people from eastern Europe or the eastern Mediterranean. Often including the Irish in Britain but rarely including white western Europeans or white Americans, Canadians, Australians or New Zealanders. 'Minority' is always defined in relation to the national population, so that where locally a BME group is in the majority it is still termed a 'minority group'. See *Ethnic categories*.

B

Body language

See *Kinesics*.

Boolean algebra/logic/symbolic logic

A binary logical system devised by George Boole to describe propositions whose outcome would be either true or false (as expressed in **truth**

tables). This is the basis of the operational logic of internet search engines and of some forms of *comparative analysis* – see *Qualitative comparative analysis (QCA)*.

Department of Electronic Engineering University of Surrey, *'Elements of Boolean Algebra'*, www.ee.surrey.ac.uk/Projects/Labview/boolalgebra/

Bootstrapping

In statistics, the creation of a virtual *population* of *data* from a small sample by cloning the sample again and again. For example if 3, 7,16,10, 12, 5, 8, 10, 7, 5 is a probability sample (*Sample, probability*) it can be cloned to produce a population such as:

> 3, 7, 16, 10, 12, 5, 8, 10, 7, 5, 3, 7, 16, 10, 12, 5, 8, 10, 7, 5, 3, 7, 16, 10, 12, 5, 8, 10, 7, 5, 3, 7, 16, 10, 12, 5, 8, 10, 7, 5, 3, 7, 16, 10, 12, 5, 8, 10, 7, 5, 3, 7, 16, 10, 12, 5, 8, 10, 7, 5, 3, 7, 16, 10, 12, 5, 8, 10, 7, 5, and so on.

Then a very large number of probability samples of 10 can be taken from this population to yield quite good estimates of the *parameters* of the population from which the original sample was drawn. Bootstrapping may also refer to the generation of more elaborate data sets, particularly in *computer simulation*, and has several other meanings in engineering, software design, and financial investment.

Box plot (box and whisker diagram)

Graphical *five number summary* of a data set. It shows the:

- *median* as a measure of central tendency.
- *range* from maximum to minimum value.
- *inter-quartile range* – the middle 50% of scores from the top of
  - the first quartile (of the second 25% of scores) shown by the bottom of the box, to
  - the bottom of the third quartile (the third 25% of scores/the score at 75%) shown by the top of the box.
- Any skew in the distribution is shown by the median not being in the middle of the box.
- Outliers may be shown separately or by a whisker which is at least three times as long as the box.

(See Figure 3 opposite) Box plots are especially useful when comparing two or more sets of data. A rough visual test for *homoscedasticity* is the extent to which the boxes are the same vertical height. See also *Inter-quartile range*.

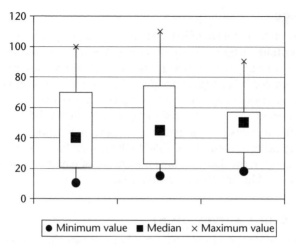

Figure 3   Box plots for three samples

Bracketing (epoché/phenomenological reduction)

From *phenomenology*: the setting aside of everyday assumptions about what is real; the suspension of belief that what is being studied has any reality beyond our perception of it. Sometimes the latter is regarded as the truth, as in strong versions of *social constructionism*: sometimes as a useful mind set to adopt for studying how phenomena are constituted in thought – see *Antropologically strange*, S*trong programme*.

Brain-storming

See *Group interviews, nominal group*.

Breaching experiments/disruption experiments/ Garfinkeling

The subversion or disruption of taken-for-granted assumptions in order to study how they are repaired and 'normalcy' sustained. For example, in the lodger experiment, Howard Garfinkel's students (1967) behaved in their own homes as if they were guests and recorded the reactions of family members to this. Thus by violating expectations for the behaviour of family members, they demonstrated what those expectations were.

Garfinkel, H. (1967) *Studies in Ethnomethodology*, Englewood Cliffs: Prentice-Hall
Rafalovitch, A. (2006) 'Making Sociology relevant: the assignment and application of breaching experiments', *Teaching Sociology* **34**(2)

Bricolage

Originally an assemblage of heterogeneous bits and pieces, put together by a **bricoleur** using a variety of *ad hoc* methods. Sometimes applied to cultures to suggest that they are not logical and consistent, but have been assembled by historical accident. In research, sometimes (though rarely) used pejoratively to claim that a piece of research is unprincipled and incoherent – see *Method slurring*. More often used to make the point that that *ethnographic research* is inevitably a bricolage because in order to achieve naturalistic validity the researcher has to respond to what happens in the field and take advantage of whatever opportunities become available. See *Validity, naturalistic.*

British Crime Survey (BCS)

www.homeoffice.gov.uk/rds/bcs1.html and see *Victim Surveys.*

British Household Panel Survey (BHPS)

Longitudinal survey, following a large panel of respondents recruited in 1991 and re-interviewed annually. See *Panel surveys.* http://www.iser.essex.ac.uk/ulsc/bhps/

British Social Attitudes Survey (BSA)

See *Opinion Polls.*

Burden analysis

Type of economic analysis estimating the cost of illness (Cost of Illness (COI) studies) or of some social problem, such as crime or unemployment, or of taxation or regulation on sections of the population or sectors of the economy, or to 'society' or the 'economy'. Such analyses are often presented as part of a political lobbying process. Estimates are highly vulnerable to different initial assumptions about what would happen in the absence of the phenomenon topicalised and on the range of parties included as experiencing costs and benefits. As an example see Black (2008). See also *Cost-[#] analysis.*

Black, C. (2008) *Working for a Healthier Tomorrow: Dame Carol Black's review of the health of Britain's working age population,* London: The Stationery Office. www.workingforhealth.gov.uk/documents/working-for-a-healthier-tomorrow-tagged.pdf

Bureaucratic data

See *Administrative data.*

B

C or c

(1) outcome of *Cochran's C test*; (2) short for column, for example in formulae for *degrees of freedom*.

CA

Categorical Analysis (see *Membership Category Analysis*), or Cellular Automata (used in *computer simulation*), or *Clinical Audit*, or *Cluster Analysis*, or *Cognitive Anthropology* or *Conversation analysis,* or Computer Aided/Assisted # (see *Computer Assisted Qualitative Data Analysis* and *Questionnaire administration*).

CACI (Consolidated Analysis Centre Incorporated)

See *ACORN*.

Caldicott guardians

Senior officials from NHS organisations and councils with social services responsibilities, appointed to protect the confidentiality of patient/client information, including that generated by research. See also *Gate-keepers, Privacy and confidentiality.*

Caldicott Committee (1997) *Report on the Review of Patient-Identifiable Information,* London: Department of Health. http://confidential.oxfordradcliffe.net/caldicott/report/

Callactic system

See *Complex adaptive system.*

Call-back

In probability sampling for surveys, once a respondent has been chosen it is important to do all that is reasonable to ensure that they actually

participate – see *Response rate, Sample, probability*. Most survey researchers will set a **call-back level**, meaning the number of attempts which
will be made to contact a respondent before giving up. Call-back is not
a routine feature of surveys with non-probability samples; see *Sample,
quota*.

Cambridge scale

Scheme for stratifying the population into social classes according to
their associations or networks by scaling survey respondents' occupational friendships and the similarity and difference between partners.
See also *Social class*.
   Supported by CAMIS web site: http://www.camsis.stir.ac.uk/
overview.html

CAMIS

Not to be confused with *CASMIN* – see *Cambridge scale*.

Campbell collaboration

Network of institutions producing systematic reviews and *meta-analyses*
of research on effective practice for education, social work and criminal
justice interventions http://www.campbellcollaboration.org/.
   See *Effectiveness Research*.

CAPI (Computer Assisted Personal Interview/(ing))

See *Questionnaire administration*.

CAQDAS

See *Computer Assisted Qualitative Data Analysis*.

Card sorting

Elicitation technique as an alternative or adjunct to *questionnaires* in
which respondents are:

  ● asked to sort cards bearing information into logical groups (see
     Affinity diagramming, Concept mapping), or
  ● arrange cards in priority order in research on *utilities* or as a group
     activity in *nominal groups, citizen juries* or *focus groups*, or
  ● given sets of three and asked to pair two as alike and, usu-
     ally, to state how they are alike and how the other differs (*triadic
     elicitation*)

Card sorting may be emulated on-screen with drag and drop software. The technique may be more effective than standard questionnaire elicitation with children and other groups for whom literacy is a problem, especially where pictures and pictograms rather than words can be used. See also *Repertory grid technique.*

Career respondents

People who habitually put themselves forwards to respond to surveys, or to be enrolled in a panel – see *Panel surveys*, or a *Group interview.* A problem particularly where *incentives* are offered for participation as a cheap and easy method of recruiting respondents, leading to selection bias – see *Bias, selection, Sample, convenience, Sample, self-selected.* Career respondents are supported by web sites such as http://highestpaysurveys.com/.

Cartesian distinction/divide/split

See *Dualism.*

CAS

Census Area Statistics, see *Output areas.*

Case-based comparative research

See *Comparative method.*

Case control studies (case referent studies)

A comparison of potentially relevant characteristics made between some naturally occurring group of subjects – the cases (for example families that have experienced a sudden infant death) – and another group of subjects recruited to be similar to them, except for the characteristic of central interest (they have not experienced a cot death). The extent to which the two groups differ may be taken to explain why one group and not the other has the characteristic of interest. See also *Control, direct and statistical, Population comparison studies.*

> Coggan, D., Rose, G. and Barker, D.(1997) 'Case control and cross-sectional studies' Chapter 8 in *Epidemiology for the Uninitiated* (4th edn), Oxford:Wiley-Blackwell www.bmj.com/epidem/epid.html

Case referent studies

See *Case control studies.*

Case study

Using *documentary research, survey,* or *ethnographic* methods to make a detailed study of some naturally occurring entity – the case –, for example, a person, a school, a village or a firm. May be conducted because the case is of intrinsic interest, or as an example of a type. The term is sometimes used to imply that the case is unique and can only be analysed in its own terms and that the study will not yield generalisations – an *idiographic study,* and sometimes, by contrast, to imply that the 'case' represents a category in a classification system (schools or villages of particular types, for example) and that the study can illuminate other instances of the same category – see G*eneralisation, theoretical, Repesentativeness, Sampling, theoretical.* It is usually agreed, however, that basing *generalisations* on case studies is hazardous. Most qualitative research is case study research. The term may also be used to refer to the more detailed treatment of some aspects within a wider study; for example, a more intense study of selected prisoners – the cases – within a study of a prison as a whole. See also *Community studies, Critical case analysis, Deviant case analysis.*

Colorado State University (2008) *Writing Guides: case studies* http://writing.colostate.edu/guides/research/casestudy/pop2a.cfm

Gomm, R., Hammersley, M. and Foster, R. (eds) (2000) *Case Study Method: Key Issues, Key Texts,* London: Sage

CASI (Computer Assisted Self-interviewing Collection)

See *Questionnaire administration.*

CASMIN (Comparative Study of Social Mobility in Industrial Nations) (not to be confused with CAMIS)

International collaboration for harmonising the classification of occupations to produce commensurate descriptions of the 'class structures' of different nations, and for comparative class and social mobility analysis (Erikson and Goldthorpe 1992). Using an approach based on *Goldthorpe Classes* sometimes termed the **CASMIN schema** The interest in social mobility was continued in the **NPSM** project 'National Patterns of Social Mobility: Convergence or Divergence?' at Oxford (Breen 2004) and in harmonising socio-economic classifications in the *ESeC Project.*

See also *CASMIN educational classification, Social class.*

Erikson, R. and J.H. Goldthorpe 1992 *The Constant Flux: A Study of Class Mobility in Industrial Societies,* Oxford: Clarendon Press

Breen, R.(2004) *Social Mobility in Europe, http://www.sidos.ch/method/RC28/abstracts/Richard%20Breen%20_keynote_.pdf*

National Patterns of Social Mobility, 1970-1995: Divergence or Convergence? http://www.nuffield.ox.ac.uk/Users/yaish/npsm/

CASMIN educational classification

Classification of levels of education according to length and required aptitude and whether vocational or academic.

Müller, W. (n.d.) *CASMIN educational classification*. http://www.nuffield.ox.ac.uk/Users/ yaish/npsm/documents.htm

See also *CASMIN (Comparative Study of Social Mobility in Industrial Nations)*

Categorical analysis

See *Membership category analysis (MCA)*.

Categorical data/variable

See *Data, levels of (nominal level data)*.

Category bound activity (CBA)

See *Membership category analysis*.

CATI (Computer Assisted Telephone Interview/(ing))

See *Questionnaire administration*.

Causal analysis

Any research designed to establish what causes what to happen – **causality**. *Experiments* are usually regarded as the superior means for this, where changes in dependent variables are said to be caused by changes in independent variables – see *Variable, dependent* and *Variable, independent*. *Empiricism* argues that causality cannot be observed. All that can be observed is that one thing regularly follows another (**constant conjunction**). This is why writers often try to avoid using terms such as cause and effect, even when the *direction of effect* is quite clear. Alternatives include talking about:

- *correlation* between independent/treatment/predictor variables on the one hand and dependent/outcome/criterion variables on the other – see also *Logistic Regression*, *Regression analysis, Variable*
- the amount of *variance* in the dependent variable accounted for by the independent variable – *variance explained*
- the extent to which one value can be predicted from another – *proportional reduction in error (PRE)*
- 'effects' and 'effect sizes' without mentioning the word 'cause' – see *Effect size (ES) measurement*.

Researchers subscribing to *realism* or *critical rationalism* have less trouble in accepting the reality of causation. Since they are prepared to accept the reality of unobservable structures and forces which can only be known about because they alter the things which can be observed, then accepting causality which can only be inferred in the same way, is not really a problem.

There are actually two different ways of thinking about causality. The more traditional way is **conjuctionalist/successonist/sequentialist casuality** where a prior *variable* is viewed as the cause of the value of a subsequent variable. This view underlies a great deal of research. The other, associated explicitly with *realism*, though adopted by many who do not call themselves realists, is generative causality, where cause is seen in terms of generative mechanisms operating when the characteristics of a context facilitates this. **Generative mechanisms** include for example, gravity, word-of-mouth or feelings of relative deprivation (Pawson 2008). The distinction between mechanism and context comes close to the Aristotelian distinction between **necessary and sufficient causes/conditions**; the latter being the generative mechanism or 'cause' and the former the conditions or context required for the cause to have its effect (Brennan 2003). But 'necessary' and 'sufficient' are often difficult to pin down , as is the distinction between context and mechanism, and *pragmatism's* **manipulability** idea of causation is another response to this problem. A cause is then what may be manipulated to create an effect and causality is relative to context, explanatory intention and research procedure (Woodwood 2002).

The idea of causality has traditionally been associated with the idea of *determinism.* One of the reasons for the reluctance of early empiricists to accept the idea of causality was that a deterministic notion was incompatible with the idea of free will (Russell 2007) – see *agency.* More recently the idea of **probabalistic causality** has become more acceptable (Hitchcock 2002) where the claim is merely that something is likely to happen under specified circumstances. See also *Causal modelling.*

Brennan, A. (2003) 'Necessary and sufficient'
Hitchcock, C. (2002) 'Probabalistic causation'
Russell, P. (2007) 'Hume on free will'
Woodwood, J. (2002) 'Causation and manipulability'
All in the *Stanford Encyclopedia of Philosophy* http://plato.stanford.edu/
Pawson, R. (2008) *Don't forget to think: Middle range theory as causal analysis,* NCRM
    http://www.ncrm.ac.uk/ and search on author

Causal modelling

Various statistical techniques such as *partial correlation* and *path analysis*, and *structural equation modelling* where the strength of *association* between *variables* is interpreted as the extent to which one influences the other, or of the influence on both of some other *variable*. See also *Causal analysis, Statistics software.*

CBA (Cost Benefit Analysis)

See *Cost-[#] Analysis.*

Ceiling and floor effects

Ceiling effects occur where the results of a test or some other instrument are clumped towards the top of the measuring scale. The test may then not discriminate adequately between those achieving the highest scores. With **floor effects** most of the scores fall towards the bottom and the test may not discriminate adequately between those with the lowest scores. Both are skewed distributions – see also *Kurtosis.* In either case the test will be said to lack discriminant validity ; see *Validity, discriminant.*

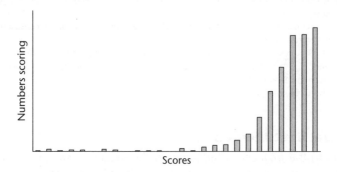

Figure 4   Showing ceiling effect: for example the results of a scholastic test which is so easy it fails to discriminate well among the most able

Depending whether they are measuring healthiness or illness either effect is common in the instruments used to measure physical and mental health, which often fail to discriminate between those who are on the verge of illness and those who are robustly healthy, because doctors are less interested in degrees of healthiness. See also *Item analysis.*

Censored data

Left censored events are those which started prior to the data collection period. Right censored events are those which continue beyond the end of the data collection period. Primarily a term used in *Event history analysis.*

Census

Social survey conducted with intention of including one hundred per cent of the target population, as opposed to sample surveys – see *Survey*. The term is used principally of censuses of the national population, although sometimes otherwise, for example in a census of the nursing workforce. The UK census have been held every 10 years in the 1st, 11th, 21st and so on, year of a millennium since 1801, with the exception of 1941. Apart from being of interest in themselves, the data provide important benchmarks for estimating whether samples in surveys are representative of populations, and for calculating rates such as morbidity and morality, *incidence and prevalence* of illness or victimisation – see *Enumerator – denominator discrepancies*. The coverage of the census is checked with a Census coverage survey (Abbot *et al.,* 2005), and data are up-dated periodically by estimates based on ad hoc surveys and other data, but inevitably become outdated as an inter-census period wears on – see also *Output areas, Response rate.*

Census England and Wales: Office for National Statistics (ONS) www.statistics.gov.uk/census/default.asp
Census Scotland www.gro-scotland.gov.uk/grosweb/grosweb.nsf/pages/censushm
Census Northern Ireland www.nisra.gov.uk
Abbot, O.,Jones, J. and Pereira, R., (2005) 'Census coverage survey: review and evaluation', Survey Methodology Bulletin No. 55: 37–42. www.statistics.gov.uk [and search for 'Survey Methodology Bulletin No. 55']
See also *Output Areas, SARs*

Central limit theorem

Refers to the *frequency distribution* of the means of samples taken at random from a *population*. If an infinite number of random samples were taken, then the *mean* (average) of their means would be identical to the mean of the population. The larger the sample, the more likely it is that its mean and *standard deviation* will be similar to those of the population. The *frequency distribution* of the means of such samples will shape up as a *normal distribution*, which allows for the calculation of the likely difference between the mean, *variance* or *standard deviation* of any sample and the mean, variance or standard deviation of the population the sample is supposed to represent – the *sampling error*. On the same principle all measurements are regarded as having two components, a true measure and a **measurement error**. Graphing the results of a very large number of measurements should result in a mean which is very close to the true measure and a normal distribution of errors. Whether for a sample, or for a measure, the central limit theorem is the basis for the calculation of *confidence intervals*.

The central limit theorem is not valid for data with a *Power (law) distribution.*

For an interactive demonstration of the central limit theorem -University of South Carolina http://www.stat.sc.edu/~west/javahtml/CLT.html

Musalia,J., (2008) *Chapter 10: Sampling* and *Chapter 11: Estimation.* University of West Kentucky. www.wku.edu/~john.musalia/soc300/

Central tendency and dispersion, measures of

These measures define the shape of a data set in terms of the way the data do, or do not, cluster around a mid-point. They are most meaningful for data distributions that approximate to a *normal distribution.* See Table 2.

Table 2   Central tendency measures and measures of dispersion

Central tendency measures define a score which is most typical of all the scores.	**Measures of dispersion** describe how the data in the set are spread out
The mode 7, 8,8,8,8,9,10,11,11,12,13,15,17, 21,21 The most common score in a set -often a poor measure of central tendency and not amenable to statistical manipulation. Data sets may have more than one mode. The mode is not a meaningful measure for *power law distributions*	**The range** 7, 8,8,8,8,9,10,11,11,12,13,15,17, 21,21 The range is between 7 and 21, or 14 points
The median 7, 8,8,8,8,9,10,11,11,12,13,15,17, 21,21 The middle score (in an odd number of scores) or the *mean* of the two middle scores (in an even number of scores) Half of all scores are on or below the median, and half are on or above the median. The median is not a meaningful measure *for power law distributions*	**The inter-quartile range** 7, 8,8,8,8,9,10,11,11,12,13,15,17, 21,21 The range which includes the middle 50% of scores. This is often the measure of dispersion used with the *median.* Sometimes analysis is conducted only on the data within the inter-quartile range, to exclude unusually high and unusually low scores, see *Inter-quartile range.*

(Continued)

Table 2 Central tendency measures and measures of dispersion

The *mean* (or arithmetic average)	The mean deviation, the *variance* and the *standard deviation* are all ways of expressing the amount by which the individual scores in a set differ from the *mean*

The *mean* (or arithmetic average)

$\boxed{11.93}$

7+8+8+8+8+9+10+11+11+12
+13+15+17+ 21+21=179

179/15= 11.93

Add up all the scores and divide by the number of scores. The mean is the most usual, and useful, measure of central tendency, providing a 'mid-point' against which the dispersion of the data set can be described. The mean is not a meaningful measure for *power law distributions*

The *mean deviation* is rarely used, except as a step on the way to calculating the *variance* or the *standard deviation*. These convert directly into each other: the *variance* is the *standard deviation* squared and the *standard deviation* is the square root of the *variance*.

The *variance* is used in the *analysis of variance (ANOVA)* and the *analysis of covariance (ANCOVA)*. The higher the figure for the variance the more scattered the scores are.

The *standard deviation* is used in a wide variety of statistical operations. It serves as a unit for measuring the distance between a particular score and the *mean* as so many *standard deviations* above or below the mean. Where scores are drawn from a population of scores which has a *normal distribution,* the *mean* and the *standard deviation* can be used to calculate how many scores will lie how many standard deviations above or Below the *mean.*

The mean deviation, the *variance* and the *standard deviation* are all ways of expressing the amount by which the individual scores in a set differ from the *mean*

Score	Mean	Difference between score and mean	Difference squared
7	11.93	−4.93	24.34
8	11.93	−3.93	15.47
8	11.93	−3.93	15.47
8	11.93	−3.93	15.47
8	11.93	−3.93	15.47
9	11.93	−2.93	8.60
10	11.93	−1.93	3.74
11	11.93	−0.93	0.87
11	11.93	−0.93	0.87
12	11.93	0.07	0.01
13	11.93	1.07	1.14
15	11.93	3.07	9.40
17	11.93	5.07	25.67
21	11.93	9.07	82.20
21	11.93	9.07	82.20
179	**total deviation**	54.77*	300.93
179/15= 11.93	**mean deviation**	54.77/15=3.65	

population variance
300.93/ 15 = 20.06

sample variance**
300.93/ 14 = 21.49

The **standard deviation** is the square root of the variance

✓ 300.93 = 17.35

coefficient of variation is the standard deviation divided by the mean 17.35/ 11.93 = 1.45

*ignore the minus signs when totalling for the mean deviation, otherwise the total will always be zero.

**Sample variance is sum of the individual variances divided by n-1 (one less than the total number of scores)

See also *Analysis of covariance (ANCOVA and MANCOVA), Analysis of variance (ANOVA and MANOVA), Coefficient of variation, Confidence intervals, Normal distribution, Statistical significance, Statistics software, Stem and leaf plots.*

Musalia, J.(2006) *Chapter 4: Measures of Central Tendency,* and *Chapter 5: Meaures of Variability,* University of West Kentucky: www.wku.edu/~john.musalia/soc300/

CER

See *Effect size (ES) measures.*

CERUK-plus (Current Educational and Children's Services Research in the UK)

NFER database of current and recently completed research in education and children's services.www.ceruk.ac.uk

Ceteris paribus

Latin for 'all other things being equal' (which they rarely are). Referring to the *context dependency* of phenomena, a phrase added to generalisations and law-like statements to account for the fact that they are only rarely precisely true.

Chaos theory

A subset of *Complexity theory.*

Children as researchers

Participative research where children are involved in data collection and analysis.

Kellett, M (2005) *Children as active researchers: a new research paradigm for the 21st century?* London, NCRM, http://www.ncrm.ac.uk/research/outputs/publications/

Children, research with

See *Criminal records, Sensitive topics and vulnerable groups.*

Chi square

See X^2.

Citation indices

Enumerate the number of times articles and books are referred to (cited) in other books and articles. **Bibliometrics** is the study of citations.

In the social and behavioural sciences the major indices are:

- **Social Sciences Citation Index** (**SSCI**) and **Social SciSearch,** recording cited references from articles found in over 1,700 scholarly social sciences journals and more selectively from another 3,300 science and technology journals. Provides access to author abstracts.
- **Arts & Humanities Citation Index** (A&HCI) and **Arts & Humanities Search,** recording cited references from articles found in nearly 1,130 of the world's leading arts & humanities journals, and more selectively from approximately 7,000 of the world's leading science and social sciences journals.

The citation indices are provided by Thomson Scientific as a subscription service http://scientific.thomson.com/

Although no longer provided by the Institute for Scientific Information this web-site by them is still a useful introduction to the citation indices: http://wos.isitrial.com/help/helpquik.html#Easy_Search

Citizen juries

See *Group interviews.*

Class intervals

See *Frequency distribution.*

Clinical audit (CA)

The *evaluation* process whereby a clinical team considers its own performance in relation to what is achieved elsewhere (benchmarking) and in relation to research evidence about effective practice – see *Effectiveness research*. Clinical audit is widespread in the NHS and in health services elsewhere, and emulated to some extent by other services.

Clinical audit support centre web sites www.clinicalauditsupport.com and www.crag.scot.nhs.uk

Closed questions

See *Question formats.*

Cluster analysis (CA)

Statistical procedures for sorting entities into categories with similar properties, involving the measurement of similarities or differences. Similar in intention to *Factor analysis.*

Statsoft Electronic Textbook: www.statsoft.com

Cluster randomisation

See *Random allocation.*

Cluster sampling

See *Sample, cluster.*

CMA (Cost Minimisation Analysis)

See *Cost-[#] analysis.*

CN

See *Confidence number.*

Cochrane collaboration

(http://www.cochrane.org/index.htm) unites a number of academic centres together for the purpose of conducting systematic reviews and *meta-analyses*, mainly in medicine but also in other human service fields. See also *Campbell collaboration, Effectiveness research.*

Coding

Assigning a number or a verbal label to some recurrent feature of data in order to index it. For *questionnaires* with forced choice questions, coding is typically done in advance of collecting the data; hence the term **pre-structured data.** In *qualitative interviews* and *ethnographic* research it is typically done in analysing the data once it has been collected. In all forms, the coding system will depend on what is of interest to the researcher. See also *Coding, open axial and selective, Computer assisted qualitative data analysis (CAQDA), Grounded theory, Question formats.*

Coding, open, axial and selective

(See also *Coding).* In the Strauss and Corbin version of *Grounded theory* **open coding** is an initial process of identifying and naming categories in the data, and, where appropriate, *dimensionalising* the categories along continua of variation (for example, from 'never' to 'always'). **Axial coding** is a process of identifying relationships between the categories established by open coding – although it may prompt some additional open coding activity. A common kind of axial coding is the classification of events or utterances on the basis of who, what, when, where, and what next. **Selective coding** involves elaborating and validating

C

the axial codes and refining the analysis. See also *Constant comparison, Validation.*

Dick,B.(2005) 'Grounded theory: a thumbnail sketch', *Resource Papers in Action Research.* www.scu.edu.au/schools/gcm/ar/arp/grounded.html

Woods, L., Priest, H., and Roberts, P.(2002) 'An overview of three different approaches to the interpretation of qualitative data: Part 2, Practical illustrations', *Nurse Researcher* **10**(1) :44–46

Strauss, B. and Corbin, J., (1990) *Basics of Qualitative Research,* London: Sage

Coding, thematic

See *Thematic analysis.*

Coefficient of alienation and coefficient of determination

See *Pearson's product moment coefficient.*

Coefficient of variation

Statistic expressing the degree of variability in a data set; the *standard deviation* divided by the *mean.* Sometimes used as a measure of income inequality. See also *Central tendency and dispersion, Inequality measures and metrics.*

Cognitive anthropology (CA) (New ethnography)

A collection of approaches to the study of culture which are diverse and which have changed through time but have in common the notion that cultures can be analysed in terms of logical rules and that such rules will derive from the way the human mind processes information; hence a close connection with cognitive psychology. These assumptions run counter to those associated with the idea of culture as a *bricolage* and the practice of creating *thick descriptions/ethnography.* Cognitive anthropology includes **ethnoscience** which is the study of the ideas people have about the natural world and the uses to which they put such ideas (as in ethno-medicine, ethno-agronomy, ethno-botany and so on) and studies of other classifications systems and the way they are employed in varying contexts. *Componential analysis* is one of the techniques used, as is the drawing of connectionist networks – see *Conceptual mapping.* More recently there has been a two way interchange between cognitive anthropology and the field of artificial intelligence. Terms used for cognitive/cultural structures include: folk taxonomies, knowledge structures, mazeways, mental scripts, prototypes, schemata, connectionist networks – see also *Actor perspectives, Consensus theory.*

Solomon, S., (2000) *A Brief History of Cognitive Anthropology* www.geocities.com/xerexes/coganth.html

Cognitive interview

Procedures for identifying problems in *questionnaires,* schedules for *interviews* or other data collecting instruments, and for validating such instruments. People chosen to be like intended respondents are interviewed using alternative forms of questions and asked questions about the questions. The focus is on the cognitive processes involved in responding to questions when posed in particular ways. See also, *Interviews, types of, Walk-through.*

Wills, G (1999) *Cognitive Interviewing: A 'How To' Guide,* Research Triangle Institute http://appliedresearch.cancer.gov/areas/cognitive/interview.pdf
As an example see the cognitive pilot study for the UK Household Longitudinal Study http://www.iser.essex.ac.uk/

Cohen's delta

See *Effect size (ES) measures.*

Cohen's kappa

See *Inter-rater reliability.*

Cohen's standards

Translations of effect size magnitudes into Strong, Medium and Weak – see *Effect size (ES) measures.*

Coherentism

See *Fallibilism as opposed to Foundationalism.*

Cohort

Group who have had some similar experience during the same period of time; usually at the outset; for example, all those MPs who entered Parliament for the first time, following a particular general election or simply a group all recruited to a survey or experiment at the same point in time.

Cohort effect

See *Age, period and cohort effects.*

Cohort study

Longitudinal research of a *cohort*, usually though not always *prospective.* The members of the cohort constituting the sample for study may or may not have been selected as a probability sample – *see Sample, probability.* In the UK, cohort study always implies that the same subjects are studied through time. In the USA cohort study may also refer to successive cross-sectional studies where the same *kind* of people are studied through time, termed *Pseudo-cohort* or quasi-cohort studies in the UK. See also *Birth cohort studies, Time series analysis.*

> As an example of a cohort study see the Whitehall II Study www.ucl.ac.uk/whitehallII/ publications/index.htm

CoI (Cost of illness studies)

See *Burden analysis.*

Collaborative research

(1) co-operation between two or more research centres/teams (2) multi-disciplinary research (3) synonym for co-operative research which is a variety of *participative research.*

Combination and permutation

In a combination, order is not relevant. In a permutation it is. Thus 2,4,7,9 is the same combination as 4,9,2,7. But these four numbers can appear as 16 permutations.

Combinatorial problem

Simulation and sampling. Imagine a situation where there are two possible outcomes, each of which has two possible outcomes, each of which has two possible outcomes, and so on. By the 5th shunt that will be 32 possible outcomes and by the 6th, 64. And that's only allowing two outcomes for each node of the system. Many social processes are as *complex,* or more complex than this. For *computer simulation* this means that simulations may have to be very elaborate to capture reality accurately. For surveys this means that very large samples may be necessary accurately to represent all the pathways in a social process: for example all the routes through education to a particular career level. Also the term for a large number of mathematical problems.

C

Commensurability/incommensurability

Precisely used, refers to the translatability of one sort of measurement into another; thus miles and kilometres are commensurate measures while kilometres and litres are incommensurable. *Standardisation* produces commensurability. More loosely refers to whether propositions or theories can be directly compared with each other, and whether one could be judged as more accurate than the other. See also *Relativism*.

Commissioned research (contract research, hired-hand research)

A large proportion of all social and behavioural research is commissioned by private sector organisations, philanthropic bodies, the NHS and local and national governments, in what is very much a buyer's market. Commissioning is often done by people who do not understand research and it is not uncommon for the research contract to be based on unrealistic expectations as to what can be achieved with what resources in what time scale. Competitive tendering for research contracts also encourages bidders to promise much more than they can reasonably be expected to deliver. In addition, commissions often include conditions which are uncongenial to researchers as to the client's right to control what is finally published. The Social Research Association provides a good practice guide for those who commission research which researchers might find useful in negotiating with commissioners.

Social Research Association (2003) *Commissioning Social Research: A good practice guide – second edition. Report of a working party* www.the-sra.org.uk

Grinyer, A.(1999) 'Anticipating the problems of contract research' *Social Research Update* Issue 27 http://sru.soc.surrey.ac.uk

Community (needs) assessment/profile

Compilation of data about a locality, usually carried out as the basis for planning, administering or evaluating service provision, and hence focussing on *demography, epidemiology*, health and social welfare topics, and perhaps, leisure, recreation and crime and disorder. Community profiling will nearly always draw on *administrative data*, perhaps augmented with social *surveys*, interviews with *key informants* and *focus groups*. Profiles are often available on the internet on local authority, health authority and *public health observatory* websites.

Hawtin, M., Hughes, G. and Percy Smith, J., (2007) *Community Profiling: A practical guide.* (Revised edition), Maidenhead: Open University Press.

Smith, M (2007) 'Community profiling', *Encyclopaedia of Informal Education.* www.infed. org/community/community_profiling.htm

University of Illinois, Extension (n.d.) *Needs Assessment Resources,* http://ppa.aces.uiuc. edu/NeedsRes.htm

C

Community study

(1) Detailed study of a village or neighbourhood – 'place communities', typically by *ethnographic* techniques, though surveys and *focus groups*, local *administrative data* and documentary sources may be used also. Researchers often express an interest in the community 'as a whole' but the resulting community studies tend to focus more on some kinds of activities and some kinds of people. Classic examples include: *Family and Kinship in East London*, and *Coal is our Life*. Many anthropological studies in Third World societies are in effect 'community studies', but the term tends to be restricted to studies in industrialised societies. It has usually proved difficult to state the bounds of a 'community', especially under modern conditions where someone may belong to one community as a resident, another as an employee, another as a participant in a sport, and so on, where these different communities are not spatially identical – see *Social network analysis*. Community studies conducted to inform planning decisions are more often called *Community (needs) profiles*.

Young, M. and Willmott, P., (2007) *Family and Kinship in East London,* Hamondsworth: Penguin Modern Classic Edition (orginally 1961).

Dennis, N.,Henriques, F. and Slaughter ,C.,(1969) *Coal is our Life* (2nd edn), London: Routledge (originally 1956, Eyre & Spottiswood)

Smith, M. K. (2001) 'Community' in *Encyclopedia of Informal Education*, 2008 www.infed.org/community/community.htm

Clark, A., (2007) *Understanding Community: a review of networks, ties and contacts,* NRCM http://www.ncrm.ac.uk/research/outputs/publications/

(2) Detailed studies of other sorts of community, for example of particular fractions of the population of a locality: the gay community, the African-Caribbean community, or of interest communities, such as 'the community of ten-pin bowlers'. For internet communities, see *Cyber-#*.

Comparative method

Although controlled experiments rely on comparison, the term comparative method is usually identical with the idea of *natural experiments* (and statistical control), and contrasted with research using controlled experiments – see *Control, direct and statistical*. The meaning of the term varies between the physical/natural sciences and the behavioural/social sciences, and within the latter, but in sociology and anthropology two main types of comparative method are often distinguished:

- **Variable-based comparative method**, as with Durkheim's study of suicide and most comparative research pursued through statistical means and *Qualitative comparative analysis*. Comparison is variable by variable – see also *Cross-case analysis*.

- **case-based comparative research** as with Weber's studies of religious organisation; comparison is case against case with a recognition that variables in one case may not be related together in the same way as variables in another case. See also *Case study.*

See also *Analytic induction, Constant comparative* method.

Levi-Faur, D. (n.d.) *Comparative Method in Political and Social Research* http://poli.haifa. ac.il/~levi/method.html

Comparative Study of Social Mobility in Industrial Nations

See *CASMIN (Comparative Study of Social Mobility in Industrial Nations)*

Comparison groups

Much research involves comparing groups. In true experiments comparison groups are created by randomly allocating subjects to groups which will be treated differently. In quasi-experiments other ways are used to form the groups, and sometimes ready-made, pre-existing groups are compared – see *Experiments, true and quasi.* Methods of creating groups include *random allocation* for true experiments, and for quasi experiments, *matched pairs* designs, and *precision-matching* – see also *Factorial designs.*

Groups are usually named to distinguish them. A group may be termed an 'experimental' or 'intervention', or 'treatment' or 'research' group to indicate that something was done to, or with them, by comparison with 'a control' group who didn't receive the treatment/intervention. Or groups may be labelled 'the (something) condition group' to indicate how they were treated differently or had an experience different from '(some other) condition group'. Ideally, comparison groups should be similar to each other in all respects irrelevant to the research, and only differ in ways that are relevant. For example, in an evaluation of different methods of teaching, the groups receiving different tuition should ideally have similar profiles of ability, age, gender and so on. Then any differences in their learning can be attributed to the differences in the way they were taught, because other differences will have been controlled out by the way the groups were composed. Often it is impossible to compose comparison groups which are similar at the outset and what seem to be differences of outcome due to differences of treatment or experience relevant to the research, may be due to other differences between the groups. Then these other differences have to be controlled by statistical analysis using techniques such as the *analysis of covariance (ANCOVA and MANCOVA)* or the *analysis of variance (ANOVA* and *MANOVA*) or *logistic regression* – see also *Control, direct and statistical, Standardisation.*

Competing risk analysis/models

Synonym for *Event history analysis/models.*

Complex

As in 'complex societies/organisations': made up of diverse kinds of components; for example many different specialist roles and different kinds of institution. As in '**complex intervention**' : a procedure in health, education, social work etc., that will be varied according to the particularities of each subject, or situation, hence presenting difficulties when featured in *controlled experiments.* As in '**complex process**': a process consisting of many possible pathways – see *Combinatorial problem.*
See also *Complex adaptive system, Complexity theory.*

Complex adaptive system (CAS)

In *Complexity theory*; applies to any complex *phenomenon* which adapts to its environment, for example a snowball rolling down a hill, a species under the conditions of natural selection, a business organisation in its market place, a national economy under the conditions of globalisation. A common topic for *Computer simulation.* Synonyms: **autopoietic system, callactic system, dissipative system.**

Fryer, P. (n.d.) '*What are complex adaptive systems and complexity theory?* www.trojanmice. com/articles/complexadaptivesystems.htm
Goldstone, R. (2001) 'Software for Simulating Complex Adaptive Systems', *University of Indiana* http://cognitrn.psych.indiana.edu/rgoldsto/complex/

Complexity theory

(Synonyms; **non-linear dynamics, open systems theory, ubiquity theory**) A body of ideas covering all fields of science. 'Complex' here does not mean complicated as such, but refers to complicated patterns being generated by the interaction of simple mechanisms. Includes **chaos theory** as a sub-division. There is no authoritative definition of complexity theory and some definitions would limit the term to a branch of mathematics (which includes fractal geometry and the well-known Mandelbrot plots). Some central tenets are that:

- Complex phenomena are usually produced by simple mechanisms.
- Such mechanisms usually involve both indeterminate *random* or stochastic elements, and *deterministic* orderly elements.

- Nearly everything prior influences nearly everything else subsequent, but not in a consistent way.
- Most processes are *historical processes*, in the sense that what happens next depends on what happened before. This is sometimes expressed as '*sensitivity to initial conditions*'.
- It is impossible in principle to predict the outcome of complex processes except in the very short term (though 'short term' for planets is different from short-term for fundamental particles).
- *Frequency distributions* of complex phenomena often take the form of *power distributions* and may be scale invariant (or fractal) in character.

Topics in complexity are often investigated using *computer simulation.* See also *Complex Adaptive Systems (CAS), Criticality, Emergence.*

MacGill, V (2007) 'Chaos and Complexity Tutorial' http://complexity.orcon.net.nz/index.html

Buchanan,M (2000) *Ubiquity: the science of history or why the world is simpler than we think.* London: Weidenfeld & Nicolson.

Byrne,D. (1997) 'Complexity theory and social research' *Social Research Update,* Issue 18. http://sru.soc.surrey.ac.uk/

Componential analysis

In linguistics and anthropology: *semantic* analysis in terms of the components of meaning that words and phrases have for native speakers. For example, in English the word 'girl' has the following components: human+female+immature, but also, human+female+mature but lower status, and human+female+mature but intimate and human+male+ effeminate. Synonyms: **contrast analysis, feature analysis, lexical decomposition**.

Habib, R.,(2007) *Lexical Semantics,* University of Florida
http://grove.ufl.edu/~rhabib/Lecture19-SemxII.pdf

Composition(al) analysis

Synonym for *Event structure analysis.*

Compositional effects

(1) The different effects of combining subjects in different ways, or of combining them rather than dealing with them individually. For example, the different educational outcomes for girls when in co-educational schools, as compared with girls in single sex schools, or the different judgements decision-makers might make when combined in different ways – see also *Bias, compositional, Interaction effects.* (2) The effects

arising from similar people gathering together in the same place, as opposed to **contextual effects**, which are the effects of that place on those people, for example, do those who are less mentally healthy congregate in inner cities (compositional) or does inner city living undermine mental health (contextual)?

Compteian positivism

see *Positivism.*

Computer Assisted Qualitative Data Analysis (CAQDA)

Software packages to aid researchers qualitatively to analyse qualitative data. They facilitate the on-screen *coding* of data and the bringing into juxtaposition of segments of data with the same code, or with interesting relations to each other. Packages include:

Atlas/ti , www.atlasti.com
Ethno: www.indiana.edu/~socpsy/ESA/ – see *Event Structure Analysis*
Ethnograph www.qualisresearch.com
QSR Nvivo and NUD*IST www.qsrinternational.com/products.aspx

The QDA site at the University of Huddersfield gives step by step guides for all the major CAQDA software , and some profiles of the packages to help users to choose between them http://onlineqda.hud.ac.uk/.

Computer Assisted Self-interviewing (CASI)

See *Questionnaire administration.*

Computer Assisted Telephone Interviewing (CATI)

See *Questionnaire administration.*

Computer simulation

Deterministic simulations designed to predict the future have a long history in *demography*, *econometrics* and business forecasting, predating computerisation – see *Determinism*. *Stochastic* simulations deal with emergent phenomena within the framework of *complexity theory* – see *emergence*. For some phenomena, actual instances in the real world are too rare to allow for confident generalisation. Thus the wars that have actually happened under post-nuclear conditions will not constitute a representative sample of all the wars that could possibly happen. Simulation goes some way towards remedying this problem by generating large numbers of possibilities.

University of Surrey, Centre for Research in Social Simulation (CRESS) http://cress.soc.surrey.ac.uk/s4ss/links.html

Gilbert, N. and Troitzsch, K. (2005) *Simulation for the Social Scientist* (2nd edition) Buckingham: Open University Press

Hasty, R., and Stasser, G. (2000) 'Computer simulation methods for social psychology', in Reis, H. and Judge, C. (eds) *Handbook of Research Methods in Social and Personality Psychology,* Cambridge: Cambridge University Press: 85–116

Concentration

Of wealth, income, market share, or of types of people in an organisation or at an organisational level, or type of housing, or types of people or enterprises in an area – see *Indices of inequality, Segregation indices.*

Concept

See *Construct.*

Concept(ual) mapping (concept webbing, mind-mapping, mind webs)

Drawings representing the way in which concepts and other kinds of ideas relate together (1) as a technique for planning a research project (2) as a way of representing the structure of an explanation (3) in *cognitive anthropology,* or *cognitive psychology,* as a way of representing the structure of cultural ideas as they are stored in the mind. Here the term used might be a **connective network** representing *mazeways, scripts* or *schemata.*

Trochim, W., (2006) 'Concept Mapping', *Social Research Methods Knowledge Base,* www.socialresearchmethods.net/kb

Concourse

A corpus of views about some topic – for example global warming, usually represented as a set of statements. Includes the various positions in a debate and thus differs from a *discourse,* when the latter implies consensus. Associated with the linguistic theories of William Stevenson and *Q methodology.*

Stephenson, W. (1978) 'Concourse theory of communication', *Communication,* **3**:21–40

Concurrent validity

See *Validity, concurrent.*

Conditional probability

See *Probability.*

Confirmationism

See *Verificationism.*

Confidence intervals/limits (CI/CL)

When the TV pathologist says 'time of death midnight, plus or minus two hours' she is expressing a point estimate (midnight) and the confidence interval (two hours either side). She is probably expressing the 95% confidence interval, meaning that she is 95% sure that the true time of death was between 10 p.m. and 2 a.m. But 99% confidence intervals are sometimes used and she might be 99% sure that the time of death was between 9.30 p.m and 2.30 a.m.

Confidence intervals are often displayed in a plot and whisker form, where the plot is the point estimate and the whiskers show the interval to the upper confidence limit (UCL) and to the lower confidence limit (LCL). See example in Figure 5.

The calculation of confidence intervals relies on the *central limit theorem.* Thus if you measured your own height again and again you would produce a range of different heights, but most of them would

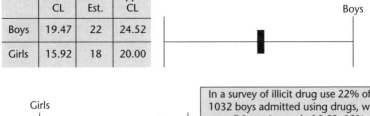

	Lower CL	Point Est.	Upper CL
Boys	19.47	22	24.52
Girls	15.92	18	20.00

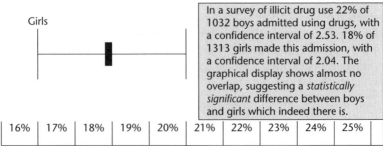

In a survey of illicit drug use 22% of 1032 boys admitted using drugs, with a confidence interval of 2.53. 18% of 1313 girls made this admission, with a confidence interval of 2.04. The graphical display shows almost no overlap, suggesting a *statistically significant* difference between boys and girls which indeed there is.

| 16% | 17% | 18% | 19% | 20% | 21% | 22% | 23% | 24% | 25% |

Figure 5 Confidence intervals in a survey of drug use among boys and girls [invented data]

cluster towards a middle score, and few would be further off. You would probably feel confident that the *mean* (average) of 100 measurements was very near the truth. If you drew a histogram (see *Graphs*) of the measures then it would take the shape of a *normal distribution*. For a normal distribution we can calculate the *standard deviation* and that will tell us what percentage of scores lie at what distance away from the *mean*. This logic allows for an estimate of how wrong a measure is likely to be. In effect we ask 'If my measure was actually the mean of a large number of measures, what would be the range within which 95% of all measures would fall?' The truth is most likely to lie within that range; between those confidence limits.

Confidence intervals are commonly cited in the results of sample survey research, and used in *meta-analysis*. Most spreadsheets, including Excel, will calculate confidence intervals from the sample size, the point estimate and the *standard deviation*. For manual calculation for confidence intervals of sample *means* at the 95% level of confidence, the formula is:

$$1.96 \times \sqrt{(\text{score as \%}) \times (100 - \text{score as \%}))/\text{sample size}}$$

For the 99% level, substitute 2.56 for 1.96

See also *Frequency distribution, Sampling error, Statistics software*.

See the interactive demonstration on the RVLS website: http://onlinestatbook.com/rvls.html

Musalia, J., (2008) *Chapter 11: Estimation,* University of West Kentucky http://www.wku.edu/~john.musalia/soc300/

Confidence level

See *Alpha level.*

Confidence limits

See *Confidence interval/limits.*

Confidence number (CN)

The minimum size a sample has to be to allow for a statistically significant result at a given level of confidence – see also *Sample size, Statistical power*.

Confidentiality

See *Anonymity, Privacy and confidentiality.*

Confirmability

Used by some qualitative researchers as a near synonym for *Objectivity* – see *Criteria for evaluating research.*

Conflict of interest

Many journals publishing research require authors to declare any potential 'conflicts of interest'. This usually refers to whether they are employed by or funded by some organisation which might benefit from the findings being in one direction or another; for example where tobacco companies fund research into cancer. See also *Bias, sympathetic, Partisan research, Value neutral or value-led.*

Confounding

To confound is mistakenly to attribute the reason for one thing to another. Avoiding confounding is the main consideration in *experimental design*: for example, creating two very similar groups of subjects to be treated differently, reduces the possibility of prior differences between the subjects confounding the experiment by the results being mistaken as due to differences in treatment. See also *Comparison groups, Control, direct and statistical.*

Conjectures

See *Hypotheses.*

Conjuctionist causality

See *Causal analysis.*

Connective network

See *Concept(ual) mapping.*

Connoisseur group

See *Group interviews.*

Connotation

See *Intension.*

Conscientisation

See *Consciousness raising.*

Consciousness raising (conscientisation)

Associated particularly with the Brazilian activist/educator Paulo Freire; facilitating oppressed groups of people to question previously taken-for-granted ideas which accommodate them to being oppressed. Sometimes this is an aim of *emancipatory* and *participatory research* rather than, or in addition to the production of research findings. See also *Critical ethnography, False consciouness, Feminist research, Ideology.*

Thompson, J. (n.d.) 'Emancipatory Learning', National Institute for Adult and Continuing Education (NIACE) www.niace.org.uk/information/briefing_sheets/Eman cipatorylearningmar00.html

Consensual definition of poverty

See *Poverty, relative.*

Consensus theory

From *cognitive anthropology,* a set of techniques for establishing how widely held among a cultural group is the meaning or application of a term, using questionnaires to produce numerical data expressing consensus or diversity in this regard. Taken as a test of the *reliability* of claims made about meanings – meaning being regarded as a social, rather than an individual matter. Not to be confused with the designation of American functionalism as a 'consensus theory', because it assumed societies based on underlying consensus of values.

Robertson, T., (2004) *Cognitive Anthropology,* University of Alabama www.as.ua.edu/ ant/Faculty/murphy/436/coganth.htm#Methodologies

Consistency

See *Reliability, internal.*

Constant comparative method (constant comparison method)

Procedure closely associated with *grounded theory,* but not confined to it, whereby researchers refine their analysis by constantly testing the interpretations they have developed so far, against new data, and refining ideas if necessary. For example, if a researcher has noted that health care assistants are more likely to wash their hands after touching a patient if they are observed by other staff, the next stage might be to see if this was true whatever staff and however many staff constituted the audience. In grounded theory the procedure is worked through the testing of the applicability of codes and their refinement. This example would be of axial coding. See also *Coding, Coding axial, open and selective, Analytic induction*.

Dye, J., Schatz,I., Rosenberg, B. and Coleman, S. (2000) 'Constant Comparison Method: A Kaleidoscope of Data', *The Qualitative Report*, **4**, no. 1/2 www.nova.edu/ ssss/QR

Construct

That which an indicator stands for; an idea, usually a component of a theory, for example 'self-image', or 'social class' – see *Construct-indicator relationship, Indicator, Validity, construct*.

Construct-indicator relationship

In mainstream science it is argued that we can never apprehend reality directly. Rather we have theoretical (hypothetical) concepts or *constructs* about reality, which we relate to empirical *indicators*. Often these indicators are brought into being, or into visibility/audibility by the research process itself. Thus the construct 'attitude' belongs to theories about human motivation. We never see an 'attitude'. Instead we see what are counted as indicators of particular attitudes in the form of responses to *questionnaires*. Differences in the way the construct indicator relationship is conceptualised illustrate a difference between *empiricism* on the one hand and *critical rationalism, realism* and *pragmatism* on the other. For the former it is the empirical observation treated as the indicator which is real, while the construct and the theory it belongs to are 'just' a convenient way we have of making sense of our observations. For the latter three the construct stands for something which exists in 'deep reality' which is itself unobservable but manifests itself in something that is observable which is treated as the indictator. See *Empiricism, Critical rationalism, Realism, Pragmatism, Validity, Construct*.

Constructionism/constructivism

(1) In psychology those theories of learning, perception and memory which place most emphasis on a person's active (constructive) interpretation, by contrast with *behavourism* which places emphasis on *determinate* reactions to stimuli.

Ryder, M., (2008) '*Constructivism*', University of Colorado http://carbon.cudenver.edu/ ~mryder/itc_data/constructivism.html

(2) Synonym for *Social Constructionism*.

Construct validity

See *Validity, construct.*

Contemporaneous research

See *Cross-sectional research.*

Content analysis

Analysis of documents and still or moving visual images, by *coding* (indexing) segments as instances of features of interest, and, usually, counting frequencies of occurrence. Most commonly used in the analysis of mass media products. Essentially the same procedure may be used in analysing transcribed interviews, but the term is rarely used for this.

Neuendorf,K (2006) *The Content Analysis Guidebook on-line,* Cleveland State University. http://academic.csuohio.edu/kneuendorf/content/

Content validity

See *Validity, content.*

Context dependency

Sensitivity of cause and effect sequences to the immediate context; a reason given for why similar situations often turn out differently. Might be regarded as a rather old fashioned way of referring to complexity as in *Complexity theory.* See also *Cetis paribus.*

Context of discovery and context of justification

The difference between the way in which a research finding was actually produced, which may have been serendipitous, untidy and inefficient, and the way a justification for the finding is written up, which may include a narrative demonstrating how the finding *might* have been made more efficiently, and how the research *might* be replicated, but which is not actually how it was done. The same idea may be expressed by the contrast between the **logic-in-use** and the **re-constructed logic of research** (Kaplan 1964). Studies in the history of science suggest that 'discovery' stories are rarely accurate – see *Bias, narrative, Reasoning.* See also *Autoethnography, Reflexivity.*

Kaplan, A., (1964) *The Conduct of Inquiry, Methodology for Behavioural Science,* San Francisco: Chandler Publishing Company.

Contextual effects

See *Compositional effects*.

Contingency/contingent

Dependent upon uncertain or accidental events; unpredictable, as in 'Research is always characterised by contingency'. Usually used to express the important role of chance in human affairs – see *Complexity theory*.

Contingency tables (cross-tabulations/cross-tabs/ X-tabs)

Show the relationship between two *variables* in tabular form (in Table 3: between gender on the one hand and smoking on the other). Such tables may have any number of rows and columns, and may contain actual numbers and or percentages: percentages may be by column or by row, or by percentages of the grand total. If there is a *direction of effect* it is usual to make the independent *variable* the column variable. Used where data is at the nominal level data, setting the data up for statistical significance testing using tests such as X^2 – see also *Data, levels of*.

Table 3 Contingency Table: Smoking by gender (numbers and percentages): invented data

	Column variable Males (%)	Column variable Females (%)	Totals
Numbers reporting they smoked (%) *Row variable*	152 (35.27)	137 (29.72)	289 *row marginal*
Numbers reporting not smoking (%) *Row variable*	279 (64.73)	324 (70.28)	603 *row marginal*
Totals	431 (100) *Column marginal*	461 (100) *Column marginal*	892 *grand total*

Musalia, J., (2008) *Chapter 6: Relationships between two variables; cross-tabulations*, University of West Kentucky www.wku.edu/~john.musalia/soc300/

Contrast(ive) analysis

See *Componential analysis*.

Control, direct and statistical

Refers to the management of *variables* which are irrelevant to the research and, if uncontrolled, might lead to mistaken conclusions ('*confound* the results'). **Direct (physical or experimental) control** (at the subject level) means selecting research subjects, or creating *comparison groups* to exclude irrelevant differences between subjects. For example, to exclude the influence of age differences, the researcher might choose subjects all of a similar age. Allocating subjects to comparison groups by *random allocation* is the preferred way of creating groups which are similar on a wide range of criteria. Direct control will also be exerted to ensure that each subject is treated in the same way as each other apart from required differences in treatment (control at the treatment level) and that all data collection and analysis is conducted in the same way for each subject. **Statistical control** means manipulating the data to identify and compensate for *confounding* variables. For example, in order to control for gender in analysing the results of a survey, subject responses will be organised into those from males and those from females and compared. S*tandardisation, logistic regression* and the *analysis of variance (ANOVA/MANOVA)* and *analysis of covariance (ANCOVA/MANCOVA)* are more sophisticated ways of accomplishing statistical control.

See also *Case control studies, Controlled experiments, Experimental design, Population control studies.*

Control group

See *Comparison groups.*

Controlled experiments

Experiments where the researcher creates a situation in which variables are controlled lest allowing them free play would make interpretation difficult – *confounding* the results. Contrasted with *natural experiments* that rely on statistical control. See *Control direct and statistical, Experimental design.*

Convergent validity

See *Validity, convergent.*

Conversation analysis (CA)

Ethnomethodological analysis of spoken language, focussing on what each utterance accomplishes in the immediate context of an interchange. Sometimes referred to as a type of *sequential analysis*, in that where an utterance appears in sequence is a crucial consideration, and as *endogenous analysis* in that it seeks to uncover the analytic decisions made by participants in order to create the situation being studied. Also employs *membership category analysis*. Similar in focus, if not in terminology, to *pragmatic linguistics*.

> Antaki, C. (n.d.) *An Introductory Tutorial in Conversation Analysis* http://www-staff.lboro. ac.uk/~ssca1/intro2.htm

Co-operation bias

See *Bias, co-operation.*

Co-operative research

See *Participative research.*

Corpus linguistics

Quantitative study of large representative samples of written or spoken language, establishing for example, letter, word or phrase frequencies, often by *text mining*; practically employed in cryptography and in the authentication of historical texts. See also *Power (law) distributions, Textual criticism.*

> Gateway to Corpus Linguistics www.corpus-linguistics.com

Correlated design

See *Related and unrelated designs.*

Correlation and correlation coefficients

Two *variables* are *correlated* when the value of one changes in step with the value of the other. The relationship can be one of positive correlation: a high value on one is associated with a high value on the other, or a low value on one is associated with a low value on the other: as with the relationship between height and weight when measured in a large population; or it can be one of negative (or inverse) correlation, as with two ends of a see-saw; when one end goes up, the other goes down. For illustrations see *Scattergrams.*

The strength of correlation is usually judged by calculating a *correlation coefficient* such as *Pearson's product moment co-efficient*, or *Spearman's Rho*, or for *curvelinear correlations, eta*. Most coefficients report values from −1 to +1:

-1 means a perfect negative correlation (two ends of a see-saw)
0 means no correlation at all,
+1 means a perfect positive correlation.

Squaring the co-efficient and multiplying by 100 gives the percentage by which one variable moves in step with the other. Sometimes it is appropriate to express this in terms of change in one causing change in the other – see *Causal analysis*.

Since correlations can occur by chance a coefficient is meaningless unless it reaches a *statistically significant* value.

A **zero order correlation** is a correlation between two variables without controlling for any other variables which might influence their relationship. **A first order correlation** is a correlation between two variables controlling for one other variable. In a **second order correlation** two other variables are controlled for. The sequence continues, **third order**, **fourth order** and so on.

See also *Association, Analysis of covariance(ANCOVA and MANCOVA), Control, direct and statistical, Covariance, Cronbach's alpha, Regression analysis, Reliability, Statistics software.*

Musalia, J., (2008) 'Chapter 8: Bivariate regression and correlation', University of West Kentucky www.wku.edu/~john.musalia/soc300/

Correspondence analysis

Analysis of tabular data at the nominal level to allow for the graphical representation of relationships between rows and columns – see *Data, levels of.*

Phillips,D.(1995) 'Correspondence analysis', Social Research Update Issue 7 http://sru. soc.surrey.ac.uk/SRU7.html#

Corrigibility as contrasted with incorrigiblity

The nature of incorrigible phenomena can only be a matter of opinion and hence such opinions cannot be scientific knowledge. But which kinds of phenomena are corrigible and which incorrigible is a contested matter. Most researchers would regard religious and similar statements as *metaphysical*, and hence incorrigible. Some researchers would regard inner mental states such as feelings, emotion, intention and such like as incorrigible, but others would argue that a researcher can be right or wrong about someone else's inner mental state – see *Intentionalism*. Whether there can be any way of being right or wrong about someone else's subjective experience is also raised by the term **qualia** (sing.,quale) sometimes used for *subjective* experiences. Usually, but not always, qualia implies incorrigbility. See also *Demarcation debate, Falsificationism.*

Tye, M., (2007) 'Qualia', Stanford Encyclopedia of Philosophy http://plato.stanford.edu/

Cost-[#] analysis

Refers to various kinds of research each of which begins with *effectiveness research* to establish whether some practice is effective in achieving what it is suppose to achieve, (or this may have been established by prior research) and followed by research to discover how much the practice, and perhaps alternatives to it, cost. These analyses are very vulnerable to price changes over time, although once the groundwork has been laid it is relatively easy to re-cost. *Generalisation* from a particular study to other sites of implementation are very vulnerable to local cost variation, and should be accompanied by local re-costing. This stage is often omitted when 'rolling-out' programs which have been run as pilots, sometimes leading to cost-overruns or under-funding in the face of higher local costs.

> **Cost-benefit analysis (CBA):** Analysis conducted solely in monetary terms, where the monetary costs of providing an intervention are compared with the monetary value of the outcomes; often involves comparison between alternative interventions, or between an intervention and doing nothing.

> **Cost-effectiveness analysis (CEA):** Where outcomes are measured in appropriate units, for example numbers of people cured, numbers of additional GCSE points for the school, scores on a consumer satisfaction questionnaire, and the inputs to achieve these outcomes costed – usually solely in monetary units. Alternative interventions can then be compared in terms of cost per additional unit of outcome.

> **Cost-minimisation analysis (CMA):** Analysis costing alternative ways of achieving the same outcomes in order to choose that of least cost. Cost may be solely in monetary terms, but might also include other considerations such as staff morale, public opinion and so on.

> **Cost of illness studies(CoI):** See *Burden analysis*

> **Cost-utility analysis (CUA):** Analysis to identify the intervention giving the greatest benefit for the least cost, where benefits (and sometimes costs) are judged in terms of *utilities*. The best known of these are quality of life years **(QALYs)** used in cost-utility analyses in health care, for example approving drugs for use in the NHS – see also *Utility*.

Greenhalgh,T. (1997) 'How to read a paper: papers that tell you what things cost (economic analysis)', *British Medical Journal* **315**: 596–99 www.bmj.com

Jefferson,T., Demicheli, V., and Mugford, M. (1996). *Elementary_economic evaluation in health care*, London: BMJ Publishing Group.

Count/count data

Synonym for frequency – see *Frequency distribution*.

Covariance

Is the amount of *variance* shared between two variables; the extent to which reducing the diversity of scores on one variable would reduce the diversity of scores on the other. Covariance is only a satisfactory measure of *association* where the two variables are measured on the same scale. *Correlation* will accommodates different scales of measurement by reference to the *standard deviation* of the two variables.

Covariance is calculated as

$$\frac{\text{Sum of ((Each X score} - \text{mean for X scores)} \times (\text{Each Y score} - \text{mean for Y scores}))}{\text{Number of data points}}$$

Covariance can be calculated on most spreadsheets including Excel.

See also *Analysis of covariance (ANCOVA and MANCOVA), Cochran's C, Correlation, Statistics software.*

Coverage error/coverage ratio

In *surveys* the **coverage error** is the extent to which a sample is not representative of the population from which it is drawn because certain sections of the population were not given a chance to be represented: often because of omissions in the *sampling frame* used. The **coverage ratio** is the percentage of the population of interest given a chance to be included; usually the percentage listed in the *sampling frame*. Coverage ratio estimates can be made for sub-groups in the population. Such estimates depend on having knowledge about or a model of the size and structure of the population of interest. For general populations this is likely to come from *census* data. **Under-coverage** refers to the extent to which the sampling frame (or the sample) omits some kinds of people, and is the usual state of affairs. **Over-coverage** occurs when some people (or other units) have more than one chance of being included in a sample. For example around 5% of patients appear as two or more individuals in NHS records so that using such records as a sampling frame might lead to over-coverage. However, the chance of double-listed people being chosen twice is low and over-coverage is rarely a problem. See *Response rate.*

Covering law explanation

See *Deductive reasoning* and *Idiographic as opposed to nomothetic.*

Covert research

see *Deceit in research, Observation, covert or overt.*

Credibility

Used by some qualitative researchers as an alternative to internal validity. See *Validity, internal, Criteria for evaluating research.*

Criminal records checks

In the UK researchers working with children and/or vulnerable adults have to undergo a check of their criminal record.

England and Wales: http://www.crb.gov.uk/
Scotland: http://www.disclosurescotland.co.uk/
Northern Ireland: http://www.accessni.gov.uk/

In England and Wales and Northern Ireland such researchers will be required to register with the *Independent Safeguarding Authority* (from 2009 in E&W, later in NI) (http://www.isa-gov.uk) A similar system of registration is being developed for Scotland. See also *Access, Gate keepers, Sensitive issues and vulnerable groups.*

Crisis of legitimation and crisis of representation

Two closely related sources of angst in the social sciences. Both are provoked by the recognition that researchers' descriptions of the social world are themselves part of the social world. Thus there are difficulties with the notion that the truth can be achieved by stepping outside what is being studied and looking at it 'objectively' – see *Objectivity.* The **crisis of legitimation** has been taken by some who espouse *social constructionism,* and by any who adopt *post modernism,* to mean that any description of the social world is as valid as any other. And along the same lines, the **crisis of representation** refers to the way in which any scene or setting is amenable to an almost infinite number of ways of representing it, between which, it is alleged, there is no principled way of choosing because a description is not the same kind of phenomenon as what is being described. The response then is to analyse the way in which any description is constructed; to deconstruct the construction to lay bare the unnoticed prejudices and preconceptions which went into it. However, both these responses are doubly problematic. First, the response is self-negating, for if every description is as valid as every other one, the description which claims to be the one and only truth is as valid as the claim that there is no description which is the one and only truth. Second, if we deconstruct a sociological representation to show that it is an ideological fabrication, then our thorough-going acceptance of these crises should prevent us from claiming that this analysis is actually true. An illegitimate way out of this impasse is *Ontological gerrymandering.* Both crises, if crises they are, are seen to undermine the authority of researchers and other scholars insofar as this derives from a claim to have superior access to the truth. This notion may be employed as part of a critique of orthodox research as unsupportably elitist (sometimes as masculinist) and hence as a prescription for *participatory research*.

Other social scientists are less perturbed by these alleged crises, or do not recognise them at all. Instead these are both taken to refer to problems which can be managed, if not entirely solved, by *critical rationalism* and a *falsificationist* approach, or by *realism*. In these views even if there is no description which can be claimed to be fully authoritative, and no representation which can claim to be the only accurate one, it is still possible to distinguish those which are false, and it is not cogent to argue that every version is as valid as every other.

See also *Dialogue/Dialogic.*

Cohen, J., (2006) *Anarchism and the crisis of representation: hermeneutics, aesthetics and politics,* Selinsgrove, PA: University of Susquenana Press.

Criteria, for evaluation

See *Evaluation studies.*

Criteria for evaluating research

Some qualitative researchers have suggested alternatives to those used in the natural sciences and more traditionally applied to social research, although many remain committed to the traditional ones. See Table 4.

Table 4   Traditional criteria for judging research compared with some alternatives proposed for qualitative social research

Traditional criteria	Alternatives for qualitative research
Internal validity* *(Validity, internal)*	Credibility or authenticity
Reliability	Dependability or auditability
Replicability	No alternative suggested
External validity or generalisability *(Validity,external, Generalisation)*	Transferability or fittingness
Objectivity	Confirmability (but see also dependability/auditability)
Usefulness	Applicability or action orientation or *validity, catalytic*

* includes naturalist or ecological validity – *Validity, naturalistic*
Source: Adapted from Miles, M. and Huberman, A. (1994) *Qualitative Data Analysis: An Expanded Sourcebook,* London, Sage: 278.

In addition there are disagreements about ethical criteria – see *Ethics*, about values in research – see *Value neutral or value led*, and about the proper relations between researcher and researched – see *Partisan research, Participative research.* These disagreements are not neces- sarily always between qualitative and quantitative researchers – see *Qualitative and quantitative.* See also *Arts based inquiry.*

Hammersley, M. (2008) 'Validity criteria for qualitative research: are they possible or even desirable ?' Chapter 9 in *Questioning Qualitative Enquiry: critical essays,* London: Sage

Criterion population

see *Reference population.*

Criterion referencing and norm referencing

Criterion referencing is comparing all subjects against an external or independent standard. Norm referencing is comparing subjects against each other; synonyms for absolute and relative standards respectively. See also *Benchmarking.*

Criterion test

See *Validity, criterion.*

Criterion validity

See *Validity, criterion.*

Critical case analysis (crucial/diacritical case analysis)

Involves the strategic choice of *case studies* which will help to decide some theoretical issue; for example, the choice of well-paid manual workers in Luton in the *Affluent Worker* studies in the 1960s to test the credibility of the prediction that manual workers were becoming middle class. See also *Deviant case analysis.*

Critical discourse analysis

See *Discourse analysis.*

Critical ethnography

Ethnographic research, often *participatory,* conducted from a *partisan* point of view usually with the aim of emancipating cultural members from taken-for-granted assumptions (*ideologies*) which oppress them. Similar in meaning to *post-colonial anthropology/ethnography.* See also *Consciousness raising, False-consciousness.*

Critical rationalism

Epistemological and ontological position most closely associated with Karl Popper. When implemented in practice difficult to distinguish from *realism*, and indeed it is part of the realism family. Probably the philosophical position most commonly declared among physical and natural scientists, and many social and behavioural ones; hence sometimes described as '*the* philosophy of science', though actual practice may be closer to other kinds of *realism*. By critics sometimes described as *positivism*, but quite wrongly since it was developed as an antidote to *logical positivism* and contrasts with that view in almost every particular. Major tenets of critical rationalism are that:

- theories develop as much from rational thinking as from evidence – the 'rationalism' in the title
- what is observable may often be emanations from a reality we cannot observe
- theories are under-determined by evidence – see *Under-determination of theory by evidence*
- no theory can ever be verified, it can only be falsified – see *falsificationism*
- the preferred procedure for scientific development is the *hypothetico- deductive method* practised in an open way such that each finding can be subject to criticism
- all scientific knowledge should be regarded as provisional – see *Fallibilism and foundationalism*
- facts can never be entirely separated from values, but all possible efforts should be made to keep them separate
- science is a distinctive area of knowledge and is restricted to those matters about which it is possible to be wrong – see *Demarcationism dispute* (Popper himself did not consider that the study of society could be 'scientific' – see *Corrigible*).

Critical rationalism group: http://groups.yahoo.com/group/CriticalRationalism/
Burnham, R. (2000) 'Critical Rationalism', *Philosophy Webring* www.telinco.co.uk/burnham/popper.htm

Critical realism

See *Realism*.

Critical theory

(1) Narrowly refers to the western marxist writings of the Frankfurt School, and even more narrowly to those of Jurgen Habermas. These are theories which place a very strong emphasis on the role of *ideology* in maintaining

power structures and in the liberating potential of the *deconstruction* of ideologies. 'Critical analysis' here means analysis in terms of power structures. (2) More broadly used as a term to cover all socially critical thinking including varieties of marxist and *feminist research*. See also *Critical ethnography, Critical realism* (see *Realism), Consciousness raising, Hermeneutic-historical, Partisan research, Participatory research*.

Boham,J.(2005) 'Critical Theory' *Stanford Encyclopedia of Philosophy* http://plato. stanford.edu

Critical values

Tables of critical values are look-up tables which express the likelihood of particular results occurring by chance, also called **inference tables**. The results of *statistical significance* tests are compared with these. Critical value calculation is built into statistical software. Each kind of test has its own equations for calculating critical values.

Criticality

State or condition of being poised on the verge of a major change.

Self-organised criticality

Mainly used in *complexity theory* to refer, for example, to the build up of a snow bank to create the conditions for an avalanche, or the build up of group dynamic factors to create the risk of a riot; a common focus for *computer simulation* – see also *Complex Adaptive Systems (CAS)*.

Cronbach's alpha (coefficient alpha of consistency)

One of several tests used to estimate the *internal consistency (internal reliability)* of a research instrument , and sometimes the consistency of judgement between different researchers – *inter-rater reliability*, or by the same researcher– *intra-rater reliability*. The *correlation* can be positive or negative, from -1 to $+1$ An alpha of 0.60 or more, indicates a level of internal consistency sufficiently high to justify the use of the instrument.

Cronbach is a parametric procedure, used where the instrument produces interval or ratio level data- see *Statistics, parametric and non-parametric, Data, levels of.* A non-parametric equivalent is *Kuder-Richardson formula 20*.

See also *Statistics software*.

Cross-case (X-case) analysis

The analysis of several *case studies* on the same dimensions or within the same framework of terms: often done within a *qualitative comparative analysis (QCA)* framework and one means of accomplishing *meta-analysis* of qualitative research.

COMPASS (Comparative Methods for the Advancement of Systematic Cross-case Analysis and Small-n Studies): www.compasss.org/WPFull.htm

Cross-over designs/trials

Experimental designs which involve exchanging *comparison groups* between treatments/conditions at some stage during the experiment, so that each group experiences each treatment/condition.

Sibbald, B. and Roberts, C.(1998) 'Understanding controlled trials: cross-over trials', *British Medical Journal,* **316**:1719–1720 www.bmj.com

Cross-sectional research (x-sectional research/ snap-shot research/contemporaneous research)

As contrasted with *prospective research* or *longitudinal resear*ch; usually refers to surveys conducted at a single point in time. Cross-sectional research often raises *direction of effect* problems. See also *Pseudo-cohort analysis.*

Cross-tabulation (cross-tab, x-tab)

See *Contingency tables.*

CUA (Cost Utility Analysis)

See *Cost-[#] analysis.*

Culture-blindness

An alleged failure to recognise important cultural differences.

Culture fair instruments

Ways of eliciting information, designed to exclude the influence of any cultural differences which should be irrelevant; used, for example, in measuring intelligence or aptitudes to avoid disadvantaging cultural minorities. Such tests usually consist of puzzles posed in terms of non-verbal symbols. However, it may be doubted whether all cultures offer the same experience of manipulating such symbols, or indeed of using the pencil and paper required to respond to them – see also *Cultural relativism.*

AllIQtest.com (2007)*Culture Fair IQ Test (Visual Spatial)* www.alliqtests.com/tests/take_ test/13/1/

Benson,E. (2003) 'Intelligence across cultures' *Monitor on Psychology:APA on-line, 32(2)* www.apa.org/monitor/feb03/intelligence.html

Cultural relativism (historical particularism)

It is uncontroversial that people from different cultures may have difficulty in understanding each other over and beyond the difficulties arising from speaking different languages; that their understandings are culturally relative; hence the representation sometimes of anthropology being a practice of translating from one culture to another, and the care taken by many historians to interpret historical materials in ways appropriate to the culture in which they were produced. Cultural relativism becomes more controversial when it is argued that one culture cannot be translated into the terms of another (incommensurability). *Social constructionism* pushes in the direction of this kind of **cognitive cultural relativism** by insisting on meanings being bound to their more immediate contexts. Cultural relativism is sometimes interpreted more narrowly to refer to systems of morality **(moral relativism)**, to the effect that the societies and the behaviour of people of one culture cannot be judged morally in terms of the moral standards of another culture. Once accepted it is difficult to prevent this notion expanding such that it appears illegitimate to make any moral judgements at all about anyone else. It is not necessary, however, to subscribe to moral relativism in order to suspend moral judgement/to be non-judgemental, while conducting research – see *Value-neutral or value-led research.*

Geertz, C. (1984) 'Anti-Anti-Relativism' *American Anthropologist* 86 (2) 263–278.

Eller, D. (n.d.) *So many ways to be human* www.geocities.com/ellerdavid/culturalrelativism. html

Cultural studies

Multi-disciplinary approach to the study of culture, combining anthropology, sociology, psychology, history, literary and other forms of artistic criticism and media studies. Variable in orientation but in Britain strongly influenced by *semiology/semiotics* and latterly, *post modernism* and post structuralism (see *Structuralism and post-structuralism*) with a focus on popular and mass culture.

Cultural Studies Central: www.culturalstudies.net/

Cumulative analysis

See *Guttman scale.*

Cumulative (frequency) distribution

Expression of the distribution of a data set where the next highest score is always added to the total of all previous scores. For the scores at the side of Figure 6, the cumulative distribution begins 5, 5+7=12, 12+10=22, and the complete series is 5,12,22,35,52,73,98,124, 150,180

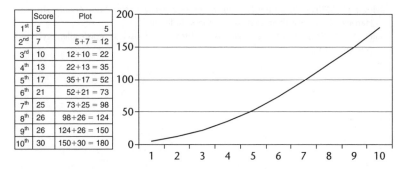

	Score	Plot
1st	5	5
2nd	7	5+7 = 12
3rd	10	12+10 = 22
4th	13	22+13 = 35
5th	17	35+17 = 52
6th	21	52+21 = 73
7th	25	73+25 = 98
8th	26	98+26 = 124
9th	26	124+26 = 150
10th	30	150+30 = 180

Figure 6 Cumulative frequency distribution

CUREE (Centre for the Use of Research Evidence in Education)

Has a website which provides access to research evidence on effective practice in education http://www.curee-paccts.com/home

Curve

In mathematics and statistics, curves include straight lines – hence linear curves (straight lines) and *curvilinea*r curves. See also *Asymptotic.*

Curvilinear relations

The *association* between two variables may be linear (straight line) or curvilinear (curved) or take other forms – for illustrations see *Regression analysis.* The usual statistic for expressing curvilinear correlations is *eta,* calculated though a one-way analysis of variance – see *Analysis of variance (ANOVA).* Alternatively, curvilinear relations may be linearised through *data transformations* or *pruning,* or avoided by working only with the *inter-quartile range* or by using *asymtotes – see Linearisation.*

Cyber-# (or e-#)

As a prefix to anthropology, *ethnography,* psychology, or sociology, indicates a research interest in the internet, its social relationships and impact on society. Lurking in on-line chat rooms as a means of research raises important ethical issues about *informed consent.* See also *Game studies, Virtual ethnography.*

Hine,C. (2001) *Virtual Ethnography,* London, Routledge

Hine,C. (2005) *Virtual Methods: issues in social research on the internet,* Oxford, Berg Publishers

Reingold,H.(2001) *The Virtual Community: homesteading on the virtual frontier,* London: HarperCollins www.rheingold.com/vc/book/index.html

Suler, J. (2008) *Psychology of Cyberspace,* http://www-usr.rider.edu/~suler/psycyber/psycyber.html

C

D/d (Δ/δ)

(1) statistical symbol for deviation or difference, usually the result of subtracting a score from a *mean*.

(2) Cohen's delta or Glass's delta – see *Effect size (ES) measures*.

(3) Index of Dissimilarity – see *Segregation indices*.

Dark number problem

See *Bias, ascertainment*.

Data

Plural: records of observations, of any kind, in any format, numerical (*quantitative*) or non-numerical (*qualitative*). Terms such as 'data point', 'score', 'measure' or 'attribute' are used more commonly than the singular – **datum**. See also *Data, levels of*.

Data archives

Repositories to store *data* sets from research projects and make them available to other researchers for *secondary analysis* and *meta-analysis*. All research projects funded by the *Economic and Social Research Council* require data to be archived at the end of the project in either the UK Data Archive (UKDA) www.data-archive.ac.uk/www.esds.ac.uk or the Qualitative Data Archive (*Qualidata*), the archive for qualitative research: www.esds.ac.uk See also *NESSTAR*.

The Institute for Social and Economic Research (ISER) , University of Essex www.iser.essex.ac.uk archives data from various longitudinal studies including the *British Household Panel Survey*, and the *UK Household Longitudinal Study*. See also *Birth Cohort Studies*.

The University of Leeds will hold the archive for the 'Timescapes' *qualitative, longitudinal study*, http://www.timescapes.leeds.ac.uk/about-archiving/Manchester Information and Associated Services (MIMAS).

University of Manchester www.mimas.ac.uk archives international data sets.

www.archiveshub.ac.uk is the portal for the archives of all British Universities.

The Cathie Marsh Centre for Census and Survey Research (CCSR), University of Manchester www.ccsr.ac.uk manages the *Samples of Anonymised Records (SARS)* from the census.

Talkbank stores audio and video recordings suitable for qualitative analysis http://talkbank.org/data/ and includes Childes where the speakers are children http://childes.psy.cmu.edu/

For guides to respositories of Anthropological field notes see:

www.nmnh.si.edu/naa/other_archives.htm and
www.nmnh.si.edu/naa/guide/_toc.htm (Smithsonian)
www.therai.org.uk/MoM/ArchiveAndManuscript.html (Royal Anthropological Institute)

For anthropological photographs and film: www.therai.org.uk/rainews/ raiCollection.html(Royal Anthropological Institute) and Beilla, P. (2001) *Ur-list of Resources for Visual Anthropology*, University of Southern California, www.usc.edu/dept/elab/urlist/

See also *Archive, Campbell collaboration, Cochrane collaboration, Corpus linguistics, Mass observation, Secondary analysis.*

Data cleaning/cleansing

Checking data and eliminating or correcting items which do not accord with the research *protocol*; for example responses to a questionnaire where two options are ticked and only one is allowed.

Data count

Creating *frequency distributions.*

Data degradation

The transformation of data at one level into data at a lower level, for example the transformation of data at the ordinal level into nominal level data (see *Data, levels of*). Or, while remaining at the same level of data, recasting it into broader categories; for example, changing the *class intervals* on a *frequency distribution* histogram from being five units wide to being ten units wide. In both cases the object is to make patterns visible at the cruder level which cannot be seen at the more refined level. See also *Graphs, Data reduction.*

Data, levels of/variables levels of

Level determines how data can be manipulated statistically and what inferences can be drawn safely from them (see Table 5). See also *Plastic interval level data.*

Table 5 Levels of data

Discrete (or discontinuous) data	**Nominal (categorical / qualitative) data** The measurement operation is counting	Data classified into categories, such as 'male/female', 'Anglican, Catholic, Methodist etc.', 'White, African-Caribbean, Asian etc. The categories are mutually exclusive and not ordered in relation to each other. No *mean* (average), nor *median* can be calculated and the only measure of central tendency possible is the *mode*. No *standard deviation* can be calculated[1]. Only non-parametric statistics[2] can be used. Sometimes expressed as dummy variables, for example 'yes ' is coded as 1 and 'no' as 0.
May be Discrete (discontinuous) or Continuous (measurable) data	**Ordinal (ranked) data** The measurement operation is ranking	Data classified by rank order, such as '1st, 2nd, 3rd...last (place in class)' or 'Most expensive, next most expensive...least expensive.' Rank order shows the positional relationship of categories but not how far apart these are. No *mean* (average) can be calculated, no *mode* identified and the only measure of central tendency possible is the *median*. No *standard deviation* can be calculated[1]. Only non-parametric statistics[2] can be used.
	Interval & Ratio level data The measurement operation is measuring in the same sense as measuring with a ruler.	Data which derive from measurement on a scale, where the intervals on the scale are equal to each other. Allow for the calculation of the *mean*, median and mode, *the variance*, and the *standard deviation* [1] and are amenable to analysis using parametric statistics. Can also be analysed using non-parametric statistics [2]. The distinction between interval and ratio level data rests on the scale having a true zero, and is rarely important in social scientific research.

(1) For *mean, mode, median, standard deviation* – see also *Central tendency and dispersion*
(2) See *Statistics, parametric and non-parametric*

D

Data mining (KDD – Knowledge Discovery in Databases)

Exploring large data sets (for example, those derived from customer loyalty cards or search engine histories) in search of consistent patterns and/or systematic relationships between *variables*, creating models to explain any patterns found, and attempting to validate or falsify the models by confronting them with new sets of data; for the purpose either of explanation and theory building, or for forecasting – see *Prediction, Validation*. The search procedures are usually automated.

Statsoft www.statsoft.com 'Data Mining'
The Data Mine www.the-data-mine.com
Dilly, R. (1996) *Data Mining: An Introduction* , Belfast: Queen's University. http://www.pcc.qub.ac.uk/tec/courses/

Data, prestructured

See *Coding*.

Data Protection Act 1998

Applies to all those who collect and keep 'personal data', which are data from which living individuals can be identified and which are not a matter of public record. Thus the Act would not apply to lists of names and addresses of prospective interviewees drawn from the telephone book or electoral register so long as these could not be associated with confidential personal data collected from them, but would apply to such a list drawn from the practice records of a GP practice. The Act does not apply to anonymised data, but in order to collect this the researcher will usually have to record personal data which may fall under the Act. Registration ('notification') by the researcher as a data controller with the Information Commission may be necessary, or the activity may have to be conducted under the auspices of the data controller of the institution to which the researcher is attached. Failure to do this, or having done so, failure to behave in conformity with the Act are offences. The process of notification is interrogative and begins with screening questions to ascertain whether notification is necessary. Notification can usually be avoided by researchers. In cases of doubt the Information Commission will advise: www.dataprotection.gov.uk

The confidentiality of data concerning NHS patients or the clients of social services/social work departments are also covered by the Caldicott provisions – see *Caldicott guardians*, and the collection of data about or from children and some vulnerable adults falls under the legislation to protect such persons from abuse – see *Sensitive topics and vulnerable groups*.

The code of practice attached to the Data Protection Act should be regarded as good research practice irrespective of whether following it is legally required. The code revolves around the principles of obtaining *informed consent* from those to whom the data apply, of accuracy of record and of keeping data securely. See also *Privacy and confidentiality*.

SRA (2005) *Data Protection Act 1998: Guide for Social Researchers*, London: Social Research Association: www.the-sra.org.uk

Data pruning

See *Pruning*.

Data reduction

The analysis of data to reduce the number of explanatory factors. For example, the grouping together of items from a questionnaire survey as all demonstrating the same variable, then the grouping together of clusters of variables as demonstrating the influence of the same factor, or a parallel process with qualitative data; often accomplished by *factor analysis* with numerical data, and by *constant comparative method* with qualitative data.

Data transformation

(1) Computing; the transformation of data from one electronic form into another, for example the modification of tabular data to be suitable for display by *geographical information system*. (2) Statistics; the transformation of data into a form more closely approximating a *normal distribution* to allow for the use of parametric statistics. For example with positively *skewed* data converting each datum into its square root or logarithm. These transformations alter the distance between each variable, and if the variables are substantively interpretable – for example as incomes, the results of transformations may be very difficult to interpret. See *Statistics, parametric and non-parametric*.

Osbourne, J. (2002) 'Notes on the use of data transformation', *Practical Assessment, Research and Evaluation* **8**(6). http://pareonline.net/Home.htm

Data triangulation

See *Triangulation*.

Debriefing

Many codes of *ethics* for research require researchers to debrief their subjects at the end of the research. In addition to any further collection of

D

research data, this includes explaining what the research was about – if that has not been explained previously (see *Deceit in research*) – , offering opportunities for subjects to have their questions answered, ascertaining whether any harm has been done to them, and offering support or counselling if necessary. Also refers to the therapeutic counselling of trauma victims and to the collection of data from (say) police, fire officers or military personnel after an incident.

Harris, B. (1988) 'Key words: a history of debriefing in social psychology' in Morawski, J. (ed.) *The Rise of Experimentation in American Psychology*, New Haven: Yale University Press: 188–212

As a research example see:

Wartburg College (n.d) *Debriefing Information'*, http://www.wartburg.edu/harrc/debriefing.html

Deceit in research

Includes:

- falsifying data or results, and falsifying accounts of how research monies were spent – both fraudulent and not to be confused with *falsification/ism*.
- misleading subjects about the risks of participating or attempting to evade responsibility for research-related harm to subjects – see *Informed consent, Safety*.
- withholding information from subjects or misleading them about the purpose of the research or parts of it.
  The last is permissible if
  - it poses no risks to research subjects, or no risks which they have not been informed about and accepted – as with participation in an experiment involving blinding
  - and if deceit is necessary for the research to be successful, as in much psychological research, for example in the psychology of perception which involves tricking the senses, or in sociology using covert participant observation to study deviant or otherwise secretive groups – see *Observation, covert or overt*.

Unless very good reasons can be advanced to the contrary, subjects who have been deceived during the research should be debriefed thereafter – see *Debriefing*. See also *Ethics*.

Decentred

(1) Of government, refers to movements away from direct government provision of services and to the increasing use of independent regula-

tors; (2) of texts, the view that the meaning of a text is not to be found in the intentions of its author, but will be different at every reading according to the interpretations of different readers; hence the waning of the tradition of textual interpretations designed to uncover the intentions of the author; (3) of people and society, the view that people are not the key units of society, but have identities constituted for them by the kinds of discourses available for characterising people; this notion is associated particularly with Michel Foucault and sometimes referred to as the 'reversal of the relationship between text/discourse and individuals' – see *Discourse analysis, Structuralism and post structuralism*. In more traditional sociology a similar 'decentering' was associated with the view that social roles, rather than individuals, were the fundamental units of society: but the term decentred was not used for this. See also *Fragmentation of identity.*

Decile

See Percentile.

Decision analysis

(1) The analysis of how decisions are made, in psychology or sociology using any means of research. (2) Techniques devised as an aid to making decisions, based on the logic of *Bayesian inference* and much used in diagnostic medicine, business decision-making and risk management (Arshan 2008, Alemi 2004).

Arsham, H. (2008) *Tools for Decision Analysis: analysis of risky decisions,* University of Baltimore. http://home.ubalt.edu/ntsbarsh/opre640a/partIX.htm#rwida

Alemi, F. (2004) *Decision analysis in health care,* George Mason University http://gunston.gmu.edu/healthscience/730/default.asp

Deconstruction/ism

Analysis of *texts* and other communications particularly by reference to the way terms have meaning in opposition to other terms; for example 'male' as 'not female' – see also *Componential analysis, Discourse analysis* (Hedges n.d). Sometimes restricted to the epistemology and textual analysis associated with Jacques Derrida (Hepburn 1999).

Hedges, W. (n.d.) *Using Deconstruction to Astonish Friends & Confound Enemies (in 2 easy steps)* www.sou.edu/English/Hedges/Sodashop/Rcenter/Theory/Howto/decon.htm

Hepburn, A. (1999) 'Derrida and psychology: deconstruction and its abuses in critical and discursive psychologies', *Theory and Psychology,* **9** (5): 641–67

Deductive reasoning/logic

The explanation of the particular by reference to *premises* about what is generally true; in the formula:

'since this is true in general where ever these conditions obtain, this must be true in this particular instance since this is an instance where the relevant conditions obtain'.

The truth about the particular – if truth it is, is already contained in the *premise*. Preferably the premises are general law-like statements, in which case, deduction may be spelled out as a **deductive-nomological explanation,** or **covering law explanation** – see also *Idiographic as opposed to nomothethic.* The models for deductive reasoning are mathematics and logic. These are so designed that (paradoxes apart) following the rules will always produce correct conclusions. Unfortunately the real world is not so tidy. Even in physics, universal laws have to be hedged with 'all other things being equal' (*ceteris paribus*) clauses. In the social sciences there are few, if any, uncontested law-like statements and reasoning from the general to the particular, while deductive in form is often from a premise which has been inductively derived – see *Inductive reasoning.* If science had to rely on deductive reasoning alone, no new theory could ever be produced, since deductive reasoning, in its requirement for starting from true premises assumes we know the truth in advance – see *Abductive reasoning, Hypothetico-deductive method, Reasoning.*

Beall, J. and Restall, G. (2005) 'Logical consequences' *Stanford Encyclopedia of Philosophy* http://plato.stanford.edu

Deductive-nomological explanation

See *Deductive reasoning.*

Deft/deff

See *Design effect.*

Degrees of freedom (df/dof or Df/Dof or ν)

(1) In experimental design the number of relevant independent variables allowed to vary/left uncontrolled; hence the more degrees of freedom the wider the range of outcomes permitted and the more difficult it will be to interpret the results – see *Causal analysis, Confounding, Controlled experiments, Variable, independent.* It is not always known how many uncontrolled variables there are, or what they are; (2) in statistics (see Table 6).

Table 6 Example of degrees of freedom in a statistical test

	Group A	Group B	Total score
Test 1	?	?	27
Test 2	?	?	35
Total score	21	41	62

For this table there is only one degree of freedom; df = 1. If the row totals and column totals are to add up correctly, you only have a free choice as to what figure to put in <u>one</u> empty cell. If there were three columns instead of two you would have two degrees of freedom. If there were ten columns and five rows you would have 36 degrees of freedom because by the time you came to fill in the 37th cell, you would find that you had no choices left. Here df is a measure of how much free play there is for chance to affect the results in a statistical test. Since testing for statistical significance is all about comparing actual results with results which might have happened by chance, degrees of freedom have to be factored into statistical testing. This just means calculating the degrees of freedom and using them to find the right place for looking up the results of the test in a table of *critical values*. Usually the formula for calculating degrees of freedom is: (rows minus 1) × (columns minus 1) but the instructions for each test will include the instructions for calculating df. In *Analysis of Variance*, **dfb** = degrees of freedom between groups; **dfw** = degrees of freedom within groups.

See also *Critical values, Statistical significance, Statistics software*.

Delphi group (connoisseur group)

See *Group interviews*.

Demand characteristics

What research subjects perceive to be expected of them:

- from what they learn from the explicit messages given to them by researchers,
- from other cues, such as the demeanour of an interviewer – see *Interviewer effect, Subject reactivity*.

Sometimes demand characteristics are investigated through *cognitive interviewing*. See also – *Bias, acquiescence, Bias, co-operation, Respondent burden*.

D

Demarcation debate/demarcationism

Debate about the distinction between 'scientific' and other forms of knowledge. The most usual demarcation line is according to whether or not bodies of knowledge are *corrigible* and amenable to refutation; to being proved false – *Falsificationism*. This leaves most sociology, anthropology, political science and economics and linguisitics as 'unscientific' – as *metaphysics*. But the demarcation line runs through, not between, disciplines, since all disciplines rely on some assumptions which cannot be falsified. There are other resolutions to the demarcation debate, including that no such distinction is possible or necessary. *Ethnomethodologists* and *social constructionist* writers in the sociology of science for example, claim that the kind of thinking in which scientists engage, is not different in kind from the everyday thinking of everyone else. See S*trong programme*.

> Provost, W. (n.d.) 'Science as paradigmatic complexity www.geocities.com/~n4bz/science/paracom.htm

Demography/demographics

The study of human populations and their vital statistics, such as births, deaths and migration patterns. For the UK the Office for National Statistics provides a wealth of data and commentary www.statistics.gov.uk, as do the regional public health observatories www.apho.org.uk. See also *Geodemography*.

Denominator and enumerator (numerator)

In a fraction, *rate* or *ratio*, the top, or first figure is the enumerator (how many) and the bottom or second figure (out of) is the denominator. For example, the rate of suicide for adult males in England in 2006 was 17.4 per 100,000. 17.4 is the enumerator and 100,000 is the denominator.

D

Denominator-enumerator discrepancies

In expressions of *rates* the *denominator* will often be drawn from a source different from that of the enumerator, perhaps giving rise to misleading estimates of *incidence/prevalence*. For example, in expressions of mortality rates for men from different occupations the enumerator figures will be drawn from the registration of deaths with the occupation of the deceased given by the person registering the death. The denominator data will be an estimate of the number of males in that occupation alive in the year of death, based on an update of the census, which may be up to 12 years out of date. People who register deaths have a strong tendency to give as the deceased's occupation, their most 'notable occupation'. Hence workers who typically retire to less strenuous occupations may nonetheless be recorded as police officers, miners, fishermen and so on at the time of their death, inflating the mortality rates for these occupations, because the census-based data which informs the denominator will only count those who were actually employed in such jobs at the time of the census or its update.

Bloor, M., Samphire, M. and Prior, L. (1987) 'Artefact explanations of inequalities in health: an assessment of the evidence', *Sociology of Health and Illness*, **9**(3): 231–64.

Denotation

See *Intension*.

Dependability

(or auditability): used by some qualitative researchers as an alternative to *reliability*. See *Criteria for evaluating research*.

Dependent interview

See *Interview, dependent*.

Dependent designs

See *Related and unrelated designs*.

Dependent variable (DV)

See *Variable*.

Deprivation indices

For the measurement of area-based inequality, these are indices based on the combination (compositing) of various indicators of deprivation and affluence, allowing geographical areas such as electoral wards or district authority areas to be put in rank order on a scale from most to least deprived. They include the **Carstairs index, Jarman indices** (Jarman 8 and Jarman 10), the **Townsend Index**, and what was the **Index of Multiple Deprivation (IMD)** for England, which was replaced first with the **Index of Deprivation 2004 (ID2004)** and then with **ID2007** (sometimes 'Index of Multiple Deprivation' 2004 or 2007). These are composed of seven components (Income, Employment, Health Deprivation and Disability, Education Skills and Training, Barriers to Housing and Services, Crime, and Living Environment) which may be presented separately or combined. Two supplementary indices are sometimes cited,

- **Income Deprivation Affecting Older People Index (IDAOPI)**
- **Income Deprivation Affecting Children Index (IDACI),** now largely superseded by the **Local Index of Child Wellbeing 2009 (CWI2009)**

For these English indices, www.communities.gov.uk – and search.

For Wales the equivalent indices are the **Welsh Index of Multiple Deprivation (WIMD2000, WIMD2005, WIMD2008 and the WIMD-Child Index** – www.dataunitwales.gov.uk – and search. For Scotland the equivalent indices are the **Scottish Index of Multiple Deprivation (SIMD2000,2003,2004,2006,2009** and the **Combined Area Child Index of Deprivation** – www.Scotland.gov.uk – and search. For Northern Ireland, the equivalent indices are the **Northern Ireland Multiple Deprivation Measure** (sometimes Northern Ireland Index of Multiple Deprivation) **NIMDM 2000** and 2005 – www.ninis.nisra.gov.uk – and search. The IMDs and the IDs have been and are used in government calculations of funding for local and health authorities. Since they do not have to be calculated by researchers they have tended to supersede the other indices. However the Townsend index is available for output areas in the UK from www.apho.org.uk. All indices place areas in roughly the same rank order of deprivation (Hoare 2003). The IDs should be available for each local authority and health authority/board in the UK from the Neighbourhood Statistics web site, www.neighbourhood.statistics.gov.uk

Hoare, J. (2003) 'Comparison of area-based inequality measures and disease morbidity in England' 1994–1998', *Health Statistics Quarterly*, no. 18, pp. 18–24. www.statistics.gov.uk and search on 'Health Statistics Quarterly'

Carr-Hill, R. and Chalmers-Dixon, P. (2005) *Public Health Observatories Handbook of Health Inequality Measurement*, in Lin, J. (ed.), Oxford: South East Health Observatory. http://www.sepho.org.uk/extras/rch_handbook.aspx

D

Descriptive statistics

Techniques for displaying the general characteristics of data; including *graphs*, measures of *central tendency and dispersion*, *contingency tables*, *cumulative frequencies*, *frequency distributions* and *scattergrams* – see also *Statistics software*, *Stem and leaf plots*.

Design-based research

See *Design experiment*.

Design effect (deft/deff)

In a *survey*, the way the *population* is sampled may shape the results so that what is shown in the sample is not true of the population from which the sample was drawn. For example, it is often convenient to use *cluster sampling* where a random sample of areas is chosen first, and then a random sample of people are chosen within each of these areas. People who live in the same area are likely to be more like each other than would be people drawn at random from the population as a whole. This reduction in diversity is the design effect for cluster sampling which is calculated as the statistic **deft/deff** from which in turn can be calculated the amount of *weighting* to be applied to correct for the design effect. Other modes of sampling will have their own design effects.

ONS (2004) *Living in Britain 2001: Appendix C*, London: Office for National Statistics. www.statistics.gov.uk/lib2001/printsection3692.html

Design ethnography

Ethnographic research to investigate consumer choice-making and use of products, as relevant to design and marketing.

Douglas, M. and Isherwood, B. (1996) *The World of Goods: Toward an Anthropology of Consumption*, London: Routledge
Aiga (n.d.) *An Ethnography Primer*, http://www.aiga.org/content.cfm/ethnography-primer

Design experiment (empirical development, design-based research/Nth-phase evaluation/

development through formative evaluation.

Applied social research modelled on 'experimentation' in engineering, design and technology, where it is often called 'the engineering approach' or the 'research and development (R&D) process'. An initial design is tried out, evaluated, improved, trialled again, evaluated, improved and so on. The terms 'design-experiment' and 'design-based research' are most commonly used in educational research. In other fields **Nth-phase evaluation** and development through formative evaluation (see *Evaluation, formative*) may be used, or this practice represented as a variety of *action research*, or represented as practice rather than as research.

Design-based Research Collective www.designbasedresearch.org

D

Design variable

In *log linear analysis*, synonym for independent variable – see *Variable*.

Determinism

The belief in robust cause and effect relationships which operate with a high degree of regularity under specified circumstances, and which can, in principle, be expressed in law-like statements – deductive-nomological explanations, or covering law explanations – see *Deductive reasoning* (Hoefer 2003). **Deterministic**: a process with outcomes highly predictable (in principle if not in practice) from a knowledge of starting condition and operating principles. Often used as a term of disapproval, for example by sociologists or historians complaining about economically deterministic theories and particularly by qualitative researchers of quantitative research in general. Determinism is often juxtaposed to freedom or free will, and most qualitative researchers reject determinism because it seems to leave no room for individual *agency* (Honderich n.d). *Behaviourism* and *positivism* are both deterministic, but most science, including social science, allows for probabilistic causality – see *Causal analysis*. *Complexity theory* is both deterministic and indeterministic at the same time seeing *phenomena* being caused by the interaction of *random* factors with deterministic ones.

Hoefer, C. (2003) 'Causal determinism', *Stanford Encyclopedia of Philosophy* http://plato.stanford.edu

Honderich, T. (n.d.) *The Determinism and Freedom Philosophy Website*, University College London www.ucl.ac.uk/~uctytho/dfwIntroIndex.htm

Deviant case analysis

The search for and the analysis of cases which seem to constitute evidence against something being proposed as generally true. An aspect of a programme of *falsification* and/or of a process of elaborating categories through *analytic induction* and through *constant comparison* in *grounded theory*.

Deviation (d)

In statistics, the difference between a score and the *mean (average)* for that set of scores. With a mean of 4, a score of 7 has a deviation of 3, and a score of 2 a deviation of −2. Sometimes termed 'the error'. See also *Central tendency and dispersion, Standard deviation, Residual*.

Df

See *Degrees of freedom.*

Dialogic/dialogical

Popular terms used in a variety of ways. A dialogic approach is contrasted with a **monological approach** which assumes a fixed notion of truth (even if we do not as yet know what this is). For the Russian philosopher Bakhtin, a major influence on *post-modernism*, there are no fixed truths, rather truth is constantly being remade through a dialogue – see *Crisis of representation and crisis of legitimation*. It is easy to accept this when applied to novels, but more controversial when applied to scientific theorising. Dialogue in this context means rethinking as well as redescribing and is applied to all kinds of thought, speech and writing. The dialogue is between people, between someone and their experiences, and between people and texts – see *Inter-textuality*. Though the dialogue may be individual, it may also be collaborative; hence the idea is consistent with *social constructionism*. In *critical theory* writers such as Hans-George Gadamer write about cultural changes being brought about through a dialogue between past texts and present experience in which the past is constantly remade (Ramberg and Gjesdal 2005), while Jurgen Habermas, another critical theorist, opines that truth can only emerge through dialogue between people in an egalitarian relationship (Bohman and Rehg 2007). This latter idea has been an important influence on *feminist research* and *feminist epistemology*. See also *Participatory research*.

In psychology a dialogic approach may be taken towards personality and identity, seeing them as produced in dialogue with experience and subject to constant change (Hermans and Dimaggio 2007).

Bohman, J. and Rehg, W. (2007) 'Jürgen Habermas', *Stanford Encyclopedia of Philosophy*, http://plato.stanford.edu

Hermans, H. and Dimaggio, G. (2007). 'Self, identity, and globalisation in times of uncertainty: A dialogical analysis', *Review of General Psychology*, **11**(1): 31–61.

Ramberg, B. and Gjesdel, K. (2005) 'Hermeneutics', *Stanford Encyclopedia of Philosophy*, http://plato.stanford.edu

Diaries

Research subjects may be asked to keep diaries to record their activities over a time period, about matters where memory may be faulty; for example to record their diet (Corti 1993). **Research diaries** (or **research logs/research journals**) are sequential records of actions, events and, possibly of emergent interpretations, tracking the course of a research project (Newbury 2001). See also *Memos*.

Newbury, D. (2001) 'Diaries and fieldnotes in the research process' Birmingham City University, www.biad.uce.ac.uk/research/rti/riadm

Corti, L. (1993) 'Using diaries in social research', *Social Research Update*, Issue 2, http://sru.soc.surrey.ac.uk

Dichotomous variables

See *Data, levels of.*

Direction of effect

Two variables may be correlated, such that it can be proposed that one 'causes' the other. But a *correlation* will not show which causes which; it will not show the direction of effect. For example does unemployment cause ill-health, or ill-health cause people to be unemployed? Because they are *prospective*, experimental techniques and *longitudinal* survey *research* can both claim to demonstrate direction of effect. See also *Causal analysis, Variables*.

Directionless tests

See *Tails (one and two tails)*.

Disability research

May refer to any kind of research into issues of disability, but the term is increasingly used to refer to such research as is conducted with the participation of people with disabilities, at least in setting the objectives for the research. The term **disability rights research** may also be used in this context. See also *Survivor research*.

> University of Leeds: Disabilities Studies Archive, www.leeds.ac.uk/disability-studies/archiveuk

Discourse analysis

The analysis of speech or *texts* or broadcasts. There are four main possibilities, depending on the conceptualisation of 'discourse':

- Discourses may be assumed to have an existence independent of individuals and of their speech and writing. Thus a piece of writing is treated as a manifestation of a more general way of thinking, understanding or doing things: as an aspect of culture. Here the term 'discourse' has replaced the more traditional term '*ideology*'. Today writers tend to write of 'patriarchal discourses', rather than of 'patriarchal ideologies'. Much of such writing goes under the title of **critical discourse analysis** where the assumption is usually that the ideas and practices constituting the discourse, favour the powerful and mislead the powerless. Where texts and mass media communication are the focus, this is the approach of some versions of *semiology/semiotics*. See also *Cultural studies*.

- As above, but rejecting the idea of *ideology* on the grounds that in referring to communication distorted to serve the interests of powerful people it assumes the possibility of 'true' communication, and assumes that power belongs to or inheres in social groups. Instead discourses are seen both as the constituting their

D

own 'regimes of truth' and as the medium of power which is independent of any social group, which indeed create social groups and individuals – see also *Decentred* and *Fragmentation of identity*. This is a view associated particularly with Michel Foucault.

• Discourses may be seen as evidence of ways individuals or groups interpret the world. They are manifested, patchily, in particular pieces of speech or writing but have an existence independent of them. Here the term 'discourse' has been added to the already over-loaded set of synonyms, including, 'perspective', 'world-view', 'interpretive scheme' and such like – see *Actor perspectives*. Speech and writing are here studied mainly in an attempt to gain insight into the minds of speakers and writers. This approach is in the broad tradition of *symbolic interactionism* or *interpretivism*.

• Discourses are the words and the way they are arranged. The interest here is in how particular kinds of communication are put together, how these formats convey the meanings they convey, and the uses to which such communications are put. This is the meaning for *conversation analysis (CA), discursive psychology, frame analysis, pragmatic linguistics, rhetorical analysis, interactive linguistics*.

Although four versions of discourse are listed above, each is associated with a range of different ways of thinking about and analysing what is termed as discourse. For the first two meanings 'discourse' may include not only speech and writing, but also pictorial material, the ideas realised in architectural forms, in processions and ceremonials, and in practices such as medical diagnosis or judicial proceedings.

See also *Narrative analysis, Textual analysis*.

Stembrouck, S. (2006) 'What is meant by discourse analysis?' http://bank.rug.ac.be/da/da.htm#lt

Antaki, C. (n.d.) 'Lecture 11: Varieties of Discourse Analysis' http://www-staff.lboro.ac.uk/~ssca1/ttlecture11DA2.htm

Discourse Analysis On-line: http://extra.shu.ac.uk/daol/

D

Discrete data/variables

Synonym for nominal level data- see *Data, levels of*.

Discriminant function analysis

Variety of *regression analysis* used to estimate the relative influence of a number of different independent variables (which are at the interval level) on a dependent variable (the 'criterion variable', which is *dichotomous* and hence at the nominal level): for example, the estimation of the different degrees of influence of income, years of education, and political attitudes on voting New Labour or voting otherwise. See also *Data, levels of, Variable, Statistics software.*

Discriminant validity

See *Internal consistency, Item analysis, Validity, discriminant.*

Discursive psychology

One of several approaches to the language of social interaction which focus on the way speech is shaped collaboratively by people in the course of accomplishing such tasks as can be accomplished linguistically, such as having an argument, or doing an interview, and on the categories speakers use which make their speech sensible; for example on the way they use psychological ideas for attributing motives or moods to other people, or in dividing them into different psychological types. Has the same area of interest as *Conversation analysis* and *Pragmatic linguistics.*

Edwards, D. (2005) 'Discursive Psychology' in Fitch, K. and Sanders, R. (eds), *Handbook of Language and Social Interaction* (pp. 257–273). Mahwah, NJ: Lawrence Erlbaum. http://www-staff.lboro.ac.uk/~ssde/index.htm

Disparity ratio

Ratio measure of difference (1) for example, in China the gender disparity ratio is 121 males to 100 females, or 12:1. In America Black people are 7× more likely to be in prison than Whites :a 7:1 disparity ratio. (2) In social mobility studies the ratio of chances of someone in a higher class moving down the social scale, compared with chances of someone in a lower social class moving up. (3) A variety of odds ratio or relative risk ratio- see *Effect size (ES) measures.* (4) Ratio between the potential and the actual: for example of the uptake of school meals measured as the ratio of those eligible against those receiving. (5) A measure of the divergence of a price or any other measure from a moving average, see *Smoothing.*

Dispersal of identity

See *Decentred, Fragmentation of identity.*

Dispersion, measures of

See *Central tendency and dispersion.*

Distribution

See *Frequency distribution.*

Distribution free tests

Synonym for non-parametric statistics, named because these tests make no assumptions about the distribution of variables (parametres) in the population from which a sample is drawn. See *Statistics, parametric and non-parametric*.

Document

Usually written or printed texts and their illustrations, but sometimes extended to cover film, TV and radio productions in the same way that the term *text* is extended.

Documentary method

In *ethnomethodology*, not a method of research and not necessarily referring to documents, but a method of everyday interpretation which might be studied by a researcher, and or used unwittingly by a researcher. Consists in treating appearances as 'the documents of' something underlying. Identical in conception to the idea of *indexicality*.

Documentary research

Social research using *documents* as a *resource* (to study what the documents refer to). The term is rarely used where the documents are numerical records (see *Administrative data*). Less often used where documents are a *topic* (to study how the documents were produced, how they are structured to convey meanings, and/or what are their effects on audiences). Then it is more usual to use terms such as *discourse analysis, narrative analysis, rhetorical analysis* and *textual analysis*. Where documents are used as a resource, questions of their authenticity and accuracy are important, which may be investigated through *textual criticism*, or checked by *validation* or *triangulation*. See also *Life history research*.

Domain assumptions

Unverifiable/unfalsifiable assumptions which have to be accepted on faith, or 'for the sake of argument', as a condition for accepting the sense of research procedures and the verity of scientific arguments; for example the assumption that the world we are dealing with today is (in some ways) the same world as yesterday's – see *Epistemology and Ontology, Episteme, Paradigm*.

Double blind

See *Blinding*.

D

Dramaturgical approach

Research orientation employing the metaphor of the theatre, such that human activity is seen in terms of production and performance, self-conscious role-playing, back-stage and front-stage and such like, and other kinds of acting, such as public relations work and confidence trickery. Most associated with the earlier work of Ervine Goffman.

> Barnhurst, A. (1994) 'Erving Goffman: The Presentation of Self in Everyday Life', http:// employees.cfmc.com/adamb/writings/goffman.htm
> ABCworld (n.d.) *Dramaturgical Perspective*: http://abcworld.net/Dramaturgical_perspective.html

Drop out

See *Attrition*.

Dualism

In philosophy, a sharp distinction made between mind and body, the physical and the mental. Synonym for **Cartesian distinction/divide/split**. Opposite of **monism,** of which *behaviourism* is the best example: monist because it denies the existence of 'mind', separate from 'brain'. See also *Epiphenominalism, Interactionism*.

> Philosophy online, 'Dualism', www.philosophyonline.co.uk/pom/pom_dualism.htm

Dummy variable

See *Variable, dummy*.

Duration analysis/models

Synonym for *Event history analysis*.

DV

See *Variable*.

D

E

See *Expected (E) frequency/value.*

e-#

See *Cyber-#.*

EBP

Evidence based practice – see *Effectiveness research.*

Ecological correlation

Association between *variables* which holds at the level of an area. An **ecological fallacy** is to assume that ecological *correlations* will also hold true at the individual level. For example, it might be true that areas with high rates of unemployment also have high crime rates, but, without further evidence it would risk an ecological fallacy to assume that it was unemployed people who committed most of the crimes. **Nosnibor effect** and **Robinson effect** are synonyms. The **reverse ecological fallacy** is the attribution to a group of the characteristics of an individual, almost synonymous with over-generalisation, and stereotyping.

Robinson, W.S. (1950), 'Ecological Correlations and the Behavior of Individuals', *American Sociological Review* **15**: 351–357.

Ecological validity

See *Validity, naturalistic.*

Econometrics

Economic research pursued through mathematics, statistics and computer modelling.

Economic and Social Data Service (ESDS)

National data archiving and dissemination service: jointly-funded initiative sponsored by the *Economic and Social Research Council (ESRC)* and the Joint Information Systems Committee (JISC). See *Data archives*.

Economic and Social Research Council (ESRC)

In the UK the principal funder of economic and social research, organiser of research training and evaluator of research quality. See also *Economic and Social Data Service* (ESDS), *National Centre for Research Methods (NCRM)*.

Economic evaluation

See *Burden analysis, Cost [#] analysis, Effectiveness research, Evaluation research*.

Editing

See *Textual criticism*.

Education evidence portal

Website displaying research evidence for effective practice in education, http://www.cfbt.com/evidenceforeducation/. See also *Campbell collaboration, CERUK-plus, Effective practice, EPPI-centre*.

EER

See *Effect size (ES) measures*.

Effect

The difference it makes doing one thing rather than another, thus 'the school effect' is the difference it makes to the educational outcomes for similar children of going to one/type of school rather than another: or, in an experiment, the difference it makes giving subjects one treatment rather than another. Note that in an experiment, natural or otherwise, what is measured as 'the effect' will include the influences of any uncontrolled variables in addition to that of interest, plus the effects of chance. See *Confounding, Effect size (ES) measures*.

Effect, fixed and random

Most calculations of *correlation, covariance* and *regression* merely compute a measure of *effect* from the actual results of the experiment or survey. This is a **fixed effect**. Alternatively these data may be regarded as being just a sample of a much larger *population* of results. A similar calculation with another sample of data drawn at random from the same population would be expected to give a different result due to *sampling error*. Calculating a **random effect** takes this into consideration by estimating the range of results which might have been achieved by conducting the same research using a very large number of random samples, thus improving the generalisability of the result – see *Central limit theorem* and *Generalisation*. Calculations to similar effect may be made in pooling results in a *meta-analysis*. The random effect will have a wider *confidence interval* than a fixed effect and a lower *statistical power*. **Variance components model** is a synonym for random effects. See also *Weighted averages/event rates*.

Newsom, J. (n.d.) 'Distinguishing Between Random and Fixed: Variables, Effects, and Coefficients', www.ioa.pdx.edu/newsom/mlrclass/ho_randfixd.doc

Effect, main

In an *analysis of variance (ANOVA and MANOVA)* this is the between-group difference. The within-group difference is termed the error.

Effect size (ES) measures

(see *Effect*). For experiments, effect size (ES) is measured in a number of different ways and used particularly in *meta-analysis*. Although the term 'effect' might not be used, the same measures are used in correlational research, such as *epidemiological* research; for example in stating the effect that housing quality might have in determining the risk of ill health. The most common measures are listed in Tables 7A and 7B. They vary according to the level of data used to express outcomes/ differences – see *Data, levels of, Forest plots, Funnel plots*. Note that the generalisation from the effect sizes found in the experiment to effect sizes which would be true if the same procedures were carried on with the wider population, depends on how *representative* were the subjects in the experiment – see *Validity, external*. Table 7C gives ways in which the size of effects may be expressed.

The *F ratio* resulting from an ANOVA or MANOVA calculation (*Analysis of variance*) or t from a *t-test* may also be used as effect size measures.

Becker, L. (2000) *Effect size (ES)* University of Hamburg, Faculty of Law, http://www2. jura.unihamburg.de/instkrim/kriminologie/Mitarbeiter/Enzmann/Lehre/StatIIKrim/ EffectSizeBecker.pdf

E

Table 7A Invented data. Effect size measures with nominal level data. In each case a X^2 test would be appropriate for judging statistical significance – see *Data, levels of*. These measures may be used in experiments, *epidemiological* and, *demographic research* and in the analysis of *survey* or *administrative data*. For research other than *controlled experiments* instead of CER and EER, read 'Event rate in this category' and 'Event rate in another category'. For example, one category might be males, and another females and the comparison might be in terms being a victim of violence within the previous year. See also *Risk, relative and absolute*

	Group A Control group	Group B Experimental group	Total
Event happened	8(6.1%)	25(18.9%)	33
Event didn't happen	123(93.9%	107(81.1%)	230
Total	131(100%)	132(100%)	263
Control event rate	CER = 8/131		= 0.06 or 6%
Experimental event rate*	EER = 25/132		= 0.19 or 19%

* these are absolute risks for these events for these subjects.

Absolute risk reduction/ increase (ARR or ARI): sometimes Absolute benefit increase (ABI)/Absolute harm increase(AHI)	EER−CER (or CER−EER) 0.19 − 0.06 =	= 0.13 For every 100 subjects enrolled in the experimental group there would be 13 more events than if they had been treated as for the experimental group
Relative Risk Ratio (RRR)	CER/ = 0.19/0.06 EER	= 0.32 0.32 to 1 in favour of an event being in the experimental rather than the control group/3 times greater chance of the event happening in the experimental group.
Relative risk increase (RRI) or if appropriate, decrease (RRD)	(EER−CER)/CER = (0.19−0.06)/ 0.06 =	= 2.17(217%) Subjects in the experimental group were 217% (2x) more likely to experienced the event than they would have had they been treated as were the control group
Odds	8 to 123 (8:123) in favour/on in control group (or 8/123 = 0.065) or 123 to 8 (123:8) against (or 123/8 = 2.8)	

(Continued)

Table 7A (Continued)

	And 25 to 117 (25:117) in favour/on in experimental group (or 25/117= 0.21) or 117 to 25 (117:25) against (or 117/25 = 4.68)
Odds Ratio (OR)	(25/117)/(8/123) = 0.21367/0.065 .... = 3.287
	Events are 3.3 times more likely to happen in the experimental rather than the control group
Numbers needed to treat (NNT) (and Numbers needed to harm (NNH))	100/ARR = 1/(EER−CER) .... = 7.69 = 8
	In the example, assume events are cures, then an NNT at 8 says that for each additional eight people treated as per the experimental group there will be one additional cure. For negative events and NNH, for each additional 8 people treated as for the experimental group 1 would be harmed. However the accuracy of NNT/NNH as a generalision depends on the representativeness of the subjects in the experiment – see *Generalisation* and *Validity, external*

Table 7B Invented data. Effect size measures with interval level data and unrelated designs see *Data, levels of, Related and unrelated designs*

Group A Control group (measure of change)	Mean 170/9	A_x- mean	A_x- mean^2	Group B Intervention group (measure of change)	Mean 159/9	B_x- mean	B_x- mean^2
Subject Score				Subject Score			
A1 13	18.89	−5.89	34.68	B1 15	17.67	−2.67	7.11
A2 15	18.89	−3.89	15.12	B2 16	17.67	−1.67	2.78
A3 22	18.89	−3.11	9.68	B3 12	17.67	−6.89	32.11
A4 12	18.89	−6.89	47.46	B4 25	17.67	7.33	53.77
A5 24	18.89	5.11	26.12	B5 27	17.67	9.33	87.05
A6 23	18.89	4.11	16.90	B6 18	17.67	0.33	0.11
A7 22	18.89	3.11	9.68	B7 20	17.67	2.33	5.44
A8 21	18.89	2.11	4.46	B8 16	17.67	−1.67	2.78
A9 18	18.89	0.89	0.79	B9 10	17.67	−7.67	58.78
Total 170			164.89	159			249.93

	Variance A=164.89/9	20.61	*Variance* B =260.7/9	31.25
	Standard Deviation A= α18.34	4.54	*Standard Deviation* Bα28.97	5.59
	Calculation to four decimal places, presented at two decimal places			

Average differences

Subtract a mean score for one group from the corresponding mean for another, for example: $18.89 - 17.67 = 1.22$ ('the results for the intervention group were on average 1.22 worse than those for the controls').

Glass' delta (Δ)/Cohen's delta (Δ) (formula 1)

((mean change in intervention group) minus (mean change in the other group)) divided by (standard deviation of mean change in other group)

$(17.67 - 18.89)/4.54 = -0.27$

Zero would indicate no difference between the groups. Assuming higher scores were preferred, plus scores would indicate that the intervention was better than the control, and minus scores the reverse. Beware ! The calculation is *asymmetric* and the result depends on which group mean is subtracted from which. If there is an intervention and a control group it is conventional to work the calculations so that a positive score indicates that things were better for the intervention group.

This formula for Cohen's delta uses either standard deviation: Glass's delta always uses the standard deviation for the control.

Cohen's delta (Δ)(formula 2)

As above, but uses the **pooled standard deviation** which is the square root of the mean of the two standard deviations each squared: here:

$$\sqrt{((4.54^2 + 5.59^2)/2)} = \sqrt{((20.61 + 31.25)/2)} = \sqrt{(51.86/2)}$$
$$= \sqrt{25.93} = 5.09 = \text{pooled SD}$$

For the example data, delta would be -0.24

This statistic is the **standardised mean difference**, and if no name other than 'effect size' is used it is this statistic which is usually meant

Beware! The calculation is *asymmetric* and the result depends on which group mean is subtracted from which. If there is an intervention and a control group it is conventional to work the calculations so that a positive score indicates that things were better for the intervention group.

Effect sizes can also be expressed as **Pearson's correlation coefficient (r)** – see *Pearson's correlation coefficient*. For these data $r = -0.12$. r^2 is often used in a meta-analysis $= 0.014$.

T-tests/student's-test

The result of a *t-test* can be used to calculate Cohen's delta, and Pearson's correlation coefficient:

Cohen's $d = \tilde{2}t/\sqrt{(degrees\ of\ freedom)}$
$r = \sqrt{t^2/(t^2 + degrees\ of\ freedom)}$

Lee Becker's pages on the University of Colorado web site will calculate both Cohen's d, second formula and Pearson's for you, using means and standard deviations http://web.uccs.edu/lbecker/Psy590/es.htm
Effect sizes can also be calculated using ANOVA
Deviations or t-test data. Http://web.uccs.edu/lbecker/Psy590/escalc3. htm

Effect sizes for related/dependent/paired/correlated designs

Here there is some controversy about the appropriate ways of expressing effect size:

> Rosnow, R. L., and Rosenthal, R. (1996). 'Computing contrasts, effect sizes, and counternulls on other people's published data: General procedures for research consumers', *Psychological Methods*, **1**, 331–340.

(Effect size (ES) measures continued)

Table 7C   Effect size magnitudes: Assuming statistical significance, ES can be said to be Large, Medium or Small, and positive or negative*

	Cohen's or Glass' d(Δ)	Pearson's r	Percentage of control group who would be below average of intervention group (positive d or r scores) or vice versa (negative d or r scores) *
Large	+/−0.80 and greater	+/−0.371 and greater	79%−99.9%
Medium	+/−0.3–0.79	+/−0.148–0.370	78%−62%
Small	+/−0.0–0.29	+/−0.000–0.147	61%−50%

* Conventionally the calculations are worked so that positive figures show differences in favour of the intervention and negative in favour of the controls, if appropriate. Squaring r obscures the direction of difference

Effectiveness research

Since the 1990s, Government pressure on both public services and research funding has focussed the research effort on providing 'evidence for practice', via *evaluation research* designed to estimate the effectiveness of health, social welfare, educational, criminal justice or other practices or programmes. For such evidence based practice (Sackett *et al.*, 1996) experimental research is preferred, and especially *randomised controlled trials*. This has led to a renewed interest in experimentation in the social sciences. See *Campbell collaboration, CERUK-plus, Clinical*

E

audit, Cochrane collaboration, Education evidence portal, EPPI-centre, Meta analysis

Sackett, D., Rosenberg, W., Gray, J., Haynes, R. and Richardson, W. (1996) 'Evidence based medicine: what it is and what it isn't', *British Medical Journal* **312**: 71–72 www.bmj.com

Oakley, A. (2000), *Experiments in Knowing: gender and method in the social science,* Cambridge: Polity Press

EGP

See *Goldthorpe Classes.*

Eigen value

In *factor analysis* the amount (not the percentage) of *variance* on the factor accounted for by the variables that constitute the factor, calculated as the sum of the squared *correlations* between the factor and each variable.

Elasticity

The *ratio* of the percentage change in one variable to the percentage change in another variable (change being variously measured). For example, **price elasticity** is the extent to which the price of something is sensitive to demand, varing between 1 (perfect elasticity) where the price changes in step with demand, to 0 (perfect **inelasticity**) where price does not change irrespective of changes of demand. Widely used in economics and elsewhere as an expression of *association* between *variables* which is independent of the units used in measurement. For example, in studies of social mobility, the elasticity of a child's (as adult) income in relation to parental income. *Sensitivity/insensitivity* are sometimes used as a synonymns.

Electronic data analysis

For a general overview see the web site for ICT Guides http://ahds. ac.uk/ictguides/methods/index.jsp.

See also *Computer Assisted Qualitative Data Analysis (CAQDA), Data mining, Statistics software.*

Emancipatory research

Research which has the object of empowering those who are its subjects, meaning improving their knowledge, competence or self-esteem, or effecting some change in their political situation. Such research is usually *participatory* with the subjects of the research being partners in the enterprise. This is intended as an antidote to the alleged power imbalances between researcher and subjects in mainstream research. See *Consciousness raising, Partisan research, Post-colonial anthropology, Survivor research.*

Barnes, C. (2000) '"Emancipatory" disability research' www.leeds.ac.uk/disability-stud-ies/archiveuk

Embodiment

(1) In general usage meaning an effective representation or symbolisation, as in 'The union flag is the embodiment of the nation'. (2) In psychology, artificial intelligence, neuroscience, *cognitive anthropology*, and *ethology* and similar disciplines the assumption that cognition and action are shaped by aspects of the body (Ziemke (2002): hence a form of monism (see *Dualism*), see also *Interactionism.* (3) In other social sciences various notions about the extent to which human beings having bodies limits, facilitates, and shapes thought and action, including for example, the sociology and psychology of physical coercion, pain experience or sexual pleasure and the cultural importance of body metaphors. See also *Kinesics.*

Ziemke, T. (2002), "What's that thing called Embodiment?", – Proceedings of the 25th Annual meeting of the Cognitive Science Society, pp. 1305–1310
Society for the Scientific Study of Embodiment http://www.ssse.org/

Emergence/Emergent phenomena

A traffic jam is an emergent phenomenon. While the cars go forward, the traffic jam stays in the same place or goes backwards. Waves, eddies, or whirlpools are created by, but different from, the movements of individual water molecules. Whether they use the term or not, most social scientists regard 'society', 'institutions', 'markets' and 'organisations' as emergent phenomena, which cannot be reduced to the thoughts and actions of individuals – but see *Methodological individualism* and *Rational choice theory.* In the past, the term 'sui generis' (self-generated) was used for the same idea. Recognising emergence is the opposite of engaging in *reductionism.* There is a close relationship between the idea of emergence and *complexity theory* and it has been claimed that *computer simulation* is the most appropriate way for studying both.

Gilbert, N (2007) 'Simulation: an emergent perspective' *Guildford, Centre for Research on Social Simulation* http://alife.ccp14.ac.uk/cress/research/simsoc/tutorial.html

Emic

Of terms, or understandings, indigenous to a culture or sub-culture – (sometimes **folk categories, members' categories, native categories, indigenous categories**, and see *Actor perspectives*). Contrasted with **etic** terms which originate with the researcher. **Emic analysis**, common in *ethnographic research*, is the analysis of a culture 'in its own terms'. Etic terms facilitate cross-cultural analysis if they provide a framework in terms of which several different cultures can be described. The terms parallel the distinction between coding with **in vivo categories** and coding in **researcher or analytic categories**. See *Coding, Cognitive anthropology, Endogenous, Grounded theory, Hermeneutic-historical, Meta-ethnography, Nominalism, Thick ethnography*.

Empirical

(1) That which can be apprehended through the senses, directly or via research instruments. The term usually assumes senses which are highly trained, disciplined and focussed to avoid errors of perception – see *Empiricism, Theory-data dependency problem*. It is a matter of debate as to what exactly can be observed. Behaviourist psychologists (see *Behaviourism*) for example, tried to restrict the term 'empirical' mainly to physical movements; hence for them a movement of the eyelid was empirically observable, but a wink was not, since to see an eyelid movement as a wink required interpretations not themselves based on observation. This restriction has proved untenable even for behaviourists and most social and behavioural scientists accept a more expansive definition of 'empirical' – see *Action*. (2) Developing theory through trial and error in everyday practice – now largely archaic except in medicine and replaced by terms such as *Action research, Formative evaluation, Design experiments*, reflective practice.

Empirical generalisation

See *Generalisation, empirical*.

Empirical representativeness

See *Representativeness*.

Empirical research

Research which involves collecting data from the real world, as opposed to other research activities such as library research or theoretical writing. The term may be restricted to **first hand empirical research** where the researcher collects and analyses the data, but may be extended to include *secondary research*, writing *systematic* or *narrative reviews*, *meta-analysis* or the analysis of *administrative data*, all of which implicate data which can be described as empirical.

Empiricism (natural realism, naïve realism)

(1) As contrasted with *rationalism, idealism or metaphysics*, this is the position in *epistemology and ontology* which assumes that to be valid, knowledge must be based on *empirical* evidence (the evidence of the senses). In this sense nearly all social and behavioural science, quantitative and qualitative (including *realism* and *social constructionism*, but excluding some forms of *marxism and post modernism*) is empiricist. (2) However, as contrasted with *realism*, empiricism refers to a narrower range of *epistemological-ontological* positions which hold that only that which can be observed is truly real and that concepts and theories are just summary statements about patterns seen in real observable entities. *Realism* ('inferential empiricism') by contrast, reverses the picture and assumes that there is a 'deep reality' of forces, structures or mechanisms which are not observable directly but which generate observable phenomena and that it is to these that theoretical statements refer. Empiricism on the narrower definition may be associated with *operationalism* and was a feature of *logical positivism*.

Markie, P. (2008) *Rationalism vs. Empiricism*, Stanford Encyclopedia of Philosophy http://plato.stanford.edu/

Empiricism, abstract

See *Logical positivism.*

Empiricism, abstracted

A term of disapproval for the kinds of research which simply collect and present data with little attempt at theoretical interpretation; perversely this is research which is weakly abstracted, for example, *opinion-poll* research. Term coined by C.Wright Mills as a contrast with 'Grand Theory' and as part of a case for something in between called '*Middle range theory*'. Sometimes described as 'mindless empiricism'. See *Empiricist, Empiricistic, Grand theory.*

Empiricist

(1) a direct synonym for *empiricism* (as in 'an empiricist approach'), (2) a term of disapproval used to indicate what is claimed is based on

insufficient theorising of data (see *Empiricism, abstracted*). (3) Or as a criticism of research which renders the subjective worlds of people in terms imposed upon them by the analyst (in *etic* rather than *emic* terms) – see *Objectification*.

Empiricistic

Always a term of disapproval along the same lines as *empiricist* when that term is used disapprovingly; almost a synonym for *scientistic*.

Endogenous

A synonym for *indigenous*, referring to animals, people or practices originating in a particular place, as in' Australian Aboriginals are endogenous/indigenous to Austrialia'. **Endogenous analysis:** in *ethnomethodology* and some fields of linguistics, particularly *Conversation Analysis*, the analysis of language and other practices in terms of their immediate context (for example the analysis of an interview as an interview rather than as a source of information about something else), with the implication that the analysis of the researcher will rediscover the analysis that was engaged in by participants in order to organise their interaction. See also *Emic*.

Schegloff, E (1997) 'Whose text? Whose Context?' *Discourse and Society* **8**(2): 165–187

Enlightenment thinking

A complex of notions which revolve around the idea of the inevitability of progress and human betterment driven by science and technology and through the application of reason to the resolution of human problems. Enlightenment thinking is *foundationalist* and comes in various forms; for example, as well as *positivism* there are several marxist and some feminist versions. The term **modernism** is often used as an alternative but usually takes a wider reference covering art, music and literature as well as science and politics. The rejection of modernism and enlightenment thinking is part of what constitutes *post modernism*.

Enumerator

See *Denominator and enumerator*.

Epidemiology

Originally the study of epidemics of disease, later the study of the geographical, temporal and social distribution of morbidity (illness) and mortality. Now extended to include the distribution of other phenomena such as crime or drug taking. See also *Public Health Observatories*.

Coggan, D., Rose, G. and Barker, D. (1997) *Epidemiology for the Uninitiated* (4th edn), Oxford: Whiley-Blackwell. www.bmj.com/epidem/epid.html

Epiphenomenalism

Position in *epistemology and ontology* which argues that what we experience consciously is secondary to neurological events which really determine our behaviour. Our conscious lives then appear as rather like what appears on the computer screen which is secondary to what happens in the processor. In this view human beings are not as *agentive* as they believe they are. There is a strain of epiphenomenalism in *behaviourism*, in *socio-biology and* in psychoanalytic theory, which allow that (sometimes) what we (consciously) experience as ourselves deciding our own actions, is mistaken. Similarly structuralism and the kinds of *discourse analysis*, where discourses drive human actors, also conceptualise consciousness at least in part as epiphenomenal – see *Structuralism and post-structuralism*. Epiphenomenalism has had a new lease of life among neuroscientists with the finding that the neurological activity associated with decision-making precedes consciousness of making decisions.

Robinson, W. (2007) 'Epiphenominalism', *Stanford Encyclopedia of Philosophy* http://plato.stanford.edu/

Episteme

(*épistémè, épistémé* but usually without accents in English texts). A body of beliefs, explicit and implicit, which ground the practices through which those who hold them decide what is true and what is false – see *Domain assumptions*. Similar to the notion of a *paradigm*, though the latter usually applies only to bodies of academic knowledge.

Michel Foucault (1980), *Power/Knowledge: selected interviews and other writings 1972– 1977*, edited Colin Gordon, New York: Pantheon (p.197).

E

Epistemic

(1) Of or pertaining to *epistemology*; synonym for epistemological, see *Epistemology and ontology*. (2) To say that explanations and theories are epistemic is to take an anti-realist position and claim that they are merely ways of organising our experience, rather than corresponding with real forces and entities. *Social constructionism*, some forms of *pragmatism* and *post modernism* are epistemic in this way – see also *Realism*.

Mayes, G. (2005) 'Theories of Explanation', *Internet Encyclopedia of Philosophy* http://www.iep.utm.edu/

Epistemic privilege

See *Standpoint epistemology*.

Epistemology and ontology

Ontology, the theory of being, refers to questions about what is meant by 'existence'; what does exist and what is the nature of existential entities? For example is there such an entity as 'society' which is different from the individuals who are members of 'it' ? **Epistemology** – the theory of knowledge – refers to questions about how we know what we know, and how we can (or cannot) know what is true. Except at a very high level of abstraction it is difficult to untangle epistemology from ontology, hence the widespread use of the compound **'epistemological-ontological'** and the use of **'epistemological'** and *'epistemic'* as if they included the ontological anyway.

The main epistemological-ontological positions in this glossary are:

Critical rationalism, Empiricism, Enlightenment thinking, Epiphenomenalism, Essentialism, Fallibilism, Falsificationism, Feminist epistemology, Foundationalism, Idealism, Instrumentalism, Logical positivism, Operationalism, Phenomomeology, Positivism, Post-modernism, Pragmatism, Realism, Social constructionism, Structuralism and post-structuralism.

Goldman, A. (2006) 'Social Epistemology'
Steup, M. (2005) 'Epistemology'
Both in the *Stanford Encyclopedia of Philosophy* http://plato.stanford.edu/

EPPI-Centre (Evidence for Policy and Practice Information and Co-ordinating Centre)

Carries out research and provides information on research eveidence for effective practice in fields of education, health promotion, employment, social care and criminal justice http://www.eppi.org.uk/

See also *Campbell collaboration, CERUK-plus, Education evidence portal*.

Equal appearing interval method/scale

See *Thurstone scale*.

Equivilisation

Process or result of making two or more measures comparable – see *commensurability*. A synonym for *standardisation*, most usually where *weighting* is used. For example the UK government definition of *poverty* is in terms of disposable, post-housing cost incomes, which fall below the 60% of the *median* income for households of a similar composition. But households with different compositions have different income needs to reach the same standard of living. Equivalisation adjusts incomes to reflect household size and age profile, using the 'OECD equivalisation scales'.

Department of Work and Pensions, *Households below average income 1994/95 to 2005/06*, www.dwp.gov.uk/asd/hbai.asp

Erikson–Goldthorpe/Erikson–Goldthorpe–Portocarero

See *Goldthope classes.*

Error bar

Synonym for *confidence intervals* when graphically represented – see *Forest plot.*

Error of central tendency

Tendency of respondents, when faced with a *rating* scale not to use the most extreme responses (for example, 'Excellent' or 'Very poor'). Commonly shown also by examiners in essay style exams who rarely use marks over 85 or under 20. A variety of positional bias – see *Bias, positional.*

Error, measurement

See *Central limit theorem.*

Error, random as opposed to systematic

A large number of *random* errors will cancel each other out, hence random errors which occur (say) at the level of an individual subject's responses, are likely to be cancelled out by errors in the opposite direction made by other respondents, and what is untrue at an individual level may nonetheless be true in aggregate. A large number of measures involving random errors will take on the form of a *normal distribution*, such that the most likely true measurement will be the *mean* (average) of all measurements, and that the extent to which this is likely to be wrong will be calculable (expressible as *confidence intervals* or as a statistic for *statistical significance*) – see *Central limit theorem*. **Systematic errors**, by contrast, will show a consistent direction away from the truth – a *bias*,

E

and cannot be easily calculated without recourse to some more accurate data. See *Bias, validation*.

ES

See *Effect size (ES) measures*.

ESA

See *Event structure analysis (ESA)*.

ESDS

See *Economic and Social Data Service*.

ESEC or ESeC Project (European Socio-economic classification)

Project to harmonise schemes of socio-economic classification across the EU, with *Goldthorpe classes* as a starting point.

> ESRC Research Centre on Microsocial change (2008) *European Socio-economic classification* http://www.iser.essex.ac.uk/esec/

Essentialism

A belief that entities have properties independently of human ideas about them – mind independent properties; for example that there are innate sexual differences in personality between males and females. The term is usually used disparagingly by *social constructionist* and *postmodernist* writers of those who do not share their constructionist views, in which case this is a synonym for *reification* or *objectification*. It is possible to adopt an essentialist position with regard to some entities, and a social constructionist position with regard to others. *Critical rationalism, empiricism, pragmatism* and *realism* are essentialist with regard to some phenomena.

Estimator/estimation rule

A rule for guessing the value of a *population parameter* based on a statistic drawn from a sample of the population. For example the sample *mean* of a random sample is an estimator for the population *mean*. See *Generalisation, empirical, Representativeness, statistical, Sample, probability, Sampling error*.

Eta (η)

The most usual correlation co-efficient used to express *curvilinear correlations.*

$$\text{Eta} = \sqrt{\frac{\text{Between sum of squares}}{\text{Total sum of squares}}}$$

The sum of squares figures are calculated through a one-way ANOVA. See *Analysis of Variance (ANOVA and MANOVA), Statistics software.*

Ethics

A branch of moral philosophy dealing with the criteria by which behaviour should be judged as morally good or bad, and the standards by which behaviour ought to be regulated. Codes of ethics for research are issued as guidance for the proper moral conduct of researchers. Compliance is often made a condition of the receipt of research grants. The codes most relevant to British researchers are those of the:

Association of Social Anthropologists: www.theasa.org/ethics.htm
British Educational Research Association: www.bera.ac.uk/publications/pdfs/ETHICA1.PDF
British Psychological Society: www.bps.org.uk/the-society/code-of-conduct/code-of-conduct_home.cfm
British Sociological Association: www.britsoc.co.uk/equality/Statement+Ethical+Practice.htm
British Society of Criminology www.britsoccrim.org/index.htm
Economic and Social Research Council: www.esrcsocietytoday.ac.uk/ESRCInfoCentre/Images/ESRC_Re_Ethics_Frame_tcm6-11291.pdf
Market Research Society www.marketresearch.org.uk/standards/guidelines.htm
Medical Research Council: www.mrc.ac.uk/PolicyGuidance/EthicsAndGovernance/index.htm
National Research Ethics Services (NHS and Social Services/Work Research) www.nres.npsa.nhs.uk
Social Research Association: www.the-sra.org.uk/ethical.htm

These guidelines are often revised and their urls changed. If you have problems, search on the name of the relevant organisation.

In addition, most Universities and many local ethics committees have their own codes of ethics.

See also *Anonymisation, Conflict of interest, Criminal records, Ethics committees, Informed consent, Privacy and confidentiality, Safety, Sensitive topics* and *Vulnerable groups.*

E

Ethics committees

Universities have ethics committees from which ethical clearance must be obtained by staff and student researchers. In England and Wales research conducted within the NHS and within Social Services, Social Work, Juvenile Justice and Probation Departments has to be approved by local research ethics committees under the overall control of the National Research Ethics Service (http://www.nres.npsa.nhs.uk/) within the 'Research Governance Framework for Health and Social Care'. Similar arrangements exist for Scotland and Northern Ireland.

Department of Health (2005) *Research Governance Framework for Health and Social Care* (2nd edition), London: The Stationery Office www.dh.gov.uk search on 'Research Governance Framework'

Research Governance in Social Care Advisory Group (2005) *Research Governance Framework*, London: Social Services Research Group www.ssrg.org.uk search on 'Research Governance Framework'

Department for Children, Schools and Families, *National Teacher Research Panel*, www.standards.dfes.gov.uk/ntrp

Scottish Executive (2006) *Research Governance Framework for Health and Social Care* (revised edition) Edinburgh: Scottish Executive www.sehd.scot.nhs.uk/cso

Office for Research Ethics Committees in Northern Ireland www.nres.npsa.nhs.uk

Ethnicity, classification

The scheme used for most government statistics and widely followed by other researchers is given on the Office for National Statistics website:

ONS (2006) Ethnic Group Statistics: a guide for the collection and classification of ethnicity data. http://www.statistics.gov.uk/about/ethnic_group_statistics/
See also *IC codes, BME*

Ethno

See *Event structure analysis (ESA), Computer Assisted Qualitative Data Analysis (CAQDA)*.

E

Ethno#

The prefix ethno- usually, but not always, stands as a synonym for 'folk', 'peoples', or 'lay'. For example, ethnobotany is the study of what ordinary people know about plants and how they use them. The prefix can be used to create a title for the study of virtually any sphere of everyday activities. See also *Cognitive anthropology*.

Ethnoarchaeology

The interpretation of archaeological evidence in the light of contemporary ethnographic research.

Ethnocentrism

A tendency to view matters from one's own cultural or sub-cultural perspective. May be used to claim that a description of the way of life of another (sub)culture has been distorted by misunderstanding or prejudice, or to claim that inappropriate moral judgements have been made, or both. Usually the implication is that the ethnocentric judge demeans the other culture, but it can apply also to the romanticising of other cultures; as for example in popular works on Eastern mysticism. See also *Culture fair, Bias, exoticism, Cultural relativism, Orientalism, Post-colonial anthropology.*

Ethnodrama

See *Performance ethnography.*

Ethnograph

See *Computer assisted qualitative data analysis.*

Ethnographic research/ethnography

Narrowly defined this refers to research conducted by the observation of naturally occurring events, often by participant observation research conducted on the assumption that it is necessary for researchers to experience life as their research subjects experience it – see *Observation, participant or non-participant.* More loosely applied to research producing any kind of qualitative data including *qualitative interviews.* The term began its life in the anthropological study of cultures exotic to the West, but is now also common in sociology. **Ethnography** (meaning **ethnographic data/materials)** may be used to refer to the *data* collected by ethnographic research and or to descriptive passages in reports of ethnographic research, or to a corpus of writing about a people or a topic. For example 'the Ethnography of the Nuer of the Southern Sudan', might be the title of a bibliography or of a museum collection – see *Ethnology.*

Hall, B. (n.d.) *How to do Ethnographic Research,* University of Pennsylvania, Department of Anthropology, www.sas.upenn.edu/anthro/CPIA/methods.html

Hammersley, M. & Atkinson, P. (2007) *Ethnography: principles and practice,* 3rd edn London: Routledge

E

Ethno-graphics

See *Visual anthropology/sociology.*

Ethnography of performance

See *Performance ethnography.*

Ethnology

Once the synonym of *ethnography*, now usually the study of material culture, usually of smaller scale societies both contemporary and archaeological. In England mainly used of museum and archaeological research. In the USA may also include *ethnographic research*.

Ethnomethodology

Literally translated means the *methods* people (ethnos) use to make sense of their lives and to make their actions sensible to others. Term coined by Howard Garfinkel. Ethnomethodology has resulted in a large body of *empirical research* displaying in fine detail the ways in which people make what they do meaningful. Typically, ethnomethodological researchers work intensively on relatively small bodies of data, such as the transcript from a single meeting, which is made available to readers of the research so that they are able, if they wish, to analyse the same data to come to a different conclusion. It is a claim of ethnomethodologists that scientific (including social) researchers use essentially the same methods of everyday practical reasoning as do other people and that there is no great difference between scientific and common-sense thinking. This is demonstrated in ethnomethodological studies in the sociology of science which *deconstruct* scientific practices to show them as *ad hoc* and context-bound – see *Strong programme*. Ethnomethodology has a social constructionist epistemology – see *Social constructionism. Conversation analysis (CA)* and *Membership category analysis* are offshoots of ethnomethodology.

Garfinkel, H. (1967) *Studies in Ethnomethodology*, Englewood Cliffs: Prentice-Hall.
Poore, S. (2000) 'Ethnomethodology; an introduction', *The Hewett School, Norfolk*. www.hewett.norfolk.sch.uk/curric/soc/ethno/intro.htm

Ethnoscience

See *Cognitive anthropology.*

Ethnostatistics

See *Ethno#*, *Administrative data.*

Ethology/ethological research

Once the study of character ('ethos') as revealed by communicative gestures, but now mainly the study of animal behaviour with a view to explanation in terms of the function of behaviour in ensuring survival.

Human ethology, sometimes termed **Human behavioural ecology,** relates common, perhaps universal, aspects of human behaviour to the evolution of the species and hence is interested in topics such as infant attachment, the preferential treatment of relatives over non-relatives, co-operation, non-verbal communication, the evolution of language, patterns of mating and sexual behaviour, and conflict resolution behaviour. In these respects overlaps in interests with **socio-biology, physical anthropology, evolutionary anthropology** and **evolutionary psychology**.

Human Behavior and Evolution Society www.hbes.com

Etic

See *Emic*.

Evaluability study

Feasibility research to establish whether a programme or a practice is amenable to worthwhile evaluation – see *Pilot studies*. Much *evaluation research* founders from being addressed to questions which are inappropriate to what is being evaluated, or because those projects or programmes are so structured, or documented as to be unevaluable. See also *Commissioned research*.

Trevisan, M. and Huang, Y.M. (2002) 'Evaluability Assessment: a primer', *Practical Assessment, Research and Evaluation* **8** (20). http://pareonline.net/Home.htm

Evaluation, formative and summative

Formative evaluation is evaluation during the development of a programme. On the basis of formative evaluation changes may be made. **Summative evaluation** occurs after the programme has finished (as a summing up), or when for some other reason there will be no opportunity to alter the programme. **Development through formative evaluation** means much the same as *Design Experiment*. See also *Clinical audit, Evaluation research*.

E

Evaluation, fourth generation/4th generation

See *Evaluation, pluralistic*.

Evaluation, illuminative

Evaluation conducted by the collection of qualitative data.

Evaluation, Nth generation

See *Design experiment.*

Evaluation, objective

Evaluation where judgements are made about how far a programme or policy has reached its objectives: synonym for **outcome evaluation**.

Evaluation, pluralistic

Evaluation studies where a practice, programme or policy is judged according to multiple sets of criteria held by various stakeholder groups; sometimes called **Stakeholder evaluation**. **Fourth Generation Evaluation** is a variety of pluralistic evaluation.

Seafield Research and Development Services (SRDS) (n.d.) www.toonloon.bizland.com/nutshell/4th.htm

Evaluation, realist/realistic

Evaluation conducted in terms of a realist *epistemology and ontology* – see *Evaluation research, Realism.*

Pawson, R. (2007) 'The promise of realist synthesis' *Realist Synthesis, supplementary reading no 5.* www.leeds.ac.uk/realistsynthesis/supreadings.htm
Pawson, R. and Tilly, N. (1997) *Realistic Evaluation,* London: Sage

Evaluation research

Applied social research conducted with the object of reaching a verdict on the value of some practice, policy, or programme and perhaps making practical recommendations for improvement; usually in the human services. Includes *effectiveness research* and *cost # analysis.* May involve any research method. There are hundreds of named varieties of evaluation, but most names appear only in one publication.

See also *Clinical audit, Design experiment, Evaluability, Evaluation formative or summative, Evaluation, illuminative, Evaluation, objective, Evaluation, pluralistic, Evaluation, realist, Meta-analysis, Mode 1 and mode 2 research, Research pure and applied, Systematic reviews.*

Trochim, W. (2006) 'Evaluation Research', *Research Methods Knowledge Base,* www.socialresearchmethods.net/kb/evaluation
Learning Technology Dissemination Initiative (ILTD) *Evaluation Cookbook* www.icbl.hw.ac.uk/ltdi/cookbook

Event history analysis/models (duration analysis, hazard models, survival analysis, competing risk models)

A range of *regression analysis* techniques for the quantitative analysis of events which change over periods of time, for example the precursors, duration, co-occurences and sequalae of unemployment. As **survival analysis**, a longstanding feature of *epidemiology* research.

Vermunt, J. K. and Moors, G. (2005). 'Event History Analysis', in Everitt, B. and Howell, D. (Eds.), *Encyclopedia of Statistics in Behavioral Science*, 568–575. Chichester: Wiley http://spitswww.uvt.nl/~vermunt/esbs2005b.pdf

Steele, F. (2005) *Event History Analysis* London: NCRM http://www.ncrm.ac.uk/research/outputs/publications/ http://www.ncrm.ac.uk/research/outputs/publications/

Event structure analysis (ESA)

Qualitative analysis of sequences of events, typically in terms of;

- **prerequisite analysis** – which events are necessary precursors to later events?
- **composition(al) analysis**, for example in terms of the agent, action, object, instrument, setting, outcome and beneficiary of an event.

Ethno is one of the software packages available for ESA – see *Computer assisted qualitative data analysis (CAQDA)*.

Heise, D. (2007) *Event Structure Analysis* (site includes Ethno software for free download) www.indiana.edu/~socpsy/ESA/

Labov, W. (2001) 'Uncovering the event structure of a narrative', University of Pennsylvania. www.ling.upenn.edu/~wlabov/uesn.pdf

Exoticism bias

See *Bias, exoticism*.

E

Expansion

In *surveys*, the grossing up of the results from a sample to give estimates of actual numbers in the population from which the sample was drawn. If the sample were perfectly representative, and 50% of respondents answered 'yes', then the expansion factor for yes sayers would be: Population size/(100/50). But no sample is ever perfectly representative so expansion factors are often weighted to compensate for the under representation of particular groups in the sample – see *Representativeness, Response rate, Weighting*. This process requires knowledge of, or a model of the population size and structure. If the survey is of a general population this information is usually derived from the *census* or periodic updates of census data.

Expectancy effect (experimenter effect, Rosenthal effect, Pygmalion effect)

Research artefacts caused by the hopes, fears and expectations of researchers, including both fraudulent actions and inadvertent actions. Inadvertently may operate through biased observation and recording (Barber and Silver 1968) or through influencing the subjects (Carrol 2007), in which case this is a special case of *subject reactivity*. May be the result of pressure from those who fund the research, or from over-identification with the subjects of the research – see *Bias patriarchal, Bias, sympathetic, Bias, value*. See also *Blinding, Commissioned research, Conflict of interest*.

Carrol, R. (2007) 'Experimenter effect', *Skeptics Dictionary* http://skepdic.com/experimentereffect.html

Barber, T. and Silver, M. (1968) 'Fact, fiction and the experimenter bias effect', *Psychological Bulletin Monograph Supplement*, **70**:6(2): 1–29

Expectancy value theory (EVA)

See *Theory of planned behaviour (TPB)*.

Expected frequency/value (E)

In a statistical calculation this is the value which would be expected to occur if the *null hypothesis* were true; usually derived from a model of what would be most likely to happen by chance or an estimation derived from a theoretical model as in a *goodness of fit* calculation. The actual value is the **Observed (O) frequency/value**. See also *Statistics, software*.

Experimental design

There are two basic designs for *controlled experiments* and modulations on these (see Figures 7A and 7B). They are:

- a similar subjects—different treatments design, or **minimum diversity design** – for investigating the effects of different conditions on similar subjects
- a different subjects—similar treatments design, or **maximum diversity design** – for investigating how different kinds of subjects respond to the similar conditions (among other things often used in *validating instruments*) for testing the range of subjects for whom a research instrument would be suitable).

E

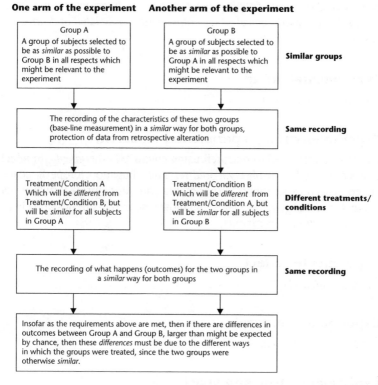

Figure 7A   Similar subjects – different treatments or minimum diversity design

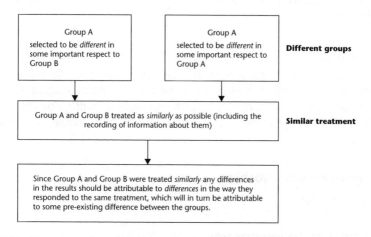

Figure 7B   A different subjects – similar treatments, or maximum diversity design

See also *Cross-over design, Factorial design, Interrupted time series design, Randomised controlled experiments (trials), Related and unrelated designs.*

Experimental group

See *Comparison groups.*

Experimentation (experimental research)

Sometimes restricted to research using *controlled experiments*, in which case contrasted with *observational research.* But more properly covering controlled experiments, experiments without controls (much *Action research* and *Design experiments* and most research in physics and chemistry) and *Natural experiments.*

Experimenter effect

See *Expectancy effect.*

Experiments, natural

See *Natural experiments.*

Experiments, true and quasi

True experiments involve *comparison groups* formed by *random allocation.* **Quasi-experiments** involve comparison groups formed by other means.

Exponent

(1) Statistics: In the expression X^2, the superscript 2 is the exponent indicating the power to which X is to be raised, here to X squared. (2) General: someone or something which expounds, explains, does or represents something, as in 'Roy Bhaskar is the main exponent of critical realism'.

Exponential smoothing

See *Smoothing.*

Ex post facto experiment

See *Natural experiment.*

E

External validity

See *Validity, external.*

Extrapolation

Extending a data set, beyond its existing values, using existing data to estimate additional data. See *Prediction.* Similar to **interpolation**, though this is restricted to estimates of additional data points between existing data points.

E

F

See *F-ratio.*

f/ϕ

Frequency – see *Frequency distribution.*

Face validity

See *Validity, face.*

Factor analysis

Comes in two forms: R and Q. **R factor analysis** is a set of statistical techniques which analyse the correlations between a large number of variables to ascertain whether a smaller number of **factors** explains their variation (*data reduction*). *Correlation coefficients* are calculated for every possible pair of variables: *pair-wise.* Where there is a high level of correlation between all variables, it is said that there is only one factor, but more usually the result is a number of clusters of variables which are associated with each other more closely than with those in another cluster. For example see Figure 8. With data from a number of scholastic examinations: English Language, English Literature, History, Media studies, Physics, Mathematics, Chemistry, factor analysis might show closer correlations in results among the first four – call this a 'linguistic ability factor', and among the last three – call this a 'scientific ability factor'. See also *Cluster analysis, Partial correlation.* Q factor analysis: the R method (above) involves finding correlations between variables across a sample of people, for example, between gender and voting intentions. Q factor analysis looks for correlations between people across a sample of variables, reducing many individual characteristics down to a few 'factors,' which represent shared ways of thinking or shared clusters of ability . For example instead of dividing academic subjects into groups as in Figure 8,

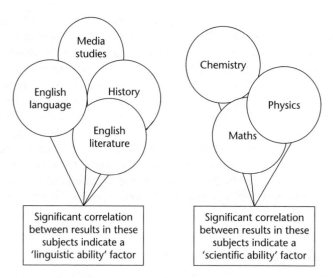

Figure 8   R factor analysis

a Q factor analysis might divide students into groups according to whether they scored well for both kinds of subject, well in one kind and poorly in another, and so on – see *Q analysis*.

Factorial design

Of experiments, modulation on similar subjects – different treatments designs where there is an interest in outcomes for sub-groups – see *Experimental design*. For example, suppose the researcher is interested not only in the effects of treating people differently, but in the different effects on males and females. This requires four *comparison groups*: males treated first way, males treated the other way, females treated first way; females treated the other way. Males and females should be *randomly allocated* to their groups separately. The *analysis of variance (ANOVA and MANOVA)* and various other statistical techniques are factorial designs used for exerting statistical control – *see Control direct and statistical.*

Trochim, W. (2006) 'Factorial design: a simple example', *Research Methods Knowledge Base*. www.socialresearchmethods.net/kb

Fact-value distinction

Accepting this distinction is a necessary precondition for adopting a value neutral approach to research: that is excluding moral judgements and personal preferences from the conduct of the research, except for those which constitute research *ethics* – see *Value neutral or value led*. The argument for this is that other moral considerations are likely to prejudice the research findings, i.e., that values may distort the facts. Not all researchers accept that such a distinction can be made. *Partisan researchers* and those who subscribe to *Critical theory, Feminist epistemology* and Critical Realism (see *realism*), who adopt a 'value-led' approach to research, may consider many so-called facts to be propositions favouring dominant groups in society and hence riddled with values, and facts only to be useful if they serve the interests of the social groups favoured by the researcher. *Social constructionist researchers* may also reject the fact-value distinction – see also *Cultural relativity, Normative research*.

Fail-safe N (or **Rosenthal's fail-safe N**)

In *meta-analysis: a sensitivity analysis* used as an antidote to publication bias (*Bias, publication*), or to what Rosenthal called the **file drawer problem,** referring to unpublished research being unavailable. The calculation works out how many additional pieces of research with statistically non-significant results it would take to overturn a meta-analysis showing a *statistically significant* result – see also *Funnel plot*.

Scargle, E. (2000) 'Publication bias: the file-drawer problem in scientific inference' *Journal of Society for Scientific Exploration* **14**(1):91–106. http://www.scientificexploration.org/jse/articles/t

Fallibilism as opposed to **Foundationalism**

Contrasting *epistemological* positions. **Fallibilism** is the belief that there are never sufficient grounds to be absolutely certain about anything. In its strongest form this is called **scepticism/skepticism**. Fallibilism may be underpinned by an anti-realist ontology that there is nothing which exists beyond our consciousness, or by an epistemological belief that entities might exist outside our consciousness, but we cannot have certain knowledge about them. It is in the nature of fallibilism that deciding between these two positions would be impossible. In the social sciences a strong form of fallibilism is associated particularly with *social constructionism* and less closely with other kinds of qualitative approaches, and with *post modernist* philosophy. A weaker form of fallibilism arises from *Falsificationism*. **Foundationalism** is the belief that science, by using the appropriate methods, can build up a corpus of explanations – a foundation – about which we can be certain. The foundation required is usually a body of scientific laws; nomothetic propositions or covering

F

laws – see *Deductive reasoning*. **Empirical/empiricist foundation-alism** argues that the foundation is secured by *empirical research*: **Coherentism** denies this is possible and looks instead to the extent to which scientific ideas hang together and support each other. Foundationalism is a less attractive idea in the 21st century than it was in the 19th. This is partly because so many apparently secure foundations have been overturned by 'scientific revolutions'; for example the replacement of Newtownian physics with Einsteinian physics – see *paradigm*. And it is partly because of the so-called 'problem of induction' – see *Inductive reasoning*. Popper's solution to this problem, *falisficationism*, which is widely accepted, suggests that the only possible foundation is one of scientific propositions which have so far survived attempts to falsify them; a much more limited conception than the foundation envisaged in *positivism* and *logical positivism*. In addition, feminists and other partisan thinkers have argued that bodies of knowledge which may look like parts of a foundation are in fact merely versions of the truth composed by and biased in favour of males, white people, or some other dominant group.

Fumerton, R. (2005) 'Foundationalist Theories of Epistemic Justification', Stanford Encyclopedia of Philosophy http://plato.stanford.edu/

Kvanvig, J. (2007) 'Coherence theories of Epistemic justification', Stanford Encyclopedia of Philosophy http://plato.stanford.edu/

Hetherington, S. (2005) 'Fallibilism', *Internet Encyclopedia of Philosophy* www.iep.utm.edu/f/fallibil.htm

Fallibility testing

Taking research findings to the people to whom they refer and asking them whether they agree with them. There is no consensus among researchers as to what should be done if subjects disagree with the researcher's interpretation, although among those favouring *participatory research*, research subjects may be given a veto over the publication of results they disagree with. In some *evaluation* studies the purpose of the research is to provide material for a debate among and with those involved. Synonym for **Member-checking** and sometimes for **Respondent validation,** though the latter can refer to questions in a *questionnaire* designed to authenticate that a respondent falls within the target group for the survey, and/or to check the consistency of respondent answers.

False consciousness

The main idea in theories of structured ignorance where some body of knowledge or corpus of communications is conceptualised as functioning to promote the interests of dominant groups. In research, false consciousness appears (1) as a topic for research with analysts deconstructing bodies of knowledge, media output and so on, to show they promote powerful interests – see *Deconstruction, Discourse* (2) as informing approaches to research where researchers believe that social, psychological or other theories are infected with false consciousness, and that hence alternative theories have to be produced as a counter (3) as a motivation for research which includes elements of *consciousness-raising.*

False negatives/positives

See *Type 1 and type 2 error.*

Falsification(ism)

Lip service at least is paid to this idea in much quantitative research in the social sciences and elsewhere. Associated with the philosopher Karl Popper who argued that because of the problem of induction, we can never be sure which knowledge claims are valid – see *Inductive reasoning.* But we can be sure about which knowledge claims are false. Therefore, he argues, science should proceed by making serious attempts to disprove (refute/falsify) what is thought to be true. At any one time the corpus of scientific knowledge will be that which has survived attempts to falsify it: not necessarily valid, but more likely to be valid – see *Validity.* Falsification is the object of the *hypothetico-deductive method.* See also *Fallibilism, Verificationism.*

Popper, K. (2002) *Conjectures and Refutations: the growth of scientific knowledge,* London: Routledge Modern Classics (originally 1963) – extract 'Science as Falsification' www.stephenjaygould.org/ctrl/popper_falsification.html#see

Reeves, C. and Brewer, J. (n.d.) *Hypothesis Testing and Proof by Contradiction: An Analogy* www.rsscse.org.uk/ts/bts/reeves/text.html

F

Family-wise error

Testing for *statistical significance* asks how often the actual results of the research might have cropped up by chance. Usually it is said that results are statistically significant if they are among those which would crop up by chance less than 5 times in 100 ($p < 0.05$, or an *alpha level* of 0.05, or 5%). But if the same set of results were subjected to 100 different statistical tests then, by chance, about 5% of tests would be expected to indicate statistical significance when they shouldn't, and, if to only 20 different statistical tests, at least one of these would give a spuriously significant result. This is the *family-wise error* and the danger is that a researcher will go on trying test after test until he or she comes up with one which gives a significant result. To reduce this possibility, researchers subjecting data to several tests usually 'raise the alpha level' meaning that instead of looking for significance at the 5% level ($p < 0.05$), they look for significance at the 1% level ($p < 0.01$). 100 different tests would still probably still give one or two false readings of statistical significance at the 1% level. A source of false leads in *data mining*. See also *Critical values, p values.*

fc

See *Cumulative frequency.*

Feature analysis

See *Componential analysis.*

Feasibility studies

See *Evaluability study, Pilot studies.*

Fidelity

See *Protocol.*

Feminist epistemology

Diverse range of theories of knowledge all proceeding from a similar critique of other knowledge-producing activities as disadvantaging women and other subordinate social groups (see *Bias, patriarchal, Ideology*) through:

- excluding them from inquiry,
- producing ideas which downgrade feminine ways of thinking and knowing,
- representing women as inferior,
- producing knowledge which is not useful to women and other subordinate groups, but which may be useful in subordinating them.

A central idea in feminist epistemology is that of the 'situated knower'; knowledge being shaped by the social, historical, political and economic context of the knower. Being a woman in an historical situation is seen as a resource for the production of knowledge rather than as an impediment to be transcended, the resource to be realised through reflexive inquiry – see *Reflexivity*. Beyond this, feminist epistemology fans out to

F

a range of positions which include feminist *empiricism*, feminist *standpoint theory,* feminist *pragmatism* and feminist *post modernism,* and in the nineteenth and early twentieth century, feminist *positivism.* However, there is also a great deal of work which declares itself to be feminist, but seems to fit none of these designations – see also *Epistemology and ontology, Historiography, Feminist research.*

Anderson, E. (2007) 'Feminist epistemology and the Philosophy of Science', *Stanford Encyclopedia of Philosophy* http://plato.stanford.edu

Feminist research

Research of nearly every kind has at one time or another been represented as 'feminist', so long as it has been motivated towards improving the social position of women – a form of *partisan research.* However, the claim to be distinctly feminist is most commonly made about research which is:

- *partisan*
- *qualitative*
- emphasises the importance of *voicing* accounts of the personal experiences (*subjectivity*) of women in ways that they agree with
- uses relationships based on shared womanhood as a resource for doing the research
- *participative*
- *emancipatory*
- credits women with knowing more and better than men – *see Standpoint theory*

See also *Feminist epistemology.*

Sarantakos, S. (2002) 'Feminist Research' in *Social Research* (3rd edn), Basingstoke: Palgrave www.palgrave.com/sociology/sarantakos/workbook/feminist.htm

F

Field experiment

Imprecise term, referring usually to experiments conducted in settings which are not in themselves created by the experimenter; for example on railways stations, or in shopping malls. But the term seems not to be used for experiments conducted in human service settings; for example, schools or hospitals.

Field notes

Most commonly the records made by *ethnographic* researchers, which may include all or some of: research data, a sequential record of research activities, and notes of emerging interpretations. In *grounded theory* such field notes are referred to as *memos*. In non-ethnographic research the term is sometimes used to refer just to a sequential record of research activities: a research *diary* or log.

Massey, A. (1995) 'Fieldnotes:breaking the silence', *Journal of OUDES Research Students* **1**(1) 12–16. www.geocities.com/Tokyo/2961/fieldnotes.htm

Field research

Usually a synonym for *empirical research*, as contrasted with desk research or library research, but alternatively, field research may be contrasted with laboratory research. See also *Field experiment, Fieldwork.*

Field testing

(1) In market research, giving research subjects some experience with a product or advertisement and collecting data about their reactions – see *A/B Research*. (2) *Piloting* research instruments and subjecting them to testing for criterion validity – see *Validity, criterion.*

Fieldwork

In sociology and anthropology usually restricted to *ethnographic research* involving face to face interaction with the subjects of the research. In psychology may refer to conducting *field experiments.*

Figuration/Figurational Studies

An approach to social research associated with Norbert Elias focusing on processes rather than structures.

The Norbert Elias Foundation: www.norberteliasfoundation.nl/index_FS.htm

F

File drawer problem

See *Fail-safe N.*

Filter/Filter question

See *Question, filter, Question, funnel.*

First order constructs/first person understanding

See *Emic, Thick ethnography, Verstehen.*

Fisherian statistics

Synonym for *Frequentist statistics*, so-called after R.A.Fisher who made a major contribution to their development. See *Statistics, inferential.*

Fisher's exact test

Non-parametric test of *statistical significance* for small samples of data in 2X2 or 2X3 tables. Used mainly where cell contents are too small for X^2 test. See *Statistics, parametric and non-parametric, Statistics software, X^2 test.*

Fit line

Synonym for line of best fit, floating mean, least squares line, regression line and trend line – see *Regression analysis.*

Fittingness

Used by some qualitative researchers instead of *generalisability or external validity – see Criteria of research quality.*

Five number summary

Summary of data set in terms of the two most extreme scores, the lower and upper quartiles and the median. Graphically displayed as a *box-plot.*

Fixed effects

See *Effects, fixed and random.*

Floating mean

See *Regression analysis.*

Floor effect

See *Ceiling effect.*

Flynn effect

A cohort effect in intelligence measurement. See *Standardisation.*

Focus groups

See *Group interviews.*

Focused enumeration

Survey technique of sampling used in absence of suitable *sampling frame*. For example, if wishing to collect a probability sample of minority ethnic people, interviewers might visit every *n*th (e.g. 5th) address in a defined area and ask about the ethnic origins of those living both at that address and at the *n*-1 (e.g. 4) addresses on either side of the visited address. If neighbouring addresses are identified as housing minority ethnic people, or if this is unknown, those addresses are visited in turn – see *Sample, probability*.

Follow-up tests

See *Post-hoc tests*.

Forced choice responses

See *Question formats*.

Forecasting

See *Prediction*.

Forest plot

Graphical display of results of statistical *meta-analysis* (see *Figure 9 overleaf*).

Figure 9 shows the odds ratios (ORs) resulting from 8 *randomised controlled trials* together with their lower (LCL) and upper (UCL) 95% *confidence limits* – see *Effect size (ES) measures* for odds ratios. Note that other ES measures can feature in a forest plot. The whiskers extend to the confidence limits. The line down the centre of the graph is the line of no difference. Results on the left (in this example) suggest that the intervention was more effective than the control condition and on the right that the control condition was more effective. Results that span the central line are inconclusive. There are various ways of producing the pooled estimate – see *Effects, fixed and random*. Although other factors influence the size of the confidence interval there is a strong tendency for the studies with larger samples to have smaller CIs: results about which we can be more certain. The pooled estimate with a sample of 2576 has the smallest confidence interval of all and suggests that the evidence from all trials combined favour the intervention. The scale used is a *log scale*. See also *Funnel plot*.

F

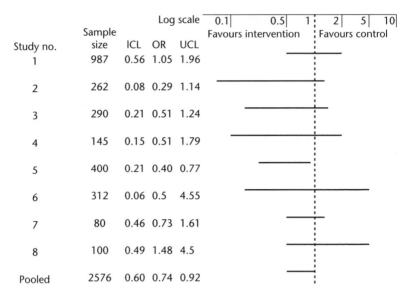

Figure 9 Example of a forest plot

Formative evaluation

See *Evaluation, formative and summative.*

Foundation

(1) In *enlightenment thinking* and early *positivism*, the notion that scientific knowledge would accumulate as a foundation of verified truth expressed in law-like terms – see *Deductive reasoning.* This is called foundationalism.

> Fumerton, R. (2005) 'Foundationalist Theories of Epistemic Justification', *Stanford Encyclopedia of Philosophy* http://plato.stanford.edu/

(2) In *logical positivism* and most other *epistemological and ontological positions* it is accepted that scientific knowledge rests on a foundation of unverifiable and *metaphysical* ideas or *domain assumptions.* See *Fallibilism as opposed to foundationalism.*

Foundationalism

See *Fallibilism as opposed to foundationalism.*

Fourth (/4th) generation evaluation

See *Evaluation, pluralistic.*

Fractal distribution

Synonym for *Power (law) distribution* and scale free/scale invariant distribution. See also *Frequency distributions.*

Fragmentation of identity

The notion associated with Michel Foucault and other post-structuralist writers that people do not have coherent identities, but rather packages of identities each constituted by the different systems of discourse that impinge upon them. Someone, for example, might have an identity given to them by the discourse of family life, another by the discourse of general practice, another by the discourse of the company they work for. The same idea is sometimes expressed as the **dispersal of identity** and as *decentred* identity. In some ways these ideas are similar in implication to traditional role-theory which sees an individual divided between the roles s/he plays. Fragmentation is a key element of *Queer theory*. It is often claimed as a (post) modern phenomenon, but there is no firm evidence that it is restricted to any particular historical period.

Sense Worldwide (2007) 'Identity' www.senseworldwide.com/categories/identity/identity/

Frame analysis

An approach to the analysis of written text and broadcast media devised by Irvine Goffman.

Thomas Koenig's *Frame Analysis* website offers resources and advice on conducting *Frame Analysis* www.ccsr.ac.uk/methods/publications/frameanalysis

Goffman, I. (1974) *Frame Analysis:An essay on the organisation of experience,* New York: Harper & Row.

F-ratio (or *F*)

The result of an *ANCOVA* or *ANOVA* calculation. It expresses the way the *total variance* in a data set is divided into the *between-group variance* (the 'main effect') and the *within-group variance* (the 'error'). A high *F* score means that most of the variance is *between-group variance* which is presumptive evidence that what groups have experienced differently makes a great deal of difference to whatever outcome is being measured. Whether *F* is *statistically significant* can be determined by looking up its value in a table of *critical values* for *F*. The critical value in the table with which F is compared, depends on the *degrees of freedom* in the calculation. Unlike most critical values tables, that for F needs two sets of *degrees of freedom*; one for the number of groups and one for the number of subjects. In practice the look-up is usually automated in a statistical computer program.

F is usually reported like this, for example: $F = (5,187)$ = 2.21, $p < 0.05$, meaning:

> (5,187) there were five *degrees of freedom* for the groups (six groups −1) and 187 *degrees of freedom* for the subjects (193 subjects minus the number of groups which was 6)
>
>   = 2.21: this was the result of the *ANOVA* calculation and is the *F ratio*
>
> $p < 0.05$: 2.21 equalled or was greater than the critical value found in the table of critical values for F for the 5% (0.05) level of statistical significance. This value was found at the intersection of the column for 5df, and the row for 187df.
>
> The interpretation is that a score for F of 2.21 or greater would only be likely to crop up by chance 5 times in 100 or less frequently. The assumption is that, therefore, it didn't occur by chance and that the result is *statistically significant*.

See also *Statistics software*.

Free school meals

Percentages of pupils receiving free school meals is often used as an easily obtainable deprivation indicator. The percentage of children who do not exercise their eligibility varies from school to school so this is not a very accurate discriminator between schools in terms of the socio-economic circumstances of pupils – see also *Deprivation indices, Income inequality indices*.

Kounali, D., Robinson, T., Goldstein, H. and Lauder, H. (2008) *The probity of free school meals as a proxy measure for disadvantage*, http://www.bath.ac.uk/research/harps/Resources/ and search on title.

Friedman's trend test

See *Trend tests*.

Frequency distribution

(See Figure 10). A frequency distribution organises data to show how many scores or measurements fall within chosen intervals (**class intervals/bins**) or where on a continuous scale. This can be shown as a line graph or frequency polygon (continuous interval level data) or a histogram (interval level data grouped in class intervals) or bar chart (nominal level data) – see *Data, levels of, Graphs*. Frequency distributions tend to be named for the ideal typical distributions to which they approximate and/or according to their *skew*, and according to their *kurtosis*. Some frequency distributions show no particular pattern. See also *Cumulative distribution, Data, transformations, Power (law) distributions, Stem and leaf plot*.

Purchasable statistics packages will sort data into frequency distributions. So will various spreadsheets including Excel. But with the exception of CountIF(only available with Excel 2007 and later) the various formulae are not easy to use (Kyd 2008, Microsoft Support 2003).

Kyd, C. (2008) 'Using Excel to calculate frequency distributions' *Exceluser* www.exceluser.com/solutions/q0001/frequency.htm

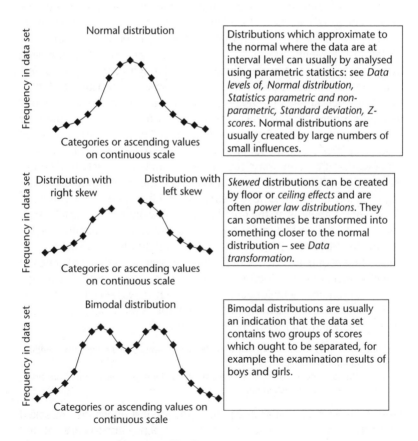

Figure 10 Types of frequency distribution

Microsoft support (2003), *How to use the frequency function,* http://support.microsoft.
com/kb/100122

Musalia, J. (2006) *Chapter 2: Frequency Distributions,* University of West Kentucky. www.
wku.edu/~john.musalia/soc300

Frequentist statistics

Synonym for Fisherian statistics, so called because they operate on the
principle of modelling the frequency with which events might occur by
chance. See also *Normal distribution, Power (law) distribution, Statistics #,
Statistical significance.*

Functional analysis/functionalism

(1) In sociology/anthropology: the analysis of social institutions in terms
of the contribution they make to the maintenance (or sometimes the
undermining) of societies. Historical functionalism assumed that social
stability was desirable and on that consideration tended to approve of
social arrangements current at the time. This was so of functionalism
in both the West and in the Soviet block, though approving of different forms of society. Functionalism was also characteristic of Marxist
thinking when applied to capitalist societies and identified institutions
as either progressive, and likely to lead to a proletarian revolution or
reactionary and helping to sustain capitalism. Functionalism stimulated
much *empirical research* but with results interpreted in terms of these
frameworks. Contemporary researchers continue to ask functionalist questions, if they ask, for example, how this or that feature of an
organisation contributes to its survival in its business environment.
Functionalist analysis on the grand scale is now unusual (Gingrich 1999)
with one exception and that is the widespread analysis of cultural ideas
and media products, allegedly to discover that they have the function of
misleading people and hence of facilitating their acceptance of states of
affairs which are not to their benefit – see *False consciousness, Ideology.*

(2) In psychology a major perspective which views behaviour in terms
of the contribution (function) it makes to various physiological and psychological systems (Philosophy online 2008).

Gingrich, P. (1999) 'Functionalism and Parsons' *University of Regina* http://uregina.
ca/~gingrich/n2f99.htm

Philosophy on line (2008) 'Functionalism' www.philosophyonline.co.uk/pom/pom_
functionalism_introduction.htm

(3) In *Ethology* and similar disciplines functionalist questions are asked
about the contribution made by patterns of behaviour to survival and
reproductive success.

Fundamental attribution error

See *Bias, attribution.*

Funnel plot

Graphical display of results of a *meta-analysis.* Results are plotted on a graph, one axis showing the precision of each study (primarily a function of sample size) and the other the magnitude of the effect size – see *Effect size (ES) measures.* Since the less precise studies are by that token more likely to show more diverse effect sizes, the data points should take the form of a funnel, with the pooled estimate at the apex. In the example in Figure 11 the combined evidence points to an effect size of 0.5 in favour of the intervention – see *Forest Plot.* Where the pattern produced does not give a funnel shape this is usually taken as evidence that the corpus of studies included in the analysis is biased. Publication bias (*Bias, publication*) is the usual suspect. Sometimes effect sizes are plotted against the *standard error* of each study, conveying the same message. See also *Fail-safe N.*

Department of Health Sciences (n.d.) 'Meta-analysis: publication bias' University of York www-users.york.ac.uk/~mb55/msc/systrev/pub_text.pdf
For software to construct funnel plots:
Basu, A. (n.d) 'How to conduct a meta analysis.' *Supercourse* www.pitt.edu/~super1/lecture/lec1171/001.htm

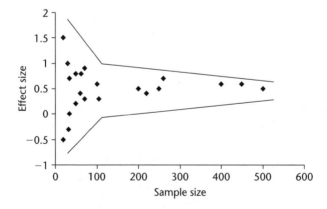

Figure 11   Funnel Plot: Sample size against effect size

Funnel question

See *Question, funnel.*

Fuzzy logic/sets

Symbolic logics such as *Boolean algebra*, require exclusive binary memberships such as 'true/false', 'yes/no' or 'belongs/does not belong'. Fuzzy logic allows for degrees of membership, such as 'true up to this point', or 'sometimes yes and sometimes no'. Hence fuzzy logic is more suitable for handling the categories of everyday speech and thought and for the probabilistic propositions characteristic of the social sciences. Fuzzy sets are principally applied in *Qualitative comparative analysis (QCA)*.

Ragin, C. (n.d.) *'Fuzzy set/Qualitative Comparative Analysis- What is QCA?* University of Arizona. www.u.arizona.edu/~cragin/fsQCA

COMPASS (Comparative Methods for the Advancement of Systemmatic Cross-case Analysis and Small-n Studies): www.compasss.org/WPFull.htm

Both sites above provide software downloads for fuzzy logical analysis as well as instructional material and academic papers.

Hajek, P. (2006) 'Fuzzy logic', *Stanford Encyclopedia of Philosophy* http://plato.stanford. edu/

F

Game studies

Mainly used for the study of the sociology, psychology, economics, strategy and structure of computer games. Supported by http://www.gamestudies.org

> Dovey, J. and Kennedy, H. (2006) *Game Cultures: computer games as new media*, Buckingham, Open University Press.

Game theory/game theoretic approaches

Body of theory and simulations concerning the way people make decisions in the face of uncertainty, including the uncertainty of not knowing how others might respond. Extended to explain institutional patterns in terms of the evolution of risk-spreading strategies, for example, in peasant agriculture or business practice. 'Prisoner's dilemma' is perhaps the best known of the games. Also employed in evolutionary biology and *ethology* to explain adaptations, particularly behavioural adaptations. Now mainly executed as computer simulations.

> McCain, R. (2006), *Strategy and Conflict: an introductory sketch of game theory* http://william-king.www.drexel.edu/top/eco/game/game.html
> For an on-line interactive version of Prisoner's Dilemma: www.open2.net/historyandthearts/philosophy_ethics/prisoners_dilemma.html

Gamma (γ)

Measure of *association* by *proportional reduction of error* with related (paired) data, used as alternative to lambda where *direction of effect* is not assumed.

$$\text{Gamma } (\gamma) = \frac{\text{number of similar pairs} - \text{number of dissimilar pairs}}{\text{number of similar pairs} + \text{number of dissimilar pairs}}$$

'Similar' and 'Dissimilar' depend on the categorisation system chosen; for example 'High','Medium', 'Low', or 'Satisfied' and 'Dissatisfied'.

Gamma × 100 = the percentage by which the value of one variable is influenced by the value of the other, which will be the same both ways.

Musalia, J. (2006) *Chapter 7: Measures of Association; nominal and ordinal variables,* University of West Kentucky. www.wku.edu/~john.musalia/soc300

Garbology

Drawing inferences about social and psychological behaviour from accretions of rubbish. Though named in the 1940s was already well-established in archaeology. Also used as a technique of industrial and state espionage, identity theft and celebrity reportage. Has recently become a common component of environmental and sustainability curricula. See also *Unobtrusive measures*.

Rathje, W., and Murphy, C. (2001) *Rubbish: The Archeology of Garbage,* Phoenix: University of Arizona Press. www.ralphmag.org/AY/garbology-one.html

Garfinkeling

Conducting *breaching experiments.*

Gate keepers

Those who control access to the subjects or site of research or repository of documents. Nowadays gaining access usually involves an *ethics committee*, but also, for example, head teachers and parents for research with school children, prison governors and the Ministry of Justice for research in prisons. For accessing or publishing information about NHS patients or social services clients, *Caldicott guardians*, and for accessing personal data held by almost any other organisation, the Data controller designated under the *Data Protection Act* may be gate keepers – see also *Privacy and confidentiality*. For research with children and vulnerable adults the researcher may have to undergo a *criminal records check*, and for research in prisons, police stations, secure units and some other government facilities a criminal records check and a security vetting. See also *Sensitive topics and vulnerable groups*.

G

Gaussian curve

Synonym for *normal distribution*. Often preferred on the grounds that there is nothing normal about the normal distribution – see also *Frequency distributions*.

Gaze

As in 'the medical gaze', refers to ways of understanding and making sense of the world characteristic of particular groups of social actors – see *Actor perspectives*.

Generalisation; empirical, naturalistic, theoretical

To generalise is to claim that something which is found in one place, for one group of people or at one time is also true of other places, for other people or other times. To generalise successfully, the claim must be true in the first instance; that is, to form the basis for a valid generalisation, a piece of research must itself have internal validity (*Validity, internal*) as well as **generalisability**/external validity/ transferability. The extent to which a generalisation from a research finding is true, will depend on how the generalisation is *specified*. Thus it may be an invalid generalisation to say that 'x will always happen under all circumstances' but it might be valid to say that 'x is likely to happen more often than not, under these specified circumstances'.

Three main forms of generalisation are distinguished:

- **Empirical generalisation:** the argument that what is true of a sample (proportionately) is also true of the population from which the sample was drawn. The validity of empirical generalisations depends (of course) on the quality of research with the sample, but particularly on the extent to which the sample is (statistically) representative of the population – see *Representativeness, statistical*.
- **Theoretical generalisation:** the claim that a principle/ mechanism/theory which explains what happened in the research study will also explain what happens more widely. Apart from the internal validity of the research, the validity of this kind of generalisation depends greatly on how the conditions under which the generalisation should be true have been specified – see *Specification*.
- **Naturalistic generalisation**: most often claimed as a benefit of *qualitative research*. Here it is the readers of the research studies who, in any way they like, relate the findings to their own lives, in much the same way as they might do with a novel or a feature film. This is associated with the idea that the purpose of much qualitative research is to develop empathy and understanding between people and enrich and expand the lives of readers.

In the last resort whether or not empirical or theoretical generalisations are valid is something to be investigated by further research; principally

G

by replicating one research study elsewhere – see *Replication*, or conducting *meta-analyses* of similar studies. The validity of a naturalistic generalisation could be tested via a study of attitude or behavioural change following exposure to a research report.

Genetic fallacy

Rejecting or accepting a claim on the basis of its origin, rather than on evidence. In social research with its many factions, shown perhaps most often in the easy acceptance of claims from 'one of us' and hostility to claims made by others. Of course there are times when the origin of a claim is important evidence, for example in judging eye-witness accounts, or assessing the authenticity of a document – see *Textual criticism*. See also *Ad hominem argument*.

Genre

Widely used loosely as a synonym for 'type of', particularly with regard to media productions, such as films or novels or types of speech or writing. Given more precision when referring to a formal typology defining different genres. Of these there are many using various criteria for definitional purposes. Hence the meaning of **genre analysis** depends of which classification of genres is used. See also *Paradigmatic analysis*.

> Chandler, D. (1997) 'An Introduction to Genre Theory', http://www.aber.ac.uk/media/ Documents/intgenre/intgenre.html

Geodemography/Geodemographics

The study of the geographical distribution of social phenomena, now usually pursued through *Geographical information systems* software.

Geographical information system (GIS)

For the software and **Geographical information science (GIS)** for the theory: software for mapping data geographically and temporally, for example for mapping the location and timing of crimes, or of outbreaks of disease. The basic technology supporting Geodemography.

> There is a good instructional package for GIS on the Ordnance Survey. website: www. ordnancesurvey.co.uk/oswebsite/gisfiles
> The Geo-ed website has a continuously updated GIS resource list: www.geo.ed.ac.uk/ home/giswww.html

A GIS crime map is planned for every neighbourhood of the UK by 2009 and information about crime mapping is available on the Home Office Crime Reduction website, including:

Gonzales, A., Schofield, R. and Hart, S. (2005) *Mapping Crime: Understanding Hot Spots*, London: Home Office http://search.crimereduction.gov.uk/ and search for 'crime mapping'.

Geographical weighting

See *Weighting, geographical.*

Georeferencing

See *Geographical information systems, Output areas.*

GHSPCD

See *Pseudo-cohort analysis.*

Gini coefficient

See *Indices of Inequality.*

GIS

See *Geographical Information System/Science.*

Glass delta

See *Effect size (ES) measures.*

Goldthorpe Classes (Hope-Goldthorpe/Erikson–Goldthorpe, Erikson–Goldthorpe–Portocarero(EGP)/CASMIN (Comparative Study of Social Mobility in Industrial Nations) classes/typology/scheme/schema

Evolving family of schemes for dividing population into social classes based on occupation. With various levels of subdivision from a simple three-fold scheme (Service/Intermediate/Working class), a sevenfold scheme to an eleven-fold scheme: the latter having being the basis for harmonising classifications between countries (see *CASMIN*) and the starting point for the *National Statistics Socio-economic Classification (NS-SEC)* and for the *ESEC project*. The Hope-Goldthorpe scale devised for the Nuffield Study of Social Mobility (Goldthorpe and Hope 1974) was the precursor of all these scales. For detailed correspondence with *Wright Classes*, see Marshall *et al.* 1989. See also *Social class.*

> http://www.encyclopedia.com/ and search on 'Goldthorpe class scheme'
> Goldthorpe, J. and Hope, K. (1974) *The Social Grading of Occupations*, Oxford Clarendon.
> Marshall, G., Rose, D., Newby, H., and Vogler, C (1989) *Social Class in Modern Britain*, London, Unwin Hyman.

Goodhart's law

Of performance management, Goodhart's law states that when a measurement becomes a target it ceases to be a good measurement. This is closely related to the idea of perverse incentives; that pursuing performance targets diverts activity away from more worthwhile ends. Given the unpopularity of government direction in public services, such claims need to be judged very carefully.

> Elton, L. (2004) 'Goodhart's Law and Performance Indicators in Higher Education', *Evaluation and Research in Education* **18**(1&2):120–128 www.multilingual-matters.net/erie/default.htm

Goodness of fit

Making *predictions* about what the data should show if such and such is true, and then comparing the actual data with this. Valid *predictions* are shown if there is no difference between what was predicted and what the actual data show, greater than might be expected by chance; i.e., valid predictions are shown by non-*statistically significant* <u>differences</u>, or by *statistically significant* <u>correlations</u>. The X^2 *goodness of fit test* is a common example, and *logistic regression* is essentially a procedure of testing models for their goodness of fit.

See also – *Prediction error, Statistics software.*

G

Grand narratives/meta narratives/meta discourses

Terms most commonly used in *cultural studies* and *post-modernism* to refer to both the more general sociological and psychological theories such as functionalism, marxism, feminism, *critical theory* or psycho-analytic theory, and to major cultural themes such as progress through science, the triumph of the market, the inevitability of democracy, or the eventual advent of the kingdom of heaven on earth. The implication is that they are just stories but also important cultural organisers bringing together and making sense of a wide variety of matters – see also *Theory*.

Sociology Central (n.d.) 'Metanarratives' *Association for the Teaching of the Social Sciences.* www.sociology.org.uk/ws1k5.htm

Graphs: bar diagrams, histograms, line graphs

(See Figures 12, 13 and 14). Graphing data for visual inspection is an important first stage of quantitative analysis. Graphs are easily created with a spreadsheet program. See also *Arithmetic and log scales, Attractors, Frequency distributions, Data transformations, Cumulative frequencies, Scattergrams*

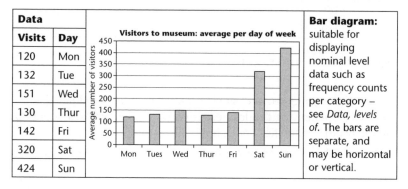

Data		Bar diagram:
Visits	**Day**	suitable for displaying nominal level data such as frequency counts per category – see *Data, levels of*. The bars are separate, and may be horizontal or vertical.
120	Mon	
132	Tue	
151	Wed	
130	Thur	
142	Fri	
320	Sat	
424	Sun	

Figure 12 Example of bar diagram

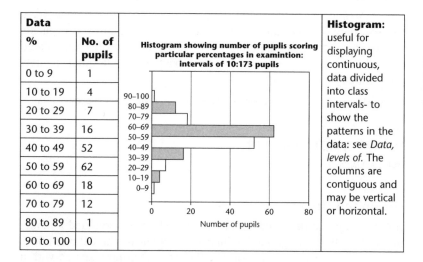

Data		Histogram:
%	**No. of pupils**	useful for displaying continuous, data divided into class intervals- to show the patterns in the data: see *Data, levels of*. The columns are contiguous and may be vertical or horizontal.
0 to 9	1	
10 to 19	4	
20 to 29	7	
30 to 39	16	
40 to 49	52	
50 to 59	62	
60 to 69	18	
70 to 79	12	
80 to 89	1	
90 to 100	0	

Figure 13 Example of histogram

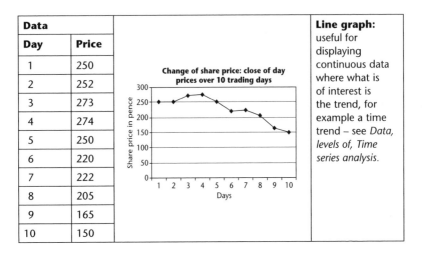

Data		
Day	**Price**	
1	250	
2	252	
3	273	
4	274	
5	250	
6	220	
7	222	
8	205	
9	165	
10	150	

Line graph: useful for displaying continuous data where what is of interest is the trend, for example a time trend – see *Data, levels of, Time series analysis.*

Figure 14 Example of line graph

The Shodor, 'Interactivate' site has a large number of animated activities on graphing, for the less experienced reader: www.shodor.org/interactivate1.0/activities/index.html

Musalia, J (2008) 'Chapter 3: Graphic Presentation', University of West Kentucky http://www.wku.edu/~john.musalia/soc300/

Grice maxims

Pragmatic linguistics. Very little ordinary speech is literal. People have to 'read between the lines' to infer what is implied but not explicitly stated – conversational *implicature.* The nine Grice maxims, formulated by Paul Grice express some assumptions people make in order to interpret ordinary conversation.

Conscious Entities (2004) 'Implicature'. www.consciousentities.com/implicature.htm

Grossing (grossing up)

See *Expansion.*

Grounded theory

Not a theory, but descriptor of any theory which is 'grounded in data'; that is, which was originated inductively by studying the data and finding theoretical explanations for it, rather than starting research with a theory and seeing if the data support or refute it – see *Inductive reasoning.*

Its core procedure is *constant comparison* The term 'grounded theory' was coined by Barney Glaser and Anselm Strauss (1967), whose subsequent disagreement has led to two distinctive proprietary brands of grounded theory; that by Strauss and Corbin (1998) being extremely prescriptive, oft quoted but apparently only rarely followed: it includes the procedures of *coding,open, axial and selective, constant comparison, negative case analysis* and the use of various kinds of *memo* for the process-recording of the research. Glaser's version is much less prescriptive.

Strauss, A. and Corbin, J. (1998) *Basics of qualitative research: grounded theory procedures and techniques.* London: Sage, is a handbook on doing grounded theory the Strauss and Corbin way.

An on-line description of their approach is given by:

Dick, B. (2005) 'Grounded theory a thumbnail sketch', *Resource Papers in Action Research.* www.scu.edu.au/schools/gcm/ar/arp/grounded.html
Glaser's version is supported by its own research institute: www.groundedtheory.com and publishing house (Sociology Press).

The seminal work is Glaser, B. and Strauss, A. (1967) *The discovery of grounded theory: strategies for qualitative research,* Chicago: Aldine.

Group interviews

Where several people participate in a group interview, for statistical purposes the group counts only as a sample of 1. This is because the performance of what one individual does is not independent of other individuals. The range of views expressed will be more restricted than if there were individual interviews – a *design effect.* There are no sharp distinctions between different types of group interview.

- **Citizen jury:** lay people are asked to discuss and decide upon issues of policy; for example how a budget should be allocated between major headings. The 'jury' are usually briefed and provided with documentary evidence. In the UK, citizen juries have only been used to gather evidence of public opinion in order to inform policy making, and never to decide policy.

  Wakeford, T. (2002) 'Citizen Juries; a radical alternative to social research', *Social Research Update* Issue 37. http://sru.soc.surrey.ac.uk/
  Community Jury Project :www.jury.org.uk

- **Delphi group (connoisseur group):** participants are credited with some expertise and the group has the task of reaching some verdict, or perhaps framing some recommendation. They may be provided with evidence to scrutinise, or a scenario to context their discussion. Used in health research to appraise the quality of research studies, and to frame consensus statements on good

G

Group interviews Continued

practice, and in various other research related to planning and policy making. See also *Vote-counting approach.*

Ali, A. (2005) 'Using Delphi technique to search for empirical measures of local planning agency power', *The Qualitative Report* **10**(4): 718–444. www.nova.edu/ssss/QR

- **Focus group:** the researcher provides questions or topics for discussion, perhaps via case study material, or with activities (for example deciding a list of priorities). Alleged by some to be a better way of investigating opinions and attitudes than using forced choice questionnaires with individuals, or even individual face to face interviews, on the grounds that discussions are more *naturalistic* and elicit views more authentically. It is argued both that focus groups provide a supportive environment for people to express themselves and, to the contrary, that they inhibit honest expression. With naturally occurring groups their talk in the group may closely match their everyday talk; for example a group of school friends, or workmates. Less frequently used than in the past in *market research* following a number of product launch disasters based on focus group research (Userfocus 2007), but remaining popular in political market research, and have recently become popular in academic social research.

Gibbs, A. (1997) 'Focus groups' *Social Research Update Issue 19* http://sru.soc.surrey.ac.uk

Userfocus (2007) 'Focus groups; is consumer research losing its focus?' www.userfocus.co.uk/articles/focuspocus.html

Parker, A. and Tritter, J. (2006) 'Focus group method and methodology; current practice and recent debate' *International Journal of Research Methods in Education* **29**(1): 23–37.

- **Nominal group:** technique for generating ideas or solving problems used in business and similar circles, where it may be described as **'brain storming'** and sometimes used for research purposes. The key feature is a task for the group to perform, which might be to solve a problem, put policies in priority order, or generate a consensus statement. They will probably be provided with stimulus material, such as a set of suggestions presented by members previously (and usually anonymously), or evidence, or a problem scenario, and their discussion will probably be facilitated. The researcher may be interested in the result of their discussion, for example as evidence of the opinions of organisation members, or may be interested in the discussion itself as a linguistic phenomenon, or in the group dynamics. Both *citizen juries* and *consensus groups* may be seen as special kinds of nominal group technique.

Manwaring, G. (1999) 'Recipes' in *The Evaluation Cookbook*, Learning Technology Dissemination Initiative (ILTD), Edinburgh, Herriot-Watt Universiry. www.icbl. hw.ac.uk/ltdi/cookbook

Guttman scale

A **scalogram** or **cumulative analysis scale** designed such that there is a high likelihood that a respondent who responds positively to a particular item will have also responded positively to all previous or subsequent items. In the example (Figure 15), an agreement to 1 would be highly predictive of affirmation of the other statements. The construction of such scales involves large numbers of people sorting candidate statements until maximum inter-predictability is achieved.

Trochim, W. (2006) 'Guttman scaling', *Social Research Knowledge Base* www. socialresearchmethods.net/kb/

	Agree	Disagree
1 I am an active member of a third world charity		
2 I donate to money to a third world charity		
3 I have considered donating money to a third world charity		
4 I am concerned about the problems of the third world		
5 I am believe I should act to help others less fortunate than myself		

Figure 15 Example of Guttman scale

G

H$_a$

Alternative *hypothesis*.

Halo effect

Subject reactivity phenomenon:(1) Respondents making approving comments about something because it is associated with something else they approve of. (2) The influence surrounding items in an instrument might have on responses to particular items. (3) Where being involved in the research of itself influences the respondents' behaviour; in which case *Hawthorne effect* would be a synonym. For all usages, usually the bias is in a positive direction. See also *Bias, Honeymoon effect*.

Haptics

See *Kinesics.*

Harmonised concepts and questions

Initiative across UK government research to use standard questions and standard definitions in order to facilitate the direct comparison of the results of different pieces of research, with some attempts to harmonise across the EU and other international agencies. Has implications for other researchers for whom it is sensible to adopt the same practice unless there are powerful reasons otherwise. See *Administrative data, CASMIN, Ethnicity classification, Equivalisation, ESEC Project, Question banks.*

ONS (2008) Harmonised Questions www.statistics.gov.uk and search on 'Harmonised concepts'
ONS (2008) *Current standard classifications* http://www.ons.gov.uk/about-statistics/classifications/current/index.html

Hawthorne effect

A form of *subject reactivity* where being observed, or simply being the subject of research, influences the subjects' behaviour.

12manage (2008) 'The Hawthorne Effect (Mayo)' www.12manage.com/methods_mayo_hawthorne_effect.html

Hazard analysis/models

See *Event history analysis/models*.

Heckman's procedure

A statistical procedure used to estimate and correct for sampling bias (see *Bias, selection*) in any surveys or *attrition* bias in longitudinal surveys.

Heckman, J. (1976) 'The common structure of statistical models of truncation, sample selection and limited dependent variables and a simple estimator for such models', *Annals of Economic and Social Measurement*, **5**(4): 475–492.

Hermeneutic-historical

Analysis in terms of the interpretations of those involved (*emic* analysis), as contrasted with **rational-empirical** analysis to uncover the facts of the matter, and as contrasted with **critical analysis** in terms of power structures and ideologies – both the latter are types of etic analysis – see *emic* analysis. Three categories of analysis from *critical theory* and especially from Jurgen Habermas.

Habermas, J. (1984), *Theory of communicative action: Lifeworld and system, Vol. I: Reason and the rationalization of society* (T. McCarthy, Trans.). Boston: Beacon Press.

Hermeneutics

(1) A tradition of biblical scholarship; (2) in sociology, anthropology, psychology and literary and artistic criticism, may refer to any approach aiming to study the meaning of texts and other communications from the viewpoint of those who produce and receive them – *emic analysis*. The aim is similar to *phenomenology, symbolic interactionism*, and *verstehen* and various psychological interpretations of communication. Like those approaches, hermeneutics involves looking at particular aspects of communication in relation to the whole; in cultural context. This is called 'the hermeneutic circle', since the understanding of the text as a whole is established by reference to the individual parts and the understanding of each individual part by reference to the whole. Varieties of hermeneutics are sometimes distinguished as Romanticist, Phenomenological – see *Phenomenology*, Dialectical, Critical – see *critical theory*, and Post structural – see *Structuralism and post structuralism*. More recently the term has been extended to include the working together of researcher and those researched to create meanings which are new to both parties in *participative research*.

H

While similar to other approaches in aims and data collecting activity, hermeneutics differs in its vocabulary and in those treated as major influences who are Wilhelm Dilthey, Edmund Husserl, Martin Heidegger, Hans-Georg Gadamer, Paul Ricoeur and Jurgen Habermas – see also *Philosophers, Semiology/semiotics.*

Ramberg, B. and Kristin Gjesdal, K. (2005) 'Hermeneutics', *Stanford Encyclopedia of Philosophy*, http://plato.stanford.edu

Demeterio, F. (2001) Introduction to Hermeneutics' *Diwatao* Vol 1(1). www.geocities.com/philodept/diwatao/introduction_to_hermeneutics.htm

Herstory

See *Historiography.*

Heteroscedasticity (heterogeneity/heteronomy of variance)

See *Homoscedasticity.*

Heuristic

(1) A rule of thumb; an experience-based approach to problem-solving; (2) a statement or criterion of good practice, widely believed, but without necessarily any strong evidential support; hence **heuristic evaluation**, which is evaluation by judgements in terms of lists of desirable features; used particularly of *usability evaluation* (Neilson n.d.) and is the process of official inspections of public services; (3) cognitive shortcuts which people use to simplify everyday reasoning and decision-making which sometimes work and sometimes lead to error (Gilovich *et al.* 2002);(4) a further usage very similar in meaning to *abductive reasoning.*

Neilson, J.(n.d) *How to Conduct a Heuristic Evaluation* www.useit.com/papers/heuristic/heuristic_evaluation.html

Gilovich, T. Griffin, D. and Kahneman, D. (eds.) (2002) *Heuristics and Biases: The Psychology of Intuitive Judgement*, Cambridge: Cambridge University Press.

Histogram

See *Graphs.*

Historical particularism

See *Cultural relativism.*

Historical processes

Processes, the direction and outcome of which are dependent on earlier states of affairs where that state of affairs is never precisely the same on different occasions; sometimes expressed through phrases such as 'sensitivity to initial conditions' or *context dependency* and sometimes by saying that the present always constitutes a memory of the past which influences the future. These ideas are closely associated both with historical research and with *complexity theory*, and imply very strict limits on the extent to which research findings in the social sciences can be generalised, or be the basis of sound predictions. See also *Idiographic research*.

Buchanan, M. (2000) *Ubiquity: The Science of History; Why the World is Simpler than we Think*, London: Weidenfeld & Nicolson.

Buchanan, M. (2000) 'New Statesman Essay: why the world is simpler than you think' *New Statesman*, 9 October www.newstatesman.com/200010090021

Historicism

A wide range of perspectives, the more traditional ones sharing the notion that history unfolds according to 'laws' of history (as in marxism, for example), and that analysis should be directed towards discovering what these are. This is rejected by the more recent perspectives (**new historicism**) which have a different focus with the idea that texts, events and so on should always be interpreted both as the product of their cultural context and its historical development and as part of the apparatus of the time for sustaining and dispersing power. The historicism of *post modernism* is actually a kind of anti-historicism and argues that 'history is always the history of the present' and that it is only possible to interpret the past in terms of our contemporary ideas.

Extracts from Karl Popper's *Poverty of Historicism* (originally 1957) http://lachlan. bluehaze.com.au/books/popper_poverty_of_historicism.html

(New Historicism) Ryn, C.(1998) 'Defining historicism', *Humanitas* **X1**(2) www.nhinet. org/ryn-rob.htm

H

Historiography

The study of the processes by which historical knowledge (accurate or otherwise) is gained and transmitted and (often) the historical accounts arising from a consideration of how history is made. Often used to include the study of the methodology of historical studies – see *Textual criticism*. Various 'standpoint' histories, such as **Feminist history/ historiography** ('**herstory**')-see *Feminist epistemology*, – black history, gay history – see *Queer theory*, – retell history from viewpoints which have often been ignored or suppressed. The **historiography of science** overlaps considerably with *social studies of science and technology*. The term can also apply to a body of historical writing about some period or topic, for example, the historiography of the second world war.

BBC (n.d) 'Nature of history', www.open2.net/historyandthearts/history/natureofhistory/index.html

Home Office model

Econometric model used by the Home Office (now Justice Ministry) to predict property crime trends and to 'level the playing field' in judging the performance of different police forces.

Dhiri, S., Brand, S., Harries, R. and Price, R. (1999) *Modelling and Predicting Crime Trends in England and Wales*, London: Home Office Research Study 198. www.homeoffice.gov.uk/rds/pdfs/hors198.pdf

Homoscedasticity/homoskedasticity (homogeneity of variance)

The condition where two or more sets of *variables* have a similar *variance*; a requirement for the use of parametric statistics with related data – see *Statistics, parametric and non-parametric, related and unrelated designs*. The opposite is **heteroscedasticity/heteroskedasticity (heterogeneity/heteronomy of variance)**. See Figures 16 and 17.

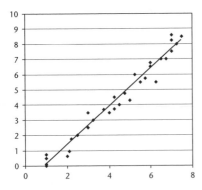
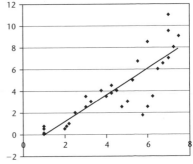

Figure 16 Data showing homoscedasticity/homogeneity or similarity of variance. The data points are at similar distances above or below the regression line

Figure 17 Data showing heteroscedasticity–heterogeneity/heteronomy/dissimilarity of variance. The data points for higher values on the horizontal axis are much more spread out vertically than the data points for lower values

See also *Box plot*, *Scattergrams*.

For statistical tests for homoscedasticity see:

Ender, P. (1999) 'Linear statistical models: checking assumptions', *Education 2/30BC*, Graduate School of Education, University of California Los Angeles www.gseis.ucla.edu/courses/ed230bc1/cnotes1/check.html

Honeymoon effect

Form of *subject reactivity* where the outcomes of a programme being tested for its effectiveness are influenced by the programme's novelty and/or by people being excited or enthused by being involved. A problem of *effectiveness research* and *action research* when conducted without adequate controls, especially with activities which depend on human competence and/or demeanour; for example reading schemes or counselling practice. Even more of a problem where research subjects are treated as partners as in *participative research*. The meaning overlaps with that of *Hawthorne effect*.

H_o

Short for null hypothesis, alternative hypotheses being designated H_a, or H_1, H_2, etc. – see *Hypothesis*.

Hoover coefficient

See *Indices of inequality*.

Hypothesis

A *prediction* or conjecture amenable to being falsified by reference to evidence – usually empirical evidence, although sometimes evidence from a computer simulation. For example:

'girls of similar prior achievement will, on average, have better educational outcomes when educated in single-sex compared with being educated in co-educational secondary schools in England'.

H

Alternative hypothesis

As opposed to **null**; the example above might be one alternative (H_{a1}) to the null hypothesis (H_0) that:

'there will be no significant difference between the educational outcomes of girls of similar prior achievement educated in single-sex as compared with co-educational secondary schools in England'.

The null hypothesis (H_0) is sometimes called the 'no difference hypothesis'. Hypotheses are an important component of the *Hypothetico-deductive method*, but are not limited to it, and in qualitative research hypotheses are often framed without the name being used, as in *analytic induction* and the process of *constant comparison*.

Hypothesise

To frame hypotheses, see *Hypothesis, Hypothetico-deductive method*.

Hypothetical

In common speech this is usually a rather disparaging term for idle speculation. But in science it refers to a proposition carefully framed so that if untrue it could be falsified. See *Corrigible, Hypothesis, Hypothetico-deductive method*.

Hypothetico-deductive method

The process of developing and refining theories through framing *hypotheses* to test them, used across the natural sciences and by many social scientists – hence often termed the 'scientific method'. The method is *falsificationist* with the main effort being to find evidence which undermines a theory, or would force a major revision of it. Thus it is usual to propose a null *hypothesis* and seek confirmation of it. If the theory were that selection at 11+ depresses educational performance overall, then the null hypothesis might be that there is no difference between children of similar ability, in their educational outcomes, whether they attend a secondary school in a comprehensive, or in a selective system. If the null hypothesis were disproved, then an alternative *hypothesis*, consistent with the theory, would remain credible (see Figure 18).

There are two well-known problems with the hypothetico-deductive method.

- the *theory data dependency problem*
- almost all theories in social science are *probabilistic* stating that such and such is likely to happen, but not inevitable. Hence, in the face of a hypothetico-deductive test which apparently disconfirms a theory, it is never quite clear whether the disconfirmation should count or not. To some extent this latter problem can be ameliorated through further research and *meta-analysis*.

Something very like hypothesis testing is practised in *analytic induction* and *grounded theory* – with *constant comparison* and *negative case analysis*. See also *Abductive reasoning*.

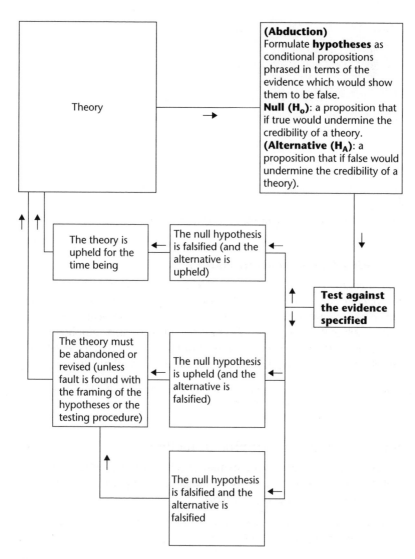

Figure 18 Hypothetico-deductive method N.B. The method does not always involve testing alternative hypotheses

Webster, S. (1998) 'The Hypothetico-deductive method', *Westminster College* New Wilmington. PA. www.psych.westminster.edu/psy201ws/Chap3/ppframe.htm

Musalia, J (2008) '*Chapter 12: Testing Hypotheses*', University of West Kentucky. http://www.wku.edu/~john.musalia/soc300/

H

I

In *time series analysis*, symbol for erratic factors.

IC codes (Identification codes)

Ethnic coding based on an official's perception of someone's race, used in policing and some other areas of penal practice where the person concerned cannot be asked to identify themselves ethnically.

IC1 – White European, IC2 – Dark European, IC3 – Afro-Caribbean, IC4 – Asian (in the British sense – i.e., Indian or Pakistani or Bangladeshi) IC5 – Oriental, IC6 – Arab/North African, IC0 – Unknown ethnicity.

Ministry of Justice (2008), *Race and the criminal justice system 2008*, http://www.justice. gov.uk/publications/raceandcjs.htm

Iconological/iconographic modelling

Pictorial representation of mathematical relationships, particularly associated with *complexity theory*. For example the representation of fractal landscapes such as Mandelbrot plots.

Byrne, D. (1997) 'Simulation – the way forward ?' *Social Research Online* **2**(2) www. socresonline.org.uk/2/2/4.html

Ideal type

A model constructed to consist of the features considered most characteristic of a class of phenomena; for example an **ideal typical** bureaucratic organisation. Each real-life example would be expected variously to share some, but not all of the ideal typical features. The use of ideal type concepts is criticised as drawing attention to cases that are extreme rather than typical in a statistical sense. The use of ideal types in social science is especially associated with Max Weber.

Weber, M. (1949) *The Methodology of the Social Sciences,* ed. A. Shils and H. Fihn, Glencoe: Free Press:90.

Buthe, T. (n.d.) 'On Ideal Types' *Duke University,* Durham. NC. www.duke.edu/~buthe/ downloads/teaching/ideal_types.pdf

Idealism

(1) As a term in *epistemology* and ontology this has a wide range of meanings, usually contrasting with *realism* (including *empiricism)*, including. **ontological idealism** which is the belief that only ideas are real, and **epistemological idealism:** the belief that (whatever the ontological truth) the only reality we can know about is the reality of our ideas. The latter characterises *social constructionism,* and *post modernism.* (2) Espousing ambitious aims, and sometimes implying over-ambitious aims; as in 'idealistic'.

Ideographic

Graphic symbolism such as writing, not to be confused with *Idiographic.*

Ideology

Sometimes used neutrally to refer to any set of ideas, but more usually to ideas which are allegedly misleading in some respects – see *Actor perspectives.* The implication may be that they are self-serving as in some uses of 'professional ideology', implying ideas that sustain the morale and the solidarity of an occupational group, or the implication may be that they are ideas which mislead those who are oppressed into accepting their situation, and their oppressors into feeling justified in privilege – *false consciousness.* The term has often been replaced with *'discourse'* as in 'patriarchal discourse' instead of 'patriarchal ideology'. The *deconstruction* of ideas to find them ideological – a *functionalist analysis,* is common in most forms of *partisan research, critical theory,* and in *semiology/semiotics.*

Idiographic research as opposed to nomothetic research

Nomothetic research (synonym for **covering law explanation** and **nomothetic-deductive explanation**) is conducted in order to draw general conclusions from specific instances and/or to test the cogency of general propositions against specific evidence – see *Deductive reasoning.* **Idiographic research,** by contrast, studies its topic as a unique constellation of circumstances. Much historical research is idiographic in that it seeks only to provide an accurate description of what happened and to explain it in its own terms, and *thick ethnography* can be described as idiographic in so far as its objective is to induct readers into the interpretive world of another culture, rather than draw any general conclusions, but see *Generalisation, naturalistic*. See also *Historical process*, *Emic*.

Illocution

Utterance classified according to what is accomplished by speaking it; for example, a request, question, or promise, as opposed to **locution**; utterances classified by what they refer to. **Perlocutions** are classified by the psychological state they induce in the hearer. In practice it has proved difficult to distinguish locutions from perlocutions and the latter are less frequently referred to. Terms from *Pragmatic Linguistics* (Speech Act Theory).

Bach, K. (n.d.) 'Speech Acts' (Reprint of *Routledge Encyclopedia of Philosophy* entry) San Francisco State University. http://online.sfsu.edu/~kbach/spchacts.html

Illuminative evaluation

See *Evaluation, illuminative*.

IMD

See *Deprivation indices*.

Implicature

Pragmatic linguistics; refers to what is meant by an utterance (implied) but not explicitly stated. For example the implicature of 'They went upstairs together' may be that they had sexual relations – see also *Grice maxims*.

Conscious Entities (2004) 'Implicature', www.consciousentities.com/implicature.htm

Imputation

Survey research. The imputing of responses to subjects who failed to make responses themselves. Involves studying the responses of those who did respond, who have similar characteristics to those who did not (age, gender, residential status and such like). On this basis, the most likely responses the non-respondents would have made are decided and entered. Alternative to, or in addition to *weighting* to offset unit or item non-response, with much the same result – see *Response rate*.

Task Force on Imputation (1997) Report of the Task Force on Imputation, *GSS Methodology paper no 8*. Government Statistical Service. www.statistics.gov.uk and search on 'GSS Methodology'

Durrant, G. (2005) *Imputation Methods for Handling Item Non-response in the Social Sciences: a methodological review*, NCRM. http://www.ncrm.ac.uk/research/outputs/publications/

Incentive payments

To encourage people to participate in research. Not uncommon in medical research and psychological research especially in the USA, and market researchers often offer incentives such as cash, prize draws or vouchers in return for completing *market research questionnaires* or participating in *focus groups* and other data producing activities. Payment for participation has greatly increased with the rise in internet surveys. For example see http://highestpaysurveys.com/. It is generally believed that incentives lead to the over-representation of the kinds of people who are motivated by gain, creating selection bias – see *Bias, selection, Career respondents*.

Simmons, E. and Wilmot, A. (2004) 'Incentive payments in social surveys: a review of the literature', *Survey Methodology Bulletin No 53*: 1–11. www.statistics.gov.uk and search on 'Survey Methodology Bulletin'.

Incidence and prevalence

In *epidemiology* and other studies of the social distribution of phenomena. **Incidence** is the number of <u>new</u> cases arising in a given time period: **prevalence** is the number of <u>all</u> cases existing during a time period, or **point prevalence:** the number of cases existing at a single point in time.

Coggan, D., Rose, G. and Barker, D. (1997) *Epidemiology for the Uninitiated*, (4th edn) Oxford: Whiley-Blackwell. www.bmj.com/epidem/epid.html

Inclusion criteria (screening criteria)

Quality criteria used in the screening of research studies to decide whether or not they should be included in a systematic review or *meta-analysis*; in health studies the usual minimum criteria are that:

- the research was an experiment.
- *comparison groups* were composed by *random allocation – see also Randomised controlled experiments/trials.*
- blinding was used.

Jadad's scale is an instrument composed of inclusion criteria. In other fields the threshold for inclusion may be less demanding.

Cochrane Collaboration (n.d.) 'Assessment of Study Quality' in *Handbook for Cochrane Reviews* Version 4.2.5. www.cochrane.dk/cochrane/handbook/hbook.htm

Income inequality indices

See *Indices of inequality, Free school meals, McLoone index, Percentile shares, Poverty, Theil index.*

Incommensurate/incommensurability

See *Commensurability.*

Incorrigible

See *Corrigible.*

Independent design

See *Related and unrelated designs.*

Independent variable (IV)

See *Variable.*

Indeterminancy of theory by data

See *Underdetermination.*

Index

(Plural, **Indices**) as in 'Retail Price Index' or 'Index of Multiple Deprivation': a measure of some phenomenon (usually) created by combining several *indicators*, see also *Construct indicator relationship, Deprivation indices, Indices of inequality, Index, to; Segregation indices.*

Index, to

As in, 'to index this year's unemployment rate against a 2001 base line': to express some measure as an **index ratio**, as a proportion of a base (or criterion) measure, perhaps the same measure at a different time, or for a wider population: synonym for **basing** or **basing out**. As an example see http://www.measuringworth.org/ukearncpi/

Index of difficulty

See *Item analysis.*

Index of discrimination

See *Item analysis.*

Index of displacement

See *Segregation indices.*

Index of dissimilarity (delta (Δ))

See *Segregation indices.*

Index ratio

See *Index, to.*

Indicator

See *Construct-indicator relation, Performance indicator.*

Indices of inequality

This term is used here for a family of indices based on the **Lorenz curve** including the **Gini coefficient**, the **Robin Hood** or **Hoover coefficient**, and the **Atkinson Index** – see also *Inequality measures and metrics.*

Calculation in each case requires interval level data – see *Data, levels of.* Where only nominal level data are available *segregation indices* might be used for some similar purposes. For an example of Lorenz curve, see Figure 19.

The **Gini coefficient** expresses the size of the area between the line of perfect equality and the line for the actual distribution. It is given either as a proportion between 0 (perfect equality) and 1 (perfect inequality) or as the corresponding percentage. The main problem with this index is that it is blind to the shape of the deviation of the actual distribution from the perfect distribution. A situation where most inequality was due to large numbers in extreme poverty, but with income fairly evenly distributed among the better off, may have the same coefficient score as one where income is fairly evenly distributed among the poorer people, but a group of super rich account for a disproportionate percentage. The Gini is also more sensitive to inequality in the middle of the range than at either end.

Miyamura, S. (2007) *How to calculate Gini Coefficient*
http://mercury.soas.ac.uk/users/sm97/teaching_intro_qm_notes_gini_coefficient.htm

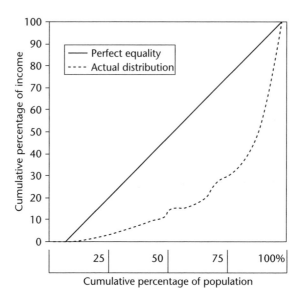

Figure 19 Example of Lorenz curve

The **Lorenz curve** is the *cumulative distribution* of whatever is unequally distributed matter – in this example, cumulative percentage of total income plotted against cumulative percentage of the adult population. This is shown in the table as the income shares of each 5% and each 25% of the population. If everyone had an equal share then the curve would take the form of a straight line running at 45% diagonally across the graph (10% of the population would get 10% of the income, 50% would get 50% and so on). If all the income was earned by just one unit of the population (here by the richest 5%) then this would approximate to a line following the bottom border of the graph to its right hand corner and then straight up the right hand margin. The actual distribution is the curve between these two extremes.

	Perfect Equality (%)	Actual Distribution (%)	Quartile shares
	0	0	The first
	5	0.25	25% of the
	10	0.75	population
	15	1.5	get 5% of the income
	20	3.5	
	25	5	
	30	5.75	The 2nd
	35	7.25	25% of the
	40	9.5	population
	45	10.6	get 10% of the income
	50	15	
	55	15.7	The 3rd 25%
	60	17.3	get 15% of the income
	65	19.5	
	70	26	
	75	30	
	80	33.5	The richest
	85	40.5	25% get 70% of the income
	90	51	
	95	75	
	100	100	

Together with *percentile shares* of aggregate income the Gini coefficient is the main index used by the UK, the USA and many other governments for tracking changes in the distribution and wealth, and by international agencies for charting the relative affluence and deprivation of different countries. See for example:

www.statistics.gov.uk – search on 'Gini'

The Gini-coefficient is also used as a measure of the extent of concentration of market share or asset ownership of companies in an economic sector, the population distribution between geographical areas, or inequality of performance in public examinations between schools, although *segregation indices* can be used for the same purpose.

The **Hoover** or **Robin Hood Coefficient** may be visualised in terms of a line showing the maximum depth of the deviation of the actual distribution from the perfect distribution on a Lorenz graph. This coefficient expresses the percentage of the unequally shared matter which would have to be redistributed to create perfect equality, that is the amount which would have to be transferred from the right-hand side of such a line to the left-hand side. This index measures only 'across-the-line' changes and is blind to changes which occur by shifts from one percentile to another on the same side of the Robin Hood line.

The **Atkinson index** improves on the Gini coefficient by weighting the calculation to make the resulting coefficient more or less sensitive to inequality at different points of the range. The weighting is described as 'setting the welfare function' or as 'setting the level of inequality aversion'. The weighting is set by a parameter of between 0 and 1. As the parameter approaches 0, the index gives more weight to the upper end of the income scale and as the parameter approaches 1 more weight to the lower end. With the welfare function set at 0.5 the result will be similar to the Gini.

Kawachi, I. (2000) 'Income Inequality', *MacArthur Research network on Socio-economic status and health* www.macses.ucsf.edu/Research/Social%20Environment/notebook/inequality.html

See also *Inequality measures and metrics*.

Indigenous

See *Endogenous*.

Inductive reasoning/inductivism/inductionism

Reasoning from the particular to the general, according to a formula such as:

'This has been true every time we have observed this set of circumstances, therefore, we claim it will always be true where ever these circumstances occur.'

Thus induction projects the properties of and explanations for known cases to unknown ones. The **'problem of induction/inductivism'** is that any proposition based on induction might be invalidated by a later contrary observation, or put another way, that generalisations based on induction could only be secure if demonstrably consistent with every possible relevant instance past, present and future. Demonstrating this is a practical impossibility. The *hypothetico-deductive method* and a falsificationist programme are proposed as partial attempts to avoid the problem of inductivism – see *Critical rationalism, Falsificationism*. The extent to which this is regarded as a problem depends on the extent to which researchers are satisfied with producing knowledge which is merely 'highly likely' to be true, rather than definitely true. Most these days are satisfied that we can know for certain what is false, and also can know that some propositions are more likely to be true than others. The problem of inductivism does not of itself force us to into *post modernism* where, it is argued, because we cannot achieve absolutely certainty, we cannot make sensible decisions about what is more and what is less likely to be true. The possibility of doing just this is central to *Bayesian inference* and to inference from *frequentist statistics*. See also *Analytic induction, Fallibilism*.

Vickers, J. (2006) 'The Problem of Induction' *Stanford Encyclopedia of Philosophy* http://plato.stanford.edu/

Inequality measures and metrics

See *Coefficient of variation, Deprivation indices, Free school meals, Indices of inequality, McLoone index, Poverty, Segregation indices, Theil's T*.

Inference tables/values

See *Critical values*.

Inferential empiricism

See *Realism*.

Inferential statistics

As contrasted with *descriptive statistics*: these are the statistical techniques for judging *statistical significance*. Although inferences are drawn from *Bayesian statistics*, the term inferential statistics has become attached to *Fisherian/frequentist statistics* See also *Statistics, descriptive*.

Information

In *statistics*, that which reduces uncertainty, hence close in meaning to *reliability*.

Informed consent

A central principle of research *ethics*: that unless good reasons can be advanced for proceeding otherwise, research should only be conducted with the fully informed consent of those being researched. Informed consent means:

> 'explain[ing] as fully as possible, and in terms meaningful to participants, what the research is about, who is undertaking it, why it is being undertaken, and how it is to be disseminated [and] not as a once-and-for-all prior event, but as a process, subject to re-negotiation over time'. *British Sociological Association* 2002

Acceptable justifications for proceeding without informed consent usually take the form that:

- no harm will befall the research subjects – see *Safety*,
- <u>and</u> the value of the results outweighs the violation of the subjects' rights to autonomy,
- <u>and</u> that the same or similar results could not be achieved if informed consent were sought.

See *Deceit in research*.

There may be difficulties in achieving consent that is *fully* informed. These include:

- The researcher's inability to predict the trajectory and outcomes of the research, as is common with *ethnographic* and *action research*, and their inability to predict what might happen when the research ceases to be under the researcher's control.
- The practical difficulties of informing those who are observed during research, for example where research is conducted in public places or by lurking on the internet (Corbin 2008).
- The inability of some subjects fully to understand the implications of being research subjects, as with people from cultures and

sub-cultures with little experience and understanding of research – a particular problem for anthropologists working in societies without a research tradition.

● Keeping informed consent continually up for negotiation runs counter to attempts to achieve naturalistic validity if subjects are always being reminded that they are being researched – see *Subject reactivity, Validity, naturalistic*.

● Meeting the requirements for fully informed consent by allowing subjects to vet and veto what gets published may run counter to the research aim of publishing honest and accurate research – see *Participative research*.

In addition, there are categories of people who are not necessarily competent to give consent to be research subjects; these include children, people who are severely ill (mentally or physically), people with learning difficulties and people who are severely distressed – see *Sensitive topics and vulnerable groups*. There are two issues here. First, there is the question of whether someone is legally competent to consent to be a research subject (which can be a complicated issue) and second, even if they are legally competent, whether it is ethically justified for a researcher to assume that their understanding is sufficient to count as informed consent. For children this issue is usually resolved by seeking consent from both the parent or legal guardian and from the child. For them and others this is usually an issue which will be decided by a local *ethics committee*.

See also *Anonymisation, Ethics committees, Privacy and Confidentiality*.

Corbyn, Z. (2008) 'MySpace and your research: will red tape hit web data use?' *Times Higher Education Supplement* 10 July

Spicker, P. (2007) 'Research without consent', *Social Research Update* Issue 51http://sru. soc.surrey.ac.uk/

Wiles, R., Heath, S., Crow, G. and Charles, V. (2005) *Informed consent in social research: a literature review*, NCRC. http://www.ncrm.ac.uk/research/outputs/publications/

Wiles, R., Crow, G., Charles, V. and Heath, S. (2007) 'Informed consent and the research process: following rules or striking balances?' *Social Research Online* Vol 12 (2) www. socresonline.org.uk/

Inheritance

In social mobility studies, see *Persistence*.

Instrument

Any formal device for eliciting data, and often facilitating the recording of data, variably named as *questionnaires*, schedules, *inventories*, tests, scales, profiles, frames, grids, examinations, assessments, forms, records, or even instruments – see also *Tests objective and projective.*

Instrumentalism

(1) *Epistemology and ontology*: position associated with *pragmatism* which argues that concepts and theories cannot be true or false in the sense of corresponding or not corresponding with reality. Rather concepts and theories should be judged by how useful they are as 'instruments' for understanding or action. 'Usefulness' includes success in explanation or as forming the basis for accurate predictions, so the distinction between this view and the more usual view of truth as correspondence with reality is subtle. Some versions of pragmatism go a little further and tie the validity of a theory to its success in guiding action – see *Validity, callactic.*

> Dutra, L. (2004) 'A pragmatic view of truth' *Principia* **8**(2):259–277 www.cfh.ufsc.br/~principi/p82-5.pdf

(2) *Epistemology and ontology*: an orientation to human activity which regards action always as a means to an end, hence predicating analysis in terms both of what people want to achieve and their ideas about how actions lead to outcomes: **instrumental rationality**. *Rational choice theory* is one version of this and *Game theoretic* approaches are usually instrumentalist in this sense, as is much of economics and political science.

> Millgram, E. (2005) 'Practical Reason and the Structure of Actions' *Stanford Encyclopedia of Philosophy* http://plato.stanford.edu/

(3) As a synonym for the practice of **instrumentation**, meaning the study of a phenomenon through the development and use of instruments to do so. The study of attitudes, personality and intelligence have largely developed in this way.

See also *Operationalism.*

Intension

Not to be confused with intention (see *Intentionalism*). The elaboration of a concept or the expansion of a term to list all its possible meanings. Includes both **denotations** (explicit meanings) and **connotations** (implied meanings).

Intentionalism

(1) A term covering all approaches which assume that the (or a) proper explanation for human activity is to be found in the intentions of those

who do it. Intentions are sometimes called 'in order to motives', but intentionalism usually goes rather wider than this to include all interpretations made by social actors. This predicates analysis which 'reads the minds' of actors to find how their motives relate to the way in which they interpret the world. Applies to all *interpretive approaches*, and to *macro-sociology* influenced by Max Weber's notion of *verstehen*, which includes American functionalism of the 1930s to 60s. Much psychology is intentionalist in this sense – see *Action, Agency, Symbolic Interactionism, Discourse analysis, Dramaturgical approach*; (2) As referring to consciousness to the effect that all thought has an *object* (something thought about) which is the **intention** of thought.

> Crane, T. (2007) 'Intentionalism' from Beckerman, A. and McLaughlin, B. (eds) *Oxford Handbook to the Philosophy of Mind* http://web.mac.com/cranetim/Tims_website/Online_papers_files/Intentionalism.pdf

(3) Linguistics: the **intention** of an utterance is either what the speaker intended to convey (a psychological phenomenon) or what a native speaker would assume to be the meaning of the utterance (a sociolinguistic phenomenon) – see also *Implicature*. Intention should not be confused with *intension*.

Interaction effect

In statistical analysis, interaction occurs when the *association* between two variables is affected by a third variable. Imagine for example, two groups of pupils receiving two different methods of teaching but sitting the same examination. The results of the two groups are much the same. The conclusion might be that the two methods of teaching were equally effective. But on closer inspection it is found that girls in the first group achieved much more than girls in the second group, while boys in the first group achieved much less than boys in the second group. This is the interaction effect of teaching method and gender. Interaction effects are of central interest in *complexity theory*. See also *Analysis of covariance* (ANCOVA and MANCOVA), *Analysis of variance* (ANOVA and MANOVA), *Association, Partial correlation, Statistics software*.

Interactionism/interactionalism

(1) synonym for *symbolic Interactionism;* (2) portmaneau term for *dramaturgical approach, ethnomethodology, phenomenology,* and s*ymbolic interactionism;* (3) in philosophy and some branches of psychology, the relations between mind and body, mental and physical (Philosophy online n.d.) – see also *Behaviourism, Epiphenominalism;* (4) the study of computer–human interaction – see *Textual interaction*.

Philosophy online (n.d.) 'Interactionism' www.philosophyonline.co.uk/pom/pom_inter-actionism.htm

Intercept

See *Regression analysis, Scattergram.*

Intercept survey

See *Survey recruitment.*

Inter judge reliability

See *Inter-rater reliability.*

Internal consistency/internal reliability

Judgements about whether all the items on a research instrument which are supposed to be measuring the same construct are indeed doing so. Judgement may be made using *factor analysis, item analysis, Cronbach's alpha coefficient* and other *correlation tests* (for interval level data), *or* **Kuder-Richardson formula 20** (for nominal and ordinal level data) – see *Data, levels of.* The same approaches can be used to judge the opposite: discriminant validity (*Validity, discriminant*), which is whether items on an instrument which are supposed to differentiate between different constructs are indeed doing so – for the index of discrimination see *Item analysis.*

One way of designing research instruments is to add and subtract items from an instrument – list-wise deletion -and then test the result with a Cronbach test or some test of internal consistency and discrimination such as *Item analysis,* and finalise the instrument as the version which shows the best result.

Internal consistency may also be used to test whether different people are making judgements in the same way – see *Inter-rater reliability* or the same person made judgements consistently – see *intra-rater reliability.*

See also *Statistics software.*

Internet data collection

See *Questionnaire administration.*

Internet studies

See *Cyber#.*

Inter-observer reliability

See *Inter-rater reliability*.

Interpolation

See *Extrapolation*.

Interpreted axiomatic system

See *Axiomatic system*.

Interpretive repertoires

Culturally given, cognitive resources that people use in order to make sense of their experience and talk about it; for example kinds of argument, anecdotes, and illustrations. Synonym for *discourse* in some usages of that term, and very close in meaning to the many terms used for the organisation of cognition such as perspective, world-view, frame of reference, (actor) ideologies, social theories, typification schemes, schemes of relevance – see *Actor perspectives*.

Interpretative/interpretive approaches/interpretivism

A wide range of qualitative approaches all with the object of elucidating the meaning that events and situations have for the people who experience them. Examples include *cognitive anthropology, cognitive psychology, conversation analysis, ethnomethodology,* most *ethnographic research, discourse analysis, discursive psychology, dramaturgical approach, hermeneutics, narrative analysis, pragmatic linguistics, rhetorical analysis, semiology/semiotics, symbolic interactionism, textual interaction, verstehen.* Various quantitative approaches such as attitude research and neuro-science also have the aim of elucidating how people interpret their experience, but they are rarely called interpretive – see also *Qualitative and quantitative*.

Interquartile range (midspread)

When scores are ranked in order, the middle 50% of scores: the scores between the top of the bottom quartile and the bottom of the top quartile – see *Percentiles*. Analysis is sometimes restricted to this range of scores in order to eliminate the effects of *outliers*. See also *Windsorisation*.

The interquartile range is often displayed as a *box plot*.

Inter-rater reliability (inter-judge/inter-observer reliability)

Refers to the extent of agreement between two or more judges. Commonly used in coding data, to see how far different judges agree on the classification of an observation as being of one type or another. And it is used to judge whether different people using the same research instrument get the same results with the same or similar subjects to investigate *interviewer effects*. The simplest method is to calculate the percentages of agreements. But two judges, deciding between two options can be expected to agree by chance alone on 50% of occasions. Thus inter-rater reliability here requires agreement in excess of 50%. The required level of agreement will be determined by the number of judges and the number of options open to them in relation to the number of agreements which might have occurred by chance. Where two judges only are involved and the data are at the nominal level **Cohen's Kappa (k)** test is the most usual, giving a reading from minus 1 to plus 1. Zero indicates that the level of agreement is what might have been expected by chance. A positive score of 0.7 or more indicates an acceptable level of agreement, but depending on estimations of how critical non-agreement is. For more than two judges and ordinal or interval level data, inter-rater reliability is judged by calculating other *correlation coefficients*, or by tests such as *Cronbach's alpha* (interval level data) or Kuder-Richardson formula 20 (ordinal and nominal level data) – see *Data, levels of*. See also *Reliability, Statistics software*.

Uebersax, J. (2008) 'Statistical Methods for Rater Agreement' http://ourworld.compuserve.com/homepages/jsuebersax/agree.htm

The Sisa freeware website has a kappa calculator, as do the proprietary packages www.quantitativeskills.com/sisa/statistics/twoby2.htm

Interrogative insertion

The analysis of a written text by inserting 'readers' questions' at various points in the texts, such as *'Why does it say this here?', 'what are you telling me this for?'* The result is a display of the text as the author's responses to the questions s/he imagines the reader will ask. A key feature of the *textual interaction* approach.

Hoey, M. (1983) *On the surface of discourse*, London: George Allen & Unwin

Interrupted time series design

Experimental procedure where subjects are studied before during and after an intervention, hence each subject stands as their own *control*. Often the form for *n-of-1 experiments*.

Glass, G. (1997) 'Interrupted time series designs', in Jaeger, R. (ed.) *Complementary Methods for Reseach in Education* (2nd edn), Washington, DC: American Educational Research Association. http://glass.ed.asu.edu/gene/papers/tsx.html

Inter-subjective

The sphere of perceived reality which is constituted by people interacting with each other, which cannot be reduced to individual consciousnesses; implies a degree of mutual understanding, and its study assumes the possibility of researchers coming to understand the world as others they are studying do. The term is particularly, but not exclusively, associated with *phenomenology*.

Interval level data

See *Data, levels of.*

Intervening variable

See *Variable.*

Interview types

Situations in which one person, the interviewer, elicits information from another or, in group interviews, others – the interviewees: may be face-to-face, by telephone, by real-time internet communication; less often using a pre-recorded set of questions on audio or video tape. Four basic types of research interview can be distinguished:

- *Group interviews.*
- *Survey* interviews featuring a *questionnaire* with restricted response options – see *Questionnaire administration, Question formats.* Most likely to be recorded on paper or by computer input into a framework already set up to facilitate analysis, producing pre-coded or pre-structured data. Administration with an emphasis on treating each respondent alike to minimise *interviewer effects.* See *Coding*
- *Qualitative interviews* are more like ordinary conversations, loosely structured around a set of topics with the interviewee allowed to introduce their own topics and expand on issues (almost) at will. More likely to be audio-recorded and then transcribed for analysis by *coding* – see *transcription.* Administration is with an emphasis on responding sensitively to the particularities of each respondent. *Interviewer effects* will be considerable.

- *Cognitive interviews* are conducted to discover how interviewees respond to research instruments, often in piloting a questionnaire.

See also *Interview, dependent*.

Zalles, D. (n.d.) 'Determining if questionnaires should be used', *Online Evaluation Resource Library (OERL)* http://oerl.sri.com/module/mod1/m1_p1.html

Colker, A. (n.d.) 'Developing Interviews – preparing an interview protocol', *Online Evaluation Resource Library (OERL)*. http://oerl.sri.com/module/mod6/m6_p1.html

Colker, A. (n.d.) 'Developing Interviews – Administering interviews', *Online Evaluation Resource Library (OERL)*. http://oerl.sri.com/module/mod7/m7_p1.html

Interview, dependent

In *longitudinal research* the use of data from a previous interview to frame questions for a subsequent interview, or to avoid asking redundant questions. Respondents are reminded of their previous responses, routed around follow-up questions if no changes have occurred (**proactive dependent interviewing**) and offered opportunities to update previous responses if changes have occurred (**reactive dependent interviewing**).

Jackle, A. (2005) 'Does Dependent Interviewing Really Increase Efficiency and Reduce Respondent Burden?' *ISER Working Papers* Number 2005–11. www.iser.essex.ac.uk/pubs/workpaps/pdf/2005–11.pdf

Interviewer effects

A form of *subject reactivity*: The extent to which the characteristics or behaviour of an interviewer influence the responses of the interviewee, usually referring only to undesired influences. Includes the effects of differences and similarities in gender, age and ethnicity between interviewer and interviewee. Social survey interviews (*Interview types*) are usually arranged to minimise interviewer effects. With multiple interviewers, interviewer effects may be monitored through *inter-rater reliability* testing. The results of *qualitative interviews* are very much a product of interviewer effects (wanted and unwanted) and it is advisable not to report or analyse the respondents' contributions separately from the contributions of the interviewer – see also *Interview types*.

Martin, J. and Beerten, R. (n.d.) 'The effect of interviewer characteristics on survey response rate', *Joint Program in Survey Methodology*. www.jpsm.umd.edu/icsn/papers/Martin.htm

Intra-rater reliability

Consistency of action or judgement of the same researcher with similar respondents or in similar circumstances on different occasions. Dealt with statistically in the same way as *Inter-rater reliability*. Note that while consistency of performance is usually desirable in quantitative research, the adaptation of the researcher's performance to changing situations and to his or her emerging understanding, or the adjustment of interviewing style to respondent characteristics may be considered desirable in qualitative research.

Introspectionism

The researcher scrutinising and reporting on his or her own conscious experience was once regarded as the appropriate method for studying consciousness. It fell into disfavour around at the beginning of the 20th Century with the realisation that it was impossible to step outside of your own consciousness in order to think about it in an objective and unbiased way and that what was in your consciousness during an episode of introspection would be a product of your investigation. The same problem arises when researchers ask research subjects about their experiences or about what is in their minds, which is in effect asking them to engage in introspection. Despite these difficulties, asking mind-searching questions remains popular, particularly in *qualitative interviews* and more recently it has become very popular for researchers to provide highly introspective, autobiographical reflexive accounts of their engagement with and experiences in doing the research – see *Autoethnography, Corrigibility, Qualia, Reflexivity*.

Intuitive data processing

(1) The on-the-spot, often ad hoc, interpretations which researchers make about what is going on in order to decide whether or not to record some observation, or ask some next question, to end an interview and so on. All research involves some intuitive data processing, but *ethnographic research*, in its early stages at least, and *action research* are dominated by intuitive data processing. Because it is impossible for a researcher to keep track of his or her own on-the-spot data processing, this kind of research has a low level of *objectivity* in the auditability sense of that term – see *Objectivity, procedural*. But in order to achieve naturalistic validity, or to engage in *participatory research* it may be necessary to rely heavily on the intuition in this way: see *Validity, naturalistic*. Carefully kept research *diaries* and *reflexity* are sometimes regarded as an antidote to the problem of accountability, but reflexive accounts of this kind of research will themselves be subject to the same problem, exaggerated by the elapse of time. (2) The claim that data processing software is user-friendly ('intuitive').

Inventory

Usually a *questionnaire* asking for affirmations or denials of given statements.

Inverse correlation

Synonymous with negative *correlation*. When one variable goes up, the other goes down.

Inverse power law

See *Power (law) distribution*.

Investigator triangulation

See *Triangulation*.

In vivo categories/codes

See *Emic*.

Ironic mode

A rhetorical trope; the style of writing which contrasts 'what everyone thinks' with 'what is really true'. Often signalled in titles such as 'The myth of...' – see *Rhetorical analysis*. The author may describe what they are doing as 'deconstructing' – see also *Deconstruction*. Particularly prone to *Ontological gerrymandering*.

IRT (Item response theory)

See *Test theory*.

Isomorphism(s)/being isomorphic with

(1) The point(s) at which a description or model (verbal, graphical, pictorial or mathematical) precisely matches whatever is being described. This is a possibility denied by *post-modernism*, but assumed by *empiricism*, *critical rationalism* and *realism*. See also *Crisis of representation*. And the term is problematic insofar as no description is ever the same as what is described, so isomorphism, if at all possible, must always be a matter of degree. **Paramorphism** can refer to a description or model which has features representing the target phenomenon, though not precisely; for example has the same 'form' as what is described but is in

a different medium. (2) Isomorphism and paramorphism plus various # morphisms are terms from computing.

Item

Usually a segment of an *instrument*, for example a single question on a *questionnaire*.

Item analysis

Much used in the construction of scholastic and aptitude tests. Consists of calculating the:

- **Index of difficulty**: for *objective tests* the percentage of wrong answers per item: for other instruments, the percentage of non-responses and spoiled responses per item. Items where the index is too high will cause floor effects, where it is too low, *ceiling effects*. May be calculated also for the test as a whole. See also *Respondent burden*.

- **Index of discrimination**: in *objective tests* for each item the percentage of right answers by the top scoring 10% minus the percentage of right answers by lowest scoring 10%. Where the scores of the top and bottom 10% are very different, the item in question is discriminating well between them. The scores from items that do not discriminate well are likely to be disregarded in the analysis of results, and/or the item deleted from the instrument when used again. Item analysis is often used in the initial design of an instrument, with the scores from a prototype version containing a very large number of items being analysed to whittle down the instrument such that it contains a only those items which discriminate best. The index may be calculated also for the test as a whole.

Michigan State University (n.d.) *Item analysis* www.msu.edu/dept/soweb/itanhand. html#guide

Item characteristic curve theory

See *Test theory*.

Item non-response/item response

See *Response rate*.

Item response theory (IRT)

See *Test theory*.

Iteration/to iterate

(1) Any shuttling backwards and forwards process, usually one which continues until a satisfactory result is reached; for example the construction of a research instrument by trial and error, or the process of *design experiments*; (2) statistical process in which different values are entered into a calculation until an optimal result is reached; (3) in complex systems, a feedback loop – see *Complexity theory*.

IV – Independent variable

See *Variable*.

Jadad scale/test

Questionnaire featuring the quality criteria used to decide whether a research study should be included in a systematic review or *meta-analysis*. See *Inclusion criteria*.

Jadad, A., Moore, R., Carroll, D., Jenkinson, C., Reynolds, D., Gavaghan, D. and McQuay, H. (1996) 'Assessing the Quality of Reports of Randomized Clinical Trials: Is Blinding Necessary? *Controlled Clinical Trials* **17**(1) pp. 10–11

Jarman index

See *Deprivation indices.*

Joint Information Systems Council Resource Guide for the social sciences

List of resources available for those researching in the social sciences, primarily those funded by the Joint Information Systems Committee (JISC) of the Higher and Further Education Funding Councils of the UK, and the *Economic and Social Research Council (ESRC).*

http://www.jisc-collections.ac.uk/catalogue/coll_subject_s.aspx

Joint probability

See *Probability.*

Jonckheere trend test

See *Trend tests.*

K/k

(1) Symbol for the number of groups in a statistical calculation (and hence for the number of columns or rows in a *contingency table*); (2) symbol for sampling interval – see *Sample, probability*; (3) symbol for Kappa coefficient – see *Inter-rater reliability.*

Kappa coefficient (k) (Cohen's k)

See *Inter-rater reliability.*

KDD

See *Data mining.*

Key informants

(1) In *ethnographic research* usually someone who is a confidant of the researcher and smooths his or her way into the world of those studied. Where observation is covert, the key informant may be in the know – see *Observation, covert or overt.* Such key informants may be untypical of the group of interest, perhaps marginal members, or of superior status, and there is a danger that an ethnographic account will be overly influenced by the view point of someone who is unrepresentative.

Labov, W. (1973) 'The linguistic consequences of being a lame', *Language in Society* **2**: 81–115

Boelen, W. (1992) 'Street Corner Society': Cornerville Revisited, *Journal of Contemporary Ethnography*, **21** (1992:Apr.–1993:Jan.) 1:11(electronic paging), together with:

Whyte, W.F. (1992) 'In Defense of 'Street Corner Society', *Journal of Contemporary Ethnography*, **21** (1992:Apr.–1993:Jan.):1:52 (electronic paging)

(2) In *community needs assessment,* a range of people with different positions in the community and different view points.

University of Illinois, Extension (n.d.) *Using key informant interviews,* http://ppa.aces. uiuc.edu/KeyInform.htm

Kinesics

The study of communicative bodily movements (**'body language'** or **non-verbal communication**) from facial expression and gestures to dance routines, and often extended to consider the decoration of the body. Includes **proxemics**:the management of distances between people; **haptics:** the use of touch in communication; and **occulesics**: eye contact routines. See also *Embodiment*.

> Birdwhistell, R. (1970) *Kinesics in Context,* Philadelphia: University of Pennsylvania Press.
> Stephen Dahl (2008) *Kinesics* http://stephan.dahl.at/nonverbal/kinesics.html
> Ickinger,W. (2001) *Proxemics Research: Improving our understanding of human behavior through research with a behavioral game methodology,* http://sharktown.com/proxemics/intro.html

Kish grid

Device used for doorstep *survey research* to decide at random which member of a household should be interviewed.

> Németh, R.(2003) 'Sampling design of Health Surveys' *Luxembourg Income Study Working Paper Series,* Working Paper No. 35
> www.lisproject.org/publications/liswps/358.pdf

Knowledge discovery in data bases (KDD)

See *Data mining.*

Kon tiki problem

A problem encountered in experimental archaeology, *computer simulation, role play research* and elsewhere; that demonstrating how something could have happened, is not necessarily demonstrating how something did happen. Thor Heyerdahl successfully sailed a balsa raft called Kon tiki from South America to Polynesia, but this did not prove that Polynesia was settled by South American raft navigators.

K

Kruskal-Wallis one way analysis of variance

See *Trend tests.*

Kuder-Richardson formula 20 test (KR20)

See *Internal consistency* and *Inter-rater reliability.*

Kurtosis

Refers to the shape of a *frequency distribution* curve as defined by its height and tails. **Normal** or **mesokurtic** – the bell-shaped curve of the *normal distribution*, **leptokurtic** – long and flat, **platykurtic** – tall and thin.

L

Statistic reported by Page's trend test – see *Trend tests*.

Lambda (λ)

See *Likelihood ratio (LR)* and *Proportional reduction in error*. Also used to symbolise effect – see *Effect size (ES) measures*.

Lamp post error

See *Bias, ascertainment*.

Latent variable

A variable that cannot be measured directly, but is hypothesised to underlie the observed (**manifest**) variables. An example of a latent variable is a factor in *factor analysis*. See also *Construct-indicator relationship, Test theory*.

Leading questions

See *Question, leading*.

Least squares line

Synonym for fit line/line of best fit/regression line/trend line – see *Regression analysis*.

Least squares method

Synonym for *regression analysis*.

Leptokurtic

See *Kurtosis*.

Lexical decomposition

See *Componential analysis.*

Life-course

See *Life history research.*

Life history research

(1) *Epidemiology, demography, ethology* and socio-biology; the study of the reproductive behaviour and life cycle of the species of interest, including human beings; (2) the study of the biographies, typically as elicited by *qualitative interview* or through facilitating the writing of auto-biographies. The interest may be in social history – see *Oral history*, in raising the self-esteem, *consciousness raising* and or improving literacy skills, or in the way people construct stories about themselves and others – see *Narrative analysis.*

Centre for Life History Research University of Sussex www.sussex.ac.uk

Likelihood ratio (LR) or **lamda** (λ)

For predictive and diagnostic tests. For example, in health screening the LR is an expression of the likelihood that a given test result would occur for a patient with a certain disorder, compared to the likelihood that that same result would occur for a patient without the disorder, thus giving an estimate of the accuracy of a test result.

Positive test result (**LR+**) = sensitivity/(1-specificity)
Negative test result (**LR−**) = (1-sensitivity)/specificity

For sensitivity and specificity see *Type 1 and type 2 errors.*

Bandolier (2008) 'Likelihood Ratio (LR)' www.jr2.ox.ac.uk/bandolier/booth/glossary/like.html
For an interactive example www.cebm.net/index.aspx?o=1161 *Centre for Evidence Based Medicine*

See also *Likelihood ratio X^2 (LRX)*

Likelihood ratio X^2 (LRX)

Based on X^2 and used in *log-linear analysis* and *logistic regression*. An LRX with more than one *degree of freedom* can be decomposed into a number of smaller tables each with its own (smaller) LRX and (lower numbers of) degrees of freedom, allowing for a fine grained analysis of the *goodness of fit* between the model employed and the data.

For an LRX calculator http://home.clara.net/sisa/two2hlp.htm

Likert scale

Originally a five point scale asking for respondents' agreement/disagreement with a given statement. Now any five or seven point scale including those asking for evaluations such as 'excellent' to 'very poor'. For example:

How strongly do you agree or disagree with this statement? Young people these days have no respect for older people

Strongly disagree	Disagree	Don't know	Agree	Strongly agree
❏	❏	❏	❏	❏

Trochim, W. (2006) 'Likert scaling' *Research Methods Knowledge Base* www.socialresearchmethods.net/kb/scallik.php

Line fitting

See *Regression analysis.*

Line of best fit

Synonym for fit line, least squares line, regression line and trend line – see *Regression analysis.*

Linear and curvilinear

Describe the relationship between two variables shown on a *scattergram* and or resulting from a *regression analysis*; straight or curved – see also *Asymtotic, Eta, Linearisation, Trend, statistical.*

Linearisation

Transformation of data so that a curvilinear correlation is converted to a straight line by *data transformation, pruning* or working only with the *inter-quartile range* or with *asymtotes.*

Linear polynomial

Straight line relationship between two variables, for example as shown on a scattergram showing the results of a *regression analysis*. See also *Trend, statistical.*

L

List wise deletion

Deleting each data point in turn from a data set to see what effect it has on aggregate measures. Often done in designing instruments – see *Internal consistency, Item analysis*.

Literature review

A scrutiny of the existing literature about the research topic preparatory to embarking on the research and as an aid to interpreting the results. It may be written up as an introduction to a report of the research, showing what was known previously and perhaps critiquing previous investigations, and drawn on in a conclusion showing how the current research has added to the stock of knowledge in the area. See also *Meta-analysis*.

University of North Carolina, (2007) *Literature reviews* http://www.unc.edu/depts/ wcweb/handouts/literature_review.html

Literature search

Hart, C. (2001), *Doing a Literature Search: A Comprehensive Guide for the Social Sciences*, London: Sage.
and see *Search engines and data bases*.

Locution

See *Illocution, Pragmatic linguisitics*.

Log scale

See *Arithmetic and log scales*.

Logical behaviourism

See *Behaviourism*.

Logical empiricism

Sometimes a synonym for *logical positivism*, sometimes meaning no more than *empiricism*, but sometimes used to refer specifically to revisions of logical positivism from the 1930s onwards, sometimes including, and sometimes not including the thinking of Karl Popper – see *Critical rationalism, Hypothetico-deductive method, Falsificationism, Philosophers*.

Logical positivism

Refers to the thinking of the Vienna circle of philosophers and scientists between the 1920s and 40s. Had a brief but limited influence on the philosophy of the natural sciences, and less so on the behavioural and social sciences, except for *behaviourism*. The originators rejected the term *'positivism'* as applied to themselves and almost all of them revised their ideas later, usually in the direction of *critical rationalism* (Popper), *realism*, or in the case of Wittgenstein, to a position which has been very influential in linguistics, *ethnomethodology* and *social constructionism*.

Today it is rare to find any one who will describe themselves as a positivist, logical, neo or otherwise. The physicist Stephen Hawking has been known to use this term for himself, but it is evident from his writings that his thinking, like that of Einstein, is better described as *critical rationalism* or *realism*.

The main tenets of logical positivism were:

- the *unity of science thesis*
- that only two kinds of truth claims or justifiable beliefs are sensible: **analytic statements** which are true *a priori*, such as those of mathematics and formal logic and **synthetic statements** which can be verified (*a posteriori*) by reference to empirical evidence – the latter is the verificationist thesis – see *Verificationism*
- the only synthetic statements which are meaningful are those which are expressed in an observation language, that is in terms of what was observed, how and when, see *Behaviourism, Empiricism, Operationalism*
- ultimately all justifiable beliefs rest on a foundation of self-evident facts, which cannot be verified otherwise – see *Foundation*

Uebel, T. (2006) 'The Vienna Circle', *Stanford Encyclopedia of Philosophy* http://plato.stanford.edu/entries

Logic-in-use

See *Context of discovery and context of justification.*

Logistic regression (logistic model, logit model, maximum-entropy calculator/calculation)

Models to estimate the probability of occurrence of an event using predictor variables which may be at any data level – see *Data, levels of.* For example, the probability that a person with a criminal record will re-offend within a specified time period might be predicted from knowledge of the person's age, sex and previous offending behaviour. Used extensively in medical research, social science and market research, both to predict (forecast) future events and by way of explanation through *prediction*.

> For a logistic regression calculator with examples: Pezzullo, J. (2005) 'Logistic regression', http://statpages.org/logistic.html

Logit/logged odds/log of the odds

Odds expressed as their natural logarithm.

-9.21 = 0.0001 probability = extremely unlikely
$+9.21$ = 0.9999 probability = almost inevitable

For *odds* see also *Effect size (ES) measures.*

Log-linear analysis

A large tool-kit of non-parametric methods for analysing the relationships between variables, where some of these are represented by data at the nominal level; for example as 'yes'/'no'/'don't know' – see *Data, levels of, Statistics, parametric and non-parametric.* Involves producing models of how the relationships between variables *might* be, and then using statistical *goodness of fit* tests to judge which of the models best fits the data. *Correlation* tests and X^2 *tests* including *Likelihood Ratio X^2 (LRX)* are commonly used.

> Statsoft (2008) 'Log-Linear Analysis of Frequency Tables' www.statsoft.com/textbook/ stathome.html?stloglin.html&1

Log-normal distribution

Data transformation where re-plotting the arithmetic data points as logarithms approximates a normal distribution more nearly. See *Normal distribution.*

Longitudinal research

As opposed to *cross-sectional* (or snap-shot) *research: Cross-sectional research* collects data from only one point in time. Longitudinal research studies its subjects through time, collecting data relating to the beginning of the period of study (or prior to it), and about other points in time thereafter. Longitudinal research may be *retrospective* as in *life history* and auto/biographical research where subjects are asked to recall their pasts, and many cross-sectional surveys have retrospective elements where respondents are asked about what happened previously. Or longitudinal research may be *prospective*, where data are collected in real time. Prospective longitudinal research includes *repeat surveys, panel surveys, longitudinal surveys, cohort studies,* qualitative longitudinal research *(QLL)* and *pseudo-cohort studies.* Although experiments also follow subjects from the beginning to the end of the experiment and are prospective, the term longitudinal is rarely used for these. Prospective longitudinal studies go some way towards resolving the problem of deciding on the *direction of effect* with regard to *correlations* found on analysis. Retrospective longitudinal studies are less successful in this respect and suffer from lapses and distortions of memory -see *Bias, narrative, Bias, recall/retrospective.*

Ruspini, E. (2000) 'Longitudinal research in the social sciences', *Social Research Update* Issue 20 http://sru.soc.surrey.ac.uk/

Lynn, P. (2005) *The Methodology of Longitudinal Surveys,* Luxembourg, Eurostat, http://www.eustat.es/prodserv/datos/Sem45_i.pdf

Longitudinal surveys

Survey through time of a *representative* sample of subjects chosen either at random or as a *cohort* with an arbitrary entry date; as with the *Birth cohort studies* – which are at one and the same time surveys and cohort studies. See also *Prospectivity, Pseudo-cohort analysis, Time series analysis.*

The University of Sterling Longitudinal Data Analysis for Social Science Researchers website (www.lscs.ac.uk) has explanatory text, training activities and links to longitudinal surveys

Links are also available at ESDS Longitudinal (www.esds.ac.uk/longitudinal)

Lorenz curve

See *Indices of inequality.*

L

m̄ or M̄

Symbol for mean: m̄ = sample mean, M̄ = population mean – see *Central tendency.*

McLoone index

Inequality measure calculated by adding together the value of the lowest 50% of income, wealth, etc., dividing this by the *median* value multiplied by the number of those in the lowest 50%. For example, if there were 400 people and the lowest paid 50% of them together shared £3,000,000, and the person who earned the most among these (the middle earner), earned £20,000, then the index would be £3,000,000/£20,000 × 200 = £3 m/£4 m = 0.75. This index is blind to inequality above the median. For other measures of inequality see *Inequality measures and metrics.*

MAD (Mixed Approach Design)

See *Mixed/multi-method research.*

MANCOVA

See *Analysis of Covariance (ANCOVA and MANCOVA).*

Mandelbrot geometry/plots

See *Power (law) distributions.*

Manifest variable

See *Latent variable.*

Manipulability

See *Causal analysis.*

Mann-Whitney U test

Non-parametric test of difference or *correlation* for unrelated ordinal level data – see *Statistical significance, Statistics, parametric and nonparametric, Related and unrelated designs, Data, levels of.*

MANOVA

See *Analysis of Variance (ANOVA and MANOVA).*

Mantel-Haenszel Methods

See *Weighted averages/event rates.*

Market research

Research directed towards gathering and analysing data relevant to making decisions about marketing goods, services, political candidates or charitable causes or improving the persuasiveness of advertisements or other communications. May involve any variety of social and behavioural research. Largely carried out by commercial research companies for private sector clients, but also engaged by or for government with regard to marketing policies and projects, or disseminating health education and other public service information.

See also *AB Testing, Design ethnography, Market research categorisations, Opinion Polls, Useability research.*

Market Research Society www.marketresearch.org.uk

Market research categorisations

Market researchers 'segment the market' by dividing individuals, households and neighbourhoods into categories as an aid to identifying who might purchase certain products, or be amenable to different kinds of advertising. The Market Research Services Limited **A,B,C1,C2,D,E** scheme is based on types of occupation but is a proxy for different income groups (A highest). Depending on the product(s) the market may also be segmented in other ways, for example by age, by gender, by life-style, by disposable income, by previous consumption behaviour, by clusters of attitudes and so on, alone or in different combinations. The best known characterisation of neighbourhoods is the *ACORN* system by CACI.

Businessballs (2007) *Demographics classification,* http://www.businessballs.com/demographicsclassifications.htm

Market segmentation analysis

See *Market research categorisations*.

Masking

See *Blinding*.

Mass media research

See *Audience effect research*, *Audience research*, *Cultural studies*, *Semiology/semiotics*, *Textual analysis*.

Mass observation

From 1937 to the mid 50s, involved over 500 untrained observers who kept journals about their experiences, snooped on other people and responded to open-ended *questionnaires*. Paid investigators were also involved covertly to record people's conversations on the street, at public events and at work. Used extensively during the war as a source of information on national morale. Reactivated in 1981, although with more concern for issues of *privacy, confidentiality* and *informed consent*. The archive is a wonderful, if anarchic, repository of social history covering the war and post-war austerity period.

Mass Observation www.massobs.org.uk/index.htm

Matched pairs

Creating *comparison groups* for *experiments* by recruiting subjects, then pairing them off according to their similarity, and then allocating one of each pair to each of the comparison groups; a much less effective way of creating two groups similar to each other than using *random allocation*. See also *Power Matching*.

Material-semiotic networks

See *Actor network theory*.

Maximum difference and maximum similarity designs

See *Experimental design*.

Maximum-entropy calculator/calculation

See *Logistic regression*.

Mazeways

See *Cognitive anthropology.*

MCA and MCD

See *Membership category analysis.*

MCS

See *Birth cohort studies.*

Mean ($\bar{m}$ or $\bar{M}$ or $\bar{Y}$ or $\bar{X}$)

The average score calculated by adding all the scores and dividing by the number of scores: symbolised: $\bar{M}$ or $\bar{Y}$ or p for population means, $\bar{m}$ or $\bar{x}$ for sample means. See *Central tendency and dispersion.*

For trimmed means see *Trimming.* See also *Weighted Averages.*

Mean deviation

See *Central tendency and dispersion.*

Mean, floating

See *Regression analysis.*

Measurement

Sometimes restricted to assigning a numerical value to an observation, but may also refer to assigning observations to categories (classifying, *coding*), thus allowing for the paradoxically sounding 'qualitative measurement'. For quantitative measurement, classification yields nominal or categorical data, *ranking* yields ordinal data, and measuring on a continuous scale yields interval or ratio level data – see *Data, levels of.*

Measurement error

See *Central limit theorem, Test theory.*

Measurement error curve

See *Normal distribution.*

Median

The middle score when all scores in a data set are arranged in order (odd number of scores), or the average of the two middle scores when there is an even number of scores – see *Central tendency and dispersion.*

M

Mediating variable

See *Variable*.

Member

In *ethnomethodology* someone who is the member of a particular (sub)cultural group, who does things as they do them and understands things as they understand them. Use of the term does not require any precision in delineating the cultural groups of which someone is 'a member' since the relevance of different kinds and criteria of membership is assumed to vary with the immediate context.

Member checking

See *Fallibility testing*.

Membership category analysis (MCA)

Closely allied to, or perhaps a feature of *Conversation Analysis (CA)*. An *ethnomethodological approach* to the analysis of speech and text which focuses on the categories people use such that they 'talk up' a social organisation. For examples see Table 8.

Table 8 Some ideas from categorical analysis illustrated with a newspaper headline.

Idea	Explanation	Headline: 'Mum's warning to beware of daughter'
Category	Any person can be labelled in many ways, so readers assume that the way they are labelled is important	'Mum' and 'daughter'*
Membership categorisation device (MCD)	Categories are (usually) written and read as grouped together in collections (MCDs)	'Mum' and 'daughter' imply the MCD 'family'
Consistency rule	If one member of a collection is identified then, unless there are indications to the contrary, the next person is likely to be a member of the *same* collection	Although the headline does not explicitly say so, we read the daughter as this mum's daughter. We read them as of the same MCD 'family'

(Continued)

Table 8 (Continued)

Idea	Explanation	Headline: 'Mum's warning to beware of 'daughter'
Standardised relational pairs (SRPs)	Pairs of categories are linked together in taken-for-granted ways	Our default expectation is that 'mums' will support and defend their daughters. Warning others against your own daughter violates this expectation. That is why this is news-worthy
Category-bound activity (CBA)	Activities may be read as tied to or 'bound to' certain categories	Warning others against their own daughters is not an activity common-sensically tied to 'mums': not a CBA for mums. This is why this is news-worthy

Lepper, G. (2000) *Categories in Text and Talk: A Practical Introduction to Categorization Analysis*, London: Sage

Antaki, C. (n.d.) 'Lecture 8: the other half of CA' and 'Lecture 9: More on categories in talk' http://www-staff.lboro.ac.uk/~ssca1/ttlecture08CAcats.htm

Memoing/memos

Writings by researchers principally addressed to themselves, in order to track their progress and facilitate the writing of later accounts of how the research was done – (aka research diary/log/journal – see *Diaries*), to clarify their thinking at particular points in the research process, and to plan further research actions. Originally named in *grounded theory* but widely practised both before and after.

Mesokurtic

See *Kurtosis*.

Meta-analysis

The synthesis of a number of different studies addressing the same research question in the same way. Refers most usually to statistical meta-analysis, where the data are quantitative, and especially where the studies are *randomised controlled trials*. Where selected studies are simply reviewed, each according to the same critieria, this is termed a **systematic review**, but some meta-analyses pool the results – expressed as effect sizes – of several pre-existing pieces of research, thus gaining the advantages of a sample size larger than that of any of these – see *Effect size (ES) measures*. Studies combined in this way are typically vetted according to *inclusion criteria*, allowing into the meta-analysis only those above a quality threshold. Meta-analysis is particularly associated with *effectiveness research* and used as a practical tool for deciding which treatments are allowed within the NHS. See also *Campbell collaboration, Cochrane collaboration, Forest plot, Funnel plot, Meta-ethnography.*

Basu, A. (n.d.) 'How to conduct a meta analysis'. *Supercourse.* www.pitt.edu/~super1/lecture/lec1171/001.htm

Neill, J. (2006) *Meta analysis, research methodology,* www.wilderdom.com/research/meta-analysis.html

Meta-analysis of qualitative research

Is often called *Meta-ethnography*, see also *Mixed method/multi-method studies.*

Meta-discourse

See *Grand narrative.*

Meta-ethnography

The most common term for attempts to synthesise and draw general conclusions from a number of pieces of qualitative research including research produced ethnographically and by set piece interviews. Without using the name, this has been stock in trade for comparative work in anthropology since the 19th century. *Ethnographic research* does not usually lend itself easily to synthesis and where studies of similar settings have been compared the *Rashomon effect* is common. However, there are *sensitising concepts* which will serve as a basis for bringing various studies into the same framework; concepts such as (moral) career, deviance, stigma, time-tables as well as 'structural' concepts such as those referring to types of kinship system or political organisation.

See the special edition of *Sociological Research On-line* (2007, Vol 12 issue no 3) on reuse of ethnographic data www.socresonline.org.uk

Economic and Social Data Services (ESDS) (2007) *Re-using qualitative data,* ESDS www.esds.ac.uk/qualidata/support/reuse.asp

Thomas, J. and Harden, A. (2007) *Methods for the thematic synthesis of qualitative research in systemmatic reviews,* NCRM http://www.ncrm.ac.uk/research/outputs/publications/

Meta-narrative

See *Grand narrative, Theory.*

Metaphysics

The branch of philosophy dealing with issues which could not in principle be resolved by science; including *ontology* and *epistemology* (or most issues within these spheres) and theology. Though all scientific thinking rests on some meta-physical (*domain*) assumptions, the scope of meta-physics (as 'not science') depends heavily on the way science is defined – see *Demarcationist debate*. In some schemes of thinking most of social 'science' would be regarded as metaphysical – see also *Corrigibility*, *Falsificationism*.

Methodological eclecticism

See *Mixed/multi method research*.

Methodological individualism

Analysis that explains social phenomena by showing how they arise from the intentional states that motivate individual actors – see *Action, Agency, Intentionalism, Interpretivism*. Proposed explicitly by Max Weber in the first chapter of 'Economy and Society', and the basis for his writings on *verstehen*. Often, however, the term is used disparagingly to the effect that an analysis failed to take sufficient account of the structural factors limiting individual action or that an analysis was overly psychological – see *Structuralism and post-structuralism*.

Weber, M. (1968) *Economy and Society* (ed. Roth, G. and Wittich, C.) Berkeley: University of California Press (originally from 1913 onwards)

Heath, J. (2005) 'Methodological individualism' *Stanford Encyclopedia of Philosophy* http://plato.stanford.edu/

Methodological pluralism

See *Mixed/multi method research*.

Methodological pragmatism

The use of whatever methods seem most convenient, or apt for purpose. Implies a lack of commitment to any particular methodological orientation.

Methodological triangulation

See *Triangulation, methodological*.

Methodology

The theory relating *epistemology and ontology* and substantive theory to the techniques (methods) of research. Social scientists subscribe to many contrasting ontological and epistemological positions, social and psychological theories and have diverse ethical and political inclinations. This is reflected in the complexity of methodological theory in the social sciences as compared with the natural sciences.

Methods

The techniques of research.

Method slurring

Pejorative way of describing research using a variety of methods. The critique rests on an epistemological assumption that all research findings are constructions created by the use of the methods employed, and do not faithfully reflect the real world – *social constructionism*. The findings from using different methods will thus be incommensurate and cannot be used to support or check each other. See *Bricolage, Crisis of representation, Epistemology and ontology, Mixed/multi-method research, Paradigm, Triangulation.*

Baker, C., Wuest, J. and Stern, P. (1992) 'Method slurring: the grounded theory/phenomenology example', *Journal of Advanced Nursing* **17**: 1355–1360

Middle range theory

See *Theory.*

Midspread

Synonym for *interquartile range* – see also *Box plot, Central tendency and dispersion.*

Millennium Cohort Study (MCS)

See *Birth cohort studies.*

Mind-mapping/mind webs

See *Concept(ual) mapping.*

Mixed methods/multi methods research/mixed approach designs (MAD)

Combining in a single research project several methods of research. In favour it is argued that different methods tap different aspects of the topic and hence provide a fuller picture than could one method alone, and that each method may provide a check on the *validity* of the findings of another. This is the argument for *triangulation*. But sometimes disparaged as *method slurring*.

There has been much interest recently in the use of *Bayesian inference* as a medium for synthesising research studies using diverse methods. The synthesis is on the basis of how much each additional study increases (or undermines) a belief based on earlier studies. Giving a numerical value to researchers' beliefs brings any kind of research, quantitative or qualitative into the sphere of numbers. See *Bayesian inference*, *Triangulation*.

Frechtling, J. and Westat, L. (1997) *User-friendly Handbook for Mixed Method Evaluation*, National Science Foundation Directorate of Education and Human Resources, Division of Research, Evaluation and Communication. www.ehr.nsf.gov/EHR/REC/pubs/NSF97-153/start.htm

Mason, J. (2006) *Six strategies for mixing methods and linking data in social science research*, NCRM http://www.ncrm.ac.uk/research/outputs/publications/

Sydenstricker-Neto, J. (1997) *Research Design and Mixed-Method Approach: A Hands-on Experience. Mixed Methods tutorial* http://www.socialresearchmethods.net/tutorial/Sydenstricker/bolsa.html

Mln

See *MLwiN*.

MlwiN

Software package for fitting multilevel models, based on the earlier Mln. www.cmm.bristol.ac.uk/MLwiN/index.shtml

UCLA Academic Technology Services (n.d.) *Resources to help you learn and use MlwiN* http://www.ats.ucla.edu/stat/mlwin/

Mode

The most common score in data set. See *Central tendency and dispersion*.

Mode 1 and mode 2 research

This terminology comes from the work of Michael Gibbons and colleagues writing about both natural and social science research. Mode 1 research, characteristic of the past, was single-discipline, driven by the theoretical concerns of a discipline and conducted by scholars with considerable autonomy from any sponsors. Mode 2 research which will be characteristic of the future, is multidisciplinary, customer-led and driven by the practical concerns of those who sponsor research.

Notwotny, H., Scott, P. and Gibbons, M. (2003) 'Mode 2 revisited; the new production of knowledge', *Minerva* 41: 179–194. www.flacso.edu.mx/openseminar/downloads/gibbons.pdf

Model

Simplified representation of some phenomenon. Simulations are 'working' models, and experiments control and simplify a local situation to 'model' processes which occur more widely, in a way that makes them more amenable to study. Testing for *statistical significance* involves creating models (usually) of what would be most likely to happen by chance and comparing what actually happened with that. See also *Ideal type, Computer simulation.*

Moderating variable

See *Variable.*

Modernism

See *Enlightenment thinking.*

Monism

See *Dualism.*

Monological

See *Dialogic.*

Motive attribution

A common-sense way of understanding human behaviour is to see it as following from the motives of the person, so that motives appear as the causes of behaviour. There are psychologists and social scientists who do use this mode of interpretation. An alternative is to view motives not as causes but as interpretations. Thus understanding someone's behaviour involves a process of attributing motives to explain it, and the research interest is not in finding a cause for the behaviour but in studying how people attribute motives to themselves and others. Note that this view assumes that individuals do not know their own motives, but that they have to interpret their own behaviour to find the motivation consistent with it, as they do with others' behaviour. Hence the idea of motive attribution undermines the sense of trying to find out why someone did something by asking him why. See also *Agent, Agentive, Epiphenominalism.*

McMaster University (n.d.) *The Psychology of Interpersonal Behavior – attribution processes*, McMaster University, CA
http://sciwebserver.science.mcmaster.ca/psychology/psych1a6/1aa3/Social/lec2-1.htm

Moving average

See *Smoothing*.

Multi-level analysis/modelling

Form of *regression analysis* used when the topic is conceptualised as being composed of nesting units: for example, pupils nested in schools, and schools in local education authority areas. For the same set of pupils, measures of prior achievement, parental occupation or the deprivation score for their area of residence might be regarded as at the pupil level, and characteristics of the school as at the school level (selective/non-selective, co-educational/single sex, with sixth form or no sixth form). Spend per pupils might be allocated to a further, LEA level. The object is to estimate the influence (say, on educational achievement) of variables at the different levels, thus addressing questions such as relative influence of home background and the school, or the difference it makes for pupils of similar ability to go to different schools – the school effect.

Plewis, I. (1998) 'Multilevel Models', *Social Research Update* Issue 23. http://sru.soc.surrey.ac.uk/
Center for Multilevel Modelling (CMM), University of Bristol: www.cmm.bristol.ac.uk
See also *MlwiN*

Multi-method research

See *Mixed method/multi-method research*.

Multiple realities

(1) Refers uncontroversially to the fact that different people, and especially people from different cultures interpret the world in different ways – see *Cultural relativism*; (2) more controversially, the relativist position that there is no ultimate reality and that all interpretations are equally valid – see *Relativism, Post modernism*; (3) In cosmology refers to parallel universes; (4) In religious contexts may refer to different supernatural realms and states of consciousness.

M

Multi-stage sample

See *Sample, (multi)-stage*.

Multivariate analysis

Any statistical method for analysis involving three or more variables at once.

Multivariate analysis of covariance

See *Analysis of Covariance (ANCOVA and MANCOVA).*

Multivariate analysis of variance

See *Analysis of Variance (ANOVA and MANOVA).*

N or n

Symbol for the number of subjects or size of population. Hence **small n studies;** studies based on very few subjects. See also *N of 1 experiments*.

Naïve realism

Synonym for *Empiricism*.

Narrative analysis (NA) / research method

The ubiquity of stories in what people say and write, means that almost all kinds of qualitative research can, and have been termed 'narrative analysis'. The interest in narratives may be:

- as evidence about whatever is the topic of the story (event narratives) for example in *event structure analysis, life history* or *oral history* – see also *Bias, narrative*
- as evidence of how someone habitually makes sense of the world (narratives of experience) – *see Actor perspectives, Hemeneutics, Phenomenology, Symbolic interactionism*
- as culturally given formats for understanding – in *mass media research* or *cognitive anthropology*, for example
- as parts of an oppressive ideological apparatus (see *ideology, false consciousness*) in *Critical theory, Emancipatory research* or *Feminist research* and some *Semiology/semiotics*
- for their mechanics – how scenes are set, plots developed, motives attributed and characters established: in *Conversation analysis, Discursive psychology, Frame Analysis, Membership category analysis, Rhetorical analysis, Semiology/semiotics, Syntagmatic analysis, Textual interaction*
- for what is accomplished by telling a story rhetorically, for example showing the narrator in a good light, or practically, for example, in the course of making a case for the defence in court – *Conversation analysis, Pragmatic linguistics, Rhetorical analysis*

- with spoken narratives, in narrator-listener interaction and how the story unfolds as a collaborative project – *Conversation analysis (CA), Discursive psychology, Pragmatic linguistics.*

The data for narrative analysis may arise from *qualitative interviews*, from naturally occurring speech heard during *ethnographic research*, from *diaries* or from other writing or broadcasting. The term **Narrative research method** is sometimes applied exclusively to research involving the collaborative creation of narratives by researcher and subjects (Moen 2005); see *Life history research, Participative research, Voicing*. See also *Narrativity*.

Moen, T. (2005) 'Reflections on the Narrative Research Approach', *International Journal of Qualitative Methods* **5**(4)

Squire, C. (2008) *Approaches to Narrative Research*, NCRM http://www.ncrm.ac.uk/ research/outputs/publications/

Clandinin, D. (ed.) (2007) *Handbook of Narrative Research Methods*, London: Sage

Narrative interviewing

(1) Interviewing where the interviewee is encouraged to develop the interview along lines of their own choosing (whether or not this results in their telling stories) and synonymous with *qualitative interviewing*; (2) synonymous with narrative research method – *Narrative analysis (NA)/ research method* and then particularly as used in *Life history research*.

Narrativity

(1) The storyness of stories; their features of intertwining plot line and characterisation; (2) the orientation in *epistemology* that suggests that people experience their lives as (or through) narratives, and that this should determine the way their lives are researched. See also *Narrative analysis(NA)/research methods*.

Strawson, G. (2004) 'Against narrativity' *Ratio* (new series) **XVII**: 428–452. http://web. gc.cuny.edu/philosophy/people/strawson/against_narrativity.pdf

N

National Centre for Research Methods (NCRM)

ESRC-funded centre for providing training and training materials for social and economic researchers. Source of useful methodological papers. http://www.ncrm.ac.uk

National Child Development Study (NCDS)

See *Birth cohort studies*.

National Foundation for Educational Research (NFER)

Major source of instruments used in educational research in the UK and of first hand educational research. Their website carries information about test construction and age-standardisation. See also *CERUK*.
http://www.nfer.ac.uk/index.cfm

National Research Ethics Service

See *Ethics, Ethics committees.*

National Statistics socio-economic classification (NS SEC)

Office of National Statistics (ONS) classification of people and households in Britain into 'social classes' based on occupations, themselves classified by the *National Statistics standard occupational classification*. Replaced the *Registrar General's Social Classes* in 2001. The classes are based on *Goldthorpe classes* (see also *CASMIN*). As shown in table 9, there are 14, 9, 8, 5 and 3 category versions but the eight category scheme is that most likely to be used most often. Which ever scheme is used, there are three additional categories, 'Students', 'Occupations not stated or inadequately described' and 'Not classifiable for other reasons' which can be combined as 'Not classified'.

The ONS warn that this classification cannot be read as hierarchical, mainly because of the wide variation in socio-economic circumstances of the self-employed, and thus it should not be regarded as producing data at the ordinal level though researchers will be tempted to treat it as if it did – See *Data, levels of.*

Office for National Statistics (2008) *National Statistics Socio-economic Classification,* http://www.ons.gov.uk/about-statistics/classifications/current/ns-sec

MISOC (ERSC Research Centre on Microsocial Change) (2008) *ISR-NSEC,* http://www.iser.essex.ac.uk/nssec/

ESRC Question Bank (n.d.) *Social Classification (SOC)* http://qb.soc.surrey.ac.uk/resources/classification/socintro.htm

N

National Statistics standard occupational classification (SOC/NS-SOC)

Listing produced by Office for National Statistics in Britain for classifying occupations and categorising them into types for various administrative and research purposes, including the use of occupation as a basis for dividing people and households into 'social classes' – See *National*

Table 9 Office of National Statistics socio-economic ('social class') classification of people and households in Britain reproduced here under the terms of PSI Licence C2008002495

Fourteen classes	Nine classes	Eight classes	Five classes	Three classes
1. Employers in large establishments	1.1 Large employers and higher managerial occupations	1. Higher managerial and professional occupations	1. Managerial and professional occupations	1. Managerial and professional occupations
2. Higher managerial occupations				
3. Higher professional occupations	1.2 Higher professional occupations			
4. Lower professional and higher technical occupations	2. Lower managerial and professional occupations	2. Lower managerial and professional occupations		
5. Lower managerial occupations				
6. Higher supervisory occupations				
7. Intermediate occupations	3. Intermediate occupations	3. Intermediate occupations	2. Intermediate occupations	2. Intermediate occupations
8. Employers in small establishments	4. Small employers and own account workers	4. Small employers and own account workers	3. Small employers and own account workers	
9. Own account workers				
10. Lower supervisory workers	5. Lower supervisory and technical occupations	5. Lower supervisory and technical occupations	4. Lower supervisory and technical occupations	3. Routine and manual occupations
11. Lower technical occupations				
12. Semi-routine occupations	6. Semi-routine occupations	6. Semi-routine occupations	5. Semi-routine and routine occupations	
13. Routine occupations	7. Routine occupations	7. Routine occupations		
14. Never worked and long term unemployed	8. Never worked and long term unemployed	8. Never worked and long term unemployed	Never worked and long term unemployed	Never worked and long term unemployed

Statistics socio-economic status. Revised every ten years; the 2000 version is referred to as SOC2000.

Office for National Statistics (2008) *About the Standard Occupational Classification 2000* http://www.ons.gov.uk/about-statistics/classifications/current/SOC2000/index.html
ESRC Question Bank (n.d.) *Social Classification (SOC)* http://qb.soc.surrey.ac.uk/resources/classification/socintro.htm

National Study of Health and Development

See *Birth cohort studies.*

Natural experiment (ex post facto experiment)

The investigation of configurations of factors of the kind which experimenters would create, if they could, where they can't, but which crop up naturally; sometimes called '*the comparative method*'. Astronomers can't shove stars and galaxies about so, if they want to know what happens when two stellar bodies of particular magnitudes are close together, then they have to look for naturally occurring examples for an answer. Similarly there are often practical or ethical reasons why social and behavioural scientists cannot, or should not, conduct controlled experiments and have to find naturally occurring ones. For example twins, identical and non-identical constitute a natural experiment with regard to issues of nature and nurture; Polynesian cultures constitute a set of experiments about the relationship between culture and natural environment in that people from the same initial cultural background spread rapidly across a range of different habitats. Any major social survey offers some opportunities for comparing groups in an experimental way. Unlike the ('controlled') experimental research where the researcher creates the conditions for research in a way that exerts direct control over variables, in natural experiments control has to be exerted statistically – see *Control, direct and statistical.*

N

Dunning, T. (2005) *Improving Causal Inference: strengths and weaknesses of natural experiments.* Arizona State University www.asu.edu/clas/polisci/cqrm/APSA2005/Dunning_Causal_Inference.pdf

Natural realism

Synonym for *Empiricism.*

Naturalism

See *Naturalistic research, Validity, naturalistic.*

Naturalistic fallacy

A failure to distinguish between facts and values, primarily taking the form of arguing that the fact of some state of affairs of itself demands some particular response, without acknowledging the need for a moral case to be made for the response. For example to say 'these people live in poverty therefore their incomes should be improved' would be to commit the naturalistic fallacy insofar as the case for improving their incomes does not follow directly from the fact that they are in poverty, but requires a moral case to be made that it is someone's moral responsibility to raise the incomes of the poor. *Partisan research* is particularly prone to the commission of naturalistic fallacies. However, declaring this to be a fallacy depends on accepting that there is an essential difference between facts and values. Not all social scientists accept this. Some of those adopting a *pragmatist* epistemology believe that what is true is what is (morally) good; hence no fact value distinction, and no naturalistic fallacy. See *Fact-value distinction, Value-led as opposed to value-neutral research.*

Naturalistic generalisation

See *Generalisation, naturalistic.*

Naturalistic research

This term has two almost directly contradictory meanings: (1) the methods of the natural sciences, particularly controlled experiments. It is with regard to this that **anti-naturalism** takes its meaning. (2) Research which studies 'how things naturally are' and achieves this by the researcher trying to disrupt what is being studied as little as possible – usually by participant observation research (see *Observation, participant or non-participant*) – and (usually) by trying to understand what happens in terms meaningful to the people involved: that is to avoid imposing interpretations and terminologies from outside – see *Emic, Grounded theory, Thick ethnography.* From this point of view much of the methodology of the natural sciences is seen as thoroughly 'unnatural', and as distorting and disrupting how things usually are and seeking to understand them in an alien way. With this second meaning, successful research is said to achieve naturalism or naturalistic or ecological validity – see *Validity, naturalistic.* However, judgements about how far this is achieved depend on assumptions made by those making the judgement about how things can naturally be – see *Theory data dependency.*

Naturalistic validity

See *Naturalistic research, Validity, naturalistic.*

NCDS

See *Birth cohort studies.*

NCRM

See *National Centre for Research Methods.*

Necessary cause / condition

See *Causal analysis.*

Nemic

Synonym for *Emic.*

Neo-positivism

(1) Used by some members of the Vienna circle for themselves, while others described them as logical positivists – see *Logical positivism.* The neo was adopted in order to express a difference with earlier forms of positivism – see *Positivism;* (2) sometimes used to refer to the later thinking of some members of the Vienna circle after they had rejected logical positivism, more usually called *logical empiricism*, although that term has a variety of meanings; (3) disparaging term used by one group of social scientists to express their dislike of another group; usually an accusation that their thinking is too close to that of the natural sciences, or that the approach is value neutral, when it should, allegedly, be value led – See *Value-neutral or value led. Ethnomethodology*, for example, has been described as neo-positivist.

NESSTAR (Networked Social Science Tools and Resources)

A software system for publishing, accessing and analysing data on-line, including conversion into diagrams, maps and graphs. Provides access to an increasing archive of data from government, commercial and academic sources including the *Economic and Social Data Service archive* – see *Data archives.* http://nesstar.esds.ac.uk/

Netic

Synonym for Etic, see *Emic.*

Network analysis

See *Social Network Analysis.*

Networked Social Science Tools and Resources

See *NESSTAR.*

New ethnography

See *Cognitive anthropology.*

New historicism

See *Historicism.*

NFER

See *National Foundation for Educational Research.*

Nihilism

See *Relativism.*

N_k

Number of groups involved or number of samples taken.

NNH and NNT

See *Effect size(ES) measures.*

Nocebo effect

See *Placebo.*

N of 1 experiments

Controlled experiments where the number of subjects is just one, and that person serves as his or her own *control*. The basic pattern is to alternate treatments (usually at random, and if possible *blind*) and observe the different effects of the different treatments (an *interrupted time series design*).This approach is not suitable for any treatment which has a persistent effect. May be adopted because of ethical objections to putting different subjects at different degrees of risk in *randomised controlled trials* and/or may be preferred because it enables the tailoring of a treatment to a subject; hence most often used first and foremost as a medical or social work practice and only secondarily as a mode of research.

Nominal group

See *Group Interviews*.

Nominalism

Has a wide range of meanings in *epistemology and ontology* but in the social sciences usually refers to analysis using *emic* rather than *etic* terms. Thus to say, 'what is deviant is what people treat as deviant' is to adopt a nominalist approach. See also *Componential analysis* and other tendencies within *Cognitive anthropology*, and *Social constructionism*, which are nominalist in this sense.

Nominal level data

See *Data, levels of.*

Nomogram

A graphical calculating device, such as a slide rule, or a body-mass index graph, from which an answer can be read off from given co-ordinates. For example a nomogram for calculating sample size according to the *confidence interval* desired.

> For an interactive nomogram for interpreting *Likelihood ratios* www.cebm.net/index. aspx?o=1161 *Centre for Evidence Based Medicine*

Nomological/nomothetic

See *Deductive reasoning* and *Idiographic as opposed to nomothetic*.

Non-judgementalism

See *Value-neutral or value-led*.

Non-linear dynamics

See *Complexity theory*.

Non-parametric statistics

See *Statistics, parametric and non-parametric*.

Non-reactive research

See *Unobtrusive measures*.

Non-response

See *Response rate*.

Non-sampling error

Survey research: portmanteau term referring to all the errors which may flaw a survey apart from *sampling error*.

Ruddock, V (1999) *Measuring and Improving Data Quality*, National Statistics Methodology Papers No. 14. London, Office for National Statistics www.statistics.gov.uk/methods_ quality/publications.asp

Non-verbal communication

See *Kinesics*.

Norm referencing

See *Criterion and norm referencing*.

Normal distribution (Guassian distribution, bell curve, measurement error curve, standard error curve, sampling error curve, z curve) (see Figure 20)

In a normal distribution, 68% of scores/measurements lie within the range of + or − 1 *standard deviation* of the *mean*, 95% within the range of + or − 2 *standard deviations* of the mean, and more than 99% within plus or minus 3SD. For *statistical significance* testing this provides the basis for estimating how wrong a particular result is likely to be, for chance reasons alone. Thus there is a 68% chance that the true value is within the range constituted by the figure you got, plus one *standard deviation* and minus one standard deviation, and a 95% chance that it is within the range constituted by the measurement you got, plus two standard deviations and minus two standard deviations, and only a 5% chance that the true value lies outside this latter range.

Similarly, in sampling for surveys, the values obtained for the sample are just estimates of the corresponding values for the population from which the sample was drawn, for example, percentage of young people experiencing serious injury in the population as estimated by a sample survey. Again the properties of the normal distribution can be used to estimate the likely error. So long as the sample was selected

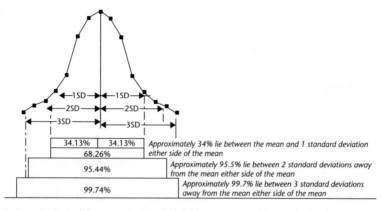

Figure 20 Example of normal distribution

on probability principles, and so long as it is of a sufficient size, there is a 95% chance that the value which is true for the population (percentage injured in the population) will lie within plus and minus 2 standard deviations of the corresponding measure in the sample (percentage injured in the sample) – see *Sample, probability, Sample size*.

These properties of the normal distribution show themselves in the *p(robability) values* quoted for tests of statistical significance, and in the *confidence intervals* often quoted with survey results. Many psychological and scholastic tests are constructed so that when used with a large number of subjects the results show a normal distribution; IQ tests for example.

See also *Central tendency and dispersion* (for the *mean* and the *standard deviation*), *Confidence intervals, p-values, Sample size*.

Jernigen, R. (2006) 'A Useful Display of a Normal Population', *The Best of Teaching Statistics*: www.rsscse.org.uk/ts/bts/jernigan/text.html

Tyell,S. (2001) *The normal distribution*, Coventry University www.coventry.ac.uk/ec/~styrrell/pages/normal.htm

N

Normal science

See *Paradigm*.

Normalisation

See *Data transformation, Standardisation*.

Normative

A normative statement is a moral proposition about how things ought to be (rather than a factual description of how things are); the opposite of descriptive, factual or actuarial. The distinction is parallel to *actuarial as opposed to contractual, value neutral as opposed to value led*, fact as opposed to value – see *Fact-value distinction*.

Norming

See *Standardisation*.

Norms

(1) Statistical typicalities, particularly *modes*, *means* or *medians*, but any entity or activity which is usual or common may be described as 'the norm' – see *Central tendency and dispersion*; (2) moral standards for behaviour. It is this latter usage that is associated with the term *Normative*.

Nosnibor effect

See *Ecological fallacy*.

Noumena

See *Phenomena*.

NPSM

See *CASMIN*.

NRES

National Research Ethics Service – See *Ethics, Ethics committees*.

NSDS

See *Birth cohort studies*.

NSPD

See *Output areas*.

NS SEC

See *National Statistics Socio-economic Classification*.

Nth phase evaluation

See *Design experiment*.

*NUD*IST*

See *Computer Assisted Qualitative Data Analysis.*

Null hypothesis

See *Hypothesis.*

Numbers needed to harm (NNH) and Numbers needed to treat (NNT)

See *Effect size (ES) measures.*

NVivo

See *Computer Assisted Qualitative Data Analysis.*

N

O

Observed (O) frequency/value – see *Expected (E) frequency/value.*

Object

(1) Non-human or non-sentient entity (2) **Object/objective**) Focus of interest, purpose or aim.

Objectification/Objectify

(1) to make public that which was private; to objectify the subjective – see *Objectivity, Subjectivity*; (2) to treat as real that which is unreal; synonym for *reification/reify*; (3) to treat a person as if they were an object.

Objective evaluation

See *Evaluation, objective.*

Objective testing as opposed to projective testing

Psychometrics. **Objective tests** are tests regarded as having right answers, such as IQ tests. **Projective tests** elicit responses which allegedly provide insight into a person's personality characteristics, emotional state, opinions and so on.

Objectivity

A term used in so many different ways that it is virtually meaningless without further definition. There are four not quite distinct meanings in research.

- **Procedural objectivity (auditability, transparency)** and the opposite of private and hidden. This was the meaning of the term at the birth of modern science in the 17th century, where knowledge based on research ('experimental knowledge') involving logical reasoning and *empirical* evidence, which (in principle) everyone could see, was juxtaposed with knowledge based on intuition, or on religious dogmatism enforced by tyrannical regimes. Hence the opposite of *objective knowledge* was dogma. Careful and accurate recording, open and honest reporting and *peer review* are related to this auditability notion of objectivity.

- Disinterestedness – having no axe to grind; regarded as desirable on the grounds both that disinterested researchers can be trusted not to knowingly mislead others, and as less likely to mislead themselves by preferring one kind of result rather than another– see *Expectancy effects*. Hence value-neutral is preferred to value-led research and strategies to make it less likely that the researchers' desires will influence the research – see *Conflict of interest, Random allocation, Blinding* and *Sampling, probability, Value neutral or value-led.* The auditability of the research (see above) should also make it easier for others to detect value bias – see *Bias, value*.

- The opposite of *subjectivity* where 'subjective' refers to private and personal experience. This relates to the demarcation between science and non-science where science is restricted to *corrigible* propositions – see *Demarcation debate*. However, other social researchers regard subjective experience as the most important domain within which humans have their being. For them the objective study of the subjective is a major enterprise, where objective means making discoveries about people's subjective experience according to the first two meanings of objectivity above; see *Hermeneutics, Phenomenology*. But feminist and anti-racist researchers in particular, critique this idea of the objective in two ways: a) that what counts as objective knowledge is distorted by having been largely produced by men or whites; that actually it is the subjectivity of white men which has been elevated into 'objective knowledge': b) that the means used to research the subjective experience of oppressed groups has given a distorted view of this. Because of the power relations involved in non-*partisan*, non-*participatory research* they have been *objectified* – treated as objects. Thus it is argued that the research task is to 'make the subjective objective', meaning to help oppressed people articulate their private (subjective) experiences so that it can be added to the stock of public (objective) knowledge – see also *Consciousness raising, Voicing*.

- Designated as true by some theory; a meaning close to the opposite of the first one above. Theologians sometimes claim that theology provides the objective truths by which we should live our lives. Marxists have argued that marxist theory provides an objective definition of the true interests of the working class. Feminist *standpoint theory* is associated with a similar view about the interests of women.

Observation

Any sense impression formed by a researcher relevant to the research, or any such, actually recorded. Includes observations of a patient's temperature in a *controlled experiment* as well as the records of protracted observation by an *ethnographic* researcher. By extension audio and video recordings are sometimes spoken of as observational data. Much of what is observed is actually spoken language. For research which mainly consists of observation there are three main dimensions of variation:

1 The extent to which subjects are aware they are being researched – see *Observation, covert or overt.*
2 The extent to which the researcher is merely an observer or plays some part the milieu being studied – see *Observation, participant or non-participant.*
3 The degree to which observation is pre-structured as opposed being determined by immediate events – see *Observation, pre-structured or intuitive.*

Observation, covert or overt

Researching people without their knowledge – covertly – is regarded as unethical unless some good reason can be advanced for it – see *Deceit in research, Ethics.* Covertness and openness range from where people have no knowledge at all that they are being studied, through situations when they know they are research subjects but don't know exactly when they are being observed, and situations where they know they are subjects of research but don't really know what the topic of the research is, through to *participatory research* where subjects have a role in the planning and execution of the research. The main reason for hiding the fact and/or the purpose of the research from subjects is that informing them would make the research impossible or produce distorting degrees of *subject reactivity.* Undercover research has been particularly common in the study of deviant groups, who would be unwilling to permit themselves to be studied if asked. Hiding the purpose, though not the fact of research is common in psychology where a great deal of research relies on deceit to be effective, although ethical codes of practice require subjects to be 'debriefed' after the research – see *debriefing*. The observation of people in public places, for example station forecourts or shopping malls, presents great difficulties in informing people that they are being observed for research purposes. The possibilities for covert research depend on whether or not the researcher is physically present in the research situation – see *Observation, participant or non-participant*. See also *Informed consent*.

Observation, naturalistic

Usually refers to *ethnographic research* conducted through participant observation of people engaged in activities ordinary to them, although in practice observation by covert recording might actually produce more naturalistic results – see *Observation, participant or non-participant, Observation, pre-structured or intuitive, Validity, naturalistic*.

Observation, participant or non-participant

One-way mirrors, video-cameras and web-cams, unobtrusive audio-recording, and lurking in internet chat rooms offer opportunities for **non-participant observation** to take place without people being aware of it and to avoid *subject reactivity* – see *Observation, covert or overt*. In **Participant observation research** the researcher joins in with the normal activities of those being researched. The extent of participation depends partly on the competence of the researcher to do what his or her subjects usually do. In some settings an observer is not a disruptive influence. For example, one more person sitting in a meeting with a note pad is unlikely to disrupt normal proceedings. In other settings an outsider would compromise *naturalism* severely. Participation may not be consistent with focussing on the task of observing, and with recording observations. Three cases for participation are where:

- joining in will be less disruptive than someone obviously just observing.
- it is necessary as a way of remaining under cover.
- it is desirable for researchers to experience life as their subjects experience it, so as to be able to give an insider's account.

Much participant observation research arises because a researchers uses an existing membership as the location for research: particularly in *practitioner research* with teachers studying teaching or nurses studying nursing. In such circumstances, and others, there may be a particular danger of sympathetic bias: see *Bias, sympathetic*.

Sanghera, B. (n.d.) 'Participant Observation' http://uk.geocities.com/balihar_sanghera/qrmparticipantobservation.html

O

Observation, pre-structured or intuitive

The observation done in controlled experiments is nearly always **pre-structured** usually involving some sort of *instrument* for guiding observation and allowing for its recording. In effect such instruments ask the researcher questions such as 'What is the time now, and which of the following is true of the subject(s) now?' **Observation schedule** would be the most common term for such an instrument. Observation may be at the time, or later in reviewing an audio or video tape. The advantages of pre-structured observation are that:

- it keeps the researcher focussed on what it is important to observe – assuming this has been correctly defined in advance.
- it allows the observational judgements of one observer to be co-ordinated with those of another, if there are more than two researchers, or if the research is a *replication* of an earlier study, and it improves the chances that the same researcher will make the same observations in the same way at different times. Consistency in observational behaviour can be checked by using *inter-rater* or *intra-rater reliability tests.*
- it leaves an audit trail in a way that intuitive observation does not, insofar as the researcher can show what was looked for at what time in what way – see *Objectivity (procedural).*

However, pre-structured observation presumes research which has reached the stage where there is a clearly articulated research question which indicates the kinds of observations which need to be made. In *ethnographic research* in particular it is often unclear as to what is most relevant to observe and record until quite late in the research project. Observation then has to be directed by what attracts the researcher's interest at the time; sometimes called **intuitive observation**, or *intuitive data processing*. Particularly if the researcher is not making notes at the time, or is not using an audio or video recording, it will often be very difficult for him or her to explain why that observation was made at that time, rather than some other observation. If research which is open-ended at the outset, later involves *constant comparison* or something similar, pre-structured observation may become appropriate at that stage.

Colker, A. (n.d.) 'Developing Observation Instruments: selecting an observation approach', *National Science Foundation On-line Evaluation Resource Library* http://oerl.sri.com/module/mod10/m10_p1.html

Observation schedule (or protocol)

See *Observation, pre-structured or intuitive.*

Observational research/study

The opposite of research by controlled experiments including *surveys* as well as *ethnographic research*.

Observed (O) frequency/value

See *Expected (E) frequency/ value*.

Occam's razor/Ockham's razor

See *Parsimony principle*.

Occulistics

See *Kinesics*.

Odds

Expression of probability (p) in the form of a ratio between the probability (p) of an event occurring and the probability of it not occurring (not-p). Thus if 70% of people with a medical condition die, the odds of survival are 30%:70%, or 3 to 7 in favour/on, or 7 to 3 against. May also be expressed as a single figure by dividing p by not-p or vice versa: here the odds of survival are 0.43, and the odds of death are 2.3. See also *Effect size (ES) measures, Logit*.

Odds ratios

See *Effect size (ES) measures*.

OLQ (On-line Questionnaire)

See *Questionnaire administration*.

Ontological/ontology

See *Epistemology and ontology*.

Ontological gerrymandering

An illegitimate practice of double standards which consists of using the anti-realist rhetoric of *social constructionism* or *post-modernism* to deny the 'real' existence of some phenomenon when this is convenient for an argument, and at the same time excluding from this kind of deconstruction something else when it is convenient that this should be regarded as real. For example, in a courtroom study, a researcher might represent the impression of the accused given by the prosecution, the defence and the witnesses as a 'social construction' (as indeed it would be) and hence as 'unreal', while treating as 'real' (and not socially constructed) the story told by the accused to the researcher.

Quine, V. (1960) *Word and Object,* Cambridge, MA: MIT Press.

Open coding

See *Coding, axial, open and selective.*

Open questions

See *Question formats.*

Operational research

See *Social research, pure and applied.*

Operationalisation/to operationalise

Defining a concept or construct in terms of the indicator(s) which would evidence it. For example, the selection of an income below a defined threshold to serve as an operational definition of 'poverty'. Sometimes used to describe the turning of a research question into a detailed plan for research.

Operationalism

(1) Most researchers practise *operationalisation* in the sense of using definitions which express the operations necessary to identify an entity as being of a particular type. (2) In *Epistemology and ontology* **operationalists** believe that there is nothing more to theoretical constructs than the operational definition. Thus intelligence would be what is measured by intelligence tests, no more and no less, and there could be as many kinds of intelligence as there are intelligence tests. A common illustration of such **operationalism** is to say that length is the number of times a stick of a certain length could be laid end to end along whatever is being measured. This illustrates one of the difficulties of operationalism, which is that each operationalisation has logically to be defined in terms of other operations – how would the length of the smaller stick be operationally defined? This problem of infinite regress makes operationalism unwieldy to say the least. In addition, as with other hard-line forms of *empiricism*, operationalism places tight limits on the

development of theory since it does not allow of the use of concepts which have no obvious operationalisations.

Bickhard, M. (n.d) *The tragedy of operationalism,* Bethlehem, PA: Lehigh University www.lehigh.edu/~mhb0/Operationalism.pdf

Opinion polls

Social *surveys* conducted to gauge opinion, usually the opinion of the general public or sections of it, but sometimes of particular occupations or members of organisations. Includes surveys of voting intentions and other topics in *psephology*. Commonly conducted by commercial polling companies, the more reputable of which belong to the British Polling Council, and paid for by news media, political parties, pressure groups and various other organisations. Also conducted for central government for the annual British Social Attitudes Survey and various consumer satisfaction questionnaires for health and social services.

British Polling Council : www.britishpollingcouncil.org/
British Social Attitudes Survey: www.esds.ac.uk/government/bsa/

Opinionnaire

Term used sometimes to refer to a *questionnaire* recording respondents' opinions.

Opportunity cost

The benefit which might have been obtained had resources been deployed differently. For example, the opportunity costs of conducting research, measured in terms of resources which could otherwise have been used to provide a service, or the opportunity costs of providing an ineffective service when the resources could have been used on research to identify a more effective one. Often feature in economic analysis, though they are usually rather speculative. See also *Burden analysis, Cost # analysis.*

O

Opportunity sample

See *Sample, convenience.*

Oral history

The reconstruction of the past from interviews with those who experienced it, and the *historiography* of this – that is, an interest in how people formulate their memories for the telling. Sometimes used as a medium in adult literacy programmes, and therapeutically as reminiscence therapy.

H-Oralhist Net www.h-net.org/~oralhist
Oral History Society www.ohs.org.uk
BBC Sound Archive (at the British Library) www.bl.uk/collections/sound-archive/history.html
Truesdell, B. (2007) *Oral History Techniques: how to organise and conduct oral history interviews,* Bloomington, University of Indiana www.indiana.edu/%7Ecshm/techniques.html

Order effect

Occurs where the outcome (usually of an experiment) depends on the order in which tasks are presented. Includes *primacy and recency effects.* See also *Bias, positional.*

Ordinal level data

See *Data, levels of.*

Ordinate

See *Y-axis.*

Orientalism

Refers to the allegedly stereotypical and biased way in which western culture, including research by western academics, treats the cultures of the near and far east. Coined by Edward Said in an important book in *post colonial anthropology.* See also *Bias, exoticism.*

Said, E. (1979) *Orientalism,* New York: Vintage
Dexheimer. J (2002) *Colonial & Postcolonial Literary Dialogues,* http://www.wmich.edu/dialogues/texts/orientalism.htm

Othering

The projection onto some person or group of characteristics contrasting with those of the speaker/writer; usually undesirable characteristics: treating them as Other (note that the upper case O is usual here). When referring to other ethnicities a fashionable synonym for *Ethnocentrism, Orientalism,* or Exoticism bias *(Bias, exoticism),* but may refer to other genders, age groups, sexual orientations or sub-cultural differences.

Outcome

The consequences of doing something, in a *controlled experiment, design experiment* or *action research* or in some programme, policy or process being evaluated. In experiments this may be expressed as the dependent variable, the response variable – see *Variable* – or as an *effect – see Effect size (ES) measures.*

Outcome, as opposed to process

A distinction sometimes made in *evaluation studies*. Evaluating a programme or policy by making judgements as to what has been achieved is termed **outcome evaluation** (or objective evaluation – see *Evaluation, objective*). However, what is meant by **process evaluation** varies and may be:

1 evaluating whether or not the programme or policy has characteristics regarded as desirable or adverse; for example, whether there is a well thought-out health and safety policy, whether there is friendly interaction between staff and clients, whether males and female have equal access to the service. These of course, are also outcomes of the actions taken to bring them about, and this distinction causes more confusion than enlightenment – see *Evaluation, heuristic*

2 an attempt to elucidate why and how outcomes have or have not been achieved. Here the juxtaposition of outcome and process implies that outcome evaluation merely records the fact of achievement or non-achievement.

Outcome evaluation is also sometimes contrasted with illuminative evaluation, see *Evaluation, illuminative.*

Outlier

Extreme values in a data *frequency distribution* which are often interpreted, rightly or wrongly, to be due to exceptional factors, and hence as distorting the overall distribution as an indication of the influence of more usual factors, and/or of the factors of greatest interest to the analyst. May be dealt with by *pruning*, by *smoothing*, by dealing only with the data in the *interquartile range*, by *Windsorisation*, by *standardising* the data for the factor(s) thought to cause the outlier. Outliers are, however, still parts of the data set, and reasons for them should be investigated. See illustration in Figure 21.

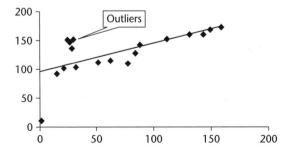

Figure 21 Illustration of outliers in a frequency distribution

See also *Power (law) distributions, Regression analysis, Spearman's rank order correlation coefficient.*

Output area

Geographical area for which survey and particularly, *census* data (*CAS – Census Area Statistics*) are summated. In the UK, common output areas are post-code areas, electoral wards, district, county council and unitary authority areas, primary care trust and health authority/board areas (in Northern Ireland Health and Social Services Board areas), administrative regions, health observatory areas, nations and the UK as a whole. In the past researchers have often had difficulty in finding statistics on different topics relating to the same area, and because of reorganisations and boundary changes, historical sequences of data have been difficult to construct. With digitisation it is becoming increasingly possible to output government statistics to user-defined output areas, subject only to safeguards preventing breaches of confidentiality. The Government standard output area classification replaced earlier ones in 2006 with a minimum area (OA) covering between 100–125 households or 250 people; smaller in some rural areas. These are aggregated into SOAs – Super Output Areas: lower tier: minimum population 1,000; middle tier: minimum population 5,000; upper tier: minimum population 25,000. These, together with administrative areas, are the geography used on the Neighbourhood Statistics website (www.neighbourhood.statistics. gov.uk).

For the classification of output areas into different types see *Area Classification of Output Areas.*

Office for National Statistics (2008) *Super Output Areas,* http://www.statistics.gov.uk/geography/soa.asp

Office for National Statistics (2008) *A beginner's guide to geographic referencing,* http://www.statistics.gov.uk/geography/geog_ref.asp

The National Statistics Postcode Directory (NSPD) (ex AFPD) gives the equivalencies between post codes and other output areas: www.statistics.gov.uk/geography/nspd.asp

Over-coverage

See *Coverage error.*

Over-rapport

See *Bias, sympathetic.*

P/p

(1) Statistic reported by Jonckheere trend test – see *Trend tests.*
(2) Upper case: used in formulae for probabilities – see *Bayesian inference*, *Probability*, *Confidence intervals.*
(3) Lower case – see *p values.*

PAF

See *Post-code address files.*

Page's trend test

See *Trend tests.*

Paired design

See *Related and unrelated designs.*

Pair wise

In *related designs*, taking each pair in turn; usually of correlations between every pair of scores in a data set, or, in **pair wise deletion**, the deletion of each pair of readings in turn to judge the effect of each pair on the aggregate.

Panel studies/surveys

Longitudinal research where a standing panel of respondents is polled from time to time. Many market research and public opinion polling companies maintain such panels. The panel might be selected through any technique of sampling – See *Sample #*. In the USA *cohort studies* are sometimes referred to as panel studies. Information on 'The British Household Panel Survey' and the new 'Understanding Society' panel survey is available at http://www.iser.essex.ac.uk/. See also *Pseudo cohort studies.*

Berrington, A., Smith, W. and Sturgis, P. (2006) *An Overview of Methods for the analysis of panel data*, NCRM http://www.ncrm.ac.uk/research/outputs/publications/

PAPI (Paper and Pencil Interview)

See *Questionnaire administration.*

Paradigm

(1) Linguisitics – see *Paradigmatic analysis.* (2) A particularly important example – as in 'mental hospitals and prisons are paradigmatic cases of total institutions'. (3) A pattern to follow, as in 'the paradigmatic approach to the problem of publication bias is Rosenthal's fail-safe N'. (4) In *epistemology and ontology,* a body of theories and less explicit beliefs constitutive of a field of study concerning what is known, what questions are sensible to ask, what methods can be used in inquiry; for example 'the interpretivist paradigm'. Similar in meaning to *episteme*, but most often used in discussions about the development of the sciences where, according to Kuhn (1996), ideas and approaches crystallise into paradigms which persist until there is a build up of problems which such **'normal science'** cannot solve, which then leads to a 'scientific revolution' (**paradigm shift**) and the emergence of a new paradigm. See also *Paradigm wars.*

Kuhn, Thomas (1996) *The Structure of Scientific Revolutions*, 3rd edn, London: Univ. of Chicago Press

Hammersley,.M. (1992) 'Paradigm Wars: the view from the front', *British Journal of the Sociology of Education*, **13**(1): 131–143

Paradigm wars

Disputes within the social and behavioural sciences as to the appropriate *epistemological and ontological* positions to adopt, and hence as to the kinds of enquiry to conduct.

Hammersley,.M. (1992) 'Paradigm Wars: the view from the front', *British Journal of the Sociology of Education*, **13**(1): 131–143

Paradigmatic analysis

Semiology/semiotics. The analysis of *texts* in terms of their being made up of selections from collections of terms (paradigms); contrasting the terms actually used with those not used: for example 'mother' rather than 'mum', 'female parent' and so on. See *Semiology/semiotics, Syntagmatic analysis.*

Chandler, D. (2006) *Semiotics for beginners: paradigmatic analysis,* University of Aberystwyth www.aber.ac.uk/media/Documents/S4B/sem05.html

Parallel forms test

See *Alternate forms test.*

Parameters

Of a *population*. Measures such as the *mean*, the range, the variance or the *standard deviation* when referring to a population from which a sample has been drawn. For all these terms see also *Central tendency and dispersion.* If applied to the sample, the *mean*, the range and so on are *statistics.*

Parametric and non-parametric statistics

See *Statistics, parametric and non-parametric.*

Pareto curve/tail

See *Power (law) distribution.*

Parsimony principle (Occam's razor/Ockham's razor)

Attributed to the 14th-century philosopher friar William of Ockham. Often paraphrased as 'All other things being equal, the simplest solution is the best.' Faced with two theories which both seem consistent with the evidence and both of which seem logically sound, the simpler one should be preferred. Sometimes finessed to imply that a theory which rests on fewer unverifiable assumptions is to be preferred to one which relies on more – see *Domain assumptions, Foundation.*

Partial association/correlation

The estimation of the influence of one variable on another net of the influence of further variables. For example (see Figure 22) investigating the contribution to academic success of ambition *and* ability *and* days of sickness absence we might expect each one of these variables to be associated with each other.

A partial correlation would calculate the correlation between:

- ability and ambition while controlling for the influence of days of sickness absence on each of them
- ambition and days of sickness absence while controlling for the influence of ability on each of them

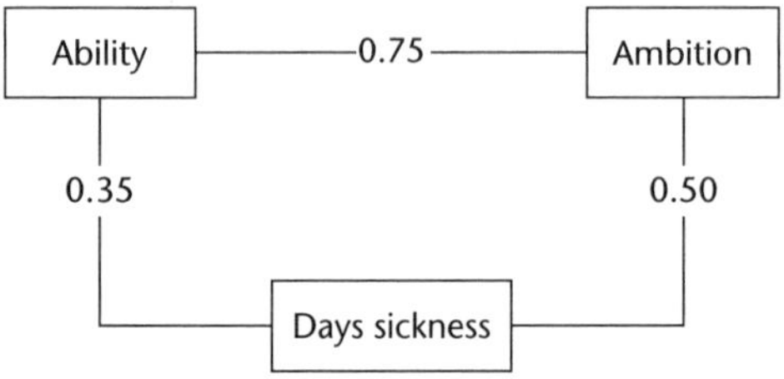

Figure 22 Example of partial correlation of 3 variables influencing an outcome variable of academic achievement.

- ability and days of sickness absence while controlling for the influence of ambition on each of them.

The results of partial correlation are reported as *correlation co-efficients.* Thus if the (partial) correlation for ability and ambition was 0.75, that would mean that there was a high correlation between these two variables, after discounting the influence of days of sickness absence. Put another way, this is an estimate of the correlation between pupils' achievements as if all had *the same level* of sickness absence. Often the result of partial correlation is assembled into a causal model by designating *variables* as independent, intervening and dependent, giving a direction to the correlations.

See also *Path analysis, Variables, Statistics software.*

Participant observation

See *Observation, participant or non-participant.*

Participative research

Research organised to overcome the traditional distinction between researcher and *subjects*, on the grounds that such research is elitist, and exploitative and that it *objectifies* those researched in treating them as objects. Subjects (partners, co-participants, collaborators) are treated as partners in the research project, usually with some role in planning it, in carrying it out and often with a veto on what is published. This is often associated with aims that have more to do with delivering benefits to the partners than with generating knowledge, hence also at the same time this is usually *action research* and *partisan research.* But the term is also applicable to research where members of the public are co-opted as co-researchers for expediential rather than ideological reasons as in much university-led local history research, and *Mass Observation.* See also *Disability research, Children as researchers, Survivor research.*

Reason, P. (ed.) (1994) *Participation in Human Enquiry,* London: Sage – republished electronically http://people.bath.ac.uk/mnspwr/Participationinhumaninquiry/titlepage.htm

Partisan research

Value-led research conducted with the specific aim of furthering the political, material or cultural interests of some fraction of society favoured by the researcher. This may include advocating their claims to better treatment, highlighting their deprivation, enhancing their public reputation, or assisting them in mobilising for action. The term is most often used of marxist, anti-racist research, *feminist research*, *disability research, survivor research*, and *queer theory*, and of the advocacy and public relations work that some anthropologists do on behalf of ethnic groups in the Third world – over land use claims for example. In these examples, partisan research tends also to be *participatory in* style and *emancipatory*. Without the emphasis on participation and empowerment, much the same characteristics are true of research conducted on behalf of companies, employers' organisations, trade unions, political parties, charities and other pressure groups – see also *value neutral or value-led research.*

Path analysis/path diagram

Statistics: constructing a causal model involving several variables by calculating *correlations* between them and assigning a *direction of effect.* May be based on *partial correlation, structural equation modelling* or otherwise. A **path diagram** is a display of the results such as shown in Figure 23. **Path analysis** following *factor analysis* may distinguish between *latent* and manifest variables.

Brannick, M. (n.d.) *Path Analysis.* University of South Florida http://luna.cas.usf.edu/~mbrannic/files/regression/Pathan.htm

Statsoft (2008) 'Structural equation modelling' *Electronic Text Book.* www.statsoft.nl/textbook/stathome.html

PAPTI (Paper and Pencil Telephone Interview)

See *Questionnaire administration.*

PDF

See *Probability density function (PDF).*

Pearson's Chi square/X^2

See X^2.

P

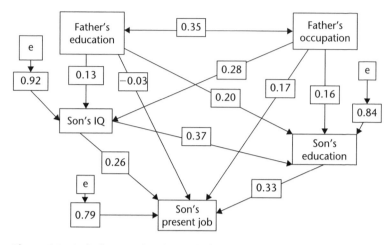

Figure 23 Path diagram showing causal relationships between father's educational achievement and occupation, son's IQ, educational achievement and present job; invented data. The figures are **path coefficients** measuring the influence of factors on each other in *standard deviation* units. Thus the 0.33 figure between son's present job and son's education means that a one standard deviation unit increase in son's educational achievement leads to a 0.33 standard deviation increase in his job status. The e(rror) figures show the unexplained *variance*: that is the variation in present job status *not* explained by the factors in the diagram. They are figures for the coefficient of alienation (*Pearson's product moment coefficient*) and the figure 0.79 means that 79% of difference in occupational status of the sons was not explained by their IQs, their education, their fathers' education or their father's occupations.

Pearson's product moment correlation coefficient (Pearson's correlation for short): synonymous with Standardised regression co-efficient

A parametric statistical calculation for *correlation* – see *Statistics, parametric and non-parametric*. The co-efficient (r or r_p) has values ranging from −1 (perfect negative/inverse) correlation, to +1 (perfect positive correl–ation) where 0 means no correlation at all. The procedure converts data into *z scores* and compares these. *Degrees of freedom* (df) are calculated as the number of rows minus 2.

Correlations of:

- 0.80 and above (plus or minus) are 'large'
- between 0.80 and 0.30 (positive or negative) are 'moderate'.
- From +0.30 through 0 to −0.30 correlations are low to non-existent.

However the coefficent must also be *statistically significant.* A significance test is usually incorporated in any calculating software.

- The **coefficient of determination** is derived by squaring r. This gives a good impression of the extent to which two variables are correlated. For example r = 0.5 means that the variance shared is $0.5^2 = 0.25 = 0.25x$ 100% = a 25% overlap. Note that on this basis a co-efficient of 0.60 shows an association 4x as great at a co-efficient of 0.30.
- The **coefficient of alienation** is the inverse of the co-efficient of determination: $1-r^2$. It can be thought of as a measure of the extent to which two variables are *not* correlated.

For data distributions containing large *outliers, Spearman's rank order correlation* is preferred.

For calculators and tutorials see *Statistics software.* See also *Phi, Point-biserial correlation.*

Peer review

The process whereby research proposals seeking funding, or ethical clearance, and papers submitted for publication in academic journals are reviewed – usually anonymously, by scholars in the field who make a judgement as to their quality. In 2003 the Royal Society established a working party on the effectiveness of peer review as a quality control procedure. www.Royalsociety.org

BMJ (n.d.) *What do we know about peer review?* http://resources.bmj.com/bmj/reviewers/ppts/preview.ppt?grp=1

Percentages and percentage points

Percentages are the most common proportional measure, much used in making comparisons which standardise for differences in group or population size by using 100 as a common *denominator.* A percentage is a rate out of 100 – see *Rates, Standarisation.*

Percentages and percentage points are commonly confused in the media, in government publications and sometimes in academic work. In Table10, Group B's success rate of fifteen out of 107 is a 14% success rate and it is 10.5 *percentage points* below the score for group A (24.5 – 14.0 = 10.5). Group B's score is *not* 10.5 *per cent* (%) below Group A. Rather the difference between groups A and B is 42.6% of Group A's success rate; so the percentage difference is 42.6% [100/((Group A%/(GroupA%−GroupB%)) which is100/(24.51/(24.51/14.02) = 42.79 = 42.8%] Note how percentage points and percentages diverge.

Table 10 Comparisons between Group A and Group B at two points in time: comparative success rates in terms of numbers, percentage points and percentages (invented data). Group A improved their success rate by 3 percentage points and 12.4%.Group B improved their success rate by 2.6 percentage points and 18.9%.

		Group A	Group B	Between group differences	
Time 1	Successes No's	25/102[1]	15/107	Points dif'[6]	% dif'[7]
	Successes%[2]	24.5%	14.0%	10.5	42.8%
Time 2	Successes No's	27/98	17/102		
	Successes %[3]	27.6%	16.7%	10.9	39.5%
Within-group Differences	Points difference[4]	3.0	2.6	The difference between the two groups at the start was 10.5 percentage points or 42.8%. At the end, the difference increased to 10.9 points and decreased to 39.5%	
	% difference[5]	12.4%	18.9%		

(1) Twenty five out of one hundred and two competitors were successful
(2) $100/(102/25) = 24.51 = 24.5\%$ & $100/(107/15) = 14.02 = 14.0\%$
(3) $100/(98/27) = 27.55 = 27.6\%$ & $100/(102/17) = 16.67 = 16.7\%$
(4) $27.55 - 24.51 = 3.06 = 3.0\text{pts}$ & $16.67 - 14.02 = 2.65 = 2.6\text{pts}$
(5) $100/(24.51/3.06) = 12.41 = 12.4\%$ & $100/(14.02/2.65) = 18.89 = 18.9\%$
(6) $24.51 - 14.02 = 10.49 = 10.5\text{pts}$ & $27.55 - 16.67 = 10.88 = 10.9\text{pts}$
(7) $100/(24.51/(24.51/14.02) = 42.79 = 42.8\%$ & $100/((27.55/(27.55/16.67) = 39.49 = 39.5\%$

Thus while group A improved its success rate more than group B in terms of percentage points, its improvement was less than group B's in terms of percentages. And the difference between the two groups was increased by 0.39 percentage points and decreased by 7.8%:

$10.88 - 10.49 = 0.39$ pts
$100/((42.79/(42.79 - 39.49) = 7.71 = 7.8\%$

The common use of percentage points rather than percentages when comparing (say) changes in public support for political parties, the relative academic achievement of boys and girls, or changing crime rates between different European countries, will often make it appear that two groups are diverging, when they are converging, or vice versa. This is much less of a problem when authors cite raw data as well as percentages or percentage points, and it is good practice to do so.

Gorard, S. (1999) 'Keeping a sense of proportion: the 'politician's error' in analysing school outcomes', *British Journal of Educational Studies,* **47**(3): 235–246

Percentiles (deciles, quantiles, quartiles)

When a set of scores is put in order, 10% of them lie on and below the 10th **percentile** – or first **decile,** 50% of them lie on or below the 50th percentile (5th decile), 10% of them lie on or above the 90th percentiles (9th decile) and so on. **Quartiles (Q_1, Q_2 etc.)** are the 25th, 50th and 75th percentiles, and *interquartile range* refers to the scores including and between the 25th and 75th percentiles. **Quantile** is a generic for any size division. See also *Interquartile range, Percentile shares, Stanines.*

Percentile shares (quantile shares)

The expression of inequality in terms of the shares of whatever is unequally shared held by different percentages of the population concerned: for example, the percentage of all income held by the poorest 20% of the population, that held by the next poorest 20% and so on – see also *Inequality, measures and metrics, Range ratio, Stanine.*

The Poverty Site, New Policy Institute and Joseph Rowntree Foundation: www.poverty.org.uk/04/index.shtml

Performance ethnography (ethnodrama)

Research conducted by working with people to create a dramatic performance and or research presented by being performed dramatically. To be distinguished from the **ethnography of performance**, which is using ethnographic research to study dramatic performances

McCall, M. (2000) 'Performance ethnography; a brief history and some advice' in Denzin, N. and Lincoln, Y. (eds) *Handbook of Qualitative Research*, London: Sage: 435–454

P

Performance indicators (PIs)

Indicators selected to provide evidence useful for monitoring the performance of an individual or organisation or the success of a programme or policy, for example the number of GCSE passes grade C and above achieved by a school, or the percentage of complaints responded to within 10 days by a social services department – see *Construct-indicator relationship.* PIs are often controversial and unpopular with the people whose performance is being monitored. Many performance indicators used in public services are poorly designed for their purpose and it is often unclear whether it is the performance of a system which is being monitored, or the performance of individuals and organisations. The latter is usually assumed, but many P.I.s do not actually measure outcomes for which those being judged should be held responsible. See also *Goodhart's law*. Some attempts have been made to 'level the playing field' of comparison. Schools, for example are now judged on a 'value-added' basis, not on the raw GCSE results, but on the results in relation to SATs scores at entry to secondary school, and police forces are judged not in comparison with all others, but in comparison only with forces with areas with similar age and social deprivation profiles – see *Home Office model*. In government circles there is a desire to make performance indication simple and easy for the public to understand, and this often runs counter to aim of performance management comparing like with like. The scoring of most public services in the UK and the descriptions of the indicators they are being scored against, are available on the internet. For example, for the performance of each NHS Trust in England see: http://2007ratings.healthcarecommission.org.uk/homepage.cfm

Pencheon, D. (2002) *The Good Indicator Guide; how to use and choose indicators,* NHS Institute for Innovation and Improvement. Available from: www.apho.org.uk

Performatives

Synonym for *Illocution.*

Periodic variation

See *Secular trend.*

Persistence

Social Mobility; the extent to which position of children (as adults) in a scheme of social stratification, matches that of their parent(s). Synonym for **Inheritance** in this context.

Personal constructs

See *Actor perspectives, Repertory grid technique.*

Perspective

As in *Interpretive perspective(s)*, or Feminist perspective(s); ways of thinking about and studying such phenomena as are made relevant by the perspective. Used as an alternative to *theory* which may imply the possibility of subjecting such bodies of ideas to empirical test – see *falsification, hypothetico-deductive method*, and used as an alternative to *paradigm* or *episteme*, though similar in meaning.

Perspectivism

See *Multiple realities, Cultural relativism, Relativism.*

Perturbation

Various techniques used to adjust data sets to prevent the subjects being identified, short of **suppression**, which is not publishing the data, or the contents of some cells in a table. Used mainly where frequencies are low and or identification might be made by cross analysing two sets of data. Perturbation includes:

- **Barnardisation** – randomly adding or subtracting small amounts from the cells of a table
- Rounding the contents of cells up or down at random by small amounts
- Data-base changes – for example swapping pairs of similar but not identical records.

ONS (2008) *GSS/GSR Data Disclosure Control Policy,* London: Office for National Statistics. www.ons.gov.uk/about/index.html and search on title

Peto method

See *Weighted averages/event rates.*

Phenomena (singular, **phenomenon**)

(1) Loosely used in the same way as 'things', but avoiding the implication of physicality; (2) refers to our experiences of the world, which might be experiences of real physical objects or imagined ones. In *epistemology and ontology* the distinction is between phenomena (our experience), and **noumena** (reality as such) which phenomena may, or may not, accurately reflect.

In social science the terms phenomenon or phenomenal should not be used to mean outstanding, exceptional or weird.

Phenomenological/ogy

(1) Most natural scientists believe that what they study in the first instance is sense data – phenomena. Thus the philosophy of natural science is phenomenological – see *Phenomena, Critical rationalism,*

P

Empiricism, Positivism, Logical positivism, Realism. (2) In the social sciences phenomenology is usually research into the way consciousness is experienced first hand and will refer to some or all of *interpretivism, hermeneutics, symbolic interactionism, dramaturgical approaches* and *ethnomethodology.* (3) More precisely, **phenomenological sociology** (or social phenomenology) refers to work influenced by Alfred Schutz, or by the rather different work of Merleau-Ponte. Appeals to phenomenology in sociological or anthropological research may take one of two contradictory forms; either as an injunction for the researcher to become a thoroughly competent member of the culture of the people being studied, and to understand matters as they understand them, or to transcend such common-sense understandings (the epoché or phenomenological reduction) – see *Anthropologically strange, Bracketing.* (4) In psychology, phenomenology also refers to consciousness and its structure. Traditionally this was studied by *introspectionism.* But these days in psychology it is not necessarily thought that qualitative methods are the most appropriate means for studying conscious experience. Indeed when the term phenomenology is used in neuro-psychology it usually involves research by brain scanning. See also *Philosophers.*

Phenomenology On-line: www.phenomenologyonline.com/

Smith, D.W. (2003) 'Phenomenology' *Stanford Encyclopedia of Philosophy* http://plato.stanford.edu/

Embrie, L. (2006) 'Alfred Schutz' *Internet Encyclopedia of Philosophy* www.iep.utm.edu/s/schutz.htm

Robbins, B. (1999) *Maurice Merleau Ponty,* Mythos and Logos http://www.mythosandlogos.com/MerleauPonty.html

Phi coefficient (Φ)

A non-parametric *correlation coefficient* calculated for nominal level dichotomous data – see *Data levels of, Statistics, parametric and nonparametric.* Calculated as the square root of X^2 over N (the number of items in the data set). Unlike most other correlation coefficients Phi runs from 0 to $+1$. Squaring the result gives an estimate of the *variance explained,* but will not indicate whether the correlation is positive or negative. Phi should only be calculated where X^2 reaches *statistical significance.* For calculators and tutorials see *Statistics, software.*

Philosophers

Introductions to the lives and thought of philosophers and other thinkers referred to elsewhere in the glossary can usually be found at:

Stanford Encyclopedia of Philosophy http://plato.stanford.edu/entries
Internet Encyclopedia of Philosophy www.iep.utm.edu/

Phronesis

The study of how and why we should act in order to change things for the better. A **phronetic** programme for the social and behavioural sciences would be based on the following questions: (1) Where are we going? (2) Who gains and who loses, by which mechanisms of power? (3) Is this development desirable? (4) What should we do about it?
See also *Praxis.*

Flyvbjerg, B. (2001) *Making Social Science Matter: Why Social Inquiry Fails and How it Can Succeed Again,* Cambridge: Cambridge University Press (Introduction available on Cambridge University Press and Amazon Books Web Sites).

Pilot study (feasibility study)

Preliminary research conducted to aid planning a more substantial study, through:

- discovering what is of interest in a research setting,
- choosing between alternative settings,
- looking for possible difficulties which might have to be overcome,
- carrying out an ethical appraisal of the research proposed (see *Ethics*) (preliminary discussions with *ethics committees* and other *gatekeepers* are advisable)
- conducting a risk assessment (see *Sensitive issues and vulnerable groups, Safety*)
- trying out techniques of research or research instruments in development.

For example, it is quite common in a pilot study to use a *questionnaire* with open questions, and on the basis of analysing the results, develop a forced choice questionnaire for the main study. See *Cognitive interview, Question formats, Validation, Walk-through.* See also *Evaluability study*

van Teijlingen, E. and Hundley, V. (2001) 'The importance of pilot studies', *Social Research Update,* Issue 35 http://sru.soc.surrey.ac.uk

Pivot table

Tool for summarising data in spreadsheet programs which will sort, count, total or otherwise manipulate data in one table and present the results in another. Particularly useful in creating *cross-tabulations.*

Kyd, C. (2008) *Excel Pivot Tables,* http://www.exceluser.com/help/pivot/long001.htm

Placebo

In *blinding,* in *controlled experiments* to disguise which treatment subjects are receiving, one *comparison group* will be given a treatment which is indistinguishable from the active treatment, but is inert; for example a tablet which looks, tastes and smells like the 'real' treatment – the placebo. Improvements in the group receiving the placebo, greater than those which might be expected by chance, may be called 'the **placebo effect**'; a *subject-reactivity* effect operating psychologically through people believing a benefit will accrue to them. This can be considerable. There are only limited circumstances in which placebos can be used in social research. The **nocebo effect** is an adverse effect created by the person's belief that this will happen.

> Carroll, R. (2005) 'The Placebo Effect', *Skeptics Dictionary* http://skepdic.com/placebo. html

Plastic interval level data

On a measurement scale, intervals which are numerically the same distance apart, but which may relate to phenomena which are not so calibrated; for example, in an examination the marks above 80 may be more difficult to achieve than those between 60 and 80. Data from such scales should be treated as being of an ordinal level, but often are treated as interval level – see *Data, levels of.*

Platykurtic

See *Kurtosis.*

Plausibility

Used by some qualitative researchers as an alternative to internal valid-ity, see *Criteria for evaluating research, Validity, internal.* But also what is achieved by successful rhetoric, hence a topic for *rhetorical analysis.*

Plot and whiskers

See *Whiskers.*

Pluralistic evaluation

See *Evaluation, pluralistic.*

Point biserial correlation

A non-parametric version of *Pearson's product moment correlation* used for *correlation* where one set of variables is dichotomous, such as gender (and is treated as a dummy variable) and the other is at the interval level

– see *Data, levels of, Statistics, parametric and non-parametric, Variable dummy.* For calculators and tutorials see *Statistics, software.*

Polysemy

Polysemic words have multiple meanings. The idea may be limited to the listings of different meanings for the same word in a dictionary, or be more fundamental with the implication that words, and the ideas they express, only have meaning in particular contexts for particular people; hence meaning is unstable and people only share meanings to a limited degree – see also *Multiple realities.*

Popperian/ism

See *Critical rationalism.*

Population

(1) A population of people; (2) a population of other entities; (3) in statistics, a population of scores or data points. Often refers to the population from which samples are taken, with regard to which the sample should be representative – see *Representativeness.*

Population at risk

That group or category of people at risk of having some characteristic or of having something happen to them; most usually as the denominator in a *rate*. In a suicide rate all ages, males in England, then the population of all males, all ages in England is the population at risk.

See also *Denominator-enumerator discrepancies, Rate.*

Population comparison/control/reference studies

Study in which data about a set of cases are compared with similar data about the population from which the cases were drawn; for example, a study comparing the characteristics of juvenile delinquents with the distribution of those same characteristics in the population as a whole. Such studies may be *cross-sectional* or *longitudinal* and the cases recruited in various ways. While researchers may have detailed and accurate knowledge about the cases they are studying, they often have no such accurate knowledge about the distribution of the same factors in the population. In this example the study might suffer from there being a large number of undetected juvenile delinquents in the population with backgrounds different from those constituting the known cases. See *Bias, ascertainment, Control, direct and statistical, Natural experiment, Standardised mortality/morbidity ratios (SMRs)*.

Population heterogeneity

Diversity in a population with regard to *variables* which interest a researcher. For example, a population considered only in terms of gender differences is less heterogeneous than the same population considered in terms of genders and age groups. In sampling this should determine the *sample size,* either directly or via the design of a stratified sample – see *Sample, stratified*.

Positional bias

See *Bias, positional*.

Positivism

Today this is mainly a term of disparagement used by some *qualitative researchers* to express dislike of quantitative research or by *partisan researchers* to express dislike of value neutral research- see *Value neutral or value-led,* and among rival groups of qualitative researchers to deprecate each other. The general thrust here is that ideas and practices characteristic of the natural sciences should not be used in the social and behavioural sciences – see *Unity of science thesis*.

Something called positivism was invented by the early nineteenth-century French philosopher Auguste Comte (**Compteian positivism**), who saw science as providing not just sound knowledge but also a new worldview as a basis for reorganising society – a positive vision, and sometimes referred to as *enlightenment thinking* or *scientism* and regarded as an important aspect of modernism – see *Post-modernism*. Science was to replace older forms of belief, including religion, and take over their social functions. In the late nineteenth and early twentieth century, positivism stood for a particular conception of scientific method, one which involved logically deriving scientific laws from empirical evidence. At the end of the nineteenth century there was a version of positivism systematised by the physicist Ernst Mach and through the Society for Positivist Philosophy, founded in 1912. **Machian positivism** prefigured much of the *logical positivism* of the Vienna circle which was briefly influential among philosophers from the 1920s to the 1940s. *Logical positivism* was not widely adopted by natural scientists, still less by social and behavioural scientists except for behaviourists – see *Behaviourism,* and was quickly found to be untenable, foundering particularly on the problem of induction – see *Inductive reasoning*.

The resulting revision of thinking constitutes what most natural scientists and many social and behavioural scientists would regard as *scientific method*. It centres on the *hypothetico-deductive method* and the idea of *falsification*. Despite its anti-positivist credentials this approach is often described as 'positivist' by social scientists, but as *critical rationalism* (and sometimes as *realism*) by those who espouse it.

Auguste Compte (2005) 'A General View of Positivism', from '*A General View of Positivism'*, (trans. Bridges, J.) London: Robert Speller & Sons (1957 and original French publication, 1856) www.marxists.org/reference/archive/comte/1856/general-view.htm

[Machian positivism] Bickhard, M. and Campbell, R. (2005) 'New Ideas in Psychology: Editorial' *New Ideas in Psychology* **23**:1–4

Post

As a prefix,with or without a hyphen, and short for 'post hoc' or 'posterior', **post** designates that something is after something else; commonly used to refer to historical periods as in post-industrial, to intellectual trends, as in *post-modernism,* or juxtaposed to *pre* where it refers (usually) to measurements taken at the end of an experiment or other intervention – see *Pre and post measurement* or juxtaposed to 'prior' in *Bayesian inference.*

Post-code address files (PAF)

A complete collection of over 27 million Royal Mail postal addresses, with a sub-set called the **Small-user post-code address file** often used as a *sampling frame* for the selection of probability samples – see *Samples, probability*. The small-user listing is of all those addresses which receive smaller amounts of mail and are therefore assumed to be residential addresses. Inevitably this will include businesses which receive little mail, and unoccupied premises, while domestic addresses which receive large deliveries, and some multi-occupied premises will not be included. See also *Output areas.*

Royal Mail (2003) *Why, what, how; guide to using the PAF File* www.royalmail.com/portal/rm

Post-colonial anthropology/ethnography

From the late 60s and early 70s, at first associated closely with writers such as Franz Fanon and Albert Memmi. Anthropological research and writing examining the impact of colonialism and neo-colonialism on third world societies and their migrants to the rich world, as a basis for liberation movements. Entails a critique of traditional anthropology as a creature and tool of colonial oppression. See also *Orientalism, Subaltern Studies.*

Reed, T. (2007) 'XI Post colonial/decolonial Theories' in *Theory and Method in American Cultural Studies.* Washington State University. *http://www.wsu.edu/~amerstu/tm/poco. html*

Loomba, A., Kaul, S., and Bunzi, M. (2005) *Postcolonial Studies and Beyond.* Durham NC: Duke University Press.

Posterior probabiity (post-)

See *Bayesian inference.*

Post hoc tests (follow-up tests)

An *analysis of variance* (*ANCOVA/MANCOVA*) or *analysis of covariance ANOVA/MANOVA* will indicate if there are *statistically significant* differences between groups, but will not identify the groups between which these statistically significant differences obtain. To establish this it is usual to conduct follow-up or *post hoc* tests, comparing all possible pairs of groups. This can be done in a single operation with tests such as the Tukey HSD test (where there are equal numbers of subjects in each group) or the Sheffe test (where there are unequal numbers in each group). Alternatively the difference between each of all the possible pairs can be compared using a series of *t-tests*.

Conducting large numbers of tests on the same data creates the risk of a *family-wise error.*

See also *Statistics, software.*

Post modernism (or postmodernism or post-modernism)

Position in *epistemology* defined mainly by its rejection of **modernism** or *enlightenment thinking*, particularly the rejection of marxism which was the most influential form of enlightenment thinking for Western European intellectuals, and of *scientism*; the notion that through science we will come to understand the human condition and improve it – see *Positivism.* Post modernism is always anti-foundationalist in rejecting the idea that through using the appropriate methods we can build up a foundation of sound knowledge about the world – see *Fallibilism and foundationalism,* and is highly relativist – see *Relativism.* The term is usually used by Anglo-American writers to cover important debates of this kind within French philosophy in the 1960s and 70s, so that it is applied to the works of Barthes, Baudrillard, Cixous, Derrida, Foucault, Irigaray, Kristeva, Lacan (see *Philosophers*), and others, although many of those named deny that they are post modernists. All of these, and others, reject modernism, but do not necessarily reject it in the same way, and they differ in what they propose instead. The rejection of science, and for most, an insistence on the processes of the social world being unstable and shifting and not being expressable in general terms and, for some, the idea that all versions of the truth are equally valid, means that post modernism has little to offer as guidance on how research should be practised. Since writings are not offered as truth claims, they are justified in other ways, for example in the same way as literature or art are justified on aesthetic grounds, or on the contribution they might make to readers' self-understanding or psycholological development. Absurdist art movements such as dada, surrealism and situationalism have been a strong influence here, as has psychoanalytic theory in some versions. Such research as is conducted in the name of post-modernism is largely through the deconstruction of *texts* to display their underlying assumptions. However, unlike the *deconstructionism* associated with *critical theory*, marxism and most *feminist research*, there is no presumption that postmodernist analysis can supply a more correct version of the truth – see *Crisis of representation and crisis of legitimation*. This denial of the superiority of expert descriptions and explanations is on ethical as well as epistemological grounds. Feminist post-modernists in particular, insist that claiming to have a grasp of the truth superior to others (or 'the Other'- see *Othering*) is authoritarian and oppressive.

Post modernism and post modern are also used as a description of the affluent societies of the late twentieth and early twenty-first centuries, globalised, dominated by mass consumerism and mass media, populated by people with uncertain and shifting identities (see *Decentred, Fragmentation of identity* and Lyotard 1984). Near synonyms for the **post modern condition**, are postindustrial (or post industrial) and post-Fordist.

Aylesworth,G. (2005) *Postmodernism,* Stanford Encyclopedia of Philosophy http://plato.stanford.edu/

Sociology Central (n.d.) 'Post Modernism', *Association for the Teaching of the Social Sciences* www.sociology.org.uk/online1.htm

Lyotard, J. (1984) *The Postmodern Condition: a report on knowledge,* Minneapolis, Minnesota University Press

Clifford, J. and Marcus, G.(1986) *Writing Culture: the poetics and politics of ethnography,* Berkeley: University of California Press

Lindholm, C. (1997) 'Logical and moral problems of postmodernism', *Journal of the Royal Anthropological Institute,* **3**(4): 747–760.

Post-structuralism

See *Structuralism and post-structuralism.*

Post-test sensitivity and pre-test sensitivity

Forms of *subject reactivity* whereby effects created by testing at the end of an experiment (post) or at the beginning (pre) are confounded with the effects of the experiment itself – see *Confounding*.

Poverty

Sometimes this term is restricted to material poverty (usually income poverty), but sometimes includes what used to be called 'poverty of opportunity' and now is more likely to be called *social exclusion* (Pantaziz *et al.*, 2006) – see *Deprivation indices, Inequality indices and metrics, McLoone's Index, Percentile shares, Poverty, absolute, Poverty relative, Poverty, Sen's index of, Segregation Indices, Theal's Index*.

Two sites which are particularly useful for information about research on poverty in the UK are:

Pantazis, C.,Gordon, D. and Levitas, R. (2006) *Poverty and Social Exclusion in Britain: the millennium survey (Studies in Poverty and Social Exclusion).* Cambridge: Polity Press
The Poverty Site: www.poverty.org.uk/04/index.shtml New Policy Institute and Joseph Rowntree Foundation
The Institute for Fiscal Affairs: www.ifs.org.uk

For Europe (and elsewhere):

The Luxembourg Income Study: www.lisproject.org

Third world poverty:

Chronic Poverty Research Center: www.chronicpoverty.org

Poverty, absolute

Defined by reference to some historically and globally fixed threshold, households with incomes below which are said to be in poverty. Classic poverty studies such as those of Booth and Rowntree employed definitions verging on the absolute, making reference to the idea of the minimum necessary to remain healthy. However, terms like 'healthy' are relative to expectations which change through time and Rowntree's definitions of poverty became more generous as time went by. Absolutist international poverty definitions such as household incomes of less than $1 a day, seem to be easily understandable, but what you can buy for $1 a day varies widely, and the implications of this level of income depend on resources drawn from the non-cash economy – see *Social capital*. Fixed definitions of poverty are useful if the interest is in historical change in standards of living, although there is rarely any reason why such an interest should be tied to a poverty threshhold rather than any other part of the income range (Burnett, J. (1993) *A History of the Cost of Living,* Farnham, Ashgate Publishing).

Absolute definitions are criticised for their social policy implications on the grounds that poverty should be defined in terms of the shares of national resources flowing to poorest sections of the community, on the ethical assumption that as living standard rise, poverty thresholds should rise also – see *Poverty, relative.*

Poverty, relative

Peter Townsend's 1979 definition is often quoted to the effect that poverty is 'where resources are so seriously below those commanded by the average individual or family that they are, in effect, excluded from average living patterns customs and activities' (1979 *Poverty in the UK,* Harmondsworth: Penguin).

Thus **relative definitions of poverty** are preferred over absolute defin-itions for policy related research. The American government approach is to define poverty in terms of an inability to purchase a given basket of goods and services. The basket is revised periodically to become more generous, but in between times (apart from up-dating for price-inflation) this bench-mark operates as a kind of short-term absolute definition – see *Poverty, absolute.* In between revisions it would allow the purchasing power of the poor to remain the same, but their share of national income to fall. The UK and most European governments use **income relative definitions**, the most common of which is that poverty is an income less than 60 per cent of the median household income after *equivalisation.* The median income is used rather than the *mean,* because the *median* is itself unaffected by changes in the distribution of income.

Department of Work and Pensions (2007) *Households below Average Incomes 1994/95 to 2005/06,* www.dwp.gov.uk/asd/hbai,asp

P

Income in this measure is from all (officially known) sources after income tax, council tax and housing costs have been deducted. Housing costs include rents, mortgage interest, buildings insurance and water charges. The measure assumes 'standard' household expenditure, and in itself takes no account of additional costs such as those of living in rural areas, or of disability over and above those costs which are recompensed in benefits. Different poverty levels are sometimes proposed to take account of such factors. More usually account is taken through the calculation of different retail price indices for different fractions of the population: for example the pensioner's RPI/Cost of Living Index. Up to a point, the question of whether 60 per cent of median income is an appropriate poverty threshold is unimportant. What is important is selecting a bench-mark figure to use in tracking changes in income distribution through time, or in comparing one geographical area with another. In this respect, *percentile shares* and other *inequality measures and metrics*, which look at the whole range of income distribution are preferable.

Since the 'poverty line' features in political debates it is important that where it is set has some degree of public legitimacy. Research on public perceptions of necessities has been an important aspect of poverty research. Typically, representative samples of the public are given a list of items and asked whether these are necessary. Those which receive (say) 50% ratings are retained. These items are then included in a questionnaire asking people whether they can afford these items. Those who say they cannot afford some number of these items (or are scored above a certain level according to the rank order of the items they cannot afford) are regarded as living in poverty, according to a **consensual definition of poverty**. The approach above, in effect, creates a poverty index based on inability to purchase what are *publicly designated* as necessities. But the usefulness of such indices is short-lived since they are dependent on majority views at a particular point in time.

Poverty, Sen's index of

Used mainly by international agencies to compare countries: defined as:

$$I = (P/N)(B - A)/A$$

where:
P = number of people below the poverty line
N = total number of people in society
B = poverty line income
A = average income of those people below the poverty line
The precise meaning depends on a definition of B – which is often 60% of *median* household income.

Power (law) distributions

Frequency distributions with properties very different from those of the *normal distribution* on which parametric inferential statistics rely – see *Statistics, parametric and non-parametric*. Called power law distributions because the line on a frequency distribution graph corresponds with an equation where one term varies according to the other term when raised (or diminished) by a power; for example height = distance^{power}

If the power were 2, then the height on the graph, showing frequency, would equal distance squared, which generates a curve of ever increasing steepness upwards on an ordinary arithmetic scaling or a diagonal straight line where *log scales* are used for both axes. With an **inverse power law** there is a curve of ever declining steepness downwards on arithmetic graphs and left to right diagonal straight lines on graphs with both scales as *log scales*. See Figure 24.

The **Pareto curve** is the best known family of power distributions. For example, the saying in business that '80% of your sales will be to 20% of your customers'. Sometimes what is graphed is frequency against rank. In the English language 'the' is the most frequently occurring word, accounting for nearly 7% of all word occurrences. The second-place word, 'of', accounts for slightly over 3.5% of words followed by 'and' at about 2.8%. Only 135 words account for half the words listed in the Brown Language Corpus – see *Corpus Linguistics*. Frequency turns out to be roughly the inverse of rank order: thus the second most common word is half as common as the most common word (percentage frequency of most common word,divided by two). The third most common word is one third as common as the most common, the fourth one fourth as common and so on; this is the **Zipf curve**.

A power distribution has no central tendency – see *Central tendency and dispersion*. Parametric tests of *statistical significance* which rely on normally distributed data may give misleading results with power distributions – see *Statistics parametric and non-parametric*. Statisticians often try to force power distributions into forms amenable to analysis by parametric statistics, using *data transformation* to recast them as something closer to a *normal distribution*. A '*log normal*' transformation is the most usual. Or perhaps they chop off the tail ('Pareto tail' or *outlier*) which contains large values but few instances, and work only with the data concerning smaller values and larger numbers of instances. This may grossly misrepresent reality. For example the major inequality in income distribution is between the super-rich and the rich, but this is hidden if the super-rich are amputated from the power-law distribution of income.

Some power distributions are also **fractal** or **scale invariant** (or scale independent) or **self-similar**. Coastlines are the iconic example. Headlands are composed of bays and headlands on a smaller scale, which on a smaller scale still are composed of smaller bays and headlands, and so on until you reach the wiggly line between grains of sand. Similar fractility is shown by stock market fluctuations, by the year, the month, the day and the hour; in urban landuse patterns, from area to sub-area to sub-sub-area; communication networks, from trunk roads to footpaths, and wars consist of small engagements within larger ones.

P

Normally distributed data	Power law distributed data/fractal data
A representative data set includes many items with middling values; fewer larger and fewer smaller than this.	With an inverse power law a representative data set has a few very large items with very high values and increasing numbers with increasingly small values.
The *mean* (arithmetic average) is a meaningful indication of the most typical value among items.	The *mean* (arithmetic average) is not a meaningful indication of the most typical value among items.
The *variance* is a meaningful measure of the amount of variety in the data set- measured as the distance of each item from the mean.	The *variance* is not a meaningful measure of the amount of variety in the data set, which will increase according to how big the data set is. The measure of variety in fractal data is the 'fractal dimension' which quantifies the ratio of small values compared to large values.
The *standard deviation* is a meaningful metric for measuring the dispersion of the data set.	The dispersion of the data set will increase according to the size of the sample, so there can be no stable *standard deviation.*
Each additional sample added to previous ones will result in less change to the grand mean.	With an inverse power law, each new sample added to the previous ones, will change the grand mean, making it smaller with most samples, and occasionally bigger.

Figure 24 Normally distributed data compared with power law distributed data
Source: Liebovitch and Scheurle 2000: 36

Power distributions, scale invariance and fractal geometry (**Mandelbrot geometry**) are actually much more common in nature and social life than are normally distributed data, because most phenomena are complex rather than linear – see *Complexity theory*. Sometimes it will be reasonable to treat the complex as linear and to transform data which is actually distributed in accordance with a power law, into more normal forms, in order to take advantage of the tool kit of parametric statistics. But in which instances this can be done is not always clear.

Liebovitch, L. and Scheurle, D. (2000) 'Two lessons from fractals and chaos', *Complexity* **5**(4):34–43

Power calculation

See *Statistical power.*

Practitioner research

Social research by members of an occupational group, often promoted on the basis that it is practitioners who best know what research needs doing. Often takes the form of *Action Research*. There are strong practitioner researcher networks among adult literacy and ESOL tutors, vocational trainers, teachers, nurses, social workers and police officers – see also *Clinical audit*. Websites of professional associations or local universities are usually the best place to locate a practitioner research network.

Practical evaluation

See *Social research, pure and applied.*

Pragmatic/pragmatism

(1) In common usage, expedient or useful in the circumstances; (2) the adoption by a researcher of any, or several methods of research which seem best fitted to the circumstances at hand; having no commitment to any particular *epistemological or ontological* assumptions – see *mixed/multi-method research, method slurring*; (3) linguistics – see *Pragmatic linguistics*. (4) In *Epistemology and ontology* pragmatism refers to a spectrum of philosophical ideas derived from Charles Sanders Peirce (who coined the term), William James, John Dewey, F.C.S. Schiller and Richard Rorty. Much of pragmatism today consists of the influence of such thinkers on positions such as *critical rationalism, empiricism, phenomenology, realism* and *symbolic interactionism* rather than being free-standing. However, a core proposal for nearly all kinds of philosophical pragmatism is that truth

should not be regarded as the correspondence between a proposition and reality, but as the usefulness of an idea in helping us understand something or accomplish some other task – see *Sensitising concepts*. This draws attention to the way in which a valid answer depends on what question was asked, and suggests that truth has not a monolithic out-there quality, but is constituted by a researcher according to how s/he asks questions and verifies the answers. It is not a large step from this position to *social constructionism* and *relativism*. It is sometimes argued that it is a step taken in effect by Richard Rorty, the most controversial of modern pragmatists. The idea of the truth as usefulness also appears in *partisan research*, for example in traditional marxism, the idea that what is true is what serves the interests of the working class, and something similar in some forms of *feminist research*. It might be appropriate to refer to these as 'pragmatic notions of truth', but only with the recognition that they go further than most pragmatic philosophers. See also *Philosophers*.

McDermid, D. (2006) 'Pragmatism'. *Internet Encyclopedia of Philosophy* www.iep.utm. edu/p/pragmati.htm

Pragmatic linguistics

Study of language in terms of the uses to which language is put. This necessitates detailed consideration of the social context of speech and of what is implied (*implicature*) but which may not necessarily be stated explicitly. **Speech act theory** – credited to J.L. Austin, is an important version focussing on what is accomplished by speaking, such as promising, persuading, misleading and so on. Similar in interests to *conversation analysis* but deploying a different vocabulary – see also *Illocution, Performative, Grice maxims, Rhetorical analysis*.

Austin, J. (1962) *How to do things with words*, Oxford: Oxford University Press
Loos, E., Day, D., Jordan, P. and Wingate, J. (2004) 'What is pragmatics?' *Glossary of Linguistic Terms*, Lingual-links, SIL International. www.sil.org/linguistics/Glossary OfLinguisticTerms

Praxis

Not just articulating a theory but acting on the basis of it, and testing and developing the theory by the experience of putting it into practice (by praxis). Rarely used except of theories which are socially critical such as marxist and feminist theories and with the pedagogy of Paulo Friere; hence associated with *partisan research*, which is *participatory* and *emancipatory* and which is *action research*. In this, the term maintains some of its meaning from the ancient Greek, which relates to economic, political and ethical action engaged in by free men.

Gibson, R. (n.d) *Paulo Freire and Revolutionary Pedagogy for Social Justice*: www.pipeline. com/%7Erougeforum/freirecriticaledu.htm

Pre-

Prior, before, usually of measurements and contrasted with *post.*

PRE

See *Proportional reduction in error.*

Pre- and post-measurement

In studying any kind of change it is important to take measurements *before* the changes occur (*pre-*, or base-line measurement) as well as afterwards (*post-*). Similarly, if two groups are to be compared it is important at the outset to establish their similarities and differences as relevant to the research. Otherwise pre-existing differences or similarities may confound the interpretation of the research. The major advantage of *longitudinal* over *cross-sectional* research, as long as it is *prospective,* is that it enables change to be measured from a base line. See also *Comparison groups, Confounding, Control, direct and statistical.*

Precision matching

Creating *comparison groups* for experiments by studying each possible subject and then composing two groups with much the same profile for the *variables* of interest. Although intuitively appealing this technique has been found less efficient than *random allocation.* Also occasionally used in the analysis of data for statistical control purposes.

Pre-post test without controls

Research design in which something about a group of subjects is recorded, something happens to them and observations are made again. Any changes pre to post might be attributed to the happenings in which the researcher is interested. But without a control group this may not be a safe assumption. The changes might have occurred anyway – see *Confounding, Control, direct and statistical, Interrupted time series design.*

Prediction

The extent to which one set of values can be accurately estimated from knowledge of another set. For example, if you know the *ranking*

of a group of neighbourhoods in terms of their affluence or depriva-
tion (which is richest, which is next richest, and so on – see *Deprivation indices*) then there is a good chance that you can roughly predict their rank order in terms of the number of crimes per head committed per year. The extent that one pattern is predictable from another is regarded as the extent to which one set of variables causes the other, or that both are caused by some third factor or set of factors – see *Causal analysis.* Prediction of itself will not indicate the *direction of effect.* The ability to predict is the primary test of a theory. The usual measurements of pre-diction are *correlation* or the *analysis of covariance (ANCOVA/MANCOVA), regression analysis and logistic/logit regression.* In everyday terms, predic-tion means **forecasting** the future. In research this is only one rather specialised use of prediction, and often involves *computer simulations.* **Retrodiction** or **backcasting** means predicting what happened in the past; for example, when testing a theory about archaeological settlement patterns by looking at archaeological evidence in the field. However, it would be just as correct to talk about the theory predicting the archae-ology as to use the term retrodiction – see also *Prediction error, Variable, predictive, Proportional reduction in error.*

Prediction error

The extent to which something cannot be predicted on the basis of know-ledge about one set of factors, is taken as evidence about the effects of other factors. This is how astronomers identified the presence of planets they could not see, by showing that the orbits of planets they could see could not be accurately predicted from knowledge of the orbits and magni-tudes of other known planets. This prediction failure meant there must be some as yet undiscovered body or bodies influencing planetary orbits. In a similar way, for example, the school effect is calculated as that difference in achievement between similar pupils going to different schools which is left over when differences *correlated* with their prior achievement, gender, social class and ethnicity have been accounted for; the prediction error – see also *Prediction, Logistic/Logit regression, Pearson's product moment co-efficient* (for co-efficient of alienation), *Regression analysis.*

Premise

The first term in a deductive argument – **syllogism,** which forms the basis of its final conclusion. For example:

All men are mortal
Robert is a man
Therefore Robert is mortal.

'All men are mortal' is the premise. More loosely the term is used for the starting assumptions of a piece of research, including *domain assumptions*. See *Axiom, Axiomatic system, Deductive reasoning.*

Pre-structured data
See *Coding.*

Pre-test sensitivity
See *Post-test sensitivity.*

Prevalence
See *Incidence.*

Primacy and recency effects
The effect of the order in which someone experiences something. To avoid these effects, research instruments may be designed in multiple versions with the order of items randomised so that different subjects get them in different order or, in experiments, it may be arranged that each group experiences both conditions but in a different order. An *order effect.*

Principal component analysis
See *Factor analysis.*

Prior probability
See *Bayesian inference.*

Prisoner's dilemma
See *Game theory.*

Privacy and confidentiality
Privacy is a poorly defined concept and there is no statute law of privacy in the UK, but in terms of research ethics, subjects are regarded as having the right not to have their privacy invaded without their *informed consent,* unless researchers can provide some compelling argument to override this right – see *Observation covert or overt.* It is almost never the case that any harm arises from breaches of privacy as such, except to

the dignity of the subjects. Such harm as might occur would come from a breach of **confidentiality**; that is disclosing matters which allegedly ought to remain private.

Confidentiality is a duty established by some kind of commitment made not to disclose whatever information is to be regarded as confidential. The duty may be established by explicit agreements with research subjects, or by the more general commitment to one of the codes of ethics under which research is practised – see *Ethics* – and is established under the terms of the *Data Protection Act* for anyone who collects and keeps identifiable personal data, and in the NHS and for Councils with Social Services responsibilities by the Caldicott provisions – see *Caldicott guardians*.

Wiles, R., Crow, G., Heath, S. and Charles, V. (2006) *Anonymity and Confidentiality*, NCRM http://www.ncrm.ac.uk/research/outputs/publications/

See also *Anonymisation, Ethics, Deceit in research, Informed consent.*

Proactive dependency

See *Interview, dependent.*

Probability

The chance or likelihood that some outcome has or will occur, or that some state of affairs will or will not obtain. Usually expressed as the ratio of that outcome/state to all possible outcomes/states. For example the probability of a coin toss being a head is 1 divided by 2: (there is a one in two probability for heads). **Conditional probability:** All probabilities are really conditional probabilities insofar as they are dependent on certain conditions being satisfied (for example the coin toss example is conditional on the coin not being biased towards heads or tails). However, the term 'conditional probability' is usually used where the probability of one thing happening is expressed explicitly on condition that something else happens or is true, for example the (conditional) probability of men who are married (the condition) committing suicide. (The suicide *rate* for married men would be a more usual way of expressing this – see *Population at risk*). Conditional probability may be written P(A|B) meaning the probability of A given B – see *Bayesian Inference*. **Joint probability** in this example is the probability of any man in the population being *both* married and committing suicide.

See also *p-values.*

Easton, V and McColl, J (1997) 'Probability' *STEPS Statistics Glossary* updated by Young S. STEPS. http://www.stats.gla.ac.uk/steps/glossary/index.html

Probability density function (PDF/ϕ(x)/f(x))

A statistic expressing the probability that a randomly selected datum will be found at any particular point in a *frequency distribution*, hence definitive of the latter– see *Statistics software*.

Easton, V. and McColl, J. (1997) 'Probability', *STEPS Statistics Glossary*, updated by Young S. STEPS. http://www.stats.gla.ac.uk/steps/glossary/index.html

Probability sampling

See *Sample, probability.*

Probability values

See *p values.*

Probes

In *qualitative interviewing* the interviewer will approach the interview with a set of topics and perhaps a set of introductory sentences – probes – designed to encourage the interviewee to cover certain aspects of each topic. *Prompt* and probe may mean the same thing.

Profile

See *Scales.*

Progressive focussing

In *ethnographic research*, or in any other research which is open-ended and where the research question is developed as part of the research process, progressive focussing refers to the trial and error process of narrowing down the possibilities towards making the final decision about the focus of the research.

Projective tests

See *Objective tests.*

Prompts

(1) In *questionnaire* research, where respondents might not quite understand the question, interviewers may be supplied with prompts to help them. For example the question might ask about someone's holiday,

which may give rise to respondents wondering if a single day counts as a holiday. In that case the prompt might be 'a couple of days or longer'. However, in survey research, questionnaire designers try to design out any ambiguity by the phrasing of questions; (2) in *qualitative interviewing* the term prompt may be used instead of question – see *probe.*

Proportional reduction in error (PRE)/Lambda (λ)

The extent to which a prediction based on one variable can be improved in accuracy by a prediction made on the basis of another variable; used as a measure of *association* with nominal level data, where the *direction of effect* is assumed – see *Data, levels of.*

Table 11 shows (invented) GCSE performance data for 300 pupils. In guessing the GCSE score of any pupil picked at random, without knowledge of gender differences, the best bet would be that s/he gained 5 GCSEs grade C or above. In effect that would be guessing that this was the outcome for all pupils. This would be wrong $300-160 = 140$ times. With knowledge of gender difference the best bets would be that all no boys and all girls got 5 grade Cs and above. The combined error here would be $(150-77) + (150-87) = 73+63 = 136$. So knowledge of gender differences reduced the number of prediction errors by $140-136 = 4$. This is expressed as a proportion with the statistic lambda (λ):

$$\text{Lambda } (\lambda) = \frac{\text{Errors using rule 1} - \text{Errors using ruke 2}}{\text{Errors using rule 1}}$$

$$= \frac{140 - 136}{140} = 0.029 = 2.9\%$$

So it can be said that gender accounts for 2.9% of the difference in GCSE results in this data set – see also *Gamma,* and *Type 1 and type 2 errors.*

Musalia, J. (2006) *Chapter 7: Measures of Association: nominal and ordinal variables,* University of West Kentucky www.wku.edu/~john.musalia/soc300/

Table 11 Performance at GCSE for 300 pupils (invented data)

	5 GCSEs Grade C+	Less than 5 GCSEs Grade C+	Total
Boys	73	77	150
Girls	87	63	150
Total	160	140	300

Prospective studies/prospectivity

Prospective studies begin before the events of interest have happened to the subjects. This provides an opportunity to gather information about them at the outset (*pre*) to provide a base-line for measuring any changes which occur. *Controlled experiments*, *longitudinal surveys*, and *action research* are prospective. *Retrospective* studies study the subjects only after the events of interest have happened. This may lead to difficulties in deciding whether any differences found were there all the time or were caused by the events of interest.

Protocol

A specification for the procedures which should be followed in conducting a piece of research, including matters such as how subjects should be briefed or debriefed, when observations should be made and such like. Protocol is built into most research *instruments* at least insofar as they indicate the order of in which questions should be asked. **Fidelity to protocol** in an *experiment* or in a *survey* means that subjects will have been treated alike when they should have been treated alike and differently when they should have been treated differently – see *Interviewer effects*. If an explicit protocol is followed it makes the auditability or procedural *objectivity* of the research easier to accomplish and would facilitate *replication*. However, for those who seek naturalistic validity, faithfully following protocols prevents the researcher responding to each subject or situation in a sensitive and 'natural' way, and protocols for *qualitative interviews* or *ethnographic research* may be little more than check lists of topics to be addressed and things to look out for – see *Validity, naturalistic*.

Proxemics

See *Kinesic*.

Proxy measure

The measurement of one thing as an indication of another. See *Concept-indicator relationship*.

Pruning (trimming)

Analysing less than the complete range of a data set in order to exclude *outliers* – see also *Inter-quartile range, Windsorisation*.

Psephology

The study of voting behaviour.

UK Political Information: www.ukpolitical.info/
British Polling Council: www.britishpollingcouncil.org/

Pseudo-anonymisation (quasi-anonymisation)

Hiding the identity of respondents by using codes known only to the researcher(s).

Pseudo cohort analysis

In a true *cohort study* the same people are studied at various points in their lives. Pseudo cohort analysis attempts to emulate this with data from repeated *cross-sectional* surveys. For example, the experiences of a sample of those aged 20 to 24 in one survey are taken as if they were the earlier experiences of those aged 21 to 25 sampled one year later. American research often describes this simply as a *cohort study* or *panel study*.

Uren, Z. (2006) *The GHS Pseudo Cohort Dataset (GHSPCD): Introduction and methodology*, UK Office for National Statistics http://www.statistics.gov.uk/articles/nojournal/Sept06SMB_Uren.pdf

Pseudo randomisation (quasi randomisation)

Using techniques such as drawing lots or tossing coins to randomise rather than using random number tables/generators. The distinction is unimportant in most social research.

Psychometrics

The theory and technique of educational and psychological trait measurement, and research into psychological traits and abilities using tests and other *instruments* – see *Attitude, Guttman scale, Objective and projective tests, Semantic differential, Standardisation, Test theory, Thurstone scale*.

Kline, T. (2005) *Psychological Testing: a practical approach to design and evaluation*, London: Sage

Public Health Observatories

Regional agencies across the UK gathering, collating and disseminating *epidemiological* information. Access to each can be made through the Association of Public Health Observatories: www.apho.org.uk

Publication bias

See *Bias, publication.*

Purposive sampling

See *Sample, purposive.*

p values

The results of tests of *statistical significance* are reported as values of *p* for probability (Table 12 shows examples). Either the precise value for *p* is cited, or a value which p is less than, as in *p<0.05* (*p* is less than 0.05).

Table 12 p values in tests of statistical significance.

p < 0.001	p is less than 0.001, there is only 1 chance in 1000 of a result like this cropping up by chance: the one in one thousand *alpha level*/level of significance.	'Very highly statistically significant' sometimes indicated ***
p < 0.01	p is less than 0.01.There is only 1 chance in one hundred of a result like this cropping up by chance: the 1% *alpha level*/level of significance.	'Highly statistically significant', sometimes indicated **
p < 0.05	p is less than 0.05. There are only five chances in 100 of a result like this cropping up by chance. The 5% *alpha level*/level of significance. This is the highest value for p which statisticians will accept for a statistically significant result	'Statistically significant', sometimes indicated *
p > 0.05	p is more than 0.05, there is a greater than 5% chance of a result like this cropping up by chance.	'Not statistically significant' – sometimes written NS, or where authors use asterisks indicated by no asterisks at all.

Note that the 5% (0.05) level of significance/*alpha level* is the same as the 95% level of confidence and the 1% level of significance/*alpha level* is the same as the 99% level of confidence as used in indicating *confidence intervals.*

Pygmalion effect

See *Expectancy effect.*

Q

Statistic reported by Tukey's HSD test – see *Post hoc tests*.

Q analysis

(Q sort, Q methodology, Q technique): procedure in which respondents are given a large number of sets of statements drawn from the same *concourse* and asked to rank order them, usually according to the strength of their agreement or disagreement. Then *factor analysis* is performed on the results, creating groupings of respondents according to the profiles of their responses. Much used in market segmentation analysis to characterise particular groups of consumers – see *Market research*, in *psephology* to characterise different categories of voters, and elsewhere.

Brown, S.(1991) *Q Methodological Tutorial*, Kent State University. http://facstaff.uww.edu/cottlec/QArchive/Primer1.html

QALY

See *Utility*.

QCA

See *Qualitative comparative analysis*.

QDA software

See *Computer Assisted Qualitative Data Analysis*.

QLL (Qualitative longitudinal research)

For example the *ESRC* 'Timescape project' http://www.timescapes.leeds.ac.uk/methods-ethics/. See also Longitudinal research.

See special 2003 edition of the *International Journal of Social Research Methodology*, 6 (3) 189–199 edited by Holland, J., Thompson, R. and Plumridge L.

And the special 2007 issue of *Social Policy and Society*, 6 (4) 529–532 edited by Corden, J. and Miller, J.

Q methodology, Q sort, Q technique

See *Q analysis*.

QnLR

Quantitative longitudinal data analysis, includes *Repeat cross-sectional surveys, Panel studies, Longitudinal survey, Cohort studies, Pseudo cohort analysis, Event analysis, Time series analysis*.

Qualia

See Corrigibility.

Qualidata

See *Data archives*.

Qualitative comparative analysis (QCA)

Variety of variable-based *comparative analysis* and of *cross-case analysis* associated with Charles Ragin which employed *Boolean algebra*, and latterly *fuzzy logic*, comparing cases, societies and or historical periods in terms of arrays of variables.

Ragin, C. (n.d.) *Fuzzy set/Qualitative Comparative Analysis – What is QCA?* University of Arizona. www.u.arizona.edu/~cragin/fsQCA provides software downloads as well as instructional material and academic papers

Qualitative interviews

Loosely structured/semi-structured interviews designed principally to collect qualitative data, although most also collect some numerical data, such as age, in order to characterise the sample. There is no agreed point at which questionnaire research using open questions (see *Question formats*) becomes a qualitative interview, but a major consideration which differentiates the two is that in survey research using *questionnaires* it is considered desirable to standardise the interview situation for all respondents – same briefing, same questions and so on, to:

- exclude the *confounding* influence of their being treated differently at interview,
- generate the same kind of data at the same level for each respondent (see *Data, levels of*),
- be able to make point by point comparison between respondents.

By contrast, in qualitative interviews it is considered desirable for the interviewer to respond to each interviewee as a unique person, and to allow, indeed encourage, interviewees to expand on topics as they wish and to raise topics of their own. Making a close, trusting relationship with respondents may be regarded as a benefit. Associated with this the latent status of the interviewer may be stressed; for example that only women are appropriate as interviewers for women – see *Interviewer effects*. The instrument for a qualitative interview, if there is one, is more likely to be a list of topics or *prompts*, which can be dealt with in any order. The results of such interviews are data which have to be analysed, usually in terms of categories decided post hoc by the contents of the corpus of interviews – by *thematic analysis, narrative analysis* or *sequential analysis,* for example, or by the techniques prescribed for *grounded theory*. It is rarely the case that comparisons can be made on a point by point basis across all respondents. The case in favour of qualitative interviews is that:

- they generate much richer data,
- responses are expressed in the language respondents would usually use – see *emic,*
- unlike *questionnaire* research, they do not force respondents to make responses to questions which may not be of great relevance to them,
- they are more likely to elicit honest disclosure.

On the final point, evidence is to the contrary suggesting that where the topics are sensitive or disreputable, the greater the social distance between interviewer and interviewee the more likely it is that responses will be honest.

Colker, A. (n.d.) 'Developing Interviews – preparing an interview protocol', *Online Evaluation Resource Library (OERL)* http://oerl.sri.com/module/mod6/m6_p1.html
Colker, A. (n.d.) 'Developing Interviews – Administering interviews', *Online Evaluation Resource Library (OERL)* http://oerl.sri.com/module/mod7/m7_p1.html

Qualitative longitudinal research

See *QLL (Qualitative longitudinal research).*

Qualitative research and quantitative research, usually juxtaposed with the following differentiating characteristics:

Table 13   Stereotypical characteristics of qualitative and quantitative research

Qualitative	Quantitative
• Collects and analyses non-numerical data	• Collects and analyses numerical data
• Investigates meaning and experience	• Investigates cause and effect
• Assumes a subject matter which is different from that of the natural sciences and hence that different methods should be adopted, such as participant *observation research* , *ethnographic research*, and *qualitative interviewing*	• Assumes a subject matter which is similar to that of the natural sciences and hence assumes that the methods of the social sciences should be similar to those of the natural science – see *Unity of Science thesis*
• Demands that qualitative research should be judged according to quality criteria which are different from those of the natural sciences. See *Criteria for evaluating research*	• Accepts that social scientific and behavioural research should be judged according to the same quality criteria as the natural sciences. See *Criteria for evaluating research*

However, there is no such neat distinction in reality:

- Many qualitative researchers, while they do not collect numerical data, nonetheless make quasi-numerical claims about what often, usually or rarely happens to many, few, or most people.
- All quantitative research begins with some qualitative decisions as to what will be regarded as an instance of this or that.
- Many *ethnographic studies* purport to describe what causes what to happen.
- There are researchers who adopt a *psychometric* and hence a quantitative approach to meaning.
- Some qualitative researchers model their research on the natural sciences and are content to be judged according to the criteria of the natural sciences.

Chenail, R. (1992) 'Qualitative Research: central tendencies and ranges', *The Qualitative Report*, **1**(4) www.nova.edu/ssss/QR

Q

Quality Adjusted Life Year (QALY)

See *Utility*.

Quartiles and Quantiles

See *Percentiles*.

Quasi-anonymisation

See *Pseudo-anonymisation, Stanines.*

Quasi-experiments

See Experiments, true and quasi.

Quasi randomisation

See *Pseudo randomisation.*

Queer theory

Applies to the study of sex and gender (first) – particularly gay and lesbian identities and secondly to all aspects of identity, to the effect that identity is always constructed through the *discourses* of the time and place. Research is largely through *deconstruction* and reflection on personal experience. Identity is considered *fragmented* and *decentered.* Queer theory spans *social constructionism* and *post-modernism* and literary and artistic criticism as well as social and psychological science.

> Green, A. (2007) 'Queer Theory and Sociology: Locating the Subject and the Self in Sexuality Studies', *Sociological Theory* **25**,1:26–45

Question banks

Questions and other elicitations used previously in surveys, banked in a repository;

- to reduce the need for unnecessary design and piloting of new *questionnaires* when adequate ones already exist,
- to encourage the use of standard instruments where possible, to facilitate direct comparison between different pieces of research.

For government research this accompanies a drive for researchers to use common definitions of terms, for example a standard classification of ethnic groups. See *Harmonised concepts and questions.*

The CASS question bank (http://qb.soc.surrey.ac.uk/) provides access to the *questionnaires* used in a wide variety of large scale surveys, sometimes directly, sometimes via links or addresses.

Question formats

Various question formats may be used on a *questionnaire* or similar *instrument.* Elicitations would be a more accurate term, since not all

Table 14   Features of open and closed questions

Closed (forced-choice) questions	Open questions (write-ins)
Framework for analysis devised before the questionnaire is used: data are *pre-structured*	Final framework for analysis devised after reviewing the responses to decide *coding* scheme
All legitimate responses provided Respondents are restricted to these Other responses will be ignored	Any response is allowable
Criticised for forcing respondents to make answers to questions: • which may not be important to them, • in language and categories they might not choose for themselves; in etic terms – see *emic*	Criticised for: • producing responses many of which cannot be used, since the researcher will not know what they mean • difficult to make point by point comparisons between respondents • producing data only at the nominal level • confounding numerical analysis because some respondents will make more than one point in response to a single question
Defended as: • producing data at a pre-specified level including internal level – see *Data, levels of* • if at the interval level, allowing for analysis of results using parametric statistics – *see Statistics, parametric and non-parametric* • confronting each respondent with the same questions allows point by point comparisons between all respondents	Defended as: • producing richer data • being expressed in terms relevant to respondents phrased as they choose. – see *emic* • considered particularly appropriate for *pilot studies*

Q

of them are grammatically questions, but questions is the usual term. A major distinction is between open and closed questions (see Table 14).

Farrall, S. Bannister, J., Ditton, J. and Gilchrist, E. (1997) 'Open and Closed Questions', *Social Research Update* Issue 17 http://sru.soc.surrey.ac.uk/

Different question formats generate data of different kinds at different levels – see *Data, levels of*:

Closed (or forced choice) questions – all permissible options are provided for

Dichotomous and closed (generating nominal level data)

Are you male or female ? Male ❏ *Female* ❏

Multiple choice and closed (generating interval level data)

Which of the following would apply to you (ring your interest): *I am interested in: Rambling, Climbing, Pony trekking, Scuba diving*

Multiple choice and closed (generating interval level data)

How many cigarettes did you smoke yesterday?

None	*1–5*	*6–10*	*11–20*	*21–30*	*30+*	*Don't know*
❏	❏	❏	❏	❏	❏	❏

Likert scale (closed, generating ordinal level data) – see *Likert scale*

How strongly do you agree or disagree with this statement?

Young people these days have no respect for older people
Strongly

Disagree	*Disagree*	*Don't know*	*Agree*	*Strongly agree*
❏	❏	❏	❏	❏

Semantic differential (closed, for each item, generates something approaching interval level data) – see *Semantic differential*

Tick the box which is closest to your feelings
Doctors are...

Warm [] [] [] [] [] [] [] *Cold*
Wise [] [] [] [] [] [] [] *Foolish*

Rating scale (closed, generating ordinal level data) – see *Rating*

Please rate the quality of the accommodation as:
Excellent 1 [ ] Good 2 [ ] Fair 3 [ ] Poor 4 [ ] Very Poor 5 [ ]

Visual analogue scale (closed, generating interval level data):

Q

Please indicate how pleased you were with your treatment by marking the thermometer:

Open-ended questions
(Generating qualitative data)

Unstructured (or better, 'loosely structured')
What does it mean to you to be a woman in a profession dominated by males?

Sentence completion
To me a good day at work means ....

Repertory grid technique – see also *Repertory grid technique*
Can you tell me in what way these two [people] are alike, and unlike this other [person] ?

In addition, responses can be elicited by asking respondents to complete half-finished stories, or to describe what is shown in a picture or on a video. Instead of answering questions respondents may be asked to put cards in rank order or in piles of different kinds – see *Card sorting*, or in experiments, to press buttons. See also *Bias, positional, Guttman scale, Questionnaire, Questionnaire administration, Questions, filter, Questions, leading, Questions positive and negative, Ranking, Thurstone Scale, Test theory.*

Smith, T. (1993) 'Little things matter: a sampler of how differences in questionnaire format can affect survey responses', Chicago, IL: General Social Survey (GSS Methodological Report No. 78). www.icpsr.umich.edu:8080/GSS

Q

Questionnaire
Instrument consisting of a set of questions, or other requests for information, for response by subjects of research, who either read or have it read to them, and respond by writing/keying/speaking their responses or having them audio recorded or written/keyed for them. Some questionnaires are given other names such as schedules, *inventories* or profiles. Used not only in survey research but also in experimental research. Instruments which consist of questions to the researcher such as observation schedules are essentially similar, but are not usually called questionnaires – see *Observation, pre-structured or intuitive.*

The position in a questionnaire may influence the pattern of responses to an item – see *Bias, positional, Primacy and recency effects* – so sometimes multiple versions of a questionnaire are produced with question order randomised so that each respondent answers questions in a different order – see also *Alternate forms tests, Questionnaire administration, Question formats, Questions, filter, Questions positive and negative.*

Punj, Girish (1997) *Questionnaire design*, Storrs, CT: University of Connecticut, School of Business Administration. www.lib.uconn.edu/~punj/m35012.pdf

Zalles, D. (n.d.) 'Determining if Questionnaires should be used', *Online Evaluation Resource Library (OERL).* http://oerl.sri.com/module/mod1/m1_p1.html

Galloway, K. (n.d.) *Questionnaire Design & Analysis: A Workbook by Alison Galloway* http://www.tardis.ed.ac.uk/~kate/qmcweb/qcont.htm

Questionnaire administration

Research on the efficacy of different methods of administering questionnaires (see Table 15) gives mixed results, except that postal questionnaires always have higher rates of non-response, and that self-completed questionnaires seem to elicit fuller disclosures of sensitive information than face-to-face administration. In this regard British

Table 15 Methods of administering questionnaires

Acronym	Description
PAPI/PAPTI	Paper and pencil personal interview – interviewer asks questions and records on paper. Face-to-face or by telephone
SAQ	Paper and pencil self-administered questionnaire; respondent answers on paper. Face-to-face briefing or delivered by post
ASAQ	Audio player administered questionnaire – respondent hears recorded questions through headphones and answers on paper. Briefing is usually face-to-face
CAPI/CATI	Interviewer reads aloud questions from computer screen and keys in respondent's answers. Face-to-face or telephone
CASI	Computer-assisted self-administered interviews where interviewer hands lap-top to respondent, questions are on screen and respondent keys in responses. Briefing may be face-to-face
ACASI	As above but questions on screen and heard though earphones
TDE	Respondent is read questions over telephone/hears recording of questions over the telephone and responds using telephone keys
OLQ	On-line questionnaires: respondent replies to questions on PC: web-based or e-mailed (Benfield 2006)
–	Loosely structured interviews: see *Qualitative interviews*

Crime Survey researchers claim that CASI administration seems to be particularly effective.

Selwyn, N. and Robson, K. (1998) 'Using e-mail as a research tool' *Social Research Update* Issue 21. http://sru.soc.surrey.ac.uk/

Sainsbury, R., Ditch, J. and Hutton, S. (1993) 'Computer Assisted Interviewing' *Social Research Update* Issue 3. http://sru.soc.surrey.ac.uk/

Benfield, J. (2006) 'Internet-based data collection: promises and realities' *Journal of Research Practice* Vol 2(2). http://jrp.icaap.org/index.php/jr

Questions, filter (routing questions)

Used to route respondents through a *questionnaire* to answer only those questions relevant to them. For example: 'If response is 'yes' go to question 14, if 'no' go to question 26'.

Questions, leading

Of *questionnaires* and *qualitative interviews*. All questions are leading in that they lead to an answer. But the term 'leading question' is used to refer to intimations to the respondent that one answer rather than another might be preferred by the researcher – see *Bias, acquiescence*, *Bias, co-operation*, or might lead the researchers to think better of the respondent – *Bias, self-serving*. The lead might be in the phrasing of the question, or its positioning, or it might be in the demeanour or characteristics of the interviewer (an *interviewer effect*). Leading questions are particularly difficult to avoid where the topic is some deviant behaviour or stigmatised status and respondents feel inclined to give an *account*. In *qualitative interviews*, interviewers often 'lead' by making encouraging responses where the interviewee says something that interests them – See *Bias, narrative, Expectancy effects*. See also *Demand characteristics*.

Questions, positive and negative

Whether questions are phrased positively or negatively can make a considerable difference to responses. For options: 'Were you happy with your treatment?' or 'Were you unhappy with your treatment?', dissatisfied people are more likely to answer 'no' to the first question than they are to answer 'yes' to the second. Since this seems to be a standard effect across all respondents it doesn't matter within the context of one survey, but it would matter in comparing the results of one survey containing the negative form and another containing the positive form.

Cohen, G., Forbes, J. and Garraway, M. (1996) 'Can different patient satisfaction surveys yield consistent results? A comparison of three surveys', *British Medical Journal*, **313** (7061): 841–4. www.bmj.com/

Queue models/simulations/theory

A family of solutions to problems which involve any kind of queue, ranging from queues at tills, to traffic flows, to production lines. Now usually implemented via computer simulations.

Jenson, P. (2004) 'Queuing' *Operations Research Models and Methods*. www.me.utexas.edu/~jensen/ORMM/models/index.html

Quicksort

See *Q analysis*.

Quixotic reliability

See *Reliability*.

Quota sample

See *Sample, quota*.

QSR Nvivo

See *Computer assisted qualitative data analysis*.

Q

r

Usually *Pearson's product moment correlation co-efficient* but sometimes spearman's rank order correlation co-efficient (r_s otherwise rho or ρ) and sometimes other correlation co-efficients.

RA

See *Rapid Appraisal*.

Racism

See *Bias, exoticism, Culture-fair, Ethnocentrism, Orientalism, Othering, Post-colonial anthropology, Subalton studies*.

Random (stochastic)

Often defined as 'determined by chance'. However, nothing is really determined by chance. For example, physics would allow an entirely adequate deterministic description of why a dice fell in a particular way on a particular occasion, without the necessity of referring to 'chance', or 'luck' (see *Determinism)*. Thus calling a dice throw 'random' really refers to the fact that the way it falls cannot accurately be predicted (except to predict that it will fall in one of six ways), and more practically, that the way it falls will be determined independently of any feature of the game of which the dice throw is a constituent and of the characteristics, hopes and position in the game of any of the players. The use of randomising devices in research – such as *random allocation*, is to effect a similar causal independence. There is philosophical debate as to whether randomness is an inherent feature of the processes to which it applies, or whether it is actually a characteristic of our limited predictive abilities. In the latter case the amount of randomness in the world would be reduced if we got better at prediction. The latter position is taken by Bayesian statisticians, who believe that probabilities are simply estimates by rational judges, rather than qualities inherent in processes – see also *Random allocation/randomisation, Random error, Bayesian inference*.

Random allocation/randomisation

Usually accomplished by using a randomising computer programme, or a table of random numbers, but for simple situations can be done by tossing a coin for each subject or writing what is to be randomised on cards, shuffling and dealing (**pseudo** or **quasi randomisation**).

In experiments, random allocation has usually proved the most effective way of producing two or more *comparison groups* which are similar, in order to control out subject characteristics which might otherwise *confound* the experimental results (Schutz *et al.*,1995). It also allows for easy *blinding* or at least allocation of subjects to groups uninfluenced by the prejudices of the researcher – see *Randomised controlled experiments/trials*.

In survey sample selection, the principle of randomisation is used for probability sampling in order to select a *representative* sample, and to generate data which are amenable to analysis using parametric statistics – see *Statistics, parametric and non-parametric*. Probability sampling is *blind* sampling to the degree that selection of subjects is not influenced by the prejudices of the researcher – see *Sample, probability*.

In instrument design, the order of items on the instrument may be randomised so as to control out the effect on responses of where an item appears in the sequence – see *Bias, positional, Order effects, Primacy and recency effects*. See also *Alternate forms test, Random*.

Schultz, K., Chalmers, I., Hayes, R. and Altman, D. (1995) 'Empirical evidence of bias: dimensions of methodic quality associated with estimates of treatment effects in controlled trials', *Journal of the American Medical Association*, **273**: 408–12

Random effect

See *Effect, fixed and random*.

Randomised/randomized controlled experiment/trial (RCT)

Sometimes distinguished from other *experiments* as 'true experiments' because the *comparison groups* are formed by *random allocation*. 'Experiment' tends to be used in theoretical research and 'trial' or RCT in the kinds of *effectiveness research* associated with evidence-based practice, where RCTs are regarded as the 'gold standard' among methods for producing evidence. This is because, if they are possible to conduct, they do provide the most convincing evidence for the causal relationships operating under the experimental conditions. But only if the same conditions obtain elsewhere will the experimental results have external validity. (see *Generalisation, Validity external*). By comparison with other kinds of experiments RCTs usually show smaller effect sizes. This is taken to indicate that with other experimental designs effect size measures are confounded by prior differences between subjects which were not controlled out by the way comparison groups were formed – see *Effect size (ES) measures, Confounding, Control direct and statistical*. RCTs are sometimes regarded as ethically suspect insofar as chance rather than a subject's informed choice determines what treatment each receives. By contrast some regard chance as the fairest way to distribute unknown risks, so long as subjects have given *informed consent* to being entered into such a lottery.

Sibbald, B. and Roland, M.(1998) 'Understanding controlled trials; why are randomised controlled trials important? *British Medical Journal 316:201*. www.bmj.com
Jadad, A. (1998) *Randomized Controlled Trials: a user's guide'*, London: BMJ Books. www. cgmh.org.tw/intr/intr5/c6700/OBGYN/F/Randomized%20tial/questions.html

Random sampling

See *Sample, probability*.

Random and systematic error

Large and significant events may occur by chance, but random error usually refers to many small errors, which in a large sample will tend towards cancelling each other out, so that they have little effect on aggregated results. This is unlike **systematic error** which will bias results systematically in a particular direction – see *Bias*. Where random errors are measurable and many, those for a single measure are likely to approximate a *normal distribution*, allowing for the calculation of an estimate of the true measure for the population and its *confidence interval* – see *Central limit theorem. Measurement error* and *Sampling error* are two important examples of random error.

Range

The distance between the highest and the lowest score in a data set, see *Central tendency and dispersion, Inter quartile range*.

Range ratio

In comparing inequality among households for income, the 95/20 ratio would be the *ratio* of the income of the household at the 95th *percentile*, to the income of the household at the 20th percentile. The 95/20, the 95/50 and the 50/20 are those most commonly used in the study of income inequality. Comparison is restricted to that between just the two percentiles chosen, and thus is blind to the overall shape of income inequality. See also *Inequality measures and metrics, Percentile shares*.

R

Ranking

Putting a number of given entities in order; 1st, 2nd, 3rd, last; producing data at the ordinal level – *see Data, levels of.*

Table 16 An example of a ranking scale, generating ordinal level data

Please put the following aspects of hotel accommodation in order of importance from 1 to 5 with 1st as the most important to you and 5th as the least. Tick the box which corresponds with your ranking.					
	1st	2nd	3rd	4th	5th
Comfortable beds					
Clean rooms					
Friendly staff					
Extensive menu					
Competitive pricing					

RAP

See *Reflective appraisal of program.*

Rapid appraisal (RA)

(1) Multi-disciplinary, *multi-method research* which began its life as **Rapid rural appraisal (RRA)** for researching the agronomic, health, nutritional, educational and other needs of third world rural communities, and often in disaster relief and reconstruction, but is increasingly used in developed countries; in the UK, especially for investigating health needs in research sponsored by Primary Health Care Trusts. Many methods of gathering data may be used. Sampling of interviewees tends to be purposive either on the maximum variability principle, or to represent all stake-holder groups – see *Sample, maximum variability, Sample, purposive.* An emphasis will be on how subjects themselves define their needs and how they envisage solutions to problems. As the name suggests, a premium is placed on speed, but to offset the possibility of inaccuracies arising from this, much attention is given to *triangulation* as a way of verifying the data from different sources. (FAO n.d., Murray 1999) See also *Community needs profile.* (2)Techniques of conducting research rapidly (Alemi 2004), sometimes identical with *Rapid Institutional appraisal.*

FAO (n.d.) Chapter 8: Rapid Rural Appraisal. *FAO Corporate Document Repository* www.fao.org/docrep/W3241E/w3241e09.htm

Murray, S. *(1999)* Experiences with "rapid appraisal" in primary care: involving the public in assessing health needs, orientating staff, and educating medical students' *British Medical Journal* **318**:440–444 www.bmj.com

Alemi, F. (2004) 'Rapid Analysis' in *Decision analysis in health care*, George Mason University http://gunston.gmu.edu/healthscience/730/default.asp

Rapid institutional appraisal (RIA)

Similar in purpose and procedure to *Rapid Appraisal*, but practised at the level of an organisation, for organisational development purposes.

Armson, R. and Ison, R.L. and Short, L. and Ramage, M. and Reynolds, M. (2001) *Rapid institutional appraisal. Systemic Practice and Action Research,* **14** (6) pp. 763–777. ISSN 1094–429X http://oro.open.ac.uk/27/

Rasch scales

See *Test theory*.

Rashomon effect

In *Ethnographic research*: named after the film 'Rashomon' by the Japanese director Akria Korosawa which tempts the audience into a number of different interpretations of the narrative between which it is difficult, if not impossible, to decide. Applied to the situation where two researchers produce radically different, incommensurate pictures of much the same phenomenon – see *commensurability*. Term coined in connection with the controversy surrounding Derek Freeman's critique of Margaret Mead's ethnographic study of Samoa to which he juxtaposed his own study (Strain 1997). But it could have been applied to an earlier controversy surrounding the repetition by Oscar Lewis of a study of a village in Mexico previously studied by Robert Redfield (Bock 1980). It is quite common that different pieces of ethnographic research give different impressions. This is sometimes mobilised in criticism of *qualitative research* as evidence of its unreliability and hence invalidity – see *reliability*. But equally it can be regarded as the result of sampling differences between two pieces of research, which were at different times, involved different subjects, and were probably not in exactly the same location, and as due to the fact that much of the descriptions offered by ethnographic researchers are of qualities which are matters of interpretation rather than matters of fact – see *Corrigible, Multiple realities*. For example, where Redfield saw co-operation, Lewis saw competition, but most societies involve both, and these manifest themselves differently at different times and in the behaviour of different people, and it would be difficult to say whether emphasising one more than the other was right or wrong. The lesson from the Rashomon effect is that

R

generalisation from what an ethnographer actually studied to those aspects of the case that s/he did not study (for example from one classroom observed to other classrooms unobserved) is highly speculative. Some of the Rashomon effect might be resolved by *triangulation*, but it refers first and foremost to those discrepancies which triangulation cannot resolve.

Strain, S. (1997) 'Margaret Mead, Derek Freeman and the Samoans', *University of South Florida*, St. Petersburg. www.stpt.usf.edu/~jsokolov/314mead1.htm

Bock, P. (1980) Tepoztlan reconsidered', *Journal of Latin American Lore*, **6**(1):129–150 www.sonoma.edu/Anthropology/wahrhaftig/bock.html

Rate

(1) A proportional measure such as a percentage (which is a rate per 100). The 'out of' figure or *denominator* is usually chosen for convenience to avoid having figures which begin on the right hand side of the decimal point and to keep the figures on the left hand side of the point to two or three digits; hence the murder rate per year for the UK is usually expressed per million, because murder is so rare, and the rate of marital breakdown is usually given as a percentage, because marital breakdown is common. Rates are used as a way of facilitating comparisons between two populations of different sizes, by *standardising* the denominator; (2) the speed at which something happens; a measure of change per time period, for example, number of examination papers marked per hour.

Rater agreement

See *Inter-rater reliability*.

Rating

Assigning a value to an entity from a given scale of values. Scoring from 1 to 100, will generate 'true' interval level data – see *Data, levels of*, but only so long as there is no bias against using parts of the scale. Such biases are common however – for example examiners rarely use the marks above 85 or below 20 – see also *Error of central tendency*. In such cases the data are better regarded as *plastic interval level* and as not suitable for analysis using parametric statistics – see *Statistics, parametric and non-parametric*. Many rating scales such as *Likert scales* assume a standard sized interval between each value; for example that the distance between 'very good' and 'good', is the same as that between 'neutral' and 'bad', but this cannot be assumed without considerable effort in validating the scale. More sophisticated rating scales are based on research and development to standardise interval size, for example, *Thurstone* and *Rasch* scales. See also *Question formats, Test theory*.

Table 17 An example of a rating scale – generating plastic interval data

	Very important	Important	Neither important nor unimportant	Not important	Very unimportant
Please indicate how important to you are the following aspects of hotel accommodation. Tick the answer closest to your own view					
Comfortable beds					
Clean rooms					
Friendly staff					
Competitive pricing					
Score each tick	5	4	3	2	1

Ratio

A measure showing the relative size of two numbers. For example if one group in an experiment has a mean score of 12 and another of 16, the ratio between them is shown as 12:16 (or 16:12) or 3:4 (or 4:3). It can also be shown as 0.75 which is derived by dividing the first figure by the second (3/4=0.75) in which case it really stands for 0.75:1, or, for the ratio expressed the other way round 4/3 = 1.33 meaning 1.33:1 spoken as '1.33 to 1'. See *Odds ratio* and *Risk ratio* in the entry for *Effect size (ES) and measures*.

R

Ratio level data

See *Data, levels of.*

Rational choice theory

Research and analysis on the assumption that the social structure and patterns of activity in society result from individuals attempting to maximise benefits and minimise costs, where these include both material and non-material benefits and losses; a common set of assumptions in micro-economics, political theory and some kinds of sociology. Inquiry is often pursued through *game theoretic models*, sometimes implemented as *computer simulations.* See also Instrumental rationality *(Instrumentalism), Methodological individualism.*

Scott, J. (2000) 'Rational choice theory', in Browning, G.,Hacli, A. and Webster, F. (eds) *Understanding Contemporary Society: theories of the present,'* London: Sage download from http://privatewww.essex.ac.uk/~scottj/socscot7.htm

Rational-empirical

See *Hermeneutic-historical.*

Rationalism

Epistemology: term for epistemological theories that maintain that (sound) reasoning is the source of sound knowledge. Originally most usually contrasted with the placing of trust in religious faith, in (allegedly) innate belief, or in ideas and practices based on emotion – all designated as **irrationalism**. From the twentieth century onwards, more problematically contrasted with the idea that testing ideas against empirical evidence is the basis of sound knowledge. Here perhaps best thought of as an assumption that our theories – so long as they are logical, should tell us what is evidence and what it means, rather than as with *empiricism,* that our theories should be determined by the evidence. In this sense the continental rationalism of René Descartes (see *Philosophers*), marxism, and *critical theory* are rationalist, as are some aspects of *feminist epistemology. Theory data dependency* means that empiricism without rationalism is impossible, hence Popper's *critical rationalism, pragmatism, and realism* are both rationalist and empiricist, while self-named empiricist approaches in practice are shaped by theorising and are also rationalist in this sense.

RCT

See *Randomised controlled experiments/trials.*

RD

See *Recipient design.*

RDS

See *Sample, respondent driven (RDS).*

Reactive dependency

See *Interview, dependent.*

Reactivity

See *Subject reactivity.*

Readership research

See *Audience research*.

Realism

(1) In *Epistemology and Ontology* the doctrine that there are entities which exist independently of our knowledge or ideas about them. This idea of mind-independent entities is a constituent of most people's common-sense and of all theories uncontroversially called 'scientific': of *critical rationalism, empiricism* (naïve realism/natural realism), *operationalism, positivism, logical positivism, pragmatism* and *realism*. S*ocial constructionism* may have, *and post-modernism* does have, strong anti-realist tendencies where realism is defined in this way. (2) As with the previous notion but more narrowly referring to a range of philosophical positions, named explicitly as 'realism', including critical realism, critical naturalism, experimental realism, feminist realism, subtle realism, scientific realism. There is considerable overlap between these positions and diversity within them, and many common points with *critical rationalism* and with the various strands of *pragmatism* which were influential in the development of realist philosophy. What these realists treat as real is illustrated by contrasting this realism with *empiricism* ("naïve realism"). A strict *empiricist* point of view tries to equate the real with what is observable via the senses, augmented or not with appropriate instruments – see *operationalism*. Since they cannot be seen, heard, smelt and so on, empiricists should find 'society/sociality/social relationships' and such like, unreal by contrast with the reality of individuals and their observable behaviour. In practice though, most empiricists operate with a more expansive definition of the empirical. Realists, by contrast, regard as real not only what can be observed, but also what is assumed to underlie what is observed and to give rise to it – **'inferential empiricism'**. Such entities, often called 'mechanisms', include electricity, gravity and so on. For an empiricist what indicates real existence are the qualities an entity has which make it possible for us to perceive it. For a realist the reality test is whether a postulated entity can bring about changes in the things that we can observe; hence forces and structures – including social structures – can be counted as among real entities in a way that it is difficult under the terms of strict empiricism. The two positions also differ in the way they think about causality – see *Causal analysis*.

The foregoing applies best to what is usually called 'scientific realism' (Sankey 2001), or 'subtle realism' (Hammersley 1992). **Critical realism**, associated with the work of Roy Bhaskar (1987) differs in its rejection of the *fact value distinction*.

R

(3) In *rhetorical analysis* realism refers to what is accomplished by those features of a text which persuade readers that what is being described is real (Atkinson 1990).

Sankey, H. (2001). 'Scientific Realism: An Elaboration and a Defence' http://philsci-archive.pitt.edu

Boyd, R. (2002) 'Scientific Realism', *Stanford Encyclopedia of Philosophy* http://plato.stanford.edu/

Miller, A. (2005) 'Realism', *Stanford Encyclopedia of Philosophy* http://plato.stanford.edu/

Hammersley, M. (1992) *What's wrong with ethnography*, London: Routledge: 50–54

Bhaskar, R. (2008) *A Realist Theory of Science*, London: Verso (earlier editions by Harvester)

Atkinson, P. (1990) *The Ethnographic Imagination: textual constructions of reality*, London: Routledge

Realist evaluation

See *Evaluation, realist(ic)*.

Reasoning

Descriptions of reasoning as *abductive, reductive, deductive* or *inductive*, do not really describe how people think, which is a rather untidy process but they can characterise the way researchers justify the conclusions they propose – see *Context of discovery and context of justification*.

Recall bias

See *Bias, recall/retrospective*.

Recension

See *Textual criticism*.

Recipient design (RD)

Principally from *conversation analysis*, the features of an utterance which can be seen as an attempt by the speaker to shape it to the perceived characteristics of the person(s) intended to hear it. An example is a 'nomination', that is a naming of the recipient as in 'What do you think John ?' Or baby-talk to babies, but RD includes more subtle features such as the use of 'we' to include or exclude the recipient, various non-verbal or intonational features to indicate non-seriousness and so on.

Reconstructed logic of research

See *Context of discovery and context of justification*.

Record linkage

Longitudinal research conducted by linking together the official records of a sample or *cohort* of people. The premier example is the *ONS* Longitudinal study (once the OPCS Longitudinal study) in which subjects are tracked through life via the records made about them by the *census*, within the NHS, the benefits system, registrations of births and deaths and so on.

The ONS Longitudinal Study *(ex OPCS LS)* www.statistics.gov.uk/services/Longitudinal.asp
Northern Ireland Longitudinal Study *(NILS)* www.nisra.gov.uk/nils/default.asp.htm

Recording

See *Audio and video recording, Fieldnotes, Diaries, Memos.*

Recursive/recursion

Of procedures in statistics or computing: repeated procedures, or self-referential procedures as in the joke:
'Recursive: see *recursive*'

Reductionism

Often used disapprovingly. **Biological, (physical) r.,**: explaining social and psychological phenomena in biological terms. **Psychological r.,**: explaining social phenomena in psychological terms (akin to some uses of *methodological individualism*). See also *Determinism*. **Phenominological reduction** – see *Bracketing*.

Reference population (criterion population)

(1) See *Standardised mortality/morbidity ratios*; (2) in the *standardisation* of tests and other instruments, the population for which norms are provided; (3) in *Population control studies*.

Reflective appraisal of program (RAP)

Evaluation of a programme using interviews to ask those affected to comment on its success or otherwise.

University of Illinois, Extension (n.d.) *Reflective Appraisal of Program (RAP)* http://ppa. aces.uiuc.edu/Data.htm

Reflective inquiry

Usually applied to research where the main aim is for the researcher him/herself to learn from the process of doing the research, hence

R

closely associated with *practitioner research*: might otherwise be called 'personal and professional development', 'practice learning' or 'reflective practice'.

Smith, M. (2008) *Donald Schön: learning, reflection and change*, INFED http://www.infed.org/thinkers/et-schon.htm

Reflexivity

(1) Principally in *ethnomethodology* , refers to self-monitoring by anyone, researcher and researched, which provides the sense of where things are at in this particular situation. (2) More generally in research, reflexivity refers to self-aware and self-critical attitude and practice where the researcher, as far as this is possible, monitors his or her own activities, and preferably records these in the form of a research *diary* or research log and with various ad hoc devices such as *memos* and by interim reports. The need to give an account of the progress of the research to a tutor or a steering committee also facilitates reflexivity. Because quantitative research uses fairly standard instruments and procedures which readers can be shown, descriptions of how the research was done are less necessary than with qualitative research. In qualitative research reflexivity is more likely to refer to reports which provide a rich narrative account of how the research was done, with its thrills and spills, and an autobiographical characterisation of the author. This is on the grounds that the results of *ethnographic research* in particular, are the product of the interaction between the researcher (as a personality rather than as a technician) and what is being researched; hence that the findings can only be understood if the reader is told in detail about the researcher and his or her engagement in the research – see *Objectivity, procedural*. Those who embrace *social constructionism* and perhaps *post-modernism* may present their reflexive account as a way of showing that it is just one story among many possible stories and has no more right to be believed than others.

Sometimes the pursuit of reflexivity goes further than providing an autobiographical narrative of the researcher doing research – *autoethnography*, with researchers trying to place their research in a wider context, for example anthropologists drawing attention to the way in which colonialism made the people they studied available as research subjects (*Post-colonial anthropology, Subalton studies*), or feminist researchers considering the implications of being privileged women, studying under-privileged ones. There is an issue here as to what context among many, researchers should reflex, or reference their accounts back to. Should this be to the autobiography of the researcher, to the doing of the research, to the political economic context of research, to the historical sequence of research of this kind, to the debates about the ethics

R

of research or to other contexts, each of which might be conceptualised and presented in a number of different ways ? Paradoxically perhaps, references to some such wider context, about which the researcher will have less secure knowledge, are sometimes taken to enhance the credibility of the account of whatever it was that the researcher studied at first hand.

Watt, D. (2007) 'On becoming a qualitative researcher: the value of reflexivity', *The Qualitative Report*, **12** (1): 82–101 www.nova.edu/ssss/QR/

Bourdieu, P. (2003) 'Participant Objectification', *Journal of the Royal Anthropological Institute* (n.s.) **9** (2): 281–316

Registrar General's Social Classes (RGSC)

An official scheme for dividing the population of adults and households into social classes based on current or last occupation; widely used in Britain from 1911 to 2000, amended from time to time. The categories were: I Professionals, II Managerial and technical, IIIN Skilled Non-manual, IIIM Skilled Manual, IV Partly skilled manual, V Unskilled Manual plus a category for those who have never been employed. Superceded in 2001 by the *National Statistics Socio-economic Classification (NS SEC)*. See also *National Statistics Standard Occupational Classification*.

Regression analysis (least squares method)

Simple regression analysis is used to define the relationship between two variables; multiple-regression analysis to find the relationships between many – see also *Multilevel analysis/modelling*.

In the *scattergrams* two variables are plotted against each other. Figure 25 shows a positive correlation. A negative correlation would show points clustered around a diagonal sloping from right to left, and lack of correlation by no apparent pattern. The line is the so-called **fit line, line of best fit, least squares line, trend line** or the **regression line**. The process is called **line fitting**. The line passes through the graph where it is closest to all data points: with the smallest error squared – hence 'least squares line'. It plots an average relationship between the two variables for all the data in the set and is sometimes called a **floating mean**. The regression line can also be regarded as the best estimate *(prediction)* of one value which can be made with knowledge of the other. The distance between each data point and the regression line is the error or **residual** (a.k.a. **random variable** and unexplained *variance*) – what is left over when any score is subtracted from this floating mean. The **intercept** is the point at which the regression line meets the vertical axis. On this scattergram the correlation is

R

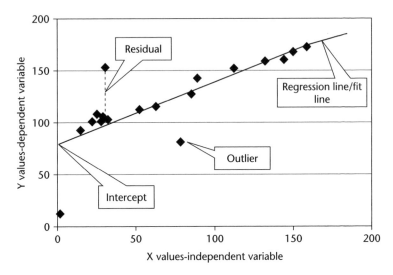

Figure 25 Scattergram showing positive correlation between X and Y:$r = 0.81$ (see *correlation coefficients*)

linear. Curvilinear *correlations* (and hence curvilinear regression lines) are possible – see *Trend, statistical*.

Scattergrams like this with fitted regression lines can be created on most spreadsheets – see also *Statistics software, Trend, statistical*.

Regression to the mean (regression fallacy/artefact, bias by selection)

Statistics; a *research artefact* likely to show itself when the same subjects are scored for some characteristic a second time, for example scores on a blood pressure scale at two consecutive points in time. Statistically there are more positions in the middle of a scale than at either extreme. Therefore on the second examination, *by chance alone,* those who scored highly are more likely to score less, and those who scored badly are more likely to score more. This is a particular problem in experiments if one group had more extreme scores than the other at the outset. The group with the more extreme scores would be likely by chance to show more improvement/deterioration by chance. A fallacy associated with evaluation of the effectiveness of speed and CCTV surveillance cameras (www.safespeed.org.uk). Not catered for in standard tests of *statistical significance*.

Trochim, W. (2006) 'Regression to the mean', *Research Methods Knowledge Base'* www.socialresearchmethods.net/kb/

Reification/to reify

(1) to treat as real, that which is not real. Principally used to claim that a researcher has mistaken what is really an analytic *construct* and hence part of the researcher's thinking, for something external and 'thing like'. Usage depends on a prior ontological decision as to what is indeed real – see *Epistemology and ontology, Realism, Social constructionism*. For example, some believe that researchers' descriptions of 'social classes' can be accurate descriptions of something real. Others believe that 'social class' is part of an analyst's attempt to understand some aspects of the way in which people in society interpret their relationships with others. In terms of this latter belief, social classes are 'reifications'. In terms of the former they are not. But in between the two beliefs it could be claimed that 'social class' is a useful metaphor (not real) but for something which is indeed real. Matters become more complex when we consider that reification is very characteristic of everyday interpretation and talk. For example, people frequently speak of something being 'all the fault of society', or of 'society needing to do something about something', as if society were the kind of entity which could be held responsible, or could take responsibility. These are reifications, but in terms of *Thomas' dictum,* if people think something is real this has real consequences, hence the argument that the reifications of ordinary folk can produce real entities for researchers to study. The concept also occupies an important place in the marxist theory of alienation and *ideology* (Burris 1988): see also *Objectification*. (2) In *computer simulation* and software engineering, to create a computer model of some real world process; synonym for realisation.

Berger, P. and Pullberg, S. (1965) 'Reification and the Sociological Critique of Consciousness', *History and Theory,* **4**, 2 pp. 196–211

Burris, V. (1988) 'Reification: a Marxist Interpretation', *California Sociologist* **10** (1): 22–43 http://darkwing.uoregon.edu/~vburris/reification.pdf

Related and unrelated designs

R

Synonym for **correlated/uncorrelated, dependent/independent, paired/unpaired** Way of characterising experimental designs (see Table 18).

Whether or not designs are related or unrelated is important in selecting an appropriate test of *statistical significance* for difference or *correlation – see Statistics parametric and non-parametric.*

Relative poverty

See *Poverty, relative.*

Table 18 Related and unrelated designs

	Related	Unrelated
Same subjects (or within group designs)	**Repeated measures design** For example; the same subjects are given words to remember under noisy conditions and also under quiet conditions. Their recall is tested after both exposures and the results compared. Comparison is each 1st score with each 2nd score.	*n-of-1 experiments* There is only one subject and he or she is subjected to a number of different conditions. Comparison is score from 1st condition with score on 2nd condition.
Different subjects (or between group designs)	For example, *matched pairs designs* Subjects are arranged as pairs according to their similarities with regard to characteristics relevant to the research. One of each pair is subjected to one experimental condition and the other to the other condition. Comparison is between each pair.	Experiments with independent samples For example, *random allocation*: a pool of subjects is divided into two groups at random. One group is assigned to one experimental condition, the other to the other. Comparison is group to group.

Relabivism

R

(1) **Epistemological relativism** or **perspectivism** refers to the notion that there is no single superior truth about social matters (and sometimes that there is no ultimate truth about anything), rather there are always several equally valid versions, some of which will be incompatible (incommensurate) with each other – see *commensurability*. This is a belief held to various degrees. Those who espouse *social constructionism* may and those who hold *post modernist* views do, hold that relativism is correct for all human knowledge. However, this is self-negating because if there is no ultimate truth and all versions of the truth are equally valid, then the claim that there is just one truth, is just as valid as the claim that there is no ultimate truth. It is not quite clear whether all those who

extend relativism to cover the natural sciences actually believe in relativism; nor is it necessary for them to do so. The *strong programme* in the sociology of science merely has to be agnostic about whether scientific or other bodies of knowledge are true or not, in order to study the social factors which form them. Many social scientists espouse relativism for some matters but not others, considering that there are some phenomena about which it is possible to be right or wrong and others which will always be a matter of interpretation – see *Corrigible*. For example, many social scientists will consider that there can only be a single correct version of what caused what, but at the same time many equally valid versions of who was to blame. Another form of limited relativism is where researchers are willing to reject some versions as false, but to regard some others as equally true. Again many will adopt an agnostic approach to the question of which version of the truth is superior, and concentrate instead on charting the various versions – see *Multiple realities*, *Evaluation*, *pluralistic*. Issues of morality sometimes influence researchers here. *Partisan* researchers, and those who favour *participatory* research may conflate truth with the right of someone to articulate their viewpoint –often this is a right they grant on the basis that this kind of person is usually prevented from expressing their view or is rarely believed when they do. Sometimes this approach results in multiple versions of the truth being presented, but sometimes researchers will select (a) particular version(s) among several as the truth – see *Standpoint theory, Voicing*. Some social scientists will switch between relativism and realism/objectivism in an unprincipled way, a practice termed *Ontological gerrymandering*.

(2) **Cultural** and **cognitive relativism:** see *Cultural relativism*.

(3) **Moral** (sometimes **value relativism**): the doctrine that the actions of members of one society should not be judged in terms of the morality of another; for example that it is wrong to used current views about racial equity as the source of criteria for judging race relations in the 1930s. The opposite of moral relativism is a subscription to a universally applicable set of human values. It is very difficult to prevent moral relativism sliding into **nihilism** which is a belief that there are no values worth subscribing to, or to a moral position which consists only in maximising one's own desires. Once we accept that people in another society should not be judged in terms of the values of our own, then there is no logical reason why the same should not apply to sub-cultures within our own society. After that step is taken, there is no logical reason why we should judge anyone else in terms of our own, rather than their own values. Moral relativism should not be confused with value neutrality (non-judgementalism) which is not a belief, but a strategic move in research to reduce the chances that a researchers' own moral views will

distort his or her approach to what is being studied – see *Value- neutral or value-led*.

Swoyer, C. (2003) 'Relativism'
Gowans, C. (2004) 'Moral Relativism'
   both in *Stanford Encyclopedia of Philosophy* http://plato.stanford.edu/

Reliability

(1) Of informants or other sources of evidence, trustworthiness, believability, but in the social sciences the second meaning is to be preferred; (2) **(consistency, stability),** consistency of measurement, or consistency of non-numerical descriptions/classifications where consistency is warranted. For research instruments there are various ways in which reliability is judged:

- **Reliability over time**, judged by *test-retest* operations: 'Does this instrument produce the same results with the same subjects on a second occasion?' The results of the first test are *correlated* with the results of the second.
- **Internal reliability**, or *internal consistency*: 'Are all the items on this instrument, or one of its sub-scales, measuring the same thing?'

Reliability is also an issue where data are produced by several researchers – are they all gathering the data in the same way, are they making decisions about coding the data in the same way? – see *inter-rater reliability*. And similarly with regard to consistency of performance of a single researcher over time or across a range of different cases – *intra-rater reliability*.

Where a method of research is unreliable the findings are (internally) invalid – see *Validity*. The converse may or may not be true. For example a stopped clock is reliable, but since it consistently tells the wrong time, what it tells is invalid: this is **Quixotic reliability**.

See also *Statistics, software*.

Garson, G. (2008) 'Reliability Analysis', North Carolina State University http://www2.chass.ncsu.edu/garson/pA765/reliab.htm

R

Repeat surveys/repeated cross-sectional studies

Surveys featuring much the same topic repeated from time to time with different samples, through samples collected in the same way to accomplish quasi longitudinalism – see *pseudo-cohort studies*. The sampling and the samples are called **sweeps** or **waves**. Repetition is in order to create time series to chart social trends but since each sweep surveys a different group of people there is some danger that changes from sweep to sweep may reflect this rather than change in the population as

Table 19 Examples of repeat surveys

Expenditure and Food Survey (once the Family Expenditure Survey and the National Food Survey)	www.statistics.gov.uk/ssd/surveys/ expenditure_food_survey.asp
General Household Survey	www.statistics.gov.uk/ghs
British Crime Survey	www.homeoffice.gov.uk/rds/bcs1.html
Offending, Crime and Justice Survey	www.homeoffice.gov.uk/rds/ offending_survey.html
National Survey of Hospital Patients and other NHS surveys	www.nhssurveys.org

a whole. Very common in public opinion polling, and with government sponsored surveys. Some examples include:

Repertory grid technique

Based on George Kelly's Personal Construct Theory which considers that consciousness is organised by classification schemes, and these can be elicited using repertory grid technique. The basic version involves asking respondents questions such as 'What do these two (people) have in common, which they don't share with this third (person)?' (**Triadic elicitation**). The objects to be compared are usually written on cards and presented in a way that allows either for all possible trios, or until no new descriptors are elicited. Going through a set of people or other entities known to the respondent in this way will elicit a finite set of descriptors in contrast pairs; for example a teacher might characterise her pupils as 'badly behaved/well-behaved, enthusiastic/bored, untidy/neat and so on. Results can be analysed by *Factor analysis*, *Item analysis* and similar techniques.

Psychologists and sociologists differ somewhat in their use of repertory grids: the former often treating a grid as a display of an individual's unique way of understanding the world; the latter as the first step towards generalising from the repertory grids of a number of respondents, to make comments about , say, an occupational culture, or a prevalent ideology – see *Actor perspectives*.

The European Personal Construct Association website provides information about personal construct theory, repertory grid technique and programs for analysing the results. www.pcp-net.de/info/index1.html

R

Replication

Close repetition of research is common in fields such as pharmacological testing, because this is required by law. Elsewhere it is more common to conduct similar research with different kinds of subjects, or with similar subjects with an allegedly superior technique. There is little kudos to be had from finding out that someone else was right. There are difficulties in interpreting a failure to produce the same results on repeating the research. These include considerations of difference in location, subjects and technique, the time and cultural change between the two pieces of research and the fact that findings from social research rarely justify a claim more confident than that such and such is *probably* true. If the probability is only (say) 70%, then there is a 30% chance that a replication will produce different results – see also *Rashomon effect, Replicability, Triangulation*.

Replicability/reproducibility

Refers to whether, in principle, a piece of research could be repeated almost exactly as the original, irrespective of whether it has actually been replicated. Thus the meaning of the term is close to that of auditability, procedural objectivity and *reliability* – see *Objectivity, procedural*. Quantitative research with its strict *protocols* , formal *instruments* and the *standardisation* of behaviour towards subjects is more replicable than *ethnographic research* where the researcher makes ad hoc, minute by minute decisions about how to respond to the immediate situation, what to focus on and what to record. However, where readers have access to the same audio or video-recorded data or documents as are available to the analyst, the analysis might be said to be replicable – as in most *ethnomethodological research* and *conversation analysis*, and some historical and sociological research with documents and texts. See also *Criteria for evaluating research*.

Representativeness

In *survey* research the object is to recruit a *sample* of people who will be representative of the population from which the sample was drawn so that what is found to be true for the sample can be confidently generalised to the population. This is called **empirical representativeness** or **statistical representativeness** and is synonymous with empirical or statistical generalisability – see *Generalisation*. Such representativeness is a relative term, depending on what level, or 'grain size' of diversity within the population the sample is supposed to represent. A sample which accurately represents the gender balance in the population may be too small to accurately represent the voting intentions of people of different genders – see *Population heterogeneity, Sample size*. Chance factors may result in a sample being less than perfectly representative, but if the sample has been properly chosen by probability, the likely deviation from representativeness (*sampling error*) can be calculated – see *Central limit theorem, Confidence interval*. Two particular ways in which probability samples can depart from representativeness, are from starting with an inadequate *sampling frame*, and from non-response – see *Response rates, Design effect*. **Theoretical representativeness** is a synonym for theoretical or explanatory generalisability – see *Generalisation, Sample theoretical*.

Reproducibility

See *Replicability*.

Research artefact (or artifact)

Misleading features of research findings, produced by the activities of the researcher, including: *expectancy effects, subject reactivity, interviewer effects, regression to the mean, family wise errors, sampling error* – see also *Bias #, Design effects, Error of central tendency, Incentives, Order effect, Positional error, Questions, closed or open, Questions, leading, Questions, positive or negative, Sampling error*. Qualitative researchers strongly committed to *naturalistic research* might argue that the findings of most kinds of research are artefactual – see *Validity, naturalistic*.

Residual

See *Regression analysis*.

Resource

See *Topic and resource*.

Respondent burden (subject burden)

Of a research technique or instrument; the extent to which respondents for a *questionnaire* or an *interview*, or subjects in an *experiment*, tire, lose interest, become alienated, or drop out. Usually measured by the number of uncompleted items, spoiled *questionnaires*, interviews prematurely ended (see *Response rate*), or by rates of *attrition* in experiments and *longitudinal surveys*.

Respondent driven sampling

See *Sample, respondent driven (RDS)*.

R

Respondent fatigue (subject fatigue)

See *Respondent burden*.

Respondent validation

See *Fallibility testing*.

Response rate/non-response rate

For a *survey* as a whole, the **unit response rate** is the number of people from whom any responses were collected, expressed as a percentage of all those selected as the sample (including any who were wrongly selected). The **unit non-response** is the sum of those selected who could not be contacted, and those selected and contacted who refused to co-operate. The term non-response is sometimes used to cover *coverage error* as well, but preferably should not. Non-respondents are rarely a representative sample of all those selected for the sample so a high non-response rate is usually an indication that the results will be biased away from statistical *representativeness*. *Imputation* and *weighting* may be used in an attempt to correct such *sampling bias*. The remarks above apply only to surveys using probability samples or systematic samples. Quota samples should not have any overall non-responses – or rather, refusals will not usually be recorded as such; see *Sample, probability, Sample quota*.

Returns are sometimes categorised in terms of categories of extent of response: for example, the percentage who completed 80%+ items/ 50–79% items/1–49% items/percentage with whom no contact was made/contact made but refused/contact made but ineligible/other, including language problems.

The **item response** rate for a particular item on a *question-naire* or interview schedule, whether in a survey or an experiment, is the number who gave a response as a percentage of either all those who were selected to be in the sample, or of all those who made any responses to any item. A high non-response rate for particular items may be an indication that there are problems with that item's compre-hensibility, or intrusiveness, or if it is late in the questionnaire an indi-cation of excessive *respondent burden*. See also *Sensitivity*. The SISA website provides explanation and software for analysing non-response: www.quantitativeskills.com/sisa/

Lynn. P., Beerten, R., Laiho, J. and Martin, J. (2001) *Recommended Standard Final Outcome Categories and Standard Definitions of Response Rate for Social Surveys*. Colchester: Essex: The Institute for Social and Economic Research www.iser.essex.ac.uk/pubs/

Foster, K. (1998) *Evaluating non-response in household surveys: a study linked to the 1991 census*, GSS Methodology Series No 8.Government Statistical Service www.statistics. gov.uk (search on GSS Methology Series)

Response variable

In *Log linear analysis* synonym for dependent variable – see *Variable*.

Retrodiction

See *Prediction*.

Retroduction/retroductive reasoning

See *Abduction/abductive reasoning*.

Retrospective bias

See *Bias, recall/retrospective*.

Retrospective study

A study, or part of study conducted after the events of interest have happened. The opposite of a *prospective study*. If by questionnaires or interviews, relying on respondent memories which are usually highly unreliable – see *Bias, narrative, Bias recall/retrospective*. Many 'cross-sectional' surveys, while conducted at a single point in time, actually include questions about the past.

RevMan method

See *Weighted averages/event rates*.

RGSC

See *Registrar General's social classes*.

Rhetoric

(1) Common usage of this term implies empty, misleading and/or grandiose speech. But this is not a good usage in the social and behavioural sciences. (2) In social science and literary criticism, refers to those features of speech or text through which a speaker or author attempts to persuade hearers or readers, and to those features which audiences find persuasive, irrespective of the intention of the originator. Since it may take just as much rhetoric to persuade people of the truth as to mislead them, rhetoric should not be equated with untruth. See *Rhetorical analysis*.

Rhetorical analysis

The analysis of written or spoken language in terms of the features included which work to persuade readers of the author's point of view, for example features which suggest that the writer of a scientific text is competent and disinterested, or features of a feminist text which suggest that the writer is imbued with the right values and loyalties. There are various schemes for conducting rhetorical analyses, most used in literary criticism. The unit of analysis is usually the **trope** referring to a figure of speech or larger unit, for example *'the ironic mode'*. Approaches differ according to whether they are corrective or not. Corrective approaches attempt to *deconstruct* the rhetoric to detect false or misleading claims. It is in this spirit that exercises in rhetorical analysis, particularly of advertisements, are set at secondary school or under-graduate level. A correctional orientation featuring rhetorical analysis has also been taken to mass media outputs by *partisan researchers* to highlight patriarchal, racist, homophobic and other kinds of *ideology*, although this practice involves treating their own analyses as non-rhetorical – see also *Critical theory, Ontological gerrymandering, Semiology/semiotics*. Other researchers have eschewed correctionalism and have regarded rhetoric as an interesting feature in its own right. These include authors who have subjected social science writing in terms of its rhetoric (Atkinson 1990, Washabaugh n.d).

Chandler, D. (2006) *Semiotics for beginners: rhetorical tropes*, University of Aberystwyth www.aber.ac.uk/media/Documents/S4B/sem07.html

Washabaugh, W. (2008) 'The Rhetoric of Ethnography', University of Wisconsin-Milwaukee www.uwm.edu/People/wash/104_3.htm

Atkinson, P. (1990) *The Ethnographic Imagination*, London: Routledge

Rho (r)

Usually *Spearman's rank order correlation co-efficient*.

RIA

See *Rapid Institutional Appraisal*.

Risk, absolute and relative

The difference between these is sometimes a source of confusion. **Absolute risk** is the likelihood of something happening, for example the likelihood of someone in a particular category being married: expressed as a proportion (a *rate*, including *percentages*) e.g., 300 per 1,000 or 30%, or a fraction, 3/10ths, or as odds, 3 to 7 or as a *ratio* 1:2.3 or 1/2.3 = 0.43,

R

or a conditional probability (*Probability*). **Relative risk** is the risk of something happening to one group by comparison with another, for example the greater risk of someone in one age group being divorced, by comparison with someone in another age group. It can be expressed simply by subtracting one absolute risk measure from another, or via a (relative)risk ratio or an *odds ratio* – see also *Effect size(ES) measures*. Confusion may arise over the difference between **absolute risk reduction/increase** on the one hand, and **relative risk reduction/increase** on the other, especially in *effectiveness research*. For example, if a disease affects in 1 in 100,000 the absolute risk is 0.001%. Suppose a medical intervention reduces the incidence to 1 in 10,000,000. The absolute risk reduction is $0.00001 - 0.001 = -0.00099$ or 0.099% – a very small reduction seemingly. But the relative risk reduction, which does not take the base-line incidence of the illness into consideration, is $1.0 - 0.1 = 0.9 = 90\%$. Understandably drug companies tend to advertise relative risk reductions, rather than absolute risk reductions – see also *Effect size (ES) measures, Risk, attributable.*

Cutforth, R., and Leighton, B. (2006) *Relative Risk Reduction(RRR) and Absolute Risk Reduction(ARR)*, Centre for Excellence in Teaching and Learning, University of Nottingham. www.nottingham.ac.uk/nursing/sonet/rlos/ebp/risk_reduction/index.html

Risk assessment

(1) A field of study in its own right, informed by *Bayesian statistics* and *decision analysis* with practical implications for many organisations, public health and investment practice. (2) A stage of the research process – see *Safety, Sensitive issues and vulnerable groups*.

Risk, attributable

A measure of the amount of some phenomenon which is due to a particular factor or set of circumstances; the magnitude of influence of a *risk factor*. For example, number of deaths from lung cancer attributable to smoking or the number of GCSE points attributable to having a father with a professional occupation. Often calculated as:

$$\frac{(\text{Amount in total relevant population}) - (\text{amount in population without the factor of interest})}{\text{amount in total relevant population}}$$

The 'amount' would usually be expressed as a *rate*, for example, so many per 1000. The same result can be reached by *correlation* or *proportional reduction of error*, and or expressed as an effect – see *Effect size (ES) measures*.

Risk factors

Characteristics making the risk of something more likely, for example, coming from a family where no adult is employed is a risk factor for juvenile delinquency. Note the probabilistic phrasing. If all children from such households were delinquent, then 'determinant' would be the more appropriate term.

Risk in research

See *Safety*.

Risk, relative

See *Effect size (ES) measures, Risk absolute and relative*.

Risk ratio (RR)

See *Effect size (ES) measures*.

Robin Hood index

See *Indices of inequality*.

Robustness

(1) generally, relatively uninfluenced by stresses and strains or changes in circumstances, (2) Of a research design or research instrument, giving accurate and/or reliable results over a wide range of circumstances; insensitive to factors which might have undermined its reliability or validity – see *Reliability, Validation, Validity external*. In this usage the threat overcome should be specified, for example: 'of robust *reliability* despite ethnic diversity in the target population'. In this context robustness (or **over-robustness**) may work against *sensitivity/specificity*. (3) Of a statistical test, giving accurate and reliable results even when the requirements for its use are violated – for example a parametric test used with ordinal level data and giving accurate results – see *Data, levels of, Statistics, parametric and non-parametric*. (4) Of relations between *variables*, one variable not being much influenced by changes in another; here a synonym for inelasticity – see *Elasticity*.

Role play (simulation experiment)

Sometimes used as a research technique, particularly where people can be asked to act out in controlled and observable conditions, activities which they often practise; for example, asking doctors to role-play diagnosis when given a case on a video-tape – see *Vignettes*. The classic example perhaps is the Stanford Prison Experiment www.prisonexp.org

Rosenthal effect

See *Expectancy effect*.

Rosenthal's fail-safe N

See Fail-safe *N*.

RR

See *Effect size(ES) measures*.

RRA

See *Rapid appraisal*.

RRD, RRI, RRR

See *Effect size (ES) measures*.

R

S

(1) Symbol for *standard deviation* of a *sample*. (2) In *time series analysis* symbol for erratic elements. (3) See *Variance*. (4) Symbol for *Sample.*

Safety

It is an important principle of research *ethics* that research should not put subjects' safety at risk unnecessarily. *Risk assessment* should identify any risks they might face. Subjects should be told and be able to make an informed decision as to whether or not to accept any risks identified – see *Informed consent*. In practice most forms of social and behavioural research pose little risk to subjects. The areas in which risks are greatest are:

- Medical research where treatments are given or withheld.
- Psycho-therapeutic research concerning sensitive and traumatic issues where close relationships are established between researcher and subject(s) (survey research on such topics seems to pose little risk).
- Some forms of *role-play* research where participants may engage in behaviour harmful to each other, for example www.prisonexp.org.
- *Action research/ participative research* where subjects (participants) may be encouraged to engage in political activism or where some form of *consciousness raising* is involved and where the psycho-dynamics of the group may be damaging to individuals.
- *Focus group* research where the psycho-dynamics of the group may be damaging to individuals.
- Covert observation research with violent groups where an informant 'in the know' may be put at risk if cover is blown – see *Observation, covert or overt.*
- Research into deviant activities where breaches of confidentiality may put subjects at risk from each other, or of criminal prosecution.

See also *Vulnerable groups and sensitive issues*.

For researchers themselves risks are greatest in *ethnographic research* with deviant groups, in anthropological research in locations far from medical facilities or other sources of assistance, and in the kinds of *action research* which involve mounting challenges to powerful opponents, and any research which places a researcher singlehanded in strange places with strangers. There are also risks associated with research into emotionally charged issues. The Social Research Association publishes guidance on how to assess the researcher risks of a research project and how to build safety into the project.

Social Research Association (2001) *A Code of Practice for the Safety of Social Researchers*, SRA www.the-sra.org.uk

Craig, G.,Corden, A. and Thornton, P. (2000) 'Safety in Social Research', *Social Research Update*, Issue 20. http://sru.soc.surrey.ac.uk

Bloor, M., Fincham, B., and Sampson, H. (2008) *Qualiti (NCRM) Commissioned Inquiry into the risk to well-being of Researchers in Qualitive Research*, NCRM. http://www.ncrm.ac.uk/research/outputs/publications/

Sample (symbolised as s)

The purpose of a sample is to represent a larger population – see *Representativeness*. In sample *surveys* a sample is selected in such a way that the proportions that are found to be true of the sample will also be approximately true of the population (empirical or statistical representativeness). Ideally such samples will be selected on probability principles or systematically (see *Sample, probability*) Then the likely differences between the sample and the population from which it is drawn, the *sampling error*, can be calculated, usually as the *confidence interval*. There are other ways of drawing survey samples, but none of these allow for the precise estimation of error. The subjects featuring in *controlled experiments* are also samples of wider populations. If other than probability samples are used it will be unclear as to whether what was found to be true in the experiment will be true of other people subjected to the same conditions – see *Generalisation, Validity, external*.
See also *Sample #, Sampling #*.

Alison Galloway (1997) *Sampling: A Workbook by Alison Galloway*, Kate Galloway. http://www.tardis.ed.ac.uk/~kate/qmcweb/scont.htm

Sample, booster

In *surveys* booster samples may be taken where sub-groups in the population are difficult to reach using the technique used for sampling the population as a whole: for example a house-to-house survey, with a booster sample drawn from hostels for homeless people. The results of

S

booster samples should not be added directly into the statistical analysis of the main survey data, because the samples were collected in different ways, but can be used as a guide to adjusting the results to compensate for the people under-represented in the main sample, and investigated in the booster – see also *Sample, Weighting*.

Sample, cluster

In *surveys* using probability samples it is often convenient to *stratify* the sampling so that first areas are chosen at random, and then within the chosen areas people are chosen at random – see *Sample (multi) staged, Sample, probability*. Clustering has the advantage of reducing travelling time where face-to-face interviewing is involved. But people who live in the same area are more likely to be like each other than like people who live in different areas. This effect is even more pronounced if, instead of selecting areas, the first stage is the selection of organisations; for example, schools or firms. Hence clustering reduces the range of diversity captured by a sample. This is one of a number of *design effects (defs)* which can arise in sampling.

Hunt, N. and Tyrell, S. (2004) *'Discuss Sampling Methods'*, Coventry University www.coventry.ac.uk/ec/~nhunt/meths/index.html

Sample, convenience (ad hoc sample, grab sample, opportunity sample)

Convenience samples are made up of the people who are conveniently available to researchers. These may not be representative of a wider population, leading to availability bias (*Bias, availability*). Most experimental work is done using convenience samples. In *randomised controlled experiments*, the total pool of subjects is usually a convenience sample which is then turned into two or more probability samples by randomly assigning subjects to *comparison groups*; see *Random allocation, Sample, probability*. But because the pool of subjects is just a convenience sample it will be difficult to know how representative these are of any wider population, and hence difficult to know how far what was true for the subjects of the experiment would be true for other people. It is often said that our knowledge of human psychology is largely our knowledge of the psychology of psychology under-graduates, the kinds of people who are most conveniently available to psychology researchers – see also *Career respondents, Validity, external*.

Convenience samples are often in the form of ready-made groups, such as school classes. This raises issues as to how representative any school class is of the total school population of that age and introduces a clustering/*design effect* – see *Sample,cluster*.

Galloway, A. (1997) *Sampling: A Workbook by Alison Galloway*, Kate Galloway http:// www.tardis.ed.ac.uk/~kate/qmcweb/scont.htm

Sample, maximum diversity

Sample selected to represent the diversity within the population of interest, such that sub-groups within the sample will be in numbers disproportionate to their numbers in the population; a disproportionate quota sample or a disproportionate random stratified sample. See *Sample, proportionate and disproportionate, Sample, stratified, Sample, quota*.

Sample, opportunity

See *Sample, convenience*.

Sample, probability (random and systematic samples)

Here each person (organisation, incident, time of day and so on) in the *population* has as equal a chance as possible of being chosen as each other. This may be done by *randomisation* by giving each unit of the population a number and then selecting numbers at random, raffle-style. Or it may be done *systematically* by selecting every nth person on a list, so long as the list orders people in a way that is arbitrary with regard to the research topic. For example, every 17th name on a list in alphabetical order of family name might be chosen: the **sampling interval (K)** would be 17. The sampling interval is derived from the size of the population divided by the required size of the sample: $k=N/s$. But if ethnicity were relevant to the research, systematic sampling from an alphabetical list might mean that people of each ethnicity would not have equal chances of being chosen, because names cluster by ethnicity. Probability samples are the preferred means of sampling in survey work, and are the only kind of sampling for which the *sampling error* can be calculated or *confidence intervals* calculated.

In survey work it is usually difficult to create a perfect probability sample: some people won't be known about and hence won't have any chance of being chosen. Some people will be chosen but then refuse to co-operate. Such people are likely to be different in important ways from the people who are chosen and do co-operate. Thus a sample chosen to be representative may turn out not to be so. However, since unavailable and uncooperative subjects are not substituted for, this survey *non-response*

S

leaves a record which can be compared with what is known about the population, and its extent estimated – see *Response rate*.

Straightforward or 'simple' probability samples tend to miss subjects who only form small percentages of the population. To overcome this, *random stratified samples* are often taken, drawing a larger percentage of the people from rarer groups than from the commoner groups; for example, drawing the same number of people from each ethnic group even though different ethnic groups make up different percentages of the population. This w*eighting* of the sample at the point of collection then has to be corrected in the analysis of the data.

In experimental work where comparison groups are created by *randomly assigning* subjects to one group or another, each group is a probability sample of the population constituted by all the subjects together. Since these samples were created on probability principles there is a good chance that they are very similar to each other – everyone had an equal chance of being in either group, and the odds of their being different can be calculated – but see *Sample, convenience, Sample size.*

See also *Call-back*, *confidence interval, sample size.*

Hunt, N. and Tyrell, S. (2004) 'Discuss Sampling Methods', Coventry University: www.coventry.ac.uk/ec/~nhunt/meths/index.html

Galloway, A. (1997) *Sampling: A Workbook by Alison Galloway*, Kate Galloway http://www.tardis.ed.ac.uk/~kate/qmcweb/scont.htm

Musalia, J (2008) *Chapter 10, Sampling* University of West Kentucky. http://www.wku.edu/~john.musalia/soc300/

Sample, purposive

Any sampling other than self-recruited samples or than those designed to produce a statistically representative sample, but particularly maximum diversity sampling, and theoretical sampling, see *Representativeness, Sample, maximum diversity, Sample, self-recruited, Sample, theoretical.*

Sample, quota

In survey work, a quota sample is an attempt to create a sample which is a small scale model of the population. Thus if 51% of the population is female, 18% of these are over 50, and 79% of these live in owner-occupied accommodation, then the researcher will collect subjects until the sample itself contains a group of females over 50 living in owner-occupied accommodation which is 79% of 18% of 51% of the sample: and similarly for all the other types of person identified as being relevant to the research. As with random stratified sampling (see *Sample, probability, Sample, stratified*) quota samples may be *weighted* to collect numbers of subjects out of proportion to their numbers in the population.

Sampling is on the first-found, first-in basis, but this means that quota samples tend to over-represent the kinds of people who are easy to find and willing to co-operate, risking availabiliity bias (*Bias, availability*). No *sampling error* or *confidence intervals* can be calculated for quota samples. Quota sampling is much cheaper than probability sampling and despite their shortcomings quota samples have proved as accurate as probability sampling in *public opinion polling* and *market research*, and are the method of choice by academics in most of continental Europe.

Hunt, N. and Tyrell, S. (2004) 'Discuss Sampling Methods', Coventry University: www.coventry.ac.uk/ec/~nhunt/meths/index.html

Galloway, A. (1997) *Sampling: A Workbook by Alison Galloway*, Kate Galloway http://www.tardis.ed.ac.uk/~kate/qmcweb/scont.htm

Sample, random

See *Sample, probability*.

Sample, random stratified

See *Sample, stratified*.

Sample, respondent driven (RDS)

Combines snowball sampling with a mathematical model for *weighting* the responses to compensate for the fact that the sample was collected in a non-probability way – see *Sample, probability, Sample, snowball*.

Respondent Driven Sampling Organisation www.respondentdrivensampling.org/

Sample, self-selected

Primarily refers to samples recruited by asking readers, listeners or viewers to write in, phone in or e-mail in their responses to questions, resulting in a sample where *representativeness* is unknown, and risking availability bias (*Bias, availability*). However, all sample recruitment involves some element of self-selection insofar as people once chosen can refuse to participate – see *Career respondents, Incentives, Response rates, Survey recruitment*.

Sample size

For surveys, the necessary size of a sample is determined by the diversity the sample is required to represent. Thus a relatively small sample will produce an accurate estimate of the sex ratio in the population – since people can only be male or female. For this a probability sample of 380

S

would be adequate irrespective of the size of the population over and above 10,000 – see *Sample, probability*. A larger sample will be required for an accurate estimate of the sex-ratio *within* each of 5 age bands, and an even larger one for an accurate estimate of differences of opinion as between people of different genders within age-bands. Thus in effect, the size a sample needs to be for statistical analysis will be determined by the number of responses the researcher allows for each item, and whether or not, or to what extent the researcher wants to *correlate* the answers to different items.The *sampling fraction* is not a good guide to the adequacy of sample size.

Nothing much can be said about an adequate sample size for samples taken by means other than probability. Larger usually means better, but larger may mean that a systematic error is magnified so that as the sample gets bigger it becomes more misleading as a guide to the proportions in the population and less *representative* – see *Error, random and systematic*.

Samples may be stratified, or otherwise *weighted*, to collect disproportionate numbers from rarely occurring groups in the population. This increases the over-all size of a sample – see *Sample, stratified*.

Experiments and quasi experiments nearly always operate with smaller sample sizes than surveys, because the purpose of experiments is not to represent diversity, but to eliminate the kinds of diversity irrelevant to the research and focus only on the differences which are relevant, though this risks eliminating differences which do turn out to be relevant. Adequate sample size here is largely a matter of creating a data set large enough for statistical manipulation. *Randomised controlled experiments* (true experiments) often involve very small samples; say 40 subjects divided into two groups of 20. They can do this because most of the diversity between subjects will have been physically controlled out in the initial selection of subjects and in the creation of the *comparison groups*. Experiments not using random allocation (quasi-experiments) need bigger samples because the comparison groups will contain diversities which are irrelevant to the research and may *confound* the results. The larger sample size is needed to provide the statistical 'elbow room' required for statistically controlling irrelevant differences – see *Experiments, true and quasi, Control, direct and statistical*. While sample size for experiments is usually set in advance, this is not the case with sequential hypothesis testing- *see Sequential analysis*.

In testing for *statistical significance* sample size is factored into the calculations. All other things being equal, it is made harder to get a statistically significant result with a small sample than with a large one. Thus in designing experiments and deciding on a sample size it is important to think backwards from the results, asking what statistically significant effect size would uphold the *null hypothesis,* and what sample size would be necessary to allow it to be produced – see *Effect size (ES) measures.* See also *Statistical power.*

For stratified samples, the calculation for adequacy of sample size should be for each stratum – see *Sample, stratified.*

The following websites carry free calculators for calculating minimum sample sizes for probability samples for a given *confidence level/ alpha level* and *confidence interval.*

Sampling for surveys
Creative Research Systems: www.surveysystem.com/resource.htm
Geocities: www.geocities.com/profemery/samplesize.htm

Sampling for experiments
Sisa: http://home.clara.net/sisa/sampshlp.htm

Sample, snowball

Sampling technique used with difficult-to-find groups or where the object is to trace out *social networks.* The researcher starts somewhere and then asks each subject to identify others who are like them in some relevant respect and goes on doing this until hardly any new names crop up. There is a question of how far, for instance, a snowball sample of drug using teenagers in Wigan will stand as representative of all drug using teenagers in, say, the North West of England – see also *Sample, respondent driven.*

Atkinson, R. and Flint, J. (2001) 'Accessing hidden and hard-to-reach populations: snowball research strategies', *Social Research Update* Issue 33 http://sru.soc.surrey.ac.uk/

Sample, (multi-) staged

Sampling is often a (multi-)staged process. For example as the first stage, researchers might first select locations in the country; perhaps at random, or perhaps purposively on the basis of their demographic or economic factors. Then as the second stage within these areas they might make a random selection of addresses from the *Post-code address files(PAF)* files and then as the third stage they might use a *Kish grid* or something similar to select who in the household to interview. Staging creates *design effects* which may be compensated for by *weighting* the results.

Galloway, A. (1997) *Sampling: A Workbook by Alison Galloway,* Kate Galloway http://www.tardis.ed.ac.uk/~kate/qmcweb/scont.htm

Sample, stratified

Where there are groups which are of research interest, but they make only small percentages of the population, a very large probability sample might be necessary to make sure sufficient of them were recruited in order for there to be a sample representative of the diversity among them. The alternative is to select a stratified sample. In effect this means collecting several samples – or **strata**, one for each group of interest. To create such sub-groups each with an adequate *sample size* will mean that they are out of proportion to their contribution to the population as a whole; disproportionate stratified probability sampling; see *Sampling, proportionate and disproportionate*. *Weighting* back to proportionality will be necessary in the analysis of the results. Quota samples may also be stratified – see *Sample, quota*.

> Hunt, N. and Tyrell, S. (2004) 'Discuss Sampling Methods', Coventry University www.coventry.ac.uk/ec/~nhunt/meths/index.html.
> Note this illustrates proportionate, rather than disproportionate stratified sampling.

Sample, systematic

See *Sample, probability*.

Sample, theoretical

The purpose of theoretical sampling is to investigate the same topic under a wide range of circumstances; each 'sample' is a different configuration of possibly relevant variables; for example the effect of government regulation might be studied in small, medium and large enterprises on the assumption that size was an important variable in mediating the impact. A range of different, but related experiments, would also constitute a theoretical sample, and *constant comparative method* is a theoretical sampling procedure, as are many procedures in the comparative analysis of qualitative data – see *Comparative qualitative analysis, Cross-case analysis*. A type of purposive sampling, see *Sample, purposive*. Theoretical sampling produces theoretical *generalisations*.

Sample, time

Different things happen at different times, and people of different sorts are available to be interviewed at different times. Consider for example the problem of getting a *representative* sample of rail-users. For this it would be necessary to recruit respondents using the railway at all times of the day and night: each time period should be given an equal chance to be represented by respondents. But equal chance means equal chance, so there should either be be fewer respondents recruited from the early hours of the morning, which might be accomplished by weighting the sample to recruit fewer respondents from this time period – time-*weighting* the sample. Or the results of the survey should be adjusted – *weighting* the results – so that the responses of those who travel in the early hours should only count towards the total in proportion to the percentage of passengers they represent. Both kinds of weighting, however, require prior knowledge of the percentages of people who travel at different times.

In *ethnographic research*, time sampling can also be an important issue. For example are observations of classrooms on Thursdays and Fridays a sound basis for generalisations which include Monday to Wednesday? Will observations in Summer term stand for what happens in the Autumn? Time sampling may be impossible and if so it is important for ethnographic researchers to specify when observations were made, and to consider how far they can generalise from one time to others.

Sample weighting

See *Weighting*.

Samples of anonymised records (SARs)

Large samples of anonymised records of individuals, families and or households from the UK censuses (1991, 2001, 2011) made available for research purposes.

Cathy Marsh Research Centre *Samples of Anonymised Records*, CMRC http://www.ccsr. ac.uk/sars/

Sampling distribution

The theoretical distribution of some *statistic* derived from taking all possible probability samples from a population. **...of the mean,** the distribution of estimates of the mean derived from taking an infinite number of samples. With a probability sample (*Sample, probability*) this will usually be a *normal distribution*, but see *Power (law) distributions*. For *mean* see *Central tendency and dispersion*. See also *Central limit theorem*.

Musalia, J. (2008) *Chapter 10: Sampling*, University of West Kentucky. http://www.wku. edu/~john.musalia/soc300/

Sampling error (sampling variability, sampling uncertainty)

This is the likely difference due to chance between a *parameter* in a population and an estimate of that parameter (*statistic*) derived from taking a probability sample (see *estimator*), for example the difference between the sample mean and the population mean – see *Sample, probability*. It is the survey equivalent of *measurement error* and similarly relates to the *central limit theorem* and the calculation of the *standard deviation* from which we can calculate the *confidence interval* and hence estimate how likely it is that this estimate is correct. It is more useful to calculate the *confidence interval* than the sampling error. See the interactive demonstration on the RVLS web site: http://onlinestatbook.com/rvls.html

Musalia, J (2008) *Chapter 10: Sampling*, University of West Kentucky. http://www.wku. edu/~john.musalia/soc300/

Sampling error curve

See *Normal distribution*.

Sampling fraction

The percentage of the population of interest which is sampled, as in 'a 5% sample' or a '10% sample'; often erroneously taken as an indication of the adequacy of *sample size*. However, this should be judged not in terms of the size of the sample as a percentage of the population, but in terms of the degree of diversity the researcher wants the sample to represent.

Sampling frame

Any list, or any resource at all, used as the basis for selecting a sample, for example the electoral register, or the list of patients registered with a GP, or a street map showing each address, or the *Post-code address files (PAF)*. Apart from research within or of organisations which have staff, client or customer lists it is a lucky survey researcher who can start with a sampling frame which is complete, and which clearly shows who is eligible for inclusion within a sample. Hence shortcomings of the sampling frame are an important source of a sample not being representative, in addition to sample non-response – see *Representativeness, Response rate*.

Sampling interval

See *Sample, probability*.

Sampling, proportional and disproportional

With a simple probability sample, sub-groups of the population will appear in the sample in more or less the same proportions as in the population and simple quota samples are designed this way. However, in order to include sub-samples which are representative of minorities it may be necessary to collect disproportionate numbers from these sub-groups. This is called stratified sampling – see *Sample, probability, Sample, stratified*. Disproportional quota sampling is also possible – see *Sample, quota. Weighting* will be necessary to restore the total sample to proportionality.

Sampling in qualitative research

Qualitative researchers can rarely produce samples which are representative of a wider *population* in the statistical or empirical sense – see *Representativeness* – and hence there may be doubts as to whether their results can be generalised – see *Generalisation* and *Validity external, Rashomon effect*. They are often unable even to present a representative sample of observations within the location in which they are studying (*sampling within the case*), and then there may be doubts as to the internal validity of their results – see *Validity, internal*. Theoretical sampling is more characteristic of qualitative research – see *Sample, theoretical*.

Onwuegbuzie, A. and Leech, N. (2007) 'Sampling Designs in Qualitative Research: making the sampling process more public', *The Qualitative Report* **12**(2): 238–254 www.nova.edu/ssss/QR

Sampling uncertainty

See *Central limit theorem, Sampling error*.

Sampling unit

Refers primarily to the unit of probability sampling – see *Sampling probability*, with the principle that each unit in the population should have an equal chance of being chosen. Units should retain their integrity throughout the research study, such that the data each produces should be produced independently of other units; in experiments, what one subject does should not influence other subjects and in surveys, interviews should be independent. Only then can the benefits of having a probability sample be used by allowing the use of parametric inferential statistics – see *Statistics, parametric and non-parametric*. For statistical analysis if the data for subjects is not independently produced, then the number of units will be less than the number of subjects. For example, two group interviews with 12 participants each is a sample of 2, not of 24. Individuals, organisations, periods of time, locations or passages of text can be sampling units.

S

Sampling variability

See *Central Limit theorem, Sampling error*.

Sampling within the case

In *case study research*, such as *ethnographic research,* the choice of people, situations or time periods to sample. The issue is whether the selection will be representative of that village, that school, that firm etc., and not whether the selection will be representative of a wider population of villages, schools, firms etc. – see *Representativeness.*

Onwuegbuzie, A. and Leech, N. (2007) 'Sampling Designs in Qualitative Research: making the sampling process more public', *The Qualitative Report* **12**(2): 238–254 www.nova.edu/ssss/QR

SAQ (Self-administered Questionnaire)

See *Questionnaire administration.*

SARs

See *Samples of anonymised records (SARs).*

SAS (Statistical Analysis System)

See *Statistics software.*

Saturation (theoretical saturation)

Term coined in *grounded theory*, but now used more widely to refer to the point at which collecting additional data does not force any revision of the explanations already developed. It is not entirely clear how such a state can be distinguished from a failure of imagination or an exhaustion of resources.

Scales

Scaling is the process of assigning numerical scores to qualitative constructs. This produces data at different levels thus determining the options for statistical analysis – see *Data, levels of, Statistics, parametric and non-parametric.*

Scales may be **unidimensional or multi-dimensional** according to the *construct* being measured. Height is a unidimensional scale, since everyone can be arranged along a single line from least to most. Academic achievement is multi-dimensional since someone can be good at maths and bad at English. There are three main kinds of unidimensional scales.

- Summative scaling – for example *Likert scaling*
- Scalogram or cumulative scaling – for example *Guttman scaling*
- Equal interval scaling – for example *Thurstone scaling*

Profiles provide a characterisation of someone or something on multi-dimensional scales.

See also *Semantic differential, Test theory*

Trochim, W. (2006) 'Scaling', *Research Methods Knowledge Base* www.socialresearch-methods.net/kb/

Scale free/scale invariant distributions

See *Power (law) distributions*.

Scalogram analysis

See *Guttman scale*.

Scattergram/scatter diagram/scatter plot/x-y graph

Graph showing the relationships between two variables with discontinuous plots. If there is a *direction of effect* it is conventional to use the horizontal (or x axis) for the independent variable and the vertical (or y) axis for the dependent variable – see *Variable*. Three dimensional versions are possible (x-y-z graphs). Scattergrams are very useful for the visual inspection of data for *correlations* and *outliers*. See also *Regression analysis* and *Funnel plot* (for illustrations). Scattergrams can be created on most spreadsheets.

Scepticism/scepticism

See *Fallibilism as opposed to foundationalism*.

Scheffe test

See *Post hoc tests*.

Science wars

Debates provoked by social constructionist studies of the natural sciences which challenge the idea that there is anything special about scientific activity and knowledge – see also *Demarcation debate, Social constructionism, Sokal affair, Strong programme*.

ABC World (n.d.) *Science Wars* http://abcworld.net/Science_wars.html
ABC World (n.d.) *The Sokal Affair*, http://abcworld.net/Sokal_affair.html

Scientific method

See *Hypothetico-deductive method*.

Scientistic

Term of disapproval used by those who believe that the use of natural science methods and thinking is inappropriate for social science. The meaning varies according how the user conceptualises natural science – see also *Unity of science thesis.*

Search engines and data bases

For social sciences, psychology and health studies. Search engines are electronic harvesting devices, such as Google, but there are more specialist engines too. Data bases here are listings, and very often full archives of articles, books and sometimes other resources. Some offer full text versions freely, some only offer contents pages and or abstracts, and some require a subscription before searching is allowed (usually the subscriber is a library). If you are attached to an institution of Higher Education your library will have a list of free and subscription data-bases.

The *Sosig* web site lists many of the most useful data-bases by varieties of social science. http://www.intute.ac.uk/socialsciences/ and go to the 'Virtual Training Suite'.

See also – BEIRC, *Campbell collaboration, CERUK-plus, Cochrane collaboration, Educational evidence portal, Eppi-centre.*

Seasonal Adjustment

See *Time series analysis.*

Secondary analysis

A not very precise term, which usually implies that one researcher has collected the data and analysed them, and another has re-analysed them. With more and more *data archiving* this is becoming increasingly common. This includes *meta-analysis* where an attempt is made to draw conclusions from several pieces of research. Sometimes used for the re-analysis of data by the same researcher, and sometimes used for the analysis of *administrative data.* The purpose of secondary analysis may be to evaluate the quality of the research and/or critique it, or to use the data for purposes not envisaged by the original researcher – however there are usually problems associated with using data for purposes other than those for which they were collected.

Mochmann, E. (n.d.) 'Data Archiving and the Uses of Secondary Analysis', Cologne, *Metadater* www.metadater.org/index.htm

SEC/S-eC

See *Socio-economic classification*.

Secular trend/variation

In a *time series analysis* the long term trend rather than **periodic variations**. Definition depends on the time frame of the analysis. For example, the secular trend might be throughout the year, with the periodic as the seasonal cycle, or the secular trend might be over 50 years and within this there might be periodic economic cycles lasting 5 to 10 years.

Segregation indices

(**dissimilarity index** or **delta (Δ), Gorard's segegration index** or **displacement index, index of isolation, index of exposure**) A family of indices expressing the extent to which groups are evenly or unevenly distributed between categories in a data set. The most common use has been to measure residential segregation, or occupational segregation, the distribution of ethnic groups within the class structure, the segregation of pupils receiving free school meals, or of minority ethnic pupils between schools in an LEA – as in the examples below. The indices can also be used to express the extent to which (say) different types of people are distributed between income categories. The indices require only nominal level data- *see Data levels of*. Where interval level data are available, indices based on the Lorenz Curve may be used instead – see *Inequality indices*. The Dissimilarity index is also sometimes used to express the degree of *goodness of fit* in *log linear analysis* (Kuha and Firth n.d.)

In the formulae in Table 20A:

A = the number of minority ethnic pupils per school
B = the number of ethnic majority pupils per school
C = total number of pupils per school
X = total minority ethnic pupils all schools
Y = total ethnic majority pupils all schools
Z = all pupils all schools
SUM (or Σ) means 'do this for all schools and add up the results'
‖ (*absolute*) means treat all numbers as positives
The data are invented.

Kuha, J. and Firth, D. (n.d.) *On the index of dissimilarity for lack of fit in long linear and log multiplicative models*

Table 20A Formulae for calculating 4 segregation indices (Examples given in Table 20B).

Index	Formulae
Dissimilarity Index or Delta Index (Δ)	$D = 0.5 \times \text{SUM} \mid ((A/X) - (B/Y)) \mid$

Reports the extent to which two groups are evenly distributed across areas, organisations or categories. Zero reports perfect similarity of distribution. 1 reports complete segregation. Compare Situations 3 and 4 below to see that this index will give the same score to what are intuitively different degrees of segregation.

Displacement Index or Gorard's Segregation Index	$S = 0.5 \times \text{SUM} \mid ((A/X) - (C/Z)) \mid$

When multiplied by 100 reports the percentage of the minority group who would have to be re-distributed in order to create perfect similarity of distribution. Minimum 0 – for perfect similarity of distribution, but maximum is not 1. Compare situations 3 and 4 (Table 20B) to see that this index will give the same score to what are intuitively different degrees of segregation.

Isolation Index	For Minority group SUM $((A/X) \times (A/C))$
	For Majority group SUM $((B/Y) \times (B/C))$

Reports for the typical member of the group the percentage of people of his or her own group who will be in the same area/organisation/category. The maximum value is 1 and the minimum value is the percentage that group comprises of the total. The minimum will register if the Dissimilarity index is 0. When the Dissimilarity Index is 0 the Isolation Index for the minority will equal the Exposure Index for the majority group and vice versa. Compare Situations 3 and 4 (Table 20B) to see that this index does discriminate between intuitively different degrees of segregation. Unfortunately it is also very much influenced by the changes in the ratio between the groups in the total population. So comparisons using the index may be difficult to interpret.

Exposure Index	For Minority group SUM $((A/X) \times (B/C))$
	For Majority group SUM $((B/Y) \times (A/C))$

Reports for the typical person of the group what percentage their area/organisation/category will be made up of the other group. The minimum value is 0. The maximum value is the percentage of the total comprised by the other group. Whatever the maximum it will equate with a Dissimilarity Index of 0. When the Dissimilarity Index is 0 the Exposure Index for the minority will equal the Isolation Index for the majority group and vice versa. Compare Situations 3 and 4 (Table 20B) to see that this index does discriminate between intuitively different degrees of segregation. Unfortunately it is also very much influenced by the changes in the ratio between the groups in the total population. So comparisons using the index may be difficult to interpret.

Table 20B

	No' Minority Ethnic	No' Ethnic Majority	C Total pupils	**Situation 1**: perfect integration. Each school has the same proportion of ethnic majority pupils	
School	A	B	C		
1	200	400	600	Dissimilarity Index	0.00
2	200	400	600	Gorard's Segregation Index	0.00
3	200	400	600	Isolation Index : minority pupils	0.33
4	200	400	600	Isolation index : majority pupils	0.66
5	200	400	600	Exposure index minority pupils	0.66
6	200	400	600	Exposure index : majority pupils	0.33
Totals	1200	2400	3600		
	X	Y	X		

	No' Minority Ethnic	No' Ethnic Majority	Total pupils	**Situation 2**: one possibility for extreme segregation with schools of same size and minority and majority ethnic populations of same size as situation 1	
School	A	B	C		
1	0	600	600	Dissimilarity Index	1.00
2	0	600	600	Gorard's Segregation Index	0.67
3	0	600	600	Isolation Index : minority pupils	1.00
4	0	600	600	Isolation index : majority pupils	1.00
5	600	0	600	Exposure index minority pupils	0
6	600	0	600	Exposure index : majority pupils	0.00
Totals	1200	2400	3600		
	X	Y	Z		

	No' Minority Ethnic	No' Ethnic Majority	Total pupils	**Situation 3**: Middling pattern of segregation with schools of same size and minority and majority ethnic populations of same size as situations 1 and 2	
School	A	B	C		
1	0	600	600	Dissimilarity Index	0.50
2	0	600	600	Gorard's Segregation Index	0.33

(Continued)

Table 20B (Continued)

3	200	400	600	Isolation Index : minority pupils	0.56
4	200	400	600	Isolation index : majority pupils	0.76
5	400	200	600	Exposure index minority pupils	0.44
6	400	200	600	Exposure index : majority pupils	0.22
Totals	1200	2400	3600		
	X	Y	Z		

	No' Minority Ethnic	No' Ethnic Majority	C Total pupils	**Situation 4**: A different middling pattern of segregation with schools of same size and minority and majority ethnic populations of same size as situations 1,2,3 and 4	
School	A	B	C		
1	0	600	600	Dissimilarity Index	0.50
2	0	600	600	Gorard's Segregation Index	0.33
3	200	400	600	Isolation Index : minority pupils	0.67
4	200	400	600	Isolation index : majority pupils	0.83
5	200	400	600	Exposure index minority pupils	0.33
6	600	0	600	Exposure index : majority pupils	0.16
Totals	1200	2400	3600		
	X	Y	Z		

http://www2.warwick.ac.uk/fac/sci/statistics/staff/academic/firth/papers/kuha_firth_delta.pdf

Noden, P. (2000) 'Rediscovering the impact of marketisation; dimensions of social segregation in England's secondary schools, 1994–99', *British Journal of the Sociology of Education*, **21**(3) 371–385

Taylor, C., Gorard, S. and Fitz, J. (2000) 'A re-examination of segregation indices in terms of compositional invariance', *Social Research Update* Issue 30: http://sru.soc.surrey.ac.uk

Racial Segregation Measurement Project, University of Michigan http://enceladus.isr.umich.edu/race/calculate.html

Selection bias

See *Bias, selection*.

Self-organisation

In *complexity theory*, refers to emergent phenomena which are unintended by people, for example the route taken by a rumour through a population, or a stock market crash. The idea is very close to what used to be expressed as the 'unintended consequences of intended action' and by the term sui generis (self-generating) – see *Complex adaptive systems*, *Emergence*.

Self-report survey

Respondents report on their own activities, feelings, experiences and so on. This is perhaps the most common strategy for generating data in the social sciences, and one highly vulnerable to the vagaries of human memory – see *Bias recall/retrospective*, and the propensity of people to try to give benign representations of themselves – see *Bias self-serving*, and other biases which make self-reports less than accurate – see also *Bias, narrative*. In criminology specifically, self-report surveys usually refer to those which ask respondents about their own criminal activities. Those which are based on a representative sample usually have among their objectives making estimates of the *incidence or prevalence* of offences independently of official records of crime – see *Administrative data* –, for example the Offending, Crime and Justice Survey. See also *Victim surveys*.

> Pudney, S. (2006) 'Rarely pure and never simple: extracting the truth from self-reported data on substance misuse' www.iser.essex.ac.uk/seminars/jess/2007/papers/pudney.pdf
> Offending Crime and Justice Survey www.homeoffice.gov.uk/rds/offending_survey.html

Self-serving bias

See *Bias, self-serving*.

Semantic and syntactic: semantic

Of or pertaining to meaning, and usually the meaning of language. Often opposed to **syntactic**, where syntax refers to the ruleful structure of language and is a near synonym for grammar. The contrast of semantic with syntactic can be misleading since the syntax of speech or *text* is crucial to conveying meaning, and to some extent what is the correct syntactic form depends on the meaning intended – see also *Polysemy*, *Syntagmatic*.

Semantic differential

Scale used in research instruments measuring attitudes, where a single idea is rated on various dimensions for its favourableness or

Table 21 Example of semantic differential scale.

Joy-riding is (*Tick the box which is closest to your feelings*)								
	6	5	4	3	2	1	0	
Fun								Boring
Not dangerous								Dangerous
Good								Bad
Healthy								Sick
Rewarding								Unrewarding

unfavourableness. In the example here (Table 21) adding all the scores would allow for a maximum of 30 for the most 'favourable' score, but the same technique is often used to give profiles to different respondents according to their differences in the way they rate different items in the scale, giving a nuanced result. Sometimes used as a preliminary stage in designing research instruments. For example, where two rows showed almost the same results for the same respondents, one of the rows could be eliminated. A final selection of dimensions might be made on the basis of which pilot dimensions most polarised respondents. See also *Componential analysis, Item analysis.*

Semi-log scale

See *Arithmetic and logarithmic scales.*

Semiology/semiotics

A diverse field of study but always concerned with the way meaning is created by signs and the way they are arranged. Signs are said to consist of two elements, the **signifier** and the **signified;** the latter being what the former 'stands for'. What is important is not the relation between signifier and signified, which is arbitrary, but the relationships between signifiers. It is the relationship of one sign to another which generates meaning, particularly through binary oppositions; thus the meaning of black is not-white, and the meaning of passive is not-active. The generation of meaning is termed **signification**.

Most work concerns the analysis of *texts*, and particularly those of popular culture, but the interest may be broader to extend to the way in which a sense of social reality is created and sustained and or to the maintenance of power structures – see also *Deconstruction, Ideology, Structuralism and post structuralism*.

Chandler, D. (2001) *Semiotics for Beginners*, London: Routledge. www.aber.ac.uk/media/Documents/S4B/

Phillips, J. (n.d.) *Structuralism and semiotics*. www.angelfire.com/de/jwp/structuralism.html

Semi-structured interview

See *Qualitative interviews*.

Sensitising concept

It may be argued that social phenomena are variable and change in relation to their immediate context, so that precise definitions akin to those of the natural sciences are inappropriate. Instead sensitising concepts are suggested to show similarities between phenomena which might otherwise be diverse The idea relates to *symbolic interactionism's* origins within pragmatic philosophy wherein the value of concepts is seen to reside in their usefulness (here as tools for thinking) rather than in their accuracy – see *Pragmatism*. Examples of sensitising concepts might be deviance, labelling, stigma, or moral career.

Blumer, H. (1969) *Symbolic Interactionism*, Engelwood Cliffs, NJ: Prentice Hall :148

Sensitive topics and vulnerable groups

For example, traumatic experiences such as rape or domestic violence, or disreputable matters such as criminal activities are sensitive topics. Research with children and vulnerable adults is often regarded as 'sensitive' whatever the topic and will usually require the researcher to undergo a *criminal record check*. Where the subjects of research might be upset by the research there are both ethical and expediential considerations. The ethical include the consideration of whether the value of the research would justify the unpleasantness experienced by the subjects, and, if so, ways of making the experience as comfortable as possible. Expediential considerations are about the accuracy of the data likely to be elicited from people who are upset, or ashamed. Many qualitative researchers have claimed that making close, trusting relationships with respondents both reduces anxiety and increases the likelihood of honest disclosure. There is no hard evidence to support this, and research evidence from social survey work suggests that disclosure is fuller and more accurate the greater the social distance between researcher and research subjects. Disreputable and deviant activities have often been studied by

S

covert participant observation research – see *Children, research with, Observation, overt or covert*. See also *Ethics, Safety, Survivor research*.

Sensitivity

(1)In *instrument* design, a sensitive instrument is one which will record more nuances of some target construct; for example, all other things being equal, a five point *Likert scale* is more sensitive than one just recording 'Like/Dislike'. However, the more sensitive an instrument is, the more possible it is that it introduces *research artefacts*. In this example, there is no way of knowing whether one person's 'Like very much' is the equivalent to another's in terms of their strength of feeling or in terms of the possibility of predicting their behaviour from their answer, and the same with the other response options. The more gradations of answer are allowed the worse the problem of **over-sensitivity** becomes. (2) In diagnostic instrument design, see *Type 1 and type 2 errors*. (3) Any way in which the results of research are influenced by *confounding* factors or speculative assumptions – see *Sensitivity analysis*. (4)) Synonym for *elasticity* (5) Refers to the extent to which a research design or the researcher's demeanour takes into account and avoids the possibility of upsetting research subjects – see *Sensitive topics and vulnerable groups*.

Sensitivity analysis

Estimating how far the findings of some piece of research were determined by (sensitive to) some factor such as the response rate of a survey, or the attrition-rate in an experiment; for example asking a question such as, ' If all the non-respondents has answered 'yes', would that have changed the results significantly?' and similarly asking 'if all the non-respondents had answered 'no' would that have changed the results significantly?' – see *Heckman's procedure*. Rosenthal's *Fail-safe N* is a sensitivity analysis estimating the likely effect of publication bias – see *Bias, publication*. In economic analysis, sensitivity analyses are often carried out to estimate the sensitivity of the results to future price changes or local costs as a way of specifying the extent to which the results might be generalised – see *Cost # analysis*.

JRC European Commission (2008) *Sensitivity Analysis Forum* http://sensitivity-analysis.jrc.ec.europa.eu/

Sequential analysis

(1) Synonym for *conversation analysis (CA)* and similar linguistic analyses, because of the analytic interest in where precisely an utterance occurred

in sequence. On the small scale this includes an interest in *adjacency pairs*, on the larger scale (for example) in the way *narratives* are developed in the course of an interchange – see also *Endogenous, Narrative analysis, Syntagmatic analysis*; (2) in statistics, short for **sequential hypothesis testing** where sample size is not fixed in advance and data are evaluated as they are collected. Collection continues until a statistically significant result is obtained, or according to a predefined stopping rule; often used in *randomised controlled trials* (Mehta 2004) and in *data mining*.

Mehta, C. (2004) *Introduction to Flexible Clinical Trials (*and other lectures), Harvard University. http://www.biostat.harvard.edu/~betensky/lecture1-intro.pdf

Sequentionalist causality

See *Causal analysis*.

Sequential paired comparison

A method of *ranking* of preference by presenting all possible pairs of alternatives and asking the respondent to make a dichotomous choice between each pair. Since this may involve a very large number of pairings, methods exist to use a decision made about one pair to avoid the need to present another – see also *Q analysis*.

Priority Search (2005) *Priority Search Ranking Process.* www.priority-research.com/images/pdf/PS_methodology.pdf

Serial effect

Form of *subject reactivity*, where an earlier question in a *questionnaire*, or an earlier action by an interviewer has (an) unwanted influence(s) on later responses.

SD

See *Standard deviation*.

SG (Social grade)

See *Market research classification*.

Sign, signified, signifier, signification

See *Semiology/semiotics*.

Sign test

See *Binomial sign test.*

Significance

See *Statistical significance, Substantive significance.*

Simulation

See *Computer simulation, Role play.*

SISS (Spacially Integrated Social Science)

See *Geographical information science.*

Skepticism/scepticism

See *Fallibilism as opposed to foundationalism.*

Skewed distribution

See *Data transformations, Frequency distributions, Power (law) distributions.*

Small-user post-code address file

See *Post-code address file (PAF).*

Small world networks

Named by Stanley Milgram following his 'Six degrees of separation' experiment, small-world networks are a combination of random and ordered relationships, wherein a few nodes (individuals, towns, websites, academic articles), have many connections and most have few, which explains why, for example some ideas, rumours and epidemics can spread rapidly through a society (and others don't), and why who you know is more important than what you know. Small world network show a *power law* (scale invariant, fractal) *distribution.* See also *Social network analysis.*

Strogatz, S. (2001) 'Exploring complex networks' *Nature,* **410** (6825): 268–276

Smoothing

Usually practised in analysing data for trends in order to identify and eliminate erratic elements, leaving only the more robust features of the data which persist either over a time period or in relation to an increasing or decreasing independent variable (see *Variable*). Calculating a **moving average** is the most usual technique, using either *means* or *medians* – see *Central tendency*. A moving average might, for example be calculated with a **smoothing window** of three months; the first data plot being the average for months 1 to 3, the second for months 2 to 4, and so on. The advantage of using medians is that they are less sensitive to *outliers* within the smoothing window. Instead of simple averaging, the averages may be computed by averaging the previously smoothed values with the next raw value i.e. the average for 1 to 3, plus the 4th value divided by 2, or other weightings may be used as in **exponential smoothing**. A disadvantage to smoothing is that it deletes information about fluctuations which, while untidy, are nonetheless real. For example, it can eliminate most of the evidence that a phenomenon has a *power law* (scale invariant or fractal) *distribution*. See also *Trend analysis*.

McLoone, J. (n.d.) 'Data Smoothing' *The Wolfram Demonstrations Project* http://demonstrations.wolfram.com/DataSmoothing/

www.statsoft.com/textbook/stathome.html search on 'timeseries/forcasting'

Snap-shot research

See Cross-sectional research, *Longitudinal research*.

SOC, SOC 90, SOC2000

See *Standard Occupational Classification*.

Social anthropology

Might be said to be the study of human social life or society, with a particular emphasis on structures of social relationships, and a tendency to pursue this in non-industrialised societies, or among 4th world populations within industrialised societies. However, the term is usually used to refer to the anthropological tradition (apart from physical anthropology) of Britain and the Commonwealth, wherever it is pursued and as a contrast with American anthropology which is more often called 'cultural anthropology'. The most favoured techniques of research are ethnographic – see *Cognitive anthropology, Ethnographic research*.

Association of Social Anthropologists of Britain and the Commonwealth www.theasa.org/

Social capital

There is some confusion whether this includes the benefits of the legally defined membership of formal organisations, as with employment, and/or the benefits of citizenship, as with welfare benefits or the rights to legal aid. However, the focus of interest is usually on resources which are provided through networks informally and outside the official economy, through friends, neighbours and relatives. The literature on social capital includes that which focuses on material benefits, that which focuses on community cohesion and on *social exclusion* – which is often linked to the theme of democratic decline, and that which focuses on psychosocial support and health (Smith 2007). The empirical study of social capital is usually through *social network analysis* via *questionnaire* research. For a questionnaire covering most of the possibilities see:

CSPP (n.d.) *Measuring Social Capital*, Centre for the Study of Public Policy, University of Aberdeen, www.abdn.ac.uk/cspp/nrb7-quest.shtml

Smith, M. (2007) 'Social Capital', *Encyclopedia of Informal Education (INFED)* www.infed. org/biblio/social_capital.htm

Social Care On-line

Includes a database of research in social care in the UK www.scie-socialcareonline.org.uk

Social class

See *Area based inequality measures, Cambridge scheme, CASMIN, CASMIN Educational classification, ESeC, Goldthorpe Classes, Market research categorisation, National Statistics socio-economic classification (NS-SEC), Registrar General's social classes, Socio-Economic classification, Wright Classes.*

Social construction/ism

(1) The term '**social construction**' is sometimes used to make a contrast between *phenomena* which are thought to represent entities with an existence independent of human thought (mind-independent entities) and phenomena which are a product of belief (socially constructed) as in a distinction between sex and gender made in this vein – see *Thomas' dictum*. Such contrasts are often made in a correctionist way, to critique the representation of what is social and changeable as something natural and inevitable – see *Objectification, Reification*. This is not social constructionism. (2) **Social constructionism** is based on the recognition that all human knowledge is cultural knowledge, produced collaboratively by social beings in particular social, economic and political relations at a particular historical moment. All knowledge is socially constructed (sex as well as gender) and cannot be corrected by an appeal to some reality which is outside socially constructed ways of knowing.

Research on this assumption is directed towards documenting the way knowledge is produced and justified and the forms of social organisation within which this happens. The results vary according to assumptions made about the nature of society as a generator of knowledge. For example, some versions focus on the importance of power structures as shaping knowledge and the ideological function of knowledge – see *false consciousness, ideology*; others regard the idea of a power structure as just another social construction; yet others focus on networks of relationships, forms of organisation or on chance and *contingency*.

Social constructionism has some difficulty in justifying its own research findings insofar as that logically they can only be social constructions of social constructions. Where this engenders *scepticism* (**radical social constructionism**), social constructionism slips into *post-modernism* with its claim that all versions of the truth are equally valid. But this is not inevitable since it can be argued that rigorous, self-aware (*reflexive*) and *objective* inquiry (procedural objectivity), even if it is by necessity a social construction job, is nonetheless superior to unreflexive and slipshod research.

See also *Science wars, Strong programme, Ontological gerrymandering*.

ABC World (n.d.) *Social Construction*, http://abcworld.net/Social_construction.html

Reichertz, J. and Zielke, B. (2008) 'Debate: Social Constructionism', *Forum for Qualitative Social Research* **9**(1) www.qualitative-research.net/fqs/fqs-e/debate-5-e.htm

Social desirability bias

See *Bias, Self-serving*

Social exclusion

Might be regarded as a non-monetary definition of relative poverty (poverty, relation) in the sense that it presumes that people have a right to access some package of opportunities and are excluded from so doing – poverty of opportunity. The target opportunities are usually defined as those to which 'the average' person, or household has access, and to which the excluded group does not. In studies of social exclusion what people are excluded from are social, health, leisure, economic, psychosocial support, employment, educational, political, personal safety and other benefits and the dimensions of exclusion most frequently studied are those of income poverty, gender, ethnicity, disability, age, sexual orientation and rural residence. Sometimes social exclusion is included within the definition of *poverty* – where poverty equals income poverty plus social exclusion (as defined above). The term 'social exclusion' has tended to replace 'inequality' in UK government and EU circles. Note the Social Exclusion Task Force in the Cabinet Office and the way each government agency has been made to commit itself to reducing social exclusion through a Public Service Agreement http://www.cabinetoffice.gov.uk/social_exclusion_task_force/

Centre for the Analysis of Social Exclusion (CASE) http://sticerd.lse.ac.uk/case/

Social grade (SG)

More often used in *market research* than *social class*.

Social network analysis

Tracing, mapping and analysing social, economic and political relationships between people and between organisations. Of long-standing – note for example the early interest of social anthropologists in kinship networks and of psychologists and sociologists in *sociometry*. However, modern social network analysis has become part of broader **network analysis**, informed by graph theory, dealing with all kinds of networks from those in deep space to those between molecules in cells. This has gained a great impetus with the development of software for *computer simulating* network development, and for creating electronic displays (see *Geographical information systems*) and by the discovery of the properties of *small world networks* which explain a great deal about complex phenomena such as the spread of epidemics, fashions, ideas and rumours and the accumulation of wealth – see *Complexity theory*. There is a lively interest in social networks in determining the resources available to people – see *Social capital, Social exclusion* and in the new networks created through the internet – see *Cyber #*.

Breiger, R. (2004) 'The analysis of social networks' in Hardy, M. and Bryman, A. (eds) *Handbook of Data Analysis*, London: Sage 505–526 (extracts available on the University of Arizona website at: www.u.arizona.edu/~breiger/NetworkAnalysis.pdf

ESRC (n.d.) 'Introduction to Social Network Analysis' www.ccsr.ac.uk/methods/publications/snacourse/snacourseweb.html

For references, visualisations, software and other resources: International Network for Social Network Analysis at www.insna.org

Social research

A term contested on several dimensions:

- according to how far 'social' covers psychological, medical and so on;
- how far 'research' means 'scientific research', with questions such as whether literary criticism counts as science and whether *semiology/semiotics* is scientific or literary. Hence the discussion relates to the dispute on the demarcation between science and non-science; see *Demarcation debate*.

- whether value-led investigatory and related activities such as *partisan* and *participatory research* should be called 'research', when their objective is often not to produce knowledge but to produce psychological, cultural or political change – see *Value-neutral or value-led*.
- on *epistemological and ontological* grounds such that if 'researchers' do not believe that the results of their research are any more valid than any other account, as seems to be the belief among *post modernists*, then can their activities count as 'research' ?
- on the 'pure and applied' dimension, with some scholars wanting the term 'research' restricted to those activities producing high quality knowledge of general validity, and excluding much inquiry into 'the social' which is to gain information of immediate practical use; for example *effectiveness research*, and the kind of 'research' done by party political and public relations researchers, or the research for media documentaries or feature films – see *Social Research, pure and applied*.

Social research, pure and applied

Applied social research is research directed principally towards finding solutions to immediate practical problems (**Operational research**) and/or to evaluating the effectiveness of practices and policies in human services (**Practical evaluation**, *Effectiveness research*, *Evaluation research*) rather than towards the development of a body of general knowledge, as in '**pure**', or 'blue-skies' research. In practice the distinction may be difficult to make, since much applied research does give rise to more general truth claims, and much 'pure research' has practical applications.

For applied research see also; *Action research, Burden analysis, Cost # analysis, Design experiments, Design ethnography, Effectiveness research, Evaluation research, Meta-analysis, Mode 1 and mode 2, n of 1 experiments, Queue theory, Randomised controlled experiments, Systematic reviews, Usability research.*

Hammersley, M. (2000) 'Varieties of social research: a typology', *International Journal of Social Research Methodology* **3**(3) 221–229

Social Science Information Gateway (SOSIG)

Freely available internet service providing high quality internet information in the social sciences including psychology, business and law: part of the Resource Discovery Network (RDN).

www.sosig.ac.uk

Social Sciences Citation Index (SSCI)

See *Citation indices.*

Social Stratification

See *Social class.*

Social Text affair/Sokal affair

Refers to a spoof article by physicist Alan Sokal (1996) satirising post-modernist writing but taken as genuine by the editors of *Social Text.* Feature in debates about the status of science – see *Science wars.*

ABC World (n.d.) *The Sokal Affair,* http://abcworld.net/Sokal_affair.html

Socio-Economic Classification (SEC or S-EC or S-eC)

(1) General, any scheme of classification designed to place individuals or households within the social structure, for example in terms of *social class* (2) UK Government statistics; until 1990 referred both to the division of the population into social classes based on occupation (*Registrar General's Social Classes)* and, separately, into Socio-economic groups (SEGs) according to position within the economy. From 1990 government research and statistics use a single socio-economic classification *National Statistics Socio-economic classification (NS-SEC)* based on a revision of *Goldthorpe classes.*

ESRC Question Bank (n.d.) *Social Classification (SOC),* http://qb.soc.surrey.ac.uk/resources/classification/socintro.htm

Socio-economic group (SEG/S-EG/S-eG)

UK Government statistics; scheme for dividing population according to occupational position within the economic structure. Superceded in 1990 by *National Statistics Socio-economic classification (NS-SEC).*

ONS (2008) *Continuity issues: SC, SEG and NS-SEC,* http://www.ons.gov.uk/about-statistics/classifications/current/ns-sec/continuity-issues/index.html

Sociogram

Graphical display of relationships between people used in *social network analysis,* and particularly in *sociometry,* usually based on a **socio-matrix** (pl, **socio-matrices**). See examples in Figures 26 and 27.

Lewejohann, L. (2005): *Sociogram (Version 1.0).* [Computer software]. Www.phenotyping.com/sociogram

Pupil no' (choosing)	Pupil no' (chosen)				
	1	2	3	4	5
1		R	R	O	R
2	R		O	O	
3	R			O	
4					R
5	R	O		R	

Figure 26 Socio-matrix extract: friendship choices for five pupils; up to four choices each.
R = reciprocated O = not reciprocated.

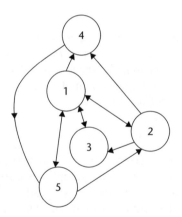

Figure 27 Detail from sociogram drawn from socio-matrix.

Socio-matrix

See *Sociogram, Sociometry*.

Sociometry

Closely associated with Jacob Moreno from the 1930s involving the quantitative and qualitative measurement of relationships using socio-matrices and usually their display in a *sociogram*. The academic aspects of sociometry have largely been absorbed into the broader *social network analysis*, while developments under the name of sociometry have been mainly in its applications in group therapy and psychodrama.

International Sociometry Training Network: www.sociometry.net

Spearman's rank order correlation co-efficient (Spearman's correlation/Spearman's rho/ρ/r_s)

A non-parametric statistical calculation for *correlation* with ordinal level data – see *Statistics, parametric and non-parametric, Data levels of*. It yields a co-efficient (ρ or rho) which ranges from -1 (perfect negative/inverse correlation) to $+1$ (perfect positive correlation) where 0 means no correlation at all. The calculation compares the rank order of one set of data with the rank order of another and estimates how likely it would be that the association shown would occur by chance. Rho is preferred to *Pearson's product moment correlation* where the data distribution includes significant *outliers*. For calculators and tutorials see *Statistics software*.

Specification

An oft unnoticed aspect of *generalisation*. While generalisations make a claim that something is likely to happen more generally than just in the circumstances of the research, the specification describes the conditions under which it is likely to happen. Sometimes a synonym for conditional probability – see *Probability*.

Specificity

Of a research *instrument*, (1) the extent to which the instrument records differences of a specific kind; for example an instrument which asks questions about a patient's satisfaction with various aspects of his or her hospital care, has more specificity than one which asks a single general 'satisfaction' question – closely related to the idea of *sensitivity* in instrument design; (2) of diagnostic instruments in particular, see *Type 1 and type 2 errors*.

Spectral analysis

In *time series analysis*, analysis to determine how far changes are cyclical.

Speech act

See *Illocution*.

Speech act theory

See *Pragmatic linguistics.*

Speech exchange (system)

Term used to apply to any multi-party situation in which speech occurs; sometimes specified more closely, for example as 'a two party speech exchange', or a 'multi-party, orchestrated speech exchange' (a seminar for example): used widely in linguistics.

SPSS (Statistical Package for the Social Sciences)

See *Statistics software.*

SS

See *Sum of the squares.*

$SSB, SS_{error}, SS_{groups}, SS_{main}, SS_{total}$ and SSW

See *Sum of the squares.*

SSCI (Social Sciences Citation Index)

See *Citation indices.*

Stability

See *Reliability.*

Stake holders

Various groups who might be said to have a legitimate interest in a programme or policy that is subject to evaluation research and such groups who might be said to have a legitimate interest in the conduct and outcome of any research activity – see also *Gate keepers, Evaluation, pluralistic.*

Standard deviation/standard error

Symbolised as SD/SE, or S for the standard deviation of a *sample* variable, and σ for the standard deviation of a *population variable*. Statistic based on the properties of the *normal distribution* which provides a standard unit for a data set, expressing the percentage of data points

S

lying at a given distance from the mean in *frequency distributions* that approximate to *normal distributions*. See also *Central tendency and dispersion, Standardisation, Z scores*.

Standard deviation of the mean/standard error of the mean

Symbolised as:

$SE_{\bar{x}} = s/\sqrt{n}$ meaning that it is calculated as the standard deviation of the sample divided by the square root of the size of the sample. This is the standard deviation of estimates of the mean which would derive from taking infinite samples from the same population. See *Central limit theorem, Normal distribution* and for standard deviation, *Central tendency and dispersion*.

Standard error curve

See *Normal distribution*.

Standard measurement error curve

See *Normal distribution*.

Standard normal distribution

See *Z scores*.

Standard occupational classification (SOC)

See *National Statistics standard occupational classification*.

Standardisation

(1) The use of rates or other proportional measures to make comparisons discounting differences in population or group size (see *rates*); (2) as **normalisation**, as in Standard Attainment Tests (SATs). Most *psychometric* instruments, such as those measuring IQ, verbal ability, or self-esteem are standardised (or normalised) (Kline 2005). Items are selected so that when the test is used with a large representative sample of the relevant population, the results take the form of a *normal distribution* with 68% of subjects scoring within the range plus and minus one *standard deviation* from the mean. A particular subject can be given a score (a *Z score or a stanine score*, both **standardised scores**) which locates him or her in relation to everyone else in the same population,

usually in terms of *percentile* or *stanine* rank. With unstandardised tests, subjects can only be located in relation to other people who have taken the test (NFER n.d.). Much hinges on which was the population for which the test was standardised/for which there are test norms: **the reference population**. If a test is standardised on an American population there is no guarantee that the *mean* and *standard deviation* for a UK population will be the same as for America. Norms become inaccurate over time For example, many IQ tests which were standardised in the past, are not standardised for the present. People have been improving their performance on IQ tests (the **Flynn effect**) so the tests have to be re-standardised from time to time (Flynn 1999). See also *Reference population, Standardised mortality/morbidity ratios (SMRs)*. (3) The use of standard questions and definitions in research – see *Harmonised concepts and questions, Question banks*; (4) controlling a variable in analysis – see *Control direct and statistical*. For example, to control for age differences in an investigation of responses to a teaching programme, the scores of all the pupils might be adjusted – standardised, so that it is as if they were all of the same age. This assumes a close *correlation* between age and score – see also *Analysis of covariance*. (5) The standardisation of behaviour by experimenters and interviewers so that all subjects are treated similarly where that is required to prevent *confounding* and to avoid some *interviewer effects*. See also *Protocol*.

National Foundation for Educational Research (NFER) (n.d.) *Standardised* Scores and Percentile Ranks http://www.nfer.ac.uk and search on title

Flynn, J. (1999) 'Searching for justice: IQ gains over time', *American Psychologist* **54**: 5–20

Standardised mean difference (Cohen's delta)

See *Effect size (ES) measures*.

Standard(ised) measurement

See *Stanines, Z scores*.

S

Standardised mortality/morbidity ratios (SMRs)

In *demography* and *epidemiology*, death rates and rates of illness vary with age. All other things being equal an older population will experience more illness and higher death rates than a younger one. To investigate the influence of factors other than age on morbidity or mortality in a particular area, the mortality/morbidity rate (usually) of the wider population *(reference population)* will be used to calculate the morbidity/mortality rate which would be expected for that area, if it had the rates of the wider population. This creates a comparison between the target population and (usually) the wider (reference) population, controlling for differences in their age profiles and gender ratio. Rates for males and females are always calculated separately because they have different mortality/morbidity rates, and the calculation is usually for each 5 or 10 year age group separately. The same principle may be followed to compare the death or morbidity rates of people within different social classes displayed as rates above or below the average for all males or all females. Sometimes social class SMRs also control for the fact that different social classes have different age profiles, sometimes they do not.

London Health Observatory *Methods- age-standardised rates.* www.lho.org.uk/DATAANDMETHODS/Methods.aspx

Standardised regression co-efficient

See *Pearson's product moment correlation.*

Standardised relational pairs (SRPs)

See *Membership category analysis.*

Standpoint epistemology

Centres on the notion that members of oppressed groups have a superior understanding of society (an **epistemic privilege)** and that by studying their views (or sharing their lives) researchers can develop important insights and lines of research. Though based on the writings of Hegel and Marx, currently the main example is **feminist standpoint epistemology** where it is argued that women have an epistemic privilege which derives from the fact that being marginalised they must learn both to get by in their own world, and to get along in the dominant patriarchal society. Their position as 'outsiders within' the dominant society is alleged to give them an insight into the social and political structures of the dominant society which less oppressed people will not have.

Janack, M. (2004) 'Feminist Epistemology', *Internet Encyclopedia of Philosophy* www.iep.utm.edu/f/fem-epis.htm#SH3a

Stanine (STAndard NINE)

Nine-point standard scale with a mean of five and a standard deviation of two, used in creating standardised/normed tests as an a variant on using *percentiles* – see *Standardisation*. Each division except the first and the last is ½ of a standard deviation. Someone at stanine 8 is among

Table 22 Stanine scale.

	lowest	next	next	Next	next	next	next	next	top
Ranking of subjects	4%	7%	12%	17%	20%	17%	12%	7%	4%
Stanine descriptor	1	2	3	4	5	6	7	8	9

those scoring more than 72% of other people in the same population and is among the top 11%. See Table 22

Statistical power

In common sense terms this is the likelihood that a statistical test will give a true result, or perhaps better put, the likelihood of not giving an inconclusive result. More technically, power is the probability that the test will correctly reject a false null hypothesis – see *Hypothesis, Type I and Type II errors*. Power is calculated as $\beta-1$ where β = the type II error probability – see *Beta level*. Power is determined mainly by:

- the differences between the means of the groups being compared – the greater the difference the greater the power
- the measurement scale used: the more discriminating the scale the greater the power – see *Data levels of*
- the significance level (alpha α *level*): 0.05 has greater power than 0.01
- the variances – the lower the variances the greater the power – see *variance*
- the *sample size* – the bigger the sample the greater the power

Researchers usually have some choice about the last four of these and this needs to be taken into consideration in planning research, particularly with regard to determining an adequate *sample size*, and/or in experiments, in deciding whether to work with a sample selected to be relatively homogeneous to reduce variances. See also *Statistical significance*.

Hyperstat on-line (n.d.) 'Power' http://davidmlane.com/hyperstat/index.html

Statistical significance

Testing data for statistical significance means asking either the question, 'Are the differences found in the results as big or bigger than the differences which might have occurred by chance ?' – **tests of difference/independence**, or 'Are the similarities found in the results as great or greater than might have occurred by chance ?' – **tests of association/similarity**, used for testing *correlation* and *covariance*. A model is created of the kinds of results which might have occurred by chance – (expected scores (E)). For tests of difference the actual results (observed scores (O)) are compared with these, then, it is calculated how often would the differences as great as or greater than that shown between E and O occur by chance. If the answer is 'not very often' then this is presumptive evidence that the results were not due to chance, and the results are said to be *statistically significant*. For a test of association the question is how often would the similarities shown between two sets of observed scores have occurred by chance. For both, the usual threshold (*alpha level/significance level*) for 'not very often' is not more than 5 times out of 100 ($p < 0.05$). Results of statistical significance testing are usually expressed in *p* (for probability) *values*, but sometimes in terms of *confidence intervals*.

Which characteristics of the data are compared with the chance model depends on the tests; sometimes, as in X^2 it is the number of items in each category of data; sometimes, as with the *Wilcoxon signed ranks test* it is rank order of the same subjects for two different tests. In the more powerful parametric tests it is the *mean*, the *standard deviation* or the *variance* – see *Statistics, parametric and non-parametric*.

Statistical significance for difference may be calculated in one direction only – *a one-tailed test*, or in either direction, *a two-tailed test* – see *Tails*.

See also, *Family wise error, Central tendency and dispersion* (for mean, standard deviation and variance), *Substantive significance* and the tests referred to above.

Statistics

Originally numerical data collected by the state as an aid to public administration, particularly for taxation and conscription. Now any numerical data and techniques for manipulating them. Narrowly, refers to measures such as the *mean*, the *range*, the *variance*, or the *standard deviation* of a sample – see *Central tendency and dispersion*. When referring to a population these are called *parameters* rather than statistics.

Statistics, Authority

See *UK Statistics Authority.*

Statistics, Bayesian

See *Bayesian inference.*

Statistics, Fisherian

See *Statistics, inferential.*

Statistics, inferential (Fisherian)

See *Inferential Statistics.*

Statistics non-parametric

See *Statistics parametric and non-parametric.*

Statistics, parametric and non-parametric
(see Table 23)

Parametric statistics tests have greater *statistical power* and are so called because their use makes assumptions about the characteristics (parameters) of the population from which the data are drawn. **Non-parametric** (or **distribution-free**) tests are used when such assumptions cannot legitimately be made. The conditions for using a parametric test are given below, although it is not unusual to find researchers using parametric tests when these conditions are not met:

Conditions for using **parametric tests** of *statistical significance*

- the level of measurement must be interval at least – see *Data, levels of*
- the intervals should be equal – see *Plastic intervals*
- the sample data must be drawn from a population which approximates a *normal distribution* – see *Data transformations*
- the *variances* of samples should not be significantly different – applies to unrelated designs only – see *Related and unrelated designs, Central tendency and dispersion (Range), Homoscedasticity.*

Non-parametric tests can be used with data that satisfy the conditions for parametric testing but not vice versa.

For selecting a test see :MicrOsiris *'Decision tree for Statistics'* : www.microsiris.com/Statistical%20Decision%20Tree/

Statistics software:

Calculators: Minitab, SAS, SYSTAT, SPSS and Analyse-it (an add-on for Microsoft Excel) are all purchasable packages allowing a wide range of statistical calculation. Most universities provide their students with access to at least one of these, usually SPSS (Statistical Package for the Social Sciences). Tuition in using them is advised and for SPSS there is:

Lee, C., Famoye, F. and Sharp, J. (1999) SPSS *On-line training workshop,* University of Central Michigan http://calcnet.mth.cmich.edu/org/spss/toc.htm

Table 23 Parametric and non-parametric tests: common examples

	Tests of difference/independence		Tests of association (correlation)
	Related designs*	Unrelated designs*	
Parametric (Interval and ratio level data)[1]	Related t-tests	Unrelated t-tests	Pearson product moment correlation coefficient.
			Cronbach's alpha
	Analysis of variance ANOVA/MANOVA	Analysis of variance ANOVA/MANOVA	
			Analysis of covariance ANCOVA/MANCOVA
Non-parametric equivalent (ordinal level data and above)[1]	Wilcoxon signed ranks	Mann–Whitney U or Wilcoxon rank sum	Spearman's rho (ρ)
			Mann–Whitney U
Non-parametric equivalent (nominal level data and above)[1]	Binomial sign test	X^2 contingency or X^2 goodness of fit test	Phi coefficient or X^2
			Kuder-Richardson formula 20
			Log-linear analysis

* see *Related and unrelated designs*

(1) see *Data, levels of.*

Free downloads vary in their comprehensiveness and user-friendliness. Openstat provides as much as most people will need and is not too difficult use in conjunction with its e-textbook (see below):

Openstat: www.statpages.org/miller/openstat

Sisa deals only with two-by-two tables but for this purpose is quick and easy to use. http://home.clara.net/sisa/two2hlp.htm

For selecting a test see :MicrOsiris *'Decision tree for Statistics'* : www.microsiris.com/Statistical%20Decision%20Tree/

Statistics on-line texts:
Absolute beginners might find the *Shodor Interactivate* web site useful : www.shodor.org/interactivate1.0/activities/index.html

John Musalia's (2008) statistics course at the University of West Kentucky is well constructed and beautifully presented on power point. www.wku.edu/~john.musalia/soc300

Statsoft http://www.statsoft.nl/textbook/stathome.html and Hyperstat http://davidmlane.com/hyperstat/index.html are both free downloadable statistics texts which start from the basics and are linked with on-line calculators.

The Rice Virtual Lab in Statistics (RVLS) carries interactive demonstrations of many statistical concepts http://onlinestatbook.com/rvls.html as does McClelland,G. (1999) *Seeing statistics*, Duxbury Press. http://psych.colorado.edu/~mcclella/java/zcalc.html

Easton, V. and McColl, J. (1997) *Statistics Glossary*, is useful for quick reference www.stats.gla.ac.uk/steps/glossary/index.html

Stem and leaf plot

Descriptive statistics; technique for laying out data so patterns can be inspected visually. A stem and leaf plot for a data array is shown in Figure 28:

Data array: 20, 79, 22, 33, 15, 27, 30, 19, 23, 21, 31, 42, 45

The stem figures are the tens, and the leaf figures are the units. Thus 15 is shown with 1 as the stem and 5 as the leaf, and 19 by adding a 9 to the same stem. From this kind of display the mode, the range, the

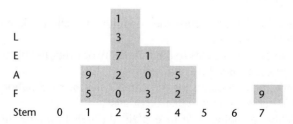

Figure 28 Example of a stem and leaf plot

overall shape of the distribution and any *outliers* can be seen – see also *Central tendency and dispersion* (for mode, and range) *Frequency distributions, Graphs.*

Stochastic

Synonym for *random*, probabilistic, determined by chance. Used principally about *computer simulations* which combine deterministic and stochastic elements – see also *Complexity theory.*

Strata (sing., stratum)

See Sample, stratified, Stratification.

Stratification

In samples – see *Sample, stratified*; **in experiments**, synonym for factorial – see *Factorial design.*

Strong programme

In the sociology of knowledge, this is *social constructionism* applied to scientific knowledge (in social studies of science and technology). The 'weak programme' although not named as such, assumed that only erroneous knowledge required a sociological explanation, as in questions such as, 'Why did the Soviets reject Darwinian evolution?' The strong programme by contrast assumes that since all knowledge is produced by human beings in social, economic and political circumstances, all knowledge, true or false, requires a sociological explanation; as in the question, 'What social/political/economic factors led to the discovery of the moons of Jupiter?' The strong programme would be agnostic about whether the moons of Jupiter exist or not; see also *Science wars, Social constructionism.* The tenets of the strong programme are that all its explanations must be:

- causal, seeking to define the conditions which enable a particular belief to come about,
- impartial with regards to the rationality or irrationality, truth or falsity, success or failure of a belief,
- symmetrical, looking for the same types of explanation whether the belief is thought to be true or false,
- reflexive in being able to explain the beliefs of the Strong programme as well as other beliefs.

The last of these is the more difficult to achieve (see *Social constructionism*).

Everything2.com 'The Strong Programme' www.everything2.com/index.pl – and search 'Strong Programme'.

Structuralism and post structuralism

Two ideas define structuralism. One is the notion that whatever is to be studied is part of an overall system or *structure* of relationships between elements, and analysis should be in terms of relating the part to the whole. The other is that appearances, which may be complicated and untidy, are underlain by simpler structures which generate what can be observed. In this sense all forms of structuralism are realist in their assumption of a deep reality of unobservable (but inferable) entities – see *Realism*. Beyond this there are a large number of structuralisms varing with the field of study and the kind structures envisaged. These include varieties where the structures are neurological, as with Chomskian linguistics, and Levi Strauss' approach to myths and kinship systems; where structures are communicational as with *semiotics/semiology*, or where they are political economic as with structural *marxism*. Structuralist thinking occurs without the term being used. The genotype-phenotype relation in genetics is a good example. And the use of the term 'structure' does not necessarily indicate a structuralist approach. In structural-functionalism, or in the use of terms such as 'kinship structure' or 'class structure', structure may simply refer to a pattern of regularities, rather than imply an underlying generative mechanism.

In *semiology/semiotics*, some fields of *hermeneutics*, some areas of literary criticism, and structural anthropology, structuralism refers to the idea that meaning arises from the differences between signs, or to the placing of one *sign* within a whole systems (or structure) of signs. Meaning is regarded as a matter of binary oppositions: what something is, is defined by what it is not: men are not women, night is not day.

Marxism and *semiotics/semiology* are the main kinds of structuralism against which **post structuralism** is defined, particularly the latter. Whereas structuralism assumes something simpler underlying complicated appearances, post-structuralism (like *post modernism*), assumes essential untidiness and incoherence. Whereas structuralism assumed that there could be a correct reading of a system of signs, post structuralism denies that this is possible and treats meaning as shifting and different from reader to reader – see *Crisis of representation, Polysemy, Relativism*. Post structuralism partially overlaps with the meaning of *post modernism* and is subject to similar problems of definition in that almost all those named as exponents deny the label, and whether they accept it or not,

S

they differ in just what they are rejecting. Thus Foucault has denied that either label applies to him, and Derrida's approach remains structuralist (on the general definition above) even though he is usually named as a post structuralist writer.

Encyclopedia of Marxism (2005) 'Structuralism' www.marxists.org/glossary/terms/s/t.htm#structuralism

ABC world (n.d.) *Structuralism* http://abcworld.net/Structuralism.html

ABC world (n.d.) *Post-structuralism* http://abcworld.net/Post-structuralism.html

Structured observation

See *Observation, structured or intuitive.*

Student's t-test

See *t-tests.*

Subaltern studies group

School of socialist historians engaged in writing the history of the Indian sub-continent from the viewpoint of the struggles of ordinary people, partly as a reaction against *orientalism*, and within the general field of *post-colonial anthropology.*

Rogall, N. (1998) *Subaltern Studies,* http://www.londonsocialisthistorians.org/index.html and search on title

Subject

Usually an uncontroversial term for someone who is the focus of research interest, but sometimes objected to on the grounds that one meaning of 'subject' is a person who is subjected to the power of another. The objection is part of a critique of mainstream research as objectifying and exploitative – see *Objectification, Partisan research, Participatory research.* Alternatives are *actor*, collaborator, informant, interviewee, *member*, narrator, operant (*behaviourism*), respondent, partner, participant, proband (now archaic), or if they are being studied as occupants of social roles, then, for example, police officer, J.P., solicitor, as appropriate.

Subject burden

See *Respondent burden.*

Subject expectancy effect

See *Subject reactivity.*

Subjective/subjectivity

The **subjective** is the world of private experience, incorrigible by definition – see *Corrigibility*. The term takes further meaning as a series of opposites to some meanings of *objective*. Thus if objective knowledge is defined as knowledge which is public and shareable, then the subjective is private and personal. If the objective is rational and disinterested, the subjective is emotional and partial (biased if you disapprove of this; committed if you approve). And if objectivity means being able to transcend your immediate situation and take an outsider's view point, then subjectivity means seeing things from one's own point of view (a blinkered viewpoint if you disapprove, and an authentic one if you approve). In much of science the subjective is viewed with grave suspicion on the grounds that emotion and bias lead to error, and the truth can only be known by rising above your own immediate concerns and perspectives. The preference for objectivity is so strong that sometimes the term 'objective knowledge' (that is desubjectivised knowledge) is used as a synonym for truth – see also *Subjectivism*.

Drapeau, M. (2002) 'Subjectivity in Research: Why Not? But…' *The Qualitative Report*, **7** (3) www.nova.edu/ssss/QR/

Subjectivism

(1) The treating of private experience as the most important sphere of human existence. In its most extreme form subjectivism denies the existence of any entities other than those subjectively experienced, and to be known about by *introspection*, or the sharing of introspection with others. It is anti-realist – see *Realism*, and a version of cognitive and moral *relativism* – see also *Multiple realities*. It runs parallel to *social constructionism* in its most radical form, except that the latter treats reality as constructed by people collaboratively, and hence treats the construction of (a sense of) reality as an *objective/inter-subjective/objectifying* or *reifying* process rather than a subjective one. Less radical forms of subjectivism may include a feminist insistence on the importance of the subjective, including the claim that what is commonly regarded as objective knowledge is actually an ideological complex which defines reality in ways favourable to dominant groups – see *ideology*. Given the diversity of feminist views it would be unwise to say in general that feminism should be regarded as subjectivist or social constructionist. In marxism, subjectivism is a term of disparagement as being in a state of *false consciousness*. (2) In probability theory subjectivism is the belief that probability is no more than an estimate of likelihood by a rational agent, as opposed to the idea that a probability is an essential feature of what ever is being estimated. Bayesian statistics takes this view. See *Bayesian inference, Prediction, Probability, Random*.

Subject reactivity (reactivity, subject expectancy effect)

General term covering all the ways in which *research artefacts* might be created by the *subjects* of research responding to the experience of being researched *per se*, and in this way create results which would not be produced in the absence of their being researched, or in the absence of their knowledge of being researched. The general effect is to undermine both the internal and the external validity of a piece of research – see *Validity, external, Validity internal*. Includes *expectancy effects*, where these work through cues conveyed by the researcher, *halo effects, Hawthorne effects, interviewer effects, pre* and *post test sensitivity* and see also *Bias, cooperative, Bias, self-effacing, Bias, self-serving, Demand characteristic Respondent burden. Blinding*, may not prevent subject reactivity, but it controls it so that the subjects' knowledge of being researched will not confound experimental results. Researchers who prioritise naturalistic/ecological validity may argue that any kind of research which alters people's normal patterns of activity creates subject reactivity which makes the results invalid in this regard – see *Validity, naturalistic*. See also *Unobtrusive measures*.

Substantive significance

As compared with *statistical significance*, substantive significance refers to the everyday practical importance of a research finding. For example, the risk of something adverse happening may be shown as statistically significant, but be so rare, and or so trivial, that it has little substantive significance.

Subtle realism

See *Realism*.

Successionist causality

See *Causal analysis*.

Successive interval scale

See *Thurstone scale*.

Sufficient cause/condition

See *Causal analysis*.

Summative evaluation

See *Evaluation, formative and summative*.

Sum of the squares (SS)

Many statistical calculations involve subtracting each score from the *mean*, squaring the result and adding all the squared differences together to produce the sum of the squares. In ANOVA calculations **SSB**, or **SS$_{groups}$** or **SS$_{main}$** stands for the sum of the squares <u>between</u> (the squared difference between each group mean and the grand *mean*, divided by the number of cases in the group and the results for each group added together). **SSW** or **SS$_{error}$** stands for the sum of the squares <u>within</u>, when each score is subtracted from its own group mean. **SS$_{total}$** expresses the total amount of variance in the data set and the purpose of ANOVA is to decide how much of this is 'within' (and attributable to diversity with each group) and how much 'between' and probably due to differences in the way each group has been treated, or what its members have experienced. See *Analysis of variance (ANOVA)*.

Suppression

See *Anonymisation, Perturbation*.

Survey

Unlike a *census* which attempts to collect data about every member of a population, a survey selects a sample to represent the population. See *Representativeness, Generalisation*. Surveys may be *cross-sectional* (snapshot) taking a sample and collecting data from them at one point in time, or *longitudinal* where the same sample of respondents is questioned at successive points in time. In *repeat surveys*, a series of cross-sectional surveys (each one a different sample, but each survey the same questions) may track characteristics of the population giving some of the advantages of longitudinal designs. See also *Pseudo cohart analysis*. Surveys vary in their:

- sampling methods – see *Sample #*
- recruitment methods – see *Survey recruitment*
- method of eliciting information see *Interview types, Question formats, Questionnaire administration*.

Statpac (2008) *Everything You Ever Wanted to Know About Surveys – Tutorial* http://www.statpac.com/surveys/

Survey analysis software

There are many software packages designed to facilitate the analysis of survey data collected by *questionnaire*. These are reviewed by the American Statistical Association at www.hcp.med.harvard.edu/statistics/survey-soft/

S

Survey recruitment

How people are found and engaged as survey respondents (see Table 24).

Table 24 How people are found and engaged as survey respondents.

Recruitment by:	Notes. For all entries see also *Questionnaire administration, Sample #, Sampling #, Incentives.*
advertising	Adverts in print or broadcast media, or, within organisations, on notice-boards and by memos are more often used to recruit subjects for *experiments* and participants for *focus groups*, than to recruit respondents for surveys, except for internet surveys. Those who sign up to be respondents are most unlikely to be *representative* of the population of interest. See *Career respondents, Incentives, Sample, self-selected.*
e-mail	May be used to recruit respondents for a later telephone or face to face interview, or for response to a down-loaded questionnaire. Those without e-mail access will be under-represented. See also *Sample, self-selected.*
door-to-door	Cold-calling, door to door may be used to recruit respondents for a later or an on-the-spot interview. Addresses may have been selected in advance on a random basis, or every nth address will be tried, see also *Focused enumeration, Kish grid.*
interception	Respondents intercepted, for example as they sit on a train or pass through a supermarket checkout. Ideally this will be within a framework for *time sampling* to allow for the fact that the supply of potential respondents and their *demography* will vary from time to time: or results should be *weighted* in retrospect to adjust sample towards *representativeness.* In intercept surveys it is usual for the respondents to be asked questions there and then. Most appropriate where the population of interest is precisely that which flows past the points of intercept; for example supermarket customers interviewed as super-market customers. Such surveys often suffer from busy targets refusing to co-operate, or doing so in a hasty and irritated way and may over-represent the more co-operative with time on their hands. See *Bias, availability.*
by intermediary	It may be necessary to use intermediaries as the first point of contact with potential respondents; for example a GP's practice register is confidential, so the practice may be asked to select every nth name on the list and telephone or mail out a request to agree to be interviewed – see also *Gatekeepers* – see also *Sample, snowball.*

(Continued)

Table 24 (Continued)

by internet	The internet may be used to advertise for respondents who will complete an on-line questionnaire. The population being sampled will be that most likely to hit the sites carrying the advertisement, but the characteristics of this population may be unknown. The sample of respondents will be biased towards those who respond to such requests, and if incentives are given, towards those most attracted by such *incentives*, see *Sample, self-selected*.
by post	A first('cold') contact with respondents by post results in very low levels of co-operation, which is why commercial companies often include prize draws and other *incentives*, but while these may increase the participation rate they will skew the sample towards those who are most attracted by such incentives – see *Sample, self selected*.
Snow-balling	See, *Sample, snowball*.
by telephone	Telephone contact may be used as an initial step in recruiting respondents who will later be interviewed face to face, or telephone interviewed at a later time more convenient to them. Telephone contact surveys under-represent those without telephones, and those who have registered to prohibit cold calling. If the *sampling frame* is a telephone directory they also under-represent ex-directory and those who only use mobile telephones, but usually random dialling is used.
write-ins, phone- ins, and e-mail-ins	Printed and broadcast media and websites, often feature *questionnaires* which they encourage their audience to complete. This includes the kind of 'survey' where respondents telephone one number to answer 'yes' and another to answer 'no'- see *Sample, self selected*. Some such surveys are better regarded as petitions in so far as recruitment is targeted on those who will support cause or oppose a development.

S

Survival analysis/models

See *Event history analysis/models*.

Survivor research

Research on behalf of, and usually by those who have experienced some traumatic event. Most commonly used of research by those who have 'survived' the mental health care system or the prison system. See also *Disability research, Participatory research*.

Faulkner, A. (2004) *The Ethics of Survivor Research: Guidelines for the ethical conduct of research carried out by mental health service users and survivors*, NCRM http://www.ncrm.ac.uk/ and search on title

Sweep

See *Repeat survey*.

Syllogism

See *Premise*.

Symbolic interactionism (SI) (sometimes foreshortened to **interactionism)**

(1) Sometimes used very generally and misleadingly to cover all *interpretive approaches*, sometimes including, sometimes excluding *ethnomethodology*; (2) more specifically used to refer to the work of George Herbert Mead and his influence on psychology and/or of Herbert Blumer and his influence on sociology, although it has always been a matter of dispute as to which aspects of Mead's work should be counted as constituents of S.I. The *epistemology* background is *pragmatism* with people pictured as practical beings adjusting their behaviour to that of others through intelligent action (rather than their behaviour being determined by forces beyond their control). For Mead this was an evolutionary theory, the interpretation of other people's actions and co-ordination of individual action one with another, being the important human adaptation; a reaction against both instinct theory and *behaviourism*. The 'symbol' in the symbolic, comes from the idea that people treat the actions of others as if they were symbols to be interpreted. Mead also noted that human beings treated the self as an object and thus he focussed interest in issues such as identity, self-esteem, and face saving activities. Selfhood is treated as a social entity. Society is not constituted by many selves coming together, rather it is the togetherness which creates the conditions for selfhood. In sociology, SI has been the inspiration for a very large number of *ethnographic* studies conducted through participant observation, although in psychology there have been laboratory experiments as well.

Oneill, G. (n.d.) 'Symbolic Interactionism'. www.geocities.com/oneill_g/symbolic_interactionism.html

Charon, J. (2006) *Symbolic Interactionism: an Introduction, an Interpretation.* Upper Saddle River, NJ: Prentice Hall

Symbolic logic

See *Boolean algebra*.

Sympathetic bias

See *Bias, sympathetic*.

Syntagmatic analysis

From *semiology/semiotics*; the analysis of the creation of meaning in texts through the way texts are structured as the kinds of texts they are, for example as narratives, arguments, montages and so on. Many writers today would use the term *discourse analysis* instead, though there are types of discourse analysis which are not syntagmatic. See also *Paradigmatic analysis, Textual interaction*.

> Chandler, D. (2006) 'Semiotics of beginners: syntagmatic analysis'. www.aber.ac.uk/ media/Documents/S4B/Sem04.html

Synthesis

The drawing together of different elements and combining them in a single (set of) conclusion(s). *Triangulation* is a synthetic process. Researchers often draw no distinction between analysis and synthesis, presenting both under a heading such as 'Findings', 'Discussion', 'Conclusion' or 'Analysis'. The term is most often used in the contexts of *mixed/multi-method research* and *meta-analysis*.

Synthetic statements

See *Logical positivism*.

Systematic reviews

See *Meta*-analysis.

S

t

(Lower case t); statistic reported by *t-test*.

T

(1) (Wilcoxon T); statistic reported by *Wilcoxon rank sum test* and *Wilcoxon signed ranks test*. (2) In *time series analysis* symbol for trend, see *trend*.

Tails (one- and two-tailed tests)

'Boys will get significantly better results than girls', is a one-tailed *hypothesis*. For a one tailed test of *statistical significance* we are interested in difference in one direction only. 'There will be significant differences between the results of boys and girls', is a two-tailed *hypothesis*. Since they don't indicate the direction of difference two-tailed tests may be called **directionless tests**. The only difference in procedure is in which column of a table of *critical values* to look up the result of the statistical test, or how to interpret the output from *statistics software*. It is made harder to get a statistically significant result on a two-tailed test than on a one-tailed test, because it is easier for chance to produce a difference in either direction than in just the one direction previously nominated.

TDE (Telephone Data Entry)

See *Questionnaire administration*.

Test of association, test of difference, test of independence

See *Statistical significance*.

Test case

See *Critical case analysis*, *Deviant case analysis*.

Test-factor elaboration

Synonym for *factorial design* where statistical control is used – see *Control, direct or statistical*.

Test theory

The theories relating to the construction of psychometric, scholastic and some health status tests. **Classical test theory (CTT) or True score theory (TSC)**, leads to tests which measure the respondent's perform-ance on the test. The 'classical' refers to the classical theory of measure-ment which divides any measure into a true score and an error and the design of tests is directed towards reducing the error – see *Central limit theorem, Measurement error*. **Item response theory (IRT)** is also known as the **2PL/3PL model, Birmbaum model, Item characteristic curve theory, Latent trait theory, Strong true score theory, or Modern test theory**. The relationship between an aptitude or disposition and the probability of a response to a test item is modelled and (so it is claimed) what is being measured is not the performance of the respondent but the (latent) trait underlying that performance. **Rasch** measurement is also a 'latent trait' theory but the modelling is more elaborate than IRT.

Klien, T. (2005) *Psychological Testing: a practical approach to design and evaluation*, London: Sage

(IRT) Baker, F. (1985) *Basics of Item Response Theory*, London, Heinemann E-published 2001 by EdRes : http://edres.org/irt/

Alagumalai, S., Curtis, D.D. and Hungi, N. (2005), *Applied Rasch Measurement: A book of exemplars* London: Springer-Kluwer.

[Rasch] Wright, B. and Stone, M. (1999) '*Measurement essentials*' Wilmington, Del. Widerange Inc. downloadable from www.rasch.org.measess/me-all.pdf

Free downloads of Rasch software are available at www.winsteps.com

Test-retest reliability

See *Reliability, test-retest*.

Text

Sometimes restricted to written materials and their illustrations, but often extended to broadcasts and websites and more rarely to any thing which can be interpreted as generating meaning; for example a street-scape, a pleasure park, a building – see *Textual analysis*.

Text mining

Automated searching of large bodies of text for particular words, word associations and word frequencies.

National Centre for Text Mining: University of Manchester: www.nactem.ac.uk/

Textual analysis

General term covering the wide range of analytic approaches to *texts*, including *content analysis, frame analysis, narrative analysis, membership category analysis, rhetorical analysis, semiology/semiotics, textual criticism and textual interaction.*

Textual criticism

The procedures used to authenticate a document, and/or to recreate an original source from later copies. Change in copying is called **recension**, restoration to the original form is called **editing**. Used by historians and other social scientists when evaluating documentary evidence, but particularly by biblical, koranic and talmudic scholars.

Textual Scholarship website: www.textualscholarship.org/index.html

Textual interaction

In linguistics and cognitive psychology the study of how readers interact with texts (Hoey 2000). Also the study of human-machine interaction via written language and of human interaction mediated by machine generated or machine displayed text (Johnson 1997).

Hoey, M. (2000) *Textual Interaction:an introduction to written discourse analysis*, London: Routledge
Johnson, C. (1997) *Interactive Systems Design* http://www.dcs.gla.ac.uk/~johnson/teaching/isd/course.html

Theil's T

An index of inequality, mathematically more complicated and less intuitive than others in this glossary, but superior in application to the analysis of material inequality. See also *Indices of inequality.*

Hale, T., (n.d.) 'A nearly painless guide to the calculation of Theil's statistic' http://utip.gov.utexas.edu/tutorials.html

Thematic analysis

The analysis of interview transcripts, written documents or broadcast media in terms of what the analyst considers to be interesting *semantic* features – initially by **thematic coding** which is labelling or tagging instances of themes as being particular types – see *Coding*. Themes may be established in advance, for example derived from a theoretical framework, or in order to produce an analysis comparable with some other previous work. Or, more usually, themes may be 'discovered' inductively in the material being analysed – see *Inductive reasoning, Grounded theory*. Thematic analysis is usually qualitative rather than quantitative –but see *Content analysis*, and is not very dissimilar to procedures in literary criticism where people write, for example about 'the theme of revenge in Webster's dramas'.

Aronson, J. (1994) 'A Pragmatic View of Thematic Analysis' *The Qualitative Report*, **2**(1): www.nova.edu/ssss/QR/

Theoretical generalisation

See *Generalisation, theoretical*.

Theoretical memos

See *Memoing/memos*.

Theoretical sampling

See *Sample, theoretical*.

Theoretical saturation

See *Saturation*.

Theory

Often used loosely to refer to any set of explanatory ideas; more narrowly, a coherently related set of ideas offering explanations in terms more abstract and general than descriptions of the particular *phenomena* they purport to explain. The possibility of a theory being testable by empirical means is sometimes made a distinguishing feature of theories by contrast with other explanatory ideas, but if this criterion is used then *epistemological and ontological* and other philosophical bodies of ideas will not qualify and most of the **grand theories** of social and behavioural science would not be regarded as theories either, because theories such as marxism, functionalism, psychoanalytic theory are not amenable to empirical falsification, which is why they are often called perspectives (and sometimes *grand or meta narratives*) rather than theories – see *Demarcationist debate, Falsificationism*. Theories which are more amenable to test are often called **middle range theories**. There are no 'bottom range' theories and the term 'middle range' was invented by Robert K Merton to name a middle way between speculative grand theories, and '**abstracted empiricism**' (Mills 1959); that is the collection of data with little attempt to theorise about it. See also *Episteme, Grand narratives, Hypotheses, Hypothetical-deductive method, Paradigm*.

Merton, R.K. (1957) *Social Theory and Social Structure*, Glencoe, IL: Free Press

Mills, C.W. (1959) *The Sociological Imagination*, Cambridge: Cambridge University Press

Theory data dependency problem/(theory ladenness of observation)

(1) A problem for the *hypothetico-deductive method* or of any process of testing the verity of a theory against evidence. Such procedures assume that the evidence, and the way of deploying it as a test, are independent of the theory being tested. However, it is the theory itself which will specify, or at least limit, what is to count as evidence, what would count as a disconfirmation and so on. For example, marxist and feminist theories include various reasons why evidence which might be taken as disconfirming is excluded as ideological – see *ideology*, while more mainstream researchers might reject evidence collected by *partisan research* on the grounds of the likelihood of alleged value *bias*; (2) a problem for what might be called naïve *naturalistic research* with regard to the notion that simply conducting unobtrusive research will discover how things naturally are, since how things appear to the researcher will be shaped by the observer's theoretical assumptions, however unformed and tacit these may be.

Newall, P. (2005) 'Theory Ladenness', Galilean Library. www.galilean-library.org/theory.html

Theory ladeness of data

See *Theory data dependency problem.*

Theory of planned behaviour (TPB)

The latest in a series of theories and related research techniques dealing with the relationship between attitudes and behaviour, particularly with regard to predicting the one from the other and for applications in creating persuasive communications as in advertising and health education. The TPB model has been shown to be superior in prediction by comparison with the **Expectancy value theory (EVT)** and the **Theory of reasoned action (TRA)** though both the latter are still sometimes used in advertising and health education research and practice.

Aizen, I.(2008) *Theory of Planned Behaviour*, University of Massachusetts www.people.umass.edu/aizen/tpb.html

Theory of reasoned action (TRA)

See *Theory of planned behaviour.*

Theory triangulation

See *Triangulation.*

Thick description/ethnography

Term invented by Gilbert Ryle (1971) who notes that if we saw a schoolboy winking we would not be able to distinguish this from a blink or a tic without knowing the social context in which the wink occurred. 'Thin description' would merely describe the movement of the eye-lid – this is a side-swipe at *behavourism* and other more extreme forms of *empiricism*. Thick description would supply the contextual information needed to understand a wink as a wink, and, more than this, to understand the meaning of that particular wink in that situation. The idea gained greater currency through the writing of Clifford Geertz (1973) who argued that the distinctive task of the ethnographer was to provide rich and detailed *ethnographic* descriptions to enable readers to approach the states of understanding that local people would have – see also *Cognitive anthropology*.

> Ryle, Gilbert (1968) The thinking of thoughts: what is le Penseur doing ?
> http://lucy.ukc.ac.uk/CSACSIA/Vol14/Papers/ryle_1.html
> Geertz, Clifford (1973) 'Thick Description: Toward an Interpretive Theory of Culture'. In *The Interpretation of Cultures: Selected Essays*, New York: Basic Books 3–30. www.stanford.edu/~davidf/qualitative151/geertz.pdf Or www.scribd.com/doc/267783/Clifford-Geertz-Thick-Description-and-other-works

Thomas' dictum/theorem

"If men define situations as real, they are real in their consequences". Originally a defining proposition of *symbolic interactionism*, but now widely accepted in the social and behavioural sciences.

> Thomas. W.I. and Thomas. D.S., (1928) *The child in America: Behavior problems and program*, New York: Knopf, 571–572

Thurstone Scale

Usually refers to a scale produced by Thurstone's **equal-appearing interval method**, although similar scales were produced by Thurstone using other methods (**successive interval method** and **paired comparison method**). Used in attitude research. Data from such scales are at the interval level, see *Data, levels of*. See also *Scales, Test theory*.

> Trochim, W. (2006) 'Thurstone Scaling', *Research Methods Knowledge Base* www.socialresearchmethods.net/kb/

'Timescapes'

See *Data archives*.

Time series analysis

Time series data are any data collected over a time period, including the results of *repeated cross-sectional surveys*, *longitudinal surveys*, *cohort*

T

studies, and time series from *administrative data*. Differences over time can be conceptualised as made up of three main components:

- *T(rend)*, the (*secular*) trend cycle (for example the growth in wages over a year or the fall in the price of electronic goods over the last decade),
- S(easonal) (or periodic) factors (for example higher wages in a holiday area in the summer),
- I erratic factors (for example particularly clement or adverse weather)

For shorter periods 'Seasonal' might refer to regular patterns within, say a week, or within a day. Time series analysis involves identifying these components of the data to identify the longer term or *secular*, *trend* and perhaps project it forward as a forecast, or to make **seasonal adjustments**. The latter re-express data net of erratic factors and with seasonal factors averaged across the year - thus showing the trend. Erratic components are usually dealt with by *smoothing*. See also *Autocorrelation*, *Event history analysis*, *Event structure analysis*, *Spectral analysis*, *Trend*, *Trend tests*.

Statsoft (n.d.) *Time series analysis/forecasting* www.statsoft.com/textbook/stathome.html

Task Force on Seasonal Adjustment (1996) *Report of the Task Force on Seasonal Adjustment*, GSS Methodology Series No. 2, Government Statistical Survey http://www.statistics.gov.uk/onlineproducts/default.asp search on 'GSS Methodology Series'

Topic, as opposed to resource

To treat something as a topic is to treat it as a matter of interest. To treat something as a resource is to treat it as evidence. For example if the way people describe their experiences is treated as a topic, then it will be of only secondary interest whether their descriptions are factually accurate. But if their descriptions are treated as a resource for finding out what happened, or what it felt like to be involved, then the accuracy of the descriptions will be crucial.

Townsend index

See *Deprivation indices*.

Transcription

The rendering of spoken words in written form; important where *audio, or video recording* is used to collect data. Transcription is sometimes by audio-typists on behalf of researchers, but the act of transcribing can be an important stage of analysis. The extent to which transcription should attempt to indicate features such as the accent and inflexion of speakers and the social interaction between them, will vary with theoretical orientation and research interest. The ESDS Qualidata archive provides a model where the result of transcription is very much like a play-script:

www.esds.ac.uk/qualidata/create/transcription.asp

The main model for transcriptions which attempt to display speech as social interaction is that used in *Conversation analysis* and developed by Gail Jepherson. The symbols used are given in

Antaki, C. (2002) *An introductory tutorial in Conversation Analysis:transcript 4* http://www-staff.lboro.ac.uk/~sscal/trans4.htm

For some purposes a phonetic transcription may be appropriate, and will be essential for material in languages without writing, in dialects which depart greatly from the written form, and languages with no phonetic relationships between spoken and written forms. Transcription representing non-verbal communication (see *Kinesics*) is particularly challenging.

Wells, J. (1996) 'Why phonetic transcription is important', *Malsori: Journal of the Phonetic Society of Korea*, Nos 31–32: 239–42 www.phon.ucl.ac.uk/home/wells/whytranscription.htm

Transferability

Used by some qualitative researchers as alternative to external validity – see *Criteria for evaluating research, Validity, external.*

Transgressive research

Research which aims that its execution or results should challenge and change features of social organisation of which the researcher disapproves. Usually applied to *action research* which is *participative*. See also *Emancipative research.*

Fox, N. (2003) 'Practice-based Evidence: Towards Collaborative and Transgressive Research', *Sociology*, **37**(1): 81–102

Transformation

See *Data transformation.*

Transparency

Up to the 1980s this meant unnoticeable, as in 'language is a transparent medium'. More recently it means easy to notice, as in 'the methods used were transparent' i.e., fully described. In research this is a recent import from business perhaps via *performance indicator* research, and most used as a synonym for auditability or procedural objectivity – see *Objectivity, procedural*.

Trend analysis

(1) Analysis of econometric data mainly as an aid to financial decision-making or economic policy making; (2) See *Time series analysis, Trend, secular* (3) see *Trend, statistical, Regression analysis*.

Trend, secular / time

In a *time series analysis* the tendency for a variable to maintain a more or less consistent trajectory over a time period, perhaps only after other factors are controlled for – see *Time series analysis*.

Trend, statistical

The overall relationship between two or more variables across their ranges, as shown for example by the trend line / regression line/ line of best fit / least squares line of a *regression analysis*. Trends are classified according to the equations which would generate them, as **first order / linear polynominal** (a straight line relationship), **second order / quadratic, third order / cubic, fourth order / quartic** and so on. For graphical representations see:http://luna.cas.usf.edu/~mbrannic/files/regression/curvilinear.html See also *Trend tests*.

Trend tests

Statistical tests for estimating whether a trend exists or not – see *Trend, statistical*. For interval level data the *F ratio* derived from an *analysis of variance (ANOVA / MANOVA)* may be used as a trend test. For ordinal data the following non-parametric tests may be used: **Kruskal-Wallis one way analysis of variance, Jonckheere trend test**, both for unrelated designs and **Friedman's trend test** and **Page trend test**, both for related designs: see *Statistics software, Statistics parametric and non-parametric, Related and unrelated designs, Data, levels of*.

Wendorf,C. (2004) *Manuals for Univariate and Multivariate Statistics*, www.uwsp.edu/psych/cw/statmanual/index.html

Triadic elicitation

See *Repertory grid technique*.

Triangulation

In social research, triangulation means cross-checking one source of evidence against another or others. From a *social constructionist* point of view triangulation makes no sense, since each version will be regarded as the outcome of the way it was produced, and there is no particular expectation that any two versions will agree. And, from any perspective, triangulation presumes some prior decision about what are the sorts of matters about which we can be right or wrong, and which matters will always be questions of interpretation or opinion (*qualia* or incorrigibles – see *corrigibility*). For incorrigible matters triangulation will not cross-check, but will only provide evidence about different (or similar) perceptions of the same phenomena – see *multiple realities*. This may be interesting however. Where sources disagree about what can be taken to be 'matters of fact', it will be necessary to decide whether this means that one source is wrong, if so it will be necessary to evaluate the alternative sources in an effort to discover which is correct, although it is possible that both or neither are correct.

Various kinds of triangulation are shown in Table 25, together with possible interpretations of agreements and disagreements between sources – see also *Rashomon effect*.

Mixed/multi-method research is often justified in terms of the triangulation opportunities built into the research design, on the grounds

Table 25 Different kinds of triangulation

Meta-analysis	See *Meta-analysis* and *Meta-ethnography*
Data source triangulation (Using two or more sources of data about the same phenomenon collected in much the same way)	• Data collected at different phases of the research • Data collected from different subjects – simply 'sampling' • Data collected at different points in time – 'time sampling' • Data collected from different settings • Observer triangulation – data collected by different members of a research team – see also *Inter-rater reliability*
Respondent validation (fallibility testing, member checking)	Subjecting the researcher's interpretations to the judgement of the subjects of the research, as to their validity. See Fallibility testing
Methodological triangulation (cross-method triangulation)	Using data collected by different methods about the same phenomenon – a characteristic of *Mixed/Multi methods research*

(Continued)

Table 25 (Continued)

Theoretical triangulation	Comparing the accounts of the same phenomenon given by research(ers) with different theoretical understandings
Reasons why lines of triangulation may contradict each other	• One is valid and another invalid • Both are valid, but one describes something exceptional/unusual and the other something more common • Both are valid, but the phenomenon in question is variable and each refers to versions of it in different places or at different times or in different sub-groups or in different kinds of situation • Both are valid, but the qualities they express are not of the kind about which anyone can be right or wrong – see *corrigibility* • Both are wrong
Reasons why lines of triangulation may support each other	• Both are right • Neither are right because this is a matter about which it is not possible to be right or wrong. • Both are wrong, but both sources are flawed by the same limitations or biases; or by different limitations or biases which have the same effect – see *Bias, Ideology*.

that findings using one kind of source are more robust if confirmed by another.

The process of triangulation is similar to that involved in validating research instruments – see *Validation, criterion*, and validating *computer simulations*

Tiainen, T. and Koivunen, E.-R. (2006) 'Exploring forms of triangulation to facilitate collaborative research practice', Journal of Research Practice Vol 2(2) http://jrp.icaap.org/index.php/jrp/

Trimming (pruning)

Analysing less than the complete *range* of a data set in order to exclude *outliers*. A **trimmed mean**, is the average of a trimmed data set – see also *Interquartile range, Winsorisation*.

Trope

See *Rhetorical analysis*.

True experiments

See *Experiments, true and quasi*.

True scores / measurements:

In measurement theory a measurement always consists of two elements: a true score and an error (although the latter may be zero) see *Central limit theorem, Measurement error*.

Trustworthiness

Used by some qualitative researchers as an alternative to internal validity, see *Criteria for evaluating research, Validity, internal*.

Truth tables

See *Boolean algebra*.

t-test (student's t)

A parametric test for determining the *statistical significance* of a difference between two sets of measurements – see *Statistics, parametric and nonparametric*. The operation takes the *variance* of both sets of measurements combined. This is a measure of the diversity within the data set as a whole. From this can be calculated the likelihood of random choices creating two samples (of the same size as the two sets of measurements) with *means* as different as or more different from those in the actual sets of measurements. Essentially this is asking 'what is the likelihood of a difference of the size observed or greater, having occurred by chance?' Or 'how often would two samples as or more different as this, be drawn at random from this same pool of scores?' If the answer is 'not very often' then this is presumptive evidence that the difference was not due to chance, and the results are said to be statistically significant. A *t*-test reports a value for the statistic *t*, which is looked up in a table of *critical values* for *t* according to the number of degrees of freedom. The results are usually expressed like this:

$$t = (50) = 2.50, p < 0.01$$

meaning
   (50) *degrees of freedom* derived from: (subjects in one group) + (subjects in the other) − the number of groups $(25 + 27 - 2 = 50)$. This identifies the row in the table of *critical values* for $t = 2.50$.

This is the *t* statistic calculated by the *t*-test $p<0.01$. At 2.50 *t* is higher than the figure shown in the table of *critical values (one* tailed) for a probability of 0.01 (but lower than that shown for 0.001) – see *Tails*.

The interpretation is that a difference of this size is likely to occur by chance only once in 100 times. This is very unlikely, so the result is highly statistically significant – see *p-values*.

The *t*-tests are essentially the same as an *analysis of variance (ANOVA)* calculation with only two groups. They are often used as *post-hoc tests* as a follow-up to *ANOVA* to compare each possible pair of groups.

T-tests come in three varieties, one each for related and unrelated designs respectively – see *Related and unrelated designs*, plus a **one sample t-test**, which compares the mean of a sample with the mean of a population to estimate the likelihood of such a sample being drawn from that population by chance. The one sample t-test is:

$$\frac{\text{Population mean} - \text{Sample mean}}{\textit{Standard error of the sample mean}} = t$$

Type 1 and Type 2 errors

(1) In statistical testing:

> Type 1 error (alpha error) – assuming that there is a difference/ association between variables when there is none
>
> Type 2 error (beta error) – assuming that there is no difference/association between variables when there is one

In theory testing (see *hypothetico-deductive method)* there is usually a preference for committing a type 2 rather than a type 1 error which means being less willing wrongly to accept a finding as *statistically significant* than to accept wrongly that a finding is not statistically significant – see *alpha level* and *beta level*. This corresponds with *falsificationism*. In practically oriented research this preference may be over-ridden by considerations of *substantive significance*, for example where making a type 2/beta error would mean regarding some outcome adverse to people as not statistically significant; for example a drug side effect, and risking the possibility of serious harm; (2) in tests such as diagnostic tests, health screening, risk assessments, selection tests, etc. See examples in Table 26.

Table 26 Examples of Type 1 and Type 2 errors in health screening

The test shows	In reality	
	it's true	it's false
It's 'true'	a) True positives [patients with cancer correctly detected as having cancer]	b) False positives (Type 1 error) [patients without cancer detected wrongly as having cancer]
It's false	c) False negatives (Type 2 error) [patients with cancer not detected as having cancer]	d) True negatives [patients without cancer detected correctly as not having cancer]

Sensitivity is the ability of a test to detect all true positives: to avoid Type 1 errors – calculated as the positives truly recognised as a proportion of all positives: $a/(a+b)$.

Specificity is the ability of a test to detect all true negatives: to avoid Type 2 errors – calculated as the negatives truly recognised as a proportion of all negatives: $d/(b+d)$.

For a test of known specificity and known sensitivity the *Likelihood ratio*(Λ can be calculated as an estimate of the accuracy of any particular result.

T

U

Statistic arising from *Mann-Whitney U tests.*

UKDA (UK data archive)

See *Data archives.*

UK household longitudinal study

http://www.iser.essex.ac.uk/ulsc/keeptrack/results/select.php.

UK Statistics Authority

Authority independent of government, to regulate the accuracy of government statistics and publish them without spin. Established in 2008 in response to widespead public and media skepticism about the accuracy of such data. See also *Administrative data.*

www.statisticsauthority.gov.uk/

Under-coverage

See *Coverage error.*

Under-determination

(1) **Indeterminancy of theory by data:** refers to a number of different problems of verifying theories by reference to data. The argument is that, in principle, no amount of data can verify a theory. But the reasons for this argument are various. They include:

- the problem of induction which relates to the abandoment of *verificationism* for *falsificationism* – see *Inductive reasoning,*
- the *theory data dependency problem,*

- the argument from the sociology of science that facts about the real world (if facts they are) are never of themselves sufficient to explain the theories we have about them; for example it may be true that germs cause disease, but germs causing disease is not enough to explain why we have a theory about germs causing disease. That needs an explanation invoking some of social, cultural, political and economic factors – see *Strong programme*.

Only hard-line exponents of *empiricism* believe that theories are or can be entirely justified with reference to data. All other *epistemological and ontological* positions recognise a gap between a theory and evidence which has to be filled by theorising, which is not itself dependent on evidence.

(2) Situations where two theories seem equally supported by the same data. See also *Parsimony principle*.

Newall, P. (2005) 'Underdetermination', *Galilean Library*. www.galilean-library.org/under.html

Unexplained variance

See *Variance explained*.

Unidimensional or multi-dimensional

See *Scales*.

Unit of sampling

See *Sampling unit*.

Unit non-response/unit response rate

See *Response rate*.

U

Unity of science thesis

Associated with *behaviourism, empiricism, positivism, logical empiricism, logical positivism* and some version of *critical rationalism;* the thesis that the methods used in the physical/natural sciences are those appropriate for all science including social science – see *Demarcationist debate, Naturalism*. This implies a rejection of those approaches which seek explanation by understanding the intentions of social actors – see *Intentionalism*.

Unobtrusive measures (non-reactive measures)

Research which does not create the conditions for *subject reactivity*. Includes:

- Physical evidence of accretion (e.g., discarded syringes) and erosion (e.g., patterns of wear on flooring) – and see *garbology*.
- Counts of traffic – motorised and pedestrian, and of car park occupancy and attendance at functions.
- The use of naturally occurring documentation – see *Administrative data*.
- Studies of sales (and remaindering) of selected commodities.
- Studies of *mass media* output.
- Unobtrusive observation – see *Observation, covert or overt*, *Observation participant and non-participant*.

These methods may be unobtrusive in the sense of not being noticed, but sometimes they are obtrusive in the sense of involving violations of *privacy and confidentiality*.

Kalman, Y. (n.d.) *Unobtrusive Methods for Social Science Research A Neglected Methodological Approach in the Social Sciences*, University of Haifa. www.kalmans.com/UnobtrusiveMeasures.ppt

Unrelated design

See *Related and unrelated designs*.

Unstructured interviews

A misleading term, since no human interchanges are 'unstructured'; a synonym for loosely or semi-structured interviews: see *Qualitative interviews*.

Usability evaluation

Primarily refers to the evaluation of the user friendliness and fitness for purpose of interfaces for computer programs, including web-based instructional programs and other websites. See also *Design ethnography*. Usability www.usabilityhome.com/

Utility

In economic analysis utility is a measurement of usefulness/preference/desirability. The utility of goods and services are usually taken as their monetary price in the market place. But price will not express the utility of non-market entities. Hence other measures of utility (other **utils**) may be used. Average composite scores on consumer-satisfaction question-naires in the NHS, for example, could be used as utils; perhaps in judging how much it would cost (in money) to raise consumer satisfaction by so many points. The best known util is the **QALY** – **Quality of Life Year**, a composite score which expresses how many additional years of life, at a given quality of life, a particular treatment will deliver per 100 patients. This measure is used in the evaluation of medical technology and in approving drugs for use in the NHS – see also *Cost(#) analysis*.

Phillips, C. (2001) 'What is a QALY?' *Whatis Series*, **1**(6):1–6. www.jr2.ox.ac.uk/bandolier/booth/glossary/QALY.html

Utility functions

Criteria for judging the usefulness of a instrument, procedure, model or theory for explaining, predicting or controlling in relation to the cost of utilising it. Thus a research instrument with lower accuracy but lower cost might be preferred to one of higher accuracy and higher cost. See also *Cost # analysis*.

U

Validation

(1) The process of testing a research *instrument*'s effectiveness in measuring the construct it is supposed to measure – see *Validity, construct, Validity, content, Validity, criterion, Validity, concurrent, Validity, discriminant, Validity, predictive* and see *Cognitive interview, Reliability*; (2) the process of testing a *computer simulation*'s ability accurately to simulate whatever it is supposed to simulate. Usually a matter of comparing data generated by the simulation with real world data – see *Validity, criterion*. See also *Fallibility testing*.

Validity

Often used in research in preference to the problematic 'true' but hardly less problematic. Given the widespread commitment to some degree of *scepticism, social constructionism, fallibilism*, and/or of *falsificationism* and/or a democratic desire to regard everyone's views as equally 'valid' (see *Relativism*), many researchers have difficulty in claiming that the results of their research are true, or valid in any uncomplicated way. With regard to falsificationism, claims that some proposition is valid, or that some *instrument* gives valid results are likely to be expressed in terms of there having been an attempt to prove its invalidity which has not done so, or that sources of invalidity have been looked for assiduously but not found. The quality of a research design is often expressed in terms of how well it counters 'threats to validity'. Various types of validity are recognised, and apart from those distinguished below, the term can also be used to indicate logicality or cogency – as in 'a valid argument', and the correct or incorrect use of instruments or techniques, for example as in 'it is an invalid use of parametric statistics to use them with data drawn from a convenience sample'.

Winter, G. (2000) 'A comparative discussion of the notion of 'validity' in qualitative and quantitative research', *The Qualitative Report* **4**(3&4) www.nova.edu/ssss/QR/
Hammersley, M. (1987). Some notes on the terms 'validity' and 'reliability. *British Educational Research Journal*, **13**(1), 73–81

Trochim, W. (2006) 'Measurement of validity types', *Social Science Knowledge Base* www.socialresearchmethods.net/kb/

Validity, catalytic

The extent to which a piece of research could lead to worthwhile change. Used mainly in connection with *action research* or in the criticism that theoretical research lacks catalytic validity. Usually similar in meaning to **Transgressive validity** – see *Transgressive research*. Both are varieties of what may be called 'pragmatic validity' – see *Pragmatism*.

Validity, comprehensiveness

See *Validity, content*.

Validity, concurrent

See *Validity, criterion*.

Validity, construct

For research *instruments* this is the premier kind of validity. Failures of most of the other kinds, and failures of *reliability* will also be failures of construct validity. Simply put, construct validity is an answer to the question of whether an *instrument* is measuring what it is supposed to be measuring (the *indicator* representing the *construct*). There are two possibilities for invalidity here:

- the method used to generate data about the indicator is faulty
- or the indicator chosen is not a very good indicator of the construct it is supposed to measure.

Construct validity may be judged in various ways, for example whether results from using the instrument are consistent with what else is known/theorised about the phenomenon of interest : whether the measures from using this instrument are uncontaminated by confounding factors and whether there are failures of other kinds of validity, or *reliability*.

V

Trochim, W. (2005) 'The idea of construct validity', *Social Science Knowledge Base* www.socialresearchmethods.net/kb/

Validity, content (coverage/item/test/domain/ dimension coverage, comprehensiveness)

Whether an *instrument* deals with all the relevant aspects of the *construct* an instrument is supposed to measure. For example, does the examination cover all the items on the syllabus; does an intelligence test cover all the domains of intelligence?

> Trochim, W. (2006) 'Measurement of validity types' *Social Science Knowledge Base* www.socialresearchmethods.net/kb/

Validity, convergent

Where two ways of measuring what is taken to be the same *construct* give similar results, these ways of measuring are described as having convergent validity, not very different from criterion validity – see *Validity, criterion*.

> Trochim, W. (2006). 'Convergent and Discriminant Validity', *Social Science Knowledge Base* www.socialresearchmethods.net/kb/

Validity, criterion

Comes in two forms both of which usually refer to research *instruments*. **Concurrent validity:** whether the results from using the instrument correlate with the results of using another instrument regarded as 'the gold standard' and called the '**Criterion test**', or if there is no such instrument with expert opinion. **Predictive validity:** whether the results using an instrument accurately predict some state of affairs. This is a common test also for validating *computer simulations*.

> Trochim, W. (2006) 'Measurement of validity types' *Social Science Knowledge Base* www.socialresearchmethods.net/kb/

Validity, dimension coverage

See *Validity, content*.

Validity, discriminant

Whether a research *instrument* or a mode of analysing data is able to discriminate accurately between instances of one construct and another – instruments which have a high degree of discriminant validity are said to be sensitive/ have *sensitivity*. See also *Internal consistency, Type 1 and type 2 errors*.

> Trochim, W. (2006) 'Measurement of validity types', *Social Science Knowledge Base* www.socialresearchmethods.net/kb/

Validity, domain coverage

See *Validity, content*.

Validity, ecological

See *Validity, naturalistic.*

Validity, external (fittingness, generalisability, transferability)

(1) Of a research *instrument*, refers to the extent to which it would produce results with the same accuracy over a wide range of subjects or settings – see also *Robustness*. The production of instruments with external validity usually involves *piloting* them and *validating* them with large representative samples of subjects – see *representativeness,*, and usually norming them – see *standardisation*. (2) When applied to research findings this is the issue of whether or how far what was found under the circumstances of the research would be true of other people, other settings or other times. Much will depend on whether the research was with a representative sample of subjects – see *Representativeness*. Note that internal validity is required before there can be external validity – see *Validity, internal*. External validity is not entirely a matter of the quality of the research. Different phenomena have more or less robust characteristics such that some will behave more consistently across a range of circumstances, and some will be highly sensitive to their local context. Hence research with some kinds of phenomena (for example human physiology) is more likely to have external validity, than research with other kinds of phenomena, for example, group dynamics. The major weakness of experiments is often said to be their low levels of external validity; experimental conditions being unlike naturally occurring ones. But this is not necessarily remedied by research conducted under naturalistic conditions if each naturally occurring set of circumstances is very different from each other – see *Validity, naturalistic*. See also *Generalisation*.

Validity, face

The weakest form of validity, but perhaps that most commonly used (with or without being named as such) is whether according to appropriate judges an instrument looks as if it measures what it is supposed to measure, or whether a piece of research seems to have avoided other threats to *validity*.

Trochim, W. (2006) 'Measurement of validity types', *Social Science Knowledge Base* www.socialresearchmethods.net/kb/

Validity, internal

The extent to which a piece of research is valid ('true') for the circumstances under which it was conducted (that is irrespective of its external validity – see *Validity, external*). This may involve judgements of any or all of the other kinds of validity listed in this glossary, plus considerations of a wide range of other factors which might flaw the research: see also *Research artefacts.*

Validity, item coverage

See *Validity, content.*

Validity, naturalistic (ecological validity)

The extent to which a piece of research accurately represents states of affairs as they 'naturally' are, uninfluenced by the activities of the researcher. In experimental research this notion may be extended to refer to the extent to which the circumstances of the experiment mirror those of any situation to which it is hoped the results can be generalised (*external validity/generalisability/transferability*). From the view point of *ethnographic, ethnomethodological* and *social constructionist* researchers, this is the most desirable kind of validity; other kinds of research being largely seen as composed of *research artefacts.* The judgement as to whether or not a piece of research has achieved naturalistic validity depends in part on demonstrating that a conscientious search has failed to find sources of distortion (research artefacts), but also on assumptions as to how matters naturally are: raising a version of the *theory data dependency problem.* Naturalistic validity is often confused with *external validity.* While a failure of naturalistic validity may undermine *generalisations* from a study to other situations, the successful achievement of naturalistic validity will only ensure successful generalisation to the extent that the circumstances of the study are similar to the circumstances to which generalisation is proposed.

Validity, predictive

See *Validity, criterion.*

Validity, test coverage

See *Validity, content.*

Value

(1) A measure of preference for goods, services, ways of living, personal characteristics and so on – see also *utilities.* (2) An abstract construct imagined to underlie a cluster of *attitudes*, themselves constructs

created to account for patterns of behaviour which express preferences or dislikes, for example the value 'Familism' underlying the attitudes 'loyalty to spouse', 'obedience to parents' and so on – see also *Test theory*. (3) Standards of morality – see *Ethics, Value-neutral or value-led research*. (4) The measurement assigned to a variable, for example male as opposed to female, 27 as opposed to 25, 'very important', 'not very important' on a five point scale – see *Variable* and *Variable #*.

Value-free research

In addition to the values concerning the humane treatment of research subjects and the integrity and honesty of researchers – see *ethics*, issues of *value* will always influence the choice of research topics, and, whatever researchers do, research findings will feed into moral and political debates and decision-making. Very few researchers claim to be able to carry out value-free research and if they do they usually mean value-neutral research. The term 'value-free' seems to be most used by *partisan* researchers who claim that since value-free research is impossible, it is necessary to do value-led research. This is not a cogent argument however – see *Value-neutral or value-led research*.

Lacey, C. (2001) 'The ways in which science is and is not value free', www.swarthmore.edu/Humanities/hlacey1/value-free.doc

Value-neutral or value-led research

Mainstream science allows that researchers may choose their research topics and questions according to their moral and political leanings; that research may be **value relevant**. But at the same time prescribes that the conduct of the research should be **value-neutral** (excepting for the values incorporated into research *ethics*). This means that researchers should do all that is possible to avoid making moral judgements about what they are observing (non-judgementalism) and to prevent their preference for one kind of finding rather than another influencing the outcome of their research (impartiality) – see *Fact value distinction, Naturalistic fallacy*. Various devices are used to exclude what would be regarded as the distorting influence of values. These include:

- the *random allocation* of subjects in experiments
- the use of probability samples in surveys – see *Samples, probability*
- *blinding* in experiments, and *masking*
- a *falsificationist* programme
- making data and analysis available for audit by others – see *Objectivity*
- the declaration of *conflicts of interest* in publications.

Partisan researchers by contrast believe that research should be **value-led**, and that it is legitimate to direct research towards the outcome they most desire. The justification for this stance may include an appeal to a pragmatic notion of truth where what is true is not what corresponds to reality, but what is considered useful or good – see *Pragmatism*. In addition, much partisan research is not directed towards the discovery of 'facts', but to goals such as empowerment, political mobilisation or the enhancement of the self-image or public reputation of the favoured group – see also *Praxis, Social research pure and applied, Transgressive research, Validity, catalytic.*

Value neutrality should not be confused with moral relativity, – see *Relativism.*

Hammersley, M. (2000) *Taking Sides in Social Research: Essays on Partisanship and Bias,* London: Routledge.

Value relevance

See *Value-neutral or value-led research.*

Variable

Anything which can take on different values; for example, gender takes the values 'male' and female' and height can take a wide range of values in centimetres. What values variables can take is partly a function of the scale of measurement used, and partly of how the construct being measured is conceptualised. For example while gender is traditionally a two value, or *dichotomous* variable, we could measure degrees of maleness and femaleness to render gender as a many valued or continuously valued variable – see *Data, levels of.*

Where a *direction of effect* is defined an **independent variable (IV)** is one that exerts a one way influence on a **dependent variable (DV).** For example, gender is an independent variable and academic achievement measured in GCSE passes is the dependent one.

The synonyms shown in Table 27 may be used for independent and dependent.

V

Table 27 Synonyms for independent and dependent (variables)

Independent (IV)	Dependent (DV)	
x	y	If only one IV and or DV are designated
Antecedent	Consequent	An antecedent variable may also be an intervening variable

(Continued)

Table 27 (Continued)

Independent (IV)	Dependent (DV)	
Condition	Response	Mainly in psychology
Design	Response	Mainly in *log linear analysis*
Exposure	Result/Response	Medical, *epidemiological* and mass media research
Factor	Variable	In *analysis of covariance* and *analysis of variance and factor analysis*
Explanatory	Explanandum	But explanandum is rarely used of variables
Input	Outcome	In statistical modelling and *evaluation research*
Predictor	Criterion	In *proportional reduction of error*, *multi-level modelling*, instrument *validation* and elsewhere – see also *Validity, criterion.*
Treatment	Outcome	Medical, social work and educational research

Variables which intervene between the independent and the dependent may be termed **intervening**, or **mediating**, and if they result in erroneous conclusions, confounding – see *Variable, confounding*.

Variable, antecedent
See *Variable*.

Variable-based comparative method
See *Comparative method*.

Variable, confounding
An independent or intervening variable whose existence may not have been detected which complicates the relationship between an(other) independent and dependent variable – see *Variable*.

Variable, continuous
See *Data, levels of*.

Variable, criterion
See *Variable*.

Variable, dependent (DV)
See *Variable*.

Variable, design

See *Variable.*

Variable, dichotomous

A variable which can take only one of two values, for example male or female – see *Data, levels of.*

Variable, dummy

With nominal data the substitution of a number for a verbal label in order to facilitate statistical manipulation. For example, 1 for male and 2 for female. *See Data, levels of.*

Variable, explandum, and Variable, explanatory

See *Variable.*

Variable, exposure

See *Variable.*

Variable, independent (IV)

See *Variable.*

Variable, interval (level)

See *Data, levels of.*

Variable, intervening-

See *Variable.*

Variable, latent

See *Latent variable.*

Variable, manifest

See *Latent variable.*

Variable, mediating

See *Variable.*

Variable, ordinal (level)

See *Data, levels of.*

Variable, predictor

See *Variable.*

Variable, random

(1) In *computer simulations* and statistical *bootstrapping* a variable generated at *random* and inserted into an equation; (2) Synonym for residual/
error/unexplained variance in *regression analysis.*

Variable, response

See *Variable.*

Variable, suppressor

Usually in *regression analysis,* an intervening variable which hides the
influence between two other variables; a variety of confounding variable; see *Variable, Variable, confounding.*

Variable, treatment

See *Variable.*

Variance

The degree of variety within a *data* set, measured by comparing each
datum with the mean. Symbolised as S^2 for the variance of a *sample*
variable, and σ^2 for the variance of a *population* variable – see *Central
tendency and dispersion.*

Variance components model

See *Effect, fixed and random.*

Variance explained

When two variables are correlated the 'variance explained' is the extent
to which the variation in one variable would be reduced if the value
of the other variable were held constant. The proportion of variance
explained is often calculated by squaring a correlation coefficient –
see *Correlation, Correlation coefficients.* The reciprocal is **unexplained**

variance, that variance in the dependent variable which is left over when the explained variance is deducted. See *Pearson's product moment coefficient*. In a *regression analysis* unexplained variance is the sum of the residuals squared. See also *Analysis of variance, Path diagram*.

Verstehen

Usually associated with Max Weber though widely used both before and after Weber's work. The meaning lies somewhere between interpretation and empathy and is usually translated as 'understanding', and refers to one aim of Weber's approach which was to assist readers to understand situations as his research subjects would understand them – first person understanding. See also *Emic*. Now sometimes used as a synonym of *interpretivism*. Weber's other aim was to explain the causes of their actions.

Verificationism

(1) The **verification principle** was associated with *logical positivism*, which claimed that the only sensible propositions referring to the real world (synthetic) were those which could (in principle) be verified by *empirical* observation. Now largely abandoned in favour of *falsificationism* on the grounds a) of the problem of induction – see *Inductive reasoning*, b) that many propositions cannot be verified by empirical observation but are nonetheless sensible, and c) that the verificationist prinicple itself cannot be verified empirically; (2) as synonym for *confirmationism*; the practice of selectively trying to find evidence to prove something true and ignoring that which does not: mainly used in criticism of non-falsificationist research. See also *Bias, confirmation*.

Victim(isation) surveys

Usually in criminology, surveys designed to elicit information about being victimised from those who have been victimised. Those which are based on representative samples usually have among their objectives estimating the *incidence or prevalence* of victimisation independent of reports to the authorities. The main part of the British Crime Survey is a victim survey and provides estimates of the incidence of crime independently of the figures collected by the police and the courts. See also *Adminstrative data, Representativeness, Self-report*.

The British Crime Survey: www.homeoffice.gov.uk/rds/bcs1.html

Video
See *Audio and video recording.*

Vignettes
Paper-based, video or audio presented character sketches or case scenarios used to stimulate discussion in a group or individual interview, or to form the basis for decision-making in research simulating real life decision-making; for example a video-tape of a patient plus case notes, used in a study of how doctors reach a diagnosis. See also *role-play, group interviews.*

Barter, C. and Renold, E. (1999) 'The use of vignettes in qualitative research', *Social Research Update* Issue 25. http://sru.soc.surrey.ac.uk/

Virtual ethnography
It is not the *ethnography* which is virtual, but the subject matter: the study of people using the internet, mainly by the researcher accessing the internet, and lurking or participating in chat rooms and game sites. May also include on-line and face-to-face interviews with users. Lurking on the web as a means of research raises important ethical issues about *informed consent.*
See also *Cyber #, Game studies.*

Hine, C. (2001) *Virtual Ethnography,* London, Routledge
Hine, C. (2005) *Virtual Methods: issues in social research on the internet,* Oxford, Berg Publishers

Visual anthropology/sociology
(1) The study within a social science framework of the making and interpretation of visual still and moving images – see also *Semiology/semiotics*; (2) the use of visual images as research evidence (Prosser 2006). Sometimes the photos and films are called ethno-graphics.

Prosser, J. (2006) *Researching with visual images: Some guidance notes and a glossary for beginners,* NCRM http://www.ncrm.ac.uk/
Beilla, P. (2001) *Ur-list of Resources for Visual Anthropology,* University of Southern California, www.usc.edu/dept/elab/urlist/
International Visual Sociology Association: http://visualsociology.org

Vital statistics
Statistics of populations most of interest to demographers such as births, deaths and migration – see *Demography.*

V

Voicing

Conducting research with the aim of articulating – voicing – the views of those studied, usually for the purpose of helping them to advocate on their own behalf, or otherwise to improve their image – see also *Consciousness raising, Participative research.*

The Joseph Rowntree Foundation has a particular interest in this kind of research: www.jrf.org.uk

Vote-counting approach

Decisions based on majority vote where Delphi groups are used to evaluate research for inclusion in *systematic reviews* or *meta analyses* – see *Group Interviews.*

V

Walk-through

Piloting a research instrument, by having subjects representing the target group work through it, perhaps giving commentary as they do so, and/or, if an on-line instrument, being video recorded or electronically monitored while using it – see also *Cognitive interview, Pilot study, Validation*

Wave

Synonym for sweep in repeated *cross sectional research.*

Web surveys

Surveys which recruit respondents on the internet and elicit and record their responses on-line. Now the premier kind of survey research in *market research.* See *Questionnaire administration, Sampling #, Survey, Survey recruitment.*

Statpac (n.d.) Web Surveys., http://www.statpac.com/

Weighted averages/event rates/mean

In combining the results from two or more groups/studies, the adjustment of each group or study's contribution to the total, in proportion to their *sample sizes.* The simplest **weighted mean** is calculated by multiplying the *mean* of each group by the number of scores for the group, adding the results together and then dividing this by the total number of scores, as shown in Table 28.

More complicated procedures includes the **Peto method**, the **RevMan (inverse variance method)** and **Mantel-Haenszel methods** as well as using random, rather than fixed effects – see *Effects, fixed and random.*

Cochrane Collaboration (2002) 'Weighted averages', *Cochrane Collaboration Open Learning Material:* www.cochrane-net.org/openlearning/HTML/mod12-3.htm

Table 28 Example of simple weighted mean calculation.

	Group *means*	Group size	Mean × size
Group 1	7	15	105
Group 2	8	10	80
Group 3	5	50	250
Sum	20	75	435
Unweighted mean		(7+8+5)/3(groups) = 20/3 = 6.66	
Weighted mean		(105+80+250)/75(scores) = 435/75 = 5.80	

Weighting

(1) In *time series analyses* – see *Smoothing*; (2) for *surveys*: many factors prevent probability samples being perfectly representative – see *Design effects, Response rate, Representativeness, Sample, probability*. In addition in a national survey different areas of the country will have populations with different *demographic* characteristics, with local implications for *representativeness*. To correct any such deviations from representativeness the sample may be weighted or the results of the survey may be weighted.

Weighting the sample, to compensate for difficulties in recruitment.

- Over-recruitment of minority or difficult to engage groups – see *Sample, stratified*.
- Selection of booster samples – see *Sample, booster*.

Weighting the results in *grossing up*, to compensate for disproportionality/unrepresentativeness by adjusting the *expansion factors* for each sub-group according to the extent of over or under-representation.

- To correct over representation via sample weighting – see above.
- For under-representation – see also *Coverage rate, Response rate*.
- To correct failures of representativeness due to *Design factors, see* also *Sample, cluster, Sample, respondent driven*.

Weighting assumes knowledge, or at least a model of, the structure of the population being sampled in order to judge over- and under-representation. For general populations the *census*, and periodic updates of census data are the usual resources for this, though they become less and less accurate over the ten year inter-census period – see also *Imputation, Weighted averages*.

Elliot, K. (1999) Report of the Task Force on Weighting and Estimation, GSS Methodology Paper No 16, Government Social Survey www.statistics.gov,uk/search on 'GSS Methodology'

Crocket, A. (2007) 'Weighting the social surveys', *Economic and Social Data Services*: www.esds.ac.uk/government/docs/weighting.pdf (although applying specifically to re-using Government social surveys this has a clear introduction weighting)

Charlton, M., Fotheringham, S and Brunsdon, C. (2005) *Geograhically weighted regression*. National Centre for Research Methods. http://www.ncrm.ac.uk/research/outputs/publications/(weighting to correct for local differences population composition in national surveys)

Whiskers

As in **plot and whiskers** – the plot is the actual value, the whiskers show the confidence interval – see *Confidence intervals*. As in **box and whiskers**, the box shows the values within the midrange/interquartile range/the middle 50% of values, the whiskers extend to the minimum and the maximum value – see *Box plot, Interquartile range*.

Wilcoxon rank sum test

Non-parametric test of *statistical significance* of difference or *correlation*, for unrelated, ordinal level data: alternative to *Mann-Whitney U Test* – reports the statistic T. See *Statistics parametric and non-parametric, Related and unrelated designs, Data, levels of.*

Wilcoxon signed ranks test

A non-parametric test of *statistical significance* used with data at the ordinal level (see *Data, levels of, Statistics, parametric and non-parametric*) which compares the rank orders of two sets of data referring to the same subjects, and asks the question 'how often would differences in ranking of the same people on different scales (or the same scale at different times) of the same size as these, happen by chance? 'If the answer is 'not very often' then the differences are regarded as *statistically significant* differences. Less likely than 5 times out of 100 ($p<0.05$) is the usual threshold, or *alpha level,* for statistical significance. This is a related design – see *Related and unrelated designs.* The results are usually reported like this:

T = 29 (N,16), $p < 0.05$, meaning:

T = 29 was the statistic produced by the test (note that this is not the same T as used in a *t-test*)

N, 16 – is the number of subjects where there was a difference in ranking between their two scores e.g., someone who came first both times is ignored.

$p<0.05$; p (for probability) is less than 5 times in 100. This is derived from looking in a table of *critical values* for this test, on the line for N=16, and finding that, if T is 29 it is equal to or <u>lower</u> than the minimum figure for $p<0.05$. The critical value for a *one-tailed test* is 35, and that for a *two-tailed test* is 29.

Note that in most other tests of statistical significance the result has to equal or beat the critical value for statistical significance, but in most rank-order tests it has to equal or fall short of the critical value – see *p values, tails*. See also *Statistics, software*.

Winsorising/Windsorizing

(Upper case W) : statistical technique to deal with *outliers/Pareto tails* in data sets which allegedly confound the analysis of the influence of (a) particular (set of) variable(s) on a data distribution, generally preferred to simple *pruning*. Consists of selecting a pair of *percentiles* – say the 5th and the 95th – then rescoring all data points below the 5th as at the 5th, and all those above the 95th as at the 95th.The extent of Windsorising is reported as the percentage by which the range is squeezed; in this example as 10% Windsorisation. Unlike pruning this maintains the number of scores while reducing the amount of *variance* in the set – see also *Smoothing, Inter quartile range*.

Within group/between group designs

See *Related and unrelated designs*.

Within group/subject variance

See *Between group/subject variance*.

Write-ins

(1) Of samples, see *Sample, self-recruited*. (2) On *questionnaires*, questions giving the respondent unconstrained choice of answer – see *Question formats*.

X

Usual designation for independent variable, see *Variable*, *X-axis*.

X (x̄ bar)

Symbol for *sample mean*.

x-axis (absissa)

The horizontal axis of a graph. Where appropriate this is the axis for the independent variable – see *Variable*. See also *y-axis*.

X-case analysis

Synonym for *cross-case analysis*.

X-tab

Synonym for *contingency table*.

X^2 test or Chi-square (pronounced Ky-square)

(1) **X^2 contingency test/test of independence** (usually just called X^2 test): A non-parametric test for *statistical significance* widely used with data at the nominal level – see *Data, levels of, Statistics, parametric and non-parametric*. It is calculated on the differences between the numbers of scores falling into different categories in a *contingency table* (for example, numbers of yeses for males as against females and the number of noes for males as against females). It may be used as a test of *statistically significant* difference. Then the question is 'how likely is it that a difference of the size observed or greater is due to chance?' and if the answer is 'not very often' then the result is regarded *as statistically significant*. The procedure here involves creating a model of the results most likely to occur by chance (the 'expected' values (E)), and comparing these with the actual values (the 'observed' values (O)).

(2) **X^2 goodness of fit test:** used to compare a theoretical prediction with what actually happened. Then the expected values are those predicted by the theory. The question is still whether the differences between the expected values and the observed values are likely to have occurred by chance, but an accurate prediction will be shown by a result which is *not* statistically significant. This 'goodness of fit' use of X^2 is common in *log linear analysis.*

The results of both X^2 tests are usually reported like this:

X^2 (5) = 8.22, ns,

meaning:

(5) – there were 5 degrees of freedom calculated as:

(Number of rows in the table, −1), multiplied by (number of columns in the table −1)

in this case there were six rows and two columns = 5df

8.22 is the statistic for X^2 resulting from the test

ns means not statistically significant. At 8.22 the figure for X^2 was lower than the minimum level for statistical significance to be found in a table of *critical values* for X^2 at 5 degrees of freedom. The lowest acceptable level (or *alpha level*) is that where the actual results are less than 5 times in 100 likely to have occurred by chance ($p < 0.05$). The figure to beat at 5 degrees of freedom was actually 11.07.

The interpretation is that the since the differences measured by the X^2 test were within a range likely to have occurred by chance the differences are not statistically significant.

The correlation coefficient *phi Φ* may be calculated from X^2.

See also *Statistics Software.*

X-Y graph

Usually a *scattergram*, although all two dimensional graphs have X and Y axes. **X-Y-Z graph**: as previously, but in three dimensional form, plotting the relationships between three variables.

Y

Usual designation for dependent variable – see *Variable, Y axis*.

Y-axis (ordinate)

The vertical axis on a graph. Where appropriate this is the axis for the dependent variable – see *Variable*. See also *X-axis*.

Yea-saying bias/set

See *Bias, acquiescence*.

Z curve/scores (standard or standardised scores)

The curve of z is a *normal distribution* curve with a *mean* of 0 and a *standard deviation* of 1. Actual data drawn from a population which approaches a normal distribution can be transformed into z scores which are units of *standard deviation*. Knowing a z score will tell you where the score stands in relation to other scores: what percentage will be higher and what percentage lower. For this reason many instruments are designed to generate z scores or transformations of them – see *Standardisation*.

For scores in any sample, randomly drawn from a population with a distribution approaching the *normal distribution*, the formula for conversion into a z scores is:

$$z = \frac{\text{score} - mean}{standard\ deviation}$$

The interpretation of a z-scores is via a table of 'Areas under the normal curve', or automatically by software. The 'Normdist' function on an Excel spreadsheet reports the same numbers as found in Table 29.

Table 29 Areas under the normal curve.

z =	.00	.01	.02	.03	.04	.05	.06	.07	.08	.09
0.0	.00000	.00399	.00789	.01197	.01595	.01994	.02392	.02790	.03188	.03586
0.1	.03983	.04380	.04776	.05172	.05567	.05962	.06356	.06749	.	.
0.2	.07926	.08317	.08706	.09095	.09483	.09871	.10257	.	.	
0.3	.11791	.12172	.12552	.12930	.13307	.	.	.		
0.4	.15542	.15910	.16276	.16640	.17003	.				

If z = 0.33.
Area = 0.12930 = 0.13 = 13% above the mean.
50% of scores lie below the mean so this score is at the 13 + 50th *percentile* = 63%.
63% of scores are below this, and 100 − 63 = 37% above this The score is 37% above average.
If z = −0.33, Area = 0.1293 = 0.13 = 13% below the mean. The score is 13% below average.

See *Normal distribution, Sample, probability, Statistics software.*

McClelland, G. (1999) 'Working with Z scores and normal probabilities' *Seeing Statistics,* Duxbury Press: *psych.colorado.edu/~mcclella/java/zcalc.html*

Zero order

See *Correlation.*

Zipf curve

See *Power (law) distributions.*

Z

Index

The more important references are in **bold** type, Cross-references are to other entries in the index and not to the main glossary pages.